The Learn2
Guide

The Learn2 *Guide*

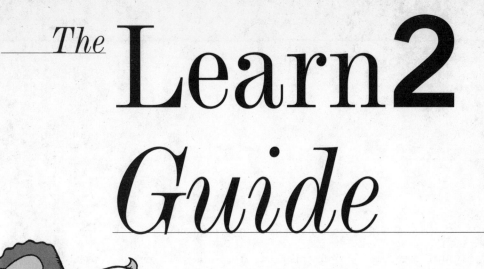

Burp a Baby,

Carve a Turkey,

and **108** Other Things

You Should Know How to Do

Edited by **Jason Roberts**

Illustrated by **Scott Hartley** and **Ethan Hay**

 Villard New York

Library of Congress Cataloging-in-Publication Data
The Learn2 guide: burp a baby, carve a turkey, and 108 other things
   you should know how to do / edited by Jason Roberts.
       p.   cm.
     ISBN 0-375-75255-2 (alk. paper)
      1. Life skills—United States.   2. Conduct of life—United States.
   I. Roberts, Jason.   II. Learn2.com.
   HQ2039.U6L43   1998
   646.7—dc21   98-24550

Random House website address: www.atrandom.com
Printed in the United States of America on acid-free paper
9 8 7 6 5 4 3 2
First Edition

DESIGNED BY BARBARA MARKS

Contents

Look Sharp: Grooming and Personal Style

Go Gourmet: Food Preparation

Hand Jive: Crafts and Activities

Around the House: Home and Garden Improvements

Introduction

I'd like to dedicate this book to someone who doesn't exist. If that person hadn't *not* been, these pages would also be nonexistent. You follow me?

Let me explain.

A few years ago I moved to Sausalito, California, to a charmingly unrenovated (read *dilapidated*) former mansion rather casually converted to apartments. I got used to the indefinably colored carpeting in the bedroom (moldy rust or rusty mold?), but the hardwood floor in the living room was another story. There was some good wood underneath the years of scrapes and scuffs, and I got it into my head that restoring its finish would be an easy, productive way to spend a relaxing afternoon.

I was wrong—about the "easy," "productive," "relaxing," and "afternoon" parts. By sundown I was on my knees in a congealing puddle of varnish, having an important two-part revelation: first, I didn't know what the hell I was doing; and second, I didn't know anyone who could straighten me out. Sure, there were preparation instructions on the varnish cans. And sure, the folks at the hardware store had been happy to discuss the merits of particular brands. But I needed someone looking over my shoulder, talking me through every step of the process, someone to help me get the hang of it.

That someone is the someone who didn't exist. Under other circumstances I might have had a handy relative, friend, or neighbor to turn to. But I hadn't met my neighbors, my closest relation was hundreds of miles away, and my friends . . . well, I had a feeling they'd be as

clueless about this particular task as I was. So I put down my brush, pulled off my sticky clothes, and went upstairs to my computer. I thought if I turned to the only other community I had access to—the global community of the World Wide Web—I'd be sure to find the guidance I needed.

Several hours later, I'd learned a lot about varnish: rock bands named Varnish; desert varnish (a dark coating on stones found in arid regions); and the use of cavity varnish in endodontic dentistry. All the search engines turned up pages and pages on marine spar varnish, violin varnish, and nail varnish (for people and pets), but nothing on the *application* of varnish itself. I gave

up; my floor was destined to dry bubbled and splotched.

My personal ineptitude didn't bother me (*that* I'm used to), but I was unsettled by the Internet's inability to help. In my job at Panmedia Corporation, a multimedia firm that produces websites, I'd long been proselytizing about the globe-transforming potential of this brave new medium. But when it came to real-world skills, what good was it? Why couldn't there be a central "ability utility" where anyone could learn to do any of a variety of tasks?

Why not? That was the question I posed to my coworkers at Panmedia the next morning, as we launched the project that became Learn2.com (and the book you're reading right now). We started by taking an inventory of our personal skills: Ian, a former electronics salesman, was a whiz at setting up stereo equipment. Jay, the son of a basketball

coach, knew not only the principles of a solid free throw, but also that cool trick of spinning a basketball on a fingertip. Dina, a for-

mer professional chef, had the knack of cooking perfect poached eggs. We set about teaching each other new skills, then distilled the process into an inventory of interactive "2torials." In October 1996, with a promotional budget of exactly $20.48 (we sent out a single press release), www.Learn2.com made its quiet debut.

Things didn't stay quiet for long. Word of mouth started to build: within a month our site was getting thousands of visitors a day. Four months later we were named by *Yahoo! Internet Life* magazine as the "#1 Most Incredibly Useful Site on the Web," edg-

ing out such big guns as Microsoft's Expedia and the FedEx website. Most important, we'd begun to receive suggestions and requests from our audience (sometimes hundreds a day), feedback that inspired an even broader range of topics. We'd publish a 2torial on changing a diaper—and then be notified that an equally important parenting skill is *improvising* a diaper.

People were grateful for the 2torial on driving a stick shift, but how about one on parallel parking?

Our audience also showed us that Learn2 needed to be more than a website. People complained that it was difficult to print out our 2torials—they'd

had to hit the Print button in their browsers multiple times, once for each step in the process. At first we dismissed that as a limitation of web publishing technology, but we couldn't deny the practicality of being able to print out Learn2 pages: What good is a 2torial on changing your oil if you have to drag your computer to the garage? We took a poll and found the vast majority of our audience printed out 2torials on a regular basis. People were tucking them into glove compartments, giving them as graduation presents, enclosing them in Christmas cards. What's more, they were eager for an official, comprehensive package. A question kept arising: *Why don't you make Learn2 into a book?*

It was a good question. And when it was asked by Jake Klisivitch, an editor at Villard, we decided to answer with a rousing *okay.* Thanks, Jake. On the subject of thanks, I'd like to rescind that earlier dedication. It may have taken the absence of someone to get Learn2 started, but it wouldn't have happened without the contributions of several Panmedians: Heather Ault, Julie Brown, Dina Camamis, Ian Cotler, Lisa Foster, Sierra Godfrey, Dane Golden, Jay Golden, Scott Hartley, Ethan Hay, Michelle Posner, Elena Stephens, Jay Ungerland, and David Weinfeld. Their dedication earns this dedication, don't you think?

The **Learn2** *Guide*

Learn2 Burp a Baby

You probably don't remember this problem from your days as a nursing infant, but every time you had a nipple in your mouth you'd get some air (along with your milk) in every swallow. Which meant you'd feel full before getting enough nutritional liquid (to use the modern term) and would need to be burped so you could nurse some more.

BEFORE YOU BEGIN

There are three classic ways to burp your baby. No matter which one you use, it's very important to properly support your baby's neck and head. An infant's neck muscles are very weak, and you should be careful not to let the head flop forward or backward.

Another very important thing to remember is to use a towel or cloth diaper to protect your clothing where your baby's face will be resting. You won't forget to do this twice.

How often to burp the baby? When bottle-feeding, every few ounces; when breast-feeding, every 5 minutes or so. When in doubt, burp your baby when she stops suckling.

STEP 1

Get in position

Position 1. On your shoulder:

This is how we commonly think of a baby being burped.

Hold the baby gently but firmly against your shoulder. Support her by placing an arm or hand under her bottom.

BE SURE BABY'S HEAD IS SUPPORTED

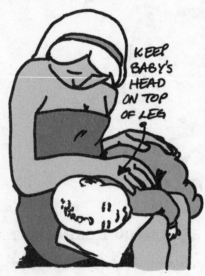

KEEP BABY'S HEAD ON TOP OF LEG

Position 2. On your lap, facedown:

This is a particularly soothing position.

Place the baby facedown across your lap. His stomach should be on one thigh, the head resting on the other. Hold the baby securely with one hand.

Position 3. Sitting up:

Be extra sure to support the baby's head when sitting her up for a burp.

Place the baby on your lap in a sitting position, leaning forward just a

bit. Support the baby's chest and chin with one hand.

If this does not produce the desired result, pat or rub a little more assertively.

STEP 2

Go for the burp

Gently rub or pat the baby on the back. If this does not produce the desired results, pat or rub a bit more firmly. But be careful: absentmindedly thumping away could harm the child.

A little experience will tell you which of the three positions works best for your baby. In any case, after everybody's finished, your baby should be placed on her side or stomach, to prevent choking on anything that might be spat up.

Learn2 Change a Flat Tire

Few people like to change a flat tire. But if you can follow simple directions, this is a good opportunity to revoke your "mechanically incompetent" status.

BEFORE YOU BEGIN

To change a tire (or more accurately, a wheel with a tire on it), you need another to replace it. Many car owners haven't checked the spare since they bought the car. Take the time now to look for your spare tire. Under the floor of the trunk and under the rear of a truck are the usual spots. Whether it's a full-sized tire or one of those small, low-quality, high-pressure ones, make sure that it's properly inflated and easily accessible.

While you're exploring the car, check the jack as well, especially if you bought the car used. It's not uncommon for the jack to be missing or incomplete. Find that out now, before you need to use it.

Most cars come with a lug-nut remover that's nearly useless—it's small, it slips, and it gives you no leverage. Go to an auto-supply store and buy one that's shaped like a cross. They generally have three different-sized sockets, plus a pry end, and give you a much better shot at removing a frozen wheel lug. Just make sure that one of the sockets fits your wheel's lugs securely before you leave the parking lot.

Tips

- There are aerosol cans that will inflate tires and spread some gunk around inside to provide a temporary fix. This is a limited repair option—these work only on punctures in the tread, not on the sidewall of a tire.
- Don't drive fast on a high-pressure spare. Your owner's manual (and sometimes the side of the tire) will indicate the top speed that the tire can sustain. Replace a high-pressure tire as soon as possible.

STEP 1

Find the right spot

Wherever you've pulled over, you'll probably have traffic passing you. Especially if it's nighttime, the oncoming cars will have a hard time seeing you crouched down at the front or the rear of the car—so choose your changing spot well.

Find a level area. It's dangerous to jack up a car on an incline. Look for a spot where you can be out of the way of traffic. A long, straight stretch of road is better than just around a bend, where traffic may come upon you unexpectedly. Turn on your emergency flashers (usually near the steering wheel).

If you have a tarp with you, spread it on the ground next to the flat tire. Weight it down with rocks or heavy objects so the wind won't pick it up. This will give you a clean space to kneel and place wheel parts. If you have gloves with you, put them on.

EMERGENCIES "ON"

LUGS LOOSENED BEFORE HOISTING

LEVEL GROUND

SPARE IS READY →

STEP 2

Get the spare and the jack

You can't remove the old wheel without a jack. The spare is probably right next to it.

The spare is usually located in the wheel well, which is often on the bottom of the side of the car. It's either an indented area or a slot of some kind where the jack is meant to reside. Your owner's manual has a diagram that will locate it for you. Most often, the spare will be held in place by a bracket or a bolt that unscrews by hand pretty easily.

If the jack is located in metal slots, slide it out and make sure that the handle is there as well. Many jack handles double as the lug remover, but if you have a real lug wrench, you won't need to use it as such.

Bring the jack and the spare over to the work area, along with the lug wrench. If you're doing this at night, take care not to lose the jack handle in the dark.

STEP 3

Loosen the lug nuts

If you try to loosen the lug nuts after jacking up the car, the wheel will just spin on you. Make it easier on yourself by doing it now.

There are generally four or five lug nuts near the center of a wheel. Sometimes they're hidden under a hubcap or a plate that needs to be pried loose. If this is the case, use the flat end of the lug wrench or jack handle. Insert it

STUCK LUG NUT?

STEP DOWN ↓

TURN COUNTER-CLOCKWISE

PULL UP ↑

into the slot provided at the edge of the plate or at the edge of the hubcap. Pry the plate or hubcap off, and don't let it roll away.

Now find the end of the wrench that fits the lug nuts properly. Place it over any nut, and turn counterclockwise to loosen it. If you have the cross-shaped lug-nut wrench, grab it at opposite ends. Use that leverage to loosen the lug nuts.

If you have trouble removing very firmly tightened lug nuts, here are a few strategies to help:

• Steady the wrench with your hand if possible, and step down hard on one end.

• Place your foot carefully onto the wrench. Holding on to the car, step with your full weight onto one end of the wrench. Bounce up and down on that end until the nut loosens.

• Find a rock, and use it to hammer on the end of the wrench.

Once the nut has loosened, continue turning the wrench until a few remaining turns with your hand will release it. Leave the nut on the threaded shaft. Repeat the process with the remaining lug nuts.

STEP 4

Jack up the car

To get the wheel off, you'll need to raise that corner of the car.

Raise the jack enough so that it just touches the car. Almost all jacks are raised by inserting the jack handle into a socket on the jack body and turning the handle. Some jacks are raised with a scissor-type motion. In this case, the socket can be hidden in the center of the jack body, while in others it may be more obvious. Don't worry about holding the jack in place while turning the handle. You can position the jack when it's raised enough to reach the car.

Now it's time to position the jack properly. Each manufacturer has a special place designated for the jack contact—that's the spot where the jack lifts the car. It's usually a foot in front of and inside the front wheel, and a foot behind and inside the rear wheel. Make sure that the jack is flat on the ground. Crank it a few more times to secure it.

When you're certain the jack is positioned properly, continue turning the handle so that the car rises off the flat tire. You'll need to fit a fully inflated tire under there, so give it a few extra turns to make sure there's enough room.

STEP 5

Remove the old wheel

You left the nuts on the old wheel so that you wouldn't lose them. Now it's

Tips

• If you have children with you, think carefully. On one hand, you don't want any extra weight in the car while it's up on a jack. On the other hand, you don't want your children near speeding cars, especially on a slick road at night. Consider the following: How's visibility? Are you on a highway or a lightly used side road? Look around: is there a safe area nearby for them to stay while you're doing this? If you have more questions, call the highway patrol now and get their recommendations.

Tips

- Be careful about using liquid-wrench or silicone sprays to loosen lug nuts. Your wrench may slip off the lubricated nut as well.
- When tightening or loosening lug nuts, are you confused about which direction to go? Remember this sage mechanical advice: "Righty-tighty, lefty loosey."

time to remove them. Spin all the lug nuts off with your hand, and put them aside, in the hubcap if you have one, or on the tarp.

Grasp the wheel by two sides of the tire (at the three o'clock and nine o'clock positions). Pull the wheel straight out and off. Keep your weight forward, or you'll fall backward and land on your butt. Roll the old wheel to one side.

STEP 6
Put on the new wheel

Holding the spare wheel, try to line up visually the holes in the center with the threaded shafts that they fit over. Shift and slide the spare wheel over the shafts until it's seated properly and can't be pushed any farther onto the shafts. If there's not enough clearance for the fully inflated tire, put the spare wheel aside and turn the jack handle a few more times.

The key step here is to tighten the lug nuts in the proper order.

TIGHTEN IN OPPOSITE PAIRS

Spin the lug nuts onto the shafts with your hands. Use the lug wrench to turn them so that they all rest against the wheel, but don't tighten them yet.

Lower the jack so that the tire just rests on the ground.

Tighten one of the lug nuts well. Give it one good turn with the wrench, but don't crank it on. Next, go to the nut opposite the one that you've just tightened, and tighten in the same way. Tighten the remaining nuts as you did the first two. If you have five nuts, tighten every other one until they're all tight.

STEP 7
Get ready to hit the road!

Turn the jack handle the other way to fully lower the car. As the weight is taken off, the jack will fall over. Lay it on its side, and finish turning the handle until the jack is fully closed.

If the wheel has a hubcap or plate, replace it by holding one edge in place and banging on the opposite edge with the jack handle, the heel of your hand, or the side of your fist.

Put the old wheel and tire in the spare's compartment or on the spare's bracket, and secure it. Secure the jack and handle in their original location.

Learn2 Cope with a Crying Child

Acrying baby can create a very frustrating situation for even the most patient adult. Something is wrong, but what? It's a big, confusing world, and babies aren't the only ones who can feel helpless.

BEFORE YOU BEGIN

Don't get frustrated. Babies can't use words, and crying is their way of communicating. Try different approaches, but give each one time enough to work before trying something new.

STEP 1
Prevent

The most important steps can be made before the baby ever begins to cry:

Be consistent in your actions; most babies like ritual. Try to prevent crying by keeping to the same schedules in feeding, changing, and nap time.

Provide the baby with as much attention as possible early on. Proximity will provide the adult with a better understanding of the baby's needs and thus create a better relationship.

Tend to the baby's diet: consult your pediatrician to understand your baby's nutritional requirements.

STEP 2
Respond

Respond quickly to the crying. There's no telling why your baby is crying until you investigate. And don't worry,

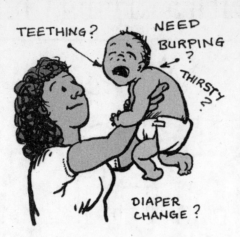

TEETHING?

NEED BURPING?

THIRSTY?

DIAPER CHANGE?

it's practically impossible to spoil a baby by rapid attention. The longer a baby cries, the more difficult the inter-pretation.

The obvious potential problems should be examined first, such as a full diaper (change), empty stomach (fill), or a full gas tank (burp). Once these have been ruled out, it's time to research.

STEP 3
Adjust

Sometimes minor physical changes are necessary to settle the baby's nerves.

- Rock gently. Rock the baby in your arms, a cradle, or a carriage. Don't shake the baby, as this can harm him.
- Take a walk. Bring the baby in a carrier, a sling, or your arms.
- Pass the baby off. A fresh set of arms can do wonders. It can be amaz-ingly straining to care for a crying baby, and the baby can sense your anguish.
- Go for a ride. When they need to

relax, babies generally respond well to car and stroller rides. Remember—you drive. Please secure the baby in an approved car seat before starting the engine.

- Adjust the excitement level. A new world, new faces, a new language: there is a lot of stimulation involved in being a baby. Limit visitors if it becomes too much for the baby.
- Adjust air intake. Gulping air can cause great discomfort for the baby. Keep the baby upright during feeding to minimize air intake.

STEP 4
Accommodate

You need not drop what you're doing and lose your composure every time the baby cries; a few minutes of crying is not going to harm the child. But here are some ways to attend to the crying when you are trying to understand the cause:

- Communicate. Entertain the baby by speaking to her and narrating your activities.
- Cuddle the baby. Hold the baby close to your chest to give him a sense of security.
- Sing, sing a song. If your baby enjoys your singing, or perhaps just one song, hurrah! Sing it again. Even your humming or the humming of a fan may relax the child.
- Give the baby a massage. Most babies enjoy being caressed, either on the back, arms, or legs.
- Give the baby a bath. Some babies enjoy a warm (not hot) bath.

Learn**2** Cure Hiccups

Time

Give at least 5 minutes to each technique before moving on to the next

What you'll need

There are several techniques, each requiring one of the following:
• A glass of water
• A lemon
• Sugar
• A paper bag
• A friend (or at least someone who's willing to stop laughing at you long enough to lend a hand)

Hiccups are often caused by too rapid eating, very hot foods, stomach problems, or stress. These can cause spasms in the diaphragm (the muscle in your upper abdomen that controls the expansion of the lungs). These in turn cause an imbalance in the carbon dioxide level in your bloodstream.

BEFORE YOU BEGIN

Your objective is to even out your carbon dioxide, the gas your breath is made of, and there are a few ways to do that. Some of these may seem odd, but keep trying—one will likely do the trick.

STEP 1

Work with the breath

These techniques can help you take in more carbon dioxide.

• Lie down on your back with your mouth wide open. Let your head hang over the edge of a couch or bed. Breathe deeply and slowly.

• The paper-bag trick: Easy now, skeptics—this one really can work. Breathing into a paper bag reuses your own air and thus allows you to inhale carbon dioxide. Don't do this for

Tips

- If someone else has the hiccups, your goal is to break the cycle of diaphragmatic contraction by suddenly giving the person's body something else to react to. That's why the scaring technique ("Boo!") sometimes works, but you can also try sudden gestures ("Look over there!") or other surprises ("Where did that llama come from?").

- For alcohol-related hiccups, eat a lemon wedge. If you can find some bitters in your great-aunt's liquor cabinet, soak the lemon wedge in that. Bitters are a liquor prepared from bitter herbs and roots, traditionally used for stomach ailments.

any longer than a minute or so, however, as this type of recycling can be dangerous.

• Hold your breath. You may also induce a cough or sneeze to change your air intake. Gargling has the same effect.

STEP 2
Drink water in an odd posture

Drink a glass of water while someone presses your ears closed. For greater effect, pinch your nose shut with one hand while you drink with the other.

Another time-honored strategy is to bend over and put your mouth on the far side of a glass of water. As you bend further, tip the glass toward your chest and drink upside down.

How come techniques like this seem to be effective? Possibly because they generate sensations that your body doesn't encounter every day. Your

body concentrates on processing these sensations, which means it stops paying attention to the repeat loop going on in your diaphragm.

STEP 3
Use a spoon

Gulp down a teaspoon of sugar. Its high carbon content and quick entry to your bloodstream will help.

Locate your uvula. It's that tear-shaped flap that hangs from the back of your throat. Touch it gently with the handle of a spoon. Breathe steadily but not too deeply—this will prevent you from gagging.

STEP 4
See a health-care professional

If the hiccups go on for longer than a day or so, consider seeing a health-care professional.

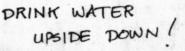

Learn2 Help a Hangover

Hangovers are nature's way of telling us that too much alcohol is not good for us. If you drink, chances are at some point in your life you've drunk way too much. No one has been able to come up with a surefire way to treat a hangover, but there are some steps to minimize the pain.

BEFORE YOU BEGIN

Sometimes you'll know in advance when you'll be facing a particularly sobriety-challenged evening. There are a few precautionary measures you can take.

Taking a gram or more of vitamin C for the few days leading up to that evening may help your body clear the alcohol more quickly than usual.

If you know that you'll be drinking in a few hours, make sure you've got something in your stomach. Breads and pasta will slow the absorption of alcohol, and there's generally a pizza joint somewhere around any bar scene.

STEP 1

Consider your beverage of choice

Congeners are toxic chemicals that are formed during fermentation, and some liquors have more of them than others. For instance:

- Vodka has fewer congeners than gin.
- Most scotch whiskey has about four times as many congeners as gin.
- Brandy, rum, and single-malt scotch have about six times as many congeners as gin.
- Bourbon drinkers ingest eight times the amount of congeners as do gin drinkers.
- Red wine has more congeners than white wine.

Time

Some people recover in a couple of hours; others take all day in a dark room

What you'll need

- Water, lots of it
- Vitamins C and B complex
- Aspirin or other nonprescription analgesic
- Simple foods such as toast and fruit
- Honey
- Sauerkraut juice
- A darkened room
- A cool compress or moist wash-cloth

Tips

- A wet washcloth or cool compress on your forehead can help soothe a headache.
- If you're too queasy to keep down water or juice, try small sips of flat, room-temperature ginger ale.

Plan for the big evening

Now that you've chosen your poison, adopt these strategies regarding mixers and other pitfalls:

- Carbonation speeds alcohol absorption, so consider mixing drinks with water instead of the fizzies.
- Stay away from sweet tropical drinks, like zombies and piña coladas, and avoid sugary foods like cookies, cake, and chocolate while drinking. Sweet flavors make it difficult to know how much alcohol you're taking in.

Safeguard against gross overindulgence

It's difficult to keep your wits about you when drinking heavily, but try to keep these things in mind:

- Drinking a big glass of water between alcoholic drinks may be the single best thing that you can do for yourself all evening.
- Whole milk and dairy products (and any other high-fat foods) retard absorption of alcohol, so eat those crackers and cheese that your gracious host put out.
- Pace yourself for the evening, rather than standing near the keg until it runs dry.
- Before you go to bed, drink more water. Down a B-complex vitamin as

NEXT DAY = SIMPLE FOODS

WATER OR JUICE - LOTS!

FRESH FRUITS

TOAST, CEREALS

well, and you'll be ahead of the game in the morning.

The morning after, part 1: Rehydrate

Carefully, placing one foot in front of the other, make your way to the kitchen. Now, drink a large glass of water, then take aspirin or other non-prescription painkiller with another big glass of water.

Got any juice around? Drink that, too.

Caffeine dehydrates your body, so stick with juice, water, and milk.

The morning after, part 2: Nourish

Eggs are more difficult to digest than some other breakfast foods, so have some toast and fruit instead, or a small bowl of cereal. Dairy products, yogurt excepted, also give some people digestive difficulty.

A tablespoon or two of honey does wonders for some of us, and believe it or not, sauerkraut juice is supposed to neutralize those nasty congeners still running around your system.

If all else fails, go lie down in a dark room. If your schedule allows you to stay there all day, you could be in pretty good shape by the evening.

Learn**2** Improvise a Diaper

Time

5 minutes

What you'll need

- A cloth napkin or soft towel, preferably square
- Safety pins

It's two o'clock in the morning, little Jamie's crying like crazy, and you've run out of diapers. As if it isn't difficult enough to even see your baby through the fog of sleepiness, now you have to solve the diaper problem. It's a scenario that makes even experienced diaper-changers join in the crying chorus.

BEFORE YOU BEGIN

Place a towel or changing cloth over the changing surface. If the baby is on a table from which he or she could fall, don't leave or take your attention from the baby, even for a second. Always keep one hand on the baby. If no safe place is available, make certain that someone holds the baby at all times, or do the change on the floor.

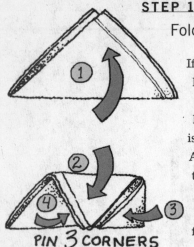

PIN 3 CORNERS

STEP 1

Fold the cloth

If your cloth is rectangular, fold it into a square. Then fold the square in half, into a triangle. This is fold 1 in the picture. Arrange the triangle so the top tip (the one that's at a 90-degree or right angle) points away from you.

STEP 2

Fold the triangle, top tip

Fold the top tip down to touch the base of the triangle (fold 2). Now your triangle looks like its tip's been cut off.

STEP 3

Fold the triangle, outside tips

Bring in the outside tips to meet the middle tip. This will create a rectangular shape.

STEP 4

Pin the tips

Pin the three tips in the middle, leaving a big hole on the top and two smaller holes on the bottom on opposite sides. Try using a single pin, and then add more as needed.

STEP 5

Lay out diaper and baby

Bring the baby over to the changing surface. Lay out the diaper so that the outside tips are closer to the baby's belly button and the top tip is closer to the baby's knees.

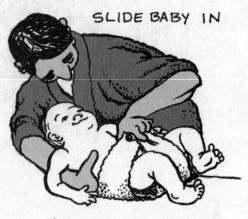

SLIDE BABY IN

LEGS THROUGH SLOTS

STEP 6

Insert baby

Guide the baby's legs through the little holes on the sides. Always keep your hand between the skin and the diaper to avoid sticking the baby. Adjust the pins. Comfort and be comforted. Go to sleep.

Learn**2** Improvise Emergency Bike Repairs

Time

5 to 30 minutes, depending on the complexity of the repair

What you'll need

- 1 foot (30 centimeters) of duct tape, rolled onto a cotton swab or other small cylinder
- 2 feet (60 centimeters) strong nylon line or twine
- 1 foot (30 centimeters) strong wire
- 3 to 5 zip ties (multipurpose plastic closures that click and lock when pulled)
- A stick, if you're in an area with any trees

Optional:

- If it's not possible to bring bike tools along, a pocketknife or other multipurpose tools

Since bicycle breakdowns are usually unexpected, you may not be prepared to make a fix. However, it's always a good idea to have some versatile repair items, like tire levels, a patch kit, and hex keys, packed with you, in either a fanny pack or an under-the-seat bag.

BEFORE YOU BEGIN

Keep your bike cleaned and tuned to prevent mishaps. It's especially important to have your bike checked out if it hasn't been ridden for several months. If you go on extended road or back-country rides, carrying a good set of tools is certainly recommended. Also, if you have the opportunity, learn basic repairs such as changing a tire and fixing a spoke.

STEP 1

Create a makeshift wrench

While more and more bikes are built with quick-release mechanisms, nuts and bolts still hold together crucial components. If these components need adjustment and you don't have a wrench, you'll need an alternative.

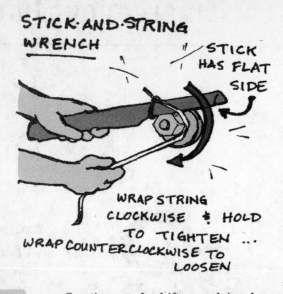

STICK·AND·STRING
WRENCH

STICK HAS FLAT SIDE

WRAP STRING CLOCKWISE & HOLD TO TIGHTEN ...

WRAP COUNTERCLOCKWISE TO LOOSEN

Tips

- Universal distress signal: If your bike needs a repair that's beyond your mechanical abilities, put it upside down, tires in the air.
- No wild rides: After improvising a bike repair, be very careful riding home. Don't confuse your patchwork with a bike mechanic's full repair. Avoid riding down any steep hills or on busy roads, and frequently check how your work is holding up.

Creating a makeshift wrench involves tying a bit of string or wire to a solid but small, preferably flat-sided stick. If no string is available, use a shoelace or a long strip of T-shirt. Note: This wrench may not tighten a component as firmly as it should be, so check the adjustment frequently to ensure it's still holding.

Tie the string around the nut, or the part you want to move. Wrap the string clockwise to tighten and counterclockwise to loosen. "Righty-tighty, lefty-loosey" is a good way to remember the direction.

Wrap the remainder of the string around the short end of the stick, and hold it steady against one of the flat sides of the hexagonal (six-sided) nut.

Use the long end as the handle. Hold your hand closer to the string for greater control. Once you have a good grip on the nut, move your hand closer to the bottom for greater leverage. At first this wrench might seem difficult

to control, but it's quite effective as long as the string or wire is tightly wound.

STEP 2
Repair it with a zip tie

You should maintain a good supply of zip ties. They're useful for replacing broken bolts or reattaching a component to the bike. A pocketknife or some paper clips can also be helpful. Second only to duct tape on the scale of versatility, zip ties are also light and easy to carry.

STEP 3
Mend a broken cable

A broken derailleur cable is the rain on any bicycle parade. To fix this problem, tie each end of the broken cable to anything that's available—a pencil, a piece of T-shirt, or a strong stick. If you tie off the cable securely, it'll respond almost as well as before.

Depending on the type of brakes you have, this method may also work for the brake cables. Don't rely heavily on this repair, however—braking power is greatly reduced by this type of breakdown.

STEP 4
Tie off flat tires

If you have a flat but no patch kit—or a patch kit in which the glue has been squashed and dried into a rock pancake—here's a way to get yourself home a little faster than walking your bike. Note: Riding on a completely flat tire can severely damage the rim (the metal portion of the wheel that holds together the spokes, inner tube, and outer tire), which is expensive to replace.

Use the handle of a fork or spoon as a tire iron, and remove the inner tube, being careful not to puncture it. Tie the inner tube in an overhand knot, exposing only that portion that has a leak.

Pull the knot as tight as possible. Then put the wheel back together, and pump up the tire. While the tire inflates, the knot should tighten and cut off air from the damaged area. If done correctly, this method will last you a few miles.

STEP 5
Tape your rims

Even if you carry a small bike-repair kit with you, there's no magic tool that can fix a cracked rim or rim strip (the thin metal strip between rim and tube). You can try to ride on without fixing it, but a creative repair is a better idea.

Try connecting the cracked ends with duct tape, or even apply grip tape from your handlebars. Use a knife or pen to cut a hole for the valve stem, if necessary.

STEP 6
Straighten the rims

While bent rims are more prevalent among mountain bikers, it's a repair

① REMOVE TUBE
② FIND HOLE
③ KNOT TUBE @ HOLE
④ REINSERT TUBE
⑤ INFLATE & RIDE CAREFULLY

with which all bicyclists should be familiar.

First, remove the wheel from your bicycle. Steady the top of the wheel against some solid object—a tree, lamppost, or street curb—and brace the bottom with your foot.

Now grasp the sides that are bending toward you. Push against them slowly until the wheel is straight. Lean into the wheel using your body weight rather than your arms and shoulders. Then use a spoke key or a stick-and-string wrench to tighten the spokes where they meet the rim. Ride home with caution.

STEP 7
Wire up the chain

Let's say the chain breaks. Maybe you've even lost the rivet, which is the small, connective rod between the links. Don't worry, you can still recover.

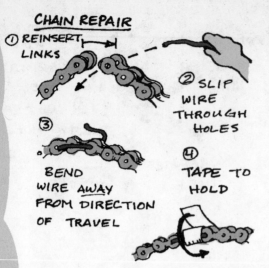

CHAIN REPAIR

① REINSERT LINKS

② SLIP WIRE THROUGH HOLES

③ BEND WIRE AWAY FROM DIRECTION OF TRAVEL

④ TAPE TO HOLD

fine. Carve the wood bolt a bit larger than the original bolt, so that you can wedge it into the space where it's going. The wooden bolt will hold the component in place long enough to get you home.

A piece of wire or a strong stick can be used to hold the links in place. Use wire from a coat hanger or even barbed wire, if you can find it.

Insert the wire where the rivet used to be and bend the ends back along the chain, opposite the direction of travel. Then wrap duct tape around the chain to hold the wire in place. As the chain moves over the cogs, they'll bite into the tape, leaving just enough tape to keep the chain together. Switch the chain to one of the larger rear cogs. This will keep it away from the other cogs, thus preventing the wire from getting stuck and causing more damage.

STEP 8

Devise an old-fashioned bolt

Use your pocketknife to carve a replacement bolt out of wood. Any piece of a hard tree stump; strong, thick stick; or old fence post will do

Learn**2** Jump-start a Car

Car batteries can lose their charge for more than a few reasons. Leaving the lights on overnight has got to top the list, though, and it catches us unprepared. It's times like these when many of us rely on the kindness of strangers, but sometimes *you* need to be the kindly stranger— or at least the one who knows which cable goes where.

BEFORE YOU BEGIN

When you're stranded in the cold rain and snow asking passing motorists if they'll give you a jump, you'll find that there are two kinds of motorists: those who have jumper cables and those who do not. Buy a good set of 100 percent copper heavy (4- to 8-gauge) cables that are at least 10 feet long.

STEP 1

Make sure the battery isn't damaged

Batteries have an electrolyte solution inside them. If that solution is frozen, don't try to jump-start the car. If your battery has removable vent caps, you can look inside to see if the liquid is frozen (then replace the caps). Otherwise, it's not easy to tell.

Time

About 5 minutes

What you'll need

- A car with the same voltage battery as your own, fully charged
- A set of jumper cables (see page 22)

Optional:

- A wire brush
- Gloves
- Safety glasses (recommended)

Tips

- Batteries produce explosive gases. Don't strike a light while jump-starting a car, and don't try to jump-start a damaged battery.
- Batteries contain sulfuric acid. If any gets on your skin or in your eyes, flush immediately with water and get medical help fast.
- If you've removed the vent caps of a battery, make sure that you replace them tightly.
- Every time a battery is discharged so much that it needs to be jumped, it is weakened. Consider buying a new one after a few jump starts, especially if you live in a cold climate.

If there are cracks in the battery casing, don't try to jump-start it. Curse a few times, call a cab, and go buy a new battery.

If there is whitish, greenish, or yellowish residue around the battery terminals, clean it off with a wire brush. Wear gloves, if possible, because that stuff can be nasty if it touches your skin. It's also a sign that you may need a new battery.

"STARTING" CAR   "DEAD" CAR

BLOCK

⊕ TO ⊕, ⊖ TO BLOCK

STEP 2
Attach the cables

Make sure that the batteries in both cars are the same voltage. You won't find many 6-volt batteries around anymore, but there's always the chance. The voltage will generally be stated on top of the battery, or look in the owner's manual.

The cars should not be touching, and both ignitions should be off.

Each battery has two metal terminals on it. One is marked positive (+); the other is negative (–). Attach one end of one cable to the dead battery's positive terminal. Attach the other end

of the same cable to the positive terminal of the battery in the starting vehicle.

Now attach one end of the other cable to the negative terminal of the battery in the starting vehicle. Attach the other end of that cable to the engine block, or frame, of the car with the dead battery. Do not attach the negative cable to the dead battery itself, and do not attach it to the frame anywhere near the battery.

STEP 3
Start the car

Stand back from the hoods of the cars. Do not smoke while you're doing this. Safety goggles are a good idea.

Start the car that's providing the jump.

Wait a moment, then try to start the car with the dead battery. If it does not start, stop trying and wait a few moments longer. Try again for no more than 30 seconds. If the car has not started by now, chances are that it's not going to.

STEP 4
Disconnect the cables

Remove the cable connections in the reverse order that you put them on. That means that the first disconnection is from the frame and the last is from the positive terminal of the car that has just been started.

Learn2 Perform the Heimlich Maneuver

The Heimlich maneuver is the most effective way to remove something stuck in an adult's or older child's throat. (Note: Another technique is used for small children and infants.) It isn't difficult, it doesn't require great strength or intelligence, and you could save a person's life with it. Since you'll also learn two techniques that you can perform on yourself, the life you save may be your own.

BEFORE YOU BEGIN

Although the Heimlich maneuver is simple and effective, it can be painful for and even injurious to the victim. It should be reserved for genuine emergencies, only when the situation meets the following guidelines:

• The person cannot talk, cough, or breathe. (If the person is coughing, he's not choking.)

• The person nods yes to the question, "Are you choking?"

• The person is unconscious, and your attempts to breathe for him or her via mouth-to-mouth resuscitation are blocked.

You'll also need to consider the age of the victim. Performing the Heimlich maneuver on small children or infants can do more harm than good, so follow the guidelines for the different age groups. And a final consideration: people come in all shapes and sizes. The force applied to a person's abdomen must be sufficient to dislodge an object, but it's appropriate to adjust the strength of the thrust depending on the body type. Use a bit less force with a skinny ten-year-old than with a heavyset forty-year-old.

Since the Heimlich maneuver can be traumatic for the victim, you can't practice the full maneuver on another person to prepare for the real event. But you can and should practice the handholds, the stance, and finding the proper location to thrust. This will prevent you from panicking in an emergency. But remember, never perform the full technique except on a choking victim.

Method 1
Perform it on a conscious person

STEP 1
Get in position

Stand close behind the victim with your thigh between his legs. Some experts recommend that you stand sideways behind the victim (with your hip at a 90-degree angle to the victim's back). This enables you to brace your hip against his lower back or buttocks.

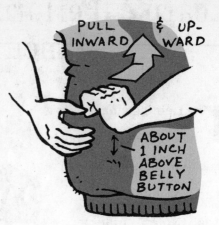

PULL INWARD & UP-WARD

ABOUT 1 INCH ABOVE BELLY BUTTON

STEP 2
Make a fist

Make a fist with one hand, and place it thumb first against the person's abdomen, an inch (about 3 centimeters) above the belly button.

STEP 3
Pull in and up

Cover that fist with your other hand. Keeping your elbows out, sharply and quickly pull your fist inward and upward.

STEP 4
Repeat

Be sure to perform this motion with sufficient force to dislodge the object; often it must be repeated up to six times. If the object remains stuck, lay the person on his back, and continue as if he were unconscious (see Method 2). If anyone else is present, have that person call 911. If you're alone, proceed directly to Method 2.

THIGH BETWEEN VICTIM'S LEGS

Method 2
Perform it on an unconscious person

STEP 1
Lay the person down

Lower the person to the floor and onto his back. If anyone else is present, have that person call 911.

STEP 2
Look in the mouth

Open his mouth and try to see the object.

STEP 3
Clear the throat

Sweep your hooked finger across the back of his throat. Remove the object if you find it.

STEP 4
Straddle

Straddle the person's thighs. This will put you in the correct position to do the thrust.

STEP 5
Put your hand in place

Place the heel of one hand over the person's abdomen just above his belly button, and cover that hand with your other one.

STEP 6
Thrust

Keeping both arms straight, press down and forward into the abdomen with a quick thrust. It may be necessary to repeat this up to four more times.

STEP 7
Clear the throat again

If the object hasn't popped out, again sweep your hooked finger across the back of his throat. Remove the object if you find it. Call 911.

STEP 8
In case of vomit

If the person vomits, turn him on his side to avoid further blockage of the air pipe.

Tips

- The Heimlich maneuver is simple and effective on choking victims when used by itself. If you also know cardiopulmonary resuscitation (CPR), you'll have another powerful life-saving technique to use on an unconscious person. Your local hospital or city-administration offices should be able to provide you with the location of CPR classes near you.

KEEP ARMS STRAIGHT

USE HEEL OF HAND

PUSH DOWN & FORWARD

STRADDLE VICTIM'S THIGHS

Method 3
Perform first aid for a choking small child or infant

Small children and infants have much more fragile bodies than the rest of us. The two methods below are designed to minimize damage to very young bones and tissue. Go to Step 2 only if Step 1 is ineffective.

STEP 1
The over-your-lap method

Sit on a chair, and place the child/infant facedown across your lap, with her upper torso hanging over the side of your knee.

Using the heel of your hand, thump the child/infant firmly but gently four times between the shoulder blades. Be especially careful with infants. Increase the amount of force only if a

gentle thump doesn't dislodge the object.

If you haven't dislodged the object with several thumps, call 911. If the victim is an infant or very small child, go on to Step 2.

STEP 2
The upside-down-by-the-ankles method

Hold the victim upside down by the ankles. You'll need to hold both ankles in one hand, with your thumb around one leg, your three last fingers around the other leg, and your index finger in between the legs.

Firmly but gently, thump the victim's back between the shoulder blades. Caution: don't search blindly in a small child or infant's mouth. You can accidently push the object further down her throat (although you should remove the object if it's readily visible). If the child vomits, turn her head to the side to keep her from choking further. If the child is unconscious, call 911.

Method 4
Perform it on yourself

Your first move is to call 911. Even though you can't speak, most 911 systems can then trace you to your address. Leave the phone off the hook and perform one of the methods below. It requires some willpower to administer this painful technique on yourself, but your life may be at stake. You have less than 2 minutes before you pass out.

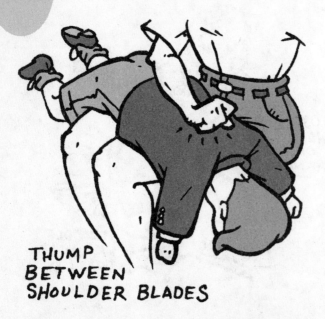

THUMP BETWEEN SHOULDER BLADES

STEP 1

Use your own hands

Make a fist with one hand, and place it thumb first against your abdomen, just above the belly button.

Cover that fist with your other hand, and pull your fist inward and upward sharply, quickly, and forcefully. Repeat several times if necessary.

STEP 2

Use a sharp-edged object

Use this method if Step 1 doesn't dislodge the object.

Locate a straight-back chair, and place it firmly against a wall or angle it in a corner. If a chair isn't available, use a sharp countertop, deck railing, staircase railing, or the sharp edge of a table, stove, or piano.

Run into the object. Attempt to meet it at the spot just above your belly button. Do this repeatedly and with as much force as you can muster until the object is dislodged.

Learn 2 Remedy a Toothache

What you'll need

- A few cotton balls (preferably sterile)
- 1 bottle oil of cloves (available at pharmacies)
- Pain reliever of your choice: aspirin, ibuprofen, acetaminophen
- 1 pint (about ½ liter) fresh, clean water
- ½ to 1 teaspoon (about 10 to 15 milligrams) salt
- A combination cold and heat pack or a bag of frozen peas and a hot-water bottle/heating pad

Most toothaches are caused by either a cavity (tooth decay) or an infection under the tooth or next to the tooth in the gums. In either case, you should be extra careful if your symptoms include fever; red, swollen, or bleeding gums; unusually bad breath despite thorough brushing and flossing; constant toothaches; or toothaches during or just after eating. If you have any of these symptoms, you should make an appointment with a dentist immediately.

Emergency care: In the rare case that a toothache is accompanied by pain in the lower jaw, neck, chest (in collarbone region), or upper arm, seek emergency care immediately. Heart attacks and angina reduce oxygen supplies to the mouth, and this can manifest as a toothache. It's better to err on the side of safety and be examined by a health-care professional.

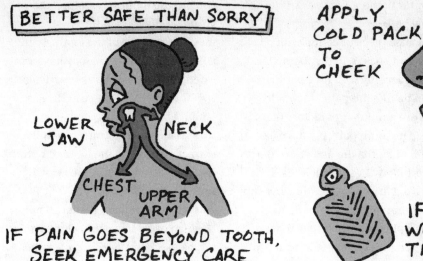

BETTER SAFE THAN SORRY

LOWER JAW

NECK

CHEST

UPPER ARM

IF PAIN GOES BEYOND TOOTH, SEEK EMERGENCY CARE

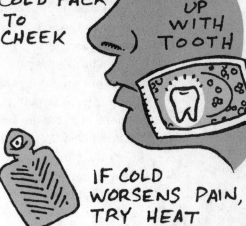

APPLY COLD PACK TO CHEEK

LINE UP WITH TOOTH

IF COLD WORSENS PAIN, TRY HEAT

BEFORE YOU BEGIN

If you turn to homeopathic remedies, be careful. Since you can purchase them without a prescription, you might have the temptation to diagnose and treat yourself without proper training. Although you're in no danger of poisoning yourself with homeopathic remedies, they won't work if you've misinterpreted your symptoms. The key to effective homeopathic treatment is very specific diagnosis, and that's where professional homeopathic practitioners come into the picture. But here's the bottom line: all the remedies presented here aren't meant to replace proper dental care: a cavity is still a cavity and will need to be filled at some point. These remedies offer relief in the meantime and may prevent the condition from worsening.

STEP 1

Try the Western approach

Your first step, not surprisingly, will be to take the pain reliever of your choice. (If you choose aspirin, don't, as some may suggest to you, crush the tablet and apply the powder directly on the tooth. Aspirin will create a burning sensation on your gums and can corrode the enamel on your teeth as well.) Since the painkiller will need some time to take effect, try the following in the meantime:

• Numb the pain. Apply an ice pack on your cheek, outside the aching tooth. Especially if you have an infection, this will reduce swelling and discomfort. Some toothaches aren't caused by infection; they respond well to moist heat and worsen with cold. If cold seems to intensify the pain in the tooth (and doesn't just feel unpleasantly cold on your cheek), then try a

Key words

Homeopathy: A two-hundred-year-old school of medical theory and practice that tries to work with the symptoms of the body rather than suppress them.

Enamel: The hard exterior of the tooth—the first line of defense against tooth decay.

hot-water bottle, a heat pack, or a heating pad.

• Soak a piece of cotton with oil of cloves, and pack it on the tooth; this works especially well for cavities.

Don't make the pain any worse. There are a number of factors that exacerbate tooth pain; if you've had your fill of toothache and you'd like it to stop, follow these guidelines:

• Avoid drinking or eating any substances that might irritate the tooth— for example, foods or drinks that are either very hot or very cold; that contain sugar; or that require a lot of crunching or chewing. Gum is also best avoided, even if it's sugar-free. If you're seeing a dentist that day, consider not eating at all until you've had a chance to meet. Unless it's baby-food consistency, any food is bound to irritate the situation and should be avoided if the pain is severe.

• Gargle. A saltwater gargle made of a pint (½ liter) of clean water and ½ to 1 teaspoon (about 10 to 15 milligrams) of salt will keep the area clean and may flush out any problem-causing bacteria.

STEP 2

Try some home remedies

These home remedies come from different parts of the world, from Russia to Central America. If one appeals to you, try it. They won't do any harm.

• Place a small piece of raw garlic directly into the cavity of the tooth. Variations include chopping some garlic, placing in cheesecloth, and apply-

ing it to the tooth; or crushing the garlic and applying it to the wrist that's on the side opposite of the tooth. By the next morning the pain may have vanished. This remedy works particularly well for infections, since garlic is a potent antibacterial agent.

• Place several drops of vanilla extract directly on the tooth. If nothing else, the alcohol in the extract will serve as an antiseptic.

• Mix ½ teaspoon (about 10 milligrams) each of salt and alum. To relieve pain and swelling, pack the mixture in the tooth cavity and around it at the gum line.

Learn2 Remove a Tick

Time

About 5 to 20 minutes, depending on how long it's been attached

What you'll need

- A pair of tweezers or forceps
- A bottle of strong antiseptic—the kind you'd use on cuts and scrapes

Optional:
- Rubbing alcohol or denatured alcohol (any beverage with a high alcohol content could also do in a pinch)
- Calamine lotion

To see a tick is to want to remove it, but unfortunately there's a lot of conflicting (and downright mistaken) lore about the right way to go about the eviction process. In this 2torial, you'll get the time-tested method generally approved of by health professionals.

BEFORE YOU BEGIN

When you discover a tick, fight the natural reaction to yank it immediately or rub it or swat it. Prompt removal is important, but your primary goal is to remove the tick in one piece, while it's still alive.

Why the emphasis on live removal? Because if you pull too hard or too quickly, you'll only get the body of the tick, leaving its tiny head embedded in the flesh, where it will almost certainly cause an infection. Worse, an injured or dying tick tends to regurgitate your blood right back into your bloodstream—with its own nasty microbes, bacteria, and viruses added to the mix.

Tips

- Obviously, the best way to minimize tick hassles is to avoid getting bitten in the first place. If you're walking through grassy areas, use a string or rubber band to close your pant legs around your socks. Lacking rubber bands, you can tuck your pant legs into your socks. Some experts recommend applying a strong bug repellent containing DEET, although others claim this chemical is too toxic for human use. If you're walking through an area with a lot of overhanging greenery, wear a hat. Remember, ticks generally drop down onto their new host.

STEP 1
Prepare to pull

Begin by getting as clear a view of the site as possible.

Wash your hands thoroughly, and sterilize the tweezers if possible. If you've got rubbing alcohol, you can wipe the tweezers with it. This should disinfect them fairly well, although it's best to follow this up with a flaming: run a lit match over the edges until well heated. If you don't have rubbing alcohol or other sterilizing solution, then just flame the tweezers and proceed (but let them cool down first!). If you don't have tweezers, then use a paper towel or other paper product. Don't grasp the tick with your bare hands.

STEP 2
Perform the patient pull

Don't hurry this step, even if you find it distasteful. Just be patient and thorough.

Using the tweezers, grasp the tick as close to the surface of the skin as possible. Then pull. Not enough to risk separating the body from the head—just enough to see the skin begin to pucker at the point of entry. Take care not to crush the tick or even squeeze it any more than necessary.

You're now applying sufficient pressure to convince the tick that it's time to vacate the premises. If you can maintain this position for anywhere from several seconds to a minute or two, it should finally relinquish its grip. You don't need to rotate the tick, although a gentle side-to-side motion may be called for.

STEP 3
Resort to stronger measures

If after several minutes the little creature isn't responding to your pressure, it's time to try a little liquid persuasion.

Place on the site a single drop of alcohol. Wait a minute, then add another drop. Do this for ten drops (and ten minutes), and you should sufficiently loosen the tick's hold. However, too much alcohol raises the possibility of regurgitation, so dose sparingly.

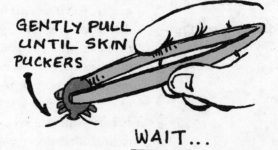

GENTLY PULL UNTIL SKIN PUCKERS

WAIT...

STEP 4

Disinfect and dispose

Once the tick is out, inspect it to determine if it's intact.

If the head has broken off, either go deeper with the tweezers (and don't worry about crushing the remains), or make an appointment with a health-care provider to have the site professionally cleared and cleaned.

Don't simply toss the tick into the trash. They're extremely tenacious beasts—even if you resorted to the alcohol drip, it's probably still alive. If you're concerned about the possibility of having contracted Lyme disease (see Step 5), you'll want to preserve the tick for testing by a doctor. Place it in a couple of nested Ziploc bags or a small glass jar with a tight-fitting lid.

If you're not going to have the tick analyzed for disease, then make sure it's permanently departed. Place it in a couple of layers of paper towels or tissue paper on a flat surface, then crush it by rolling a can or jar over it repeatedly. Finally, drop it in the toilet, to be flushed down with the next use.

Swab the site of the bite thoroughly with an antiseptic, and try to keep it clean and dry for a while. If there's an irritation or itching sensation, apply calamine lotion.

STEP 5

Live safely in a Lyme-disease area

If you're in an area with Lyme disease, do a very careful inspection of your clothes and exposed body parts—and your pets—every time you come in from a forest or a meadow. If you find a tick, it's very important to avoid contact with your bare fingers during the removal process. If the tick is difficult to remove, it may have been attached for some time. In this case, you definitely want to save it for laboratory analysis. Take the time to get it checked out.

Tips

- If you're deticking a pet or other animal, ask someone else to be the designated holder, keeping the creature steady while you perform the plucking routine.

Learn**2** <u>Stop a Nosebleed</u>

Time

5 to 10 minutes

What you'll need

- A handkerchief or towel

Optional:

- A humidifier
- A few drops of tea-tree oil (lacking that, a small blob of white petroleum jelly or first-aid cream)

Nosebleeds are one of those annoying little trials, like paper cuts and hangnails: they cause more frustration than pain, and they're soon forgotten as the day goes on. But kids, parents, and older folks take nosebleeds a bit more seriously, especially when they occur frequently or a significant amount of blood is lost.

BEFORE YOU BEGIN

Be familiar with the two types of nosebleeds: upper and lower. Most nosebleeds begin in the lower part of the septum, the semirigid wall that separates the two channels of the nose. The septum contains blood vessels, which can be broken by a blow to the nose or the edge of a sharp fingernail. With

MORE COMMON

MORE SERIOUS

lower-septum nosebleeds, the blood flows out of one or both nostrils while you're sitting upright or standing. More rarely, a nosebleed can begin high and deep within your nose; the blood will flow down the back of your mouth and throat even while you're sitting up or standing. This type of nosebleed is considered more serious, so don't bother to perform the steps detailed below—just get the person to a clinic or health-care professional right away.

STEP 1
Stop the blood flow

Get the sufferer in the right position. Keeping the head above the heart (that is, sitting or standing erect) reduces the pressure on the broken blood vessel and therefore reduces the flow of blood from the nose.

Have the person sit up straight or stand up, and keep the head level. Tilting the head back, as was sometimes advised in the past, can cause the blood to flow down the throat and into the stomach. This can cause nausea and vomiting, which would clearly aggravate the situation.

Calm the victim down, especially if it's a young child. A person who's agitated may bleed more profusely than someone who's been reassured and supported.

STEP 2
Add pressure

Option 1:

Applying pressure will reduce the flow of blood to the nose, which will give the blood a better chance to clot.

With your thumb and finger, pinch the nostrils together. Then, using gentle but firm pressure, push the pinched nostrils slightly upward and inward. Take care not to push too forcefully, especially with kids. This upward and inward pressure will reduce the flow of blood to the broken blood vessel on the septum.

Option 2:

Although virtually all health-care professionals agree that applying pressure is essential, some contend that squeezing the nostrils isn't the optimal method. The method described below places direct pressure on a major blood vessel that feeds a nosebleed.

Keeping the person's head level (or very slightly tilted back), take your index, middle, and ring fingers, and place them slightly below the nostrils, where the nose meets the upper lip. Press gently but firmly, applying pressure upward and inward. Hold this position for several minutes. Wipe away any blood that flows out—if necessary, you can gently pinch the nostrils together to prevent further mess.

If the blood continues to flow, you can apply pressure inside the mouth on the upper gum—at close to the same point as before. Wash your hands

Tips

- If the bleeding won't stop or keeps recurring, see a health-care professional immediately. If a nosebleed repeatedly occurs from the same nostril, you may have a weakened blood vessel that is prone to bleeding. In this case, you may want to ask your health-care professional about cauterizing, a procedure that uses a heated instrument to seal off the weakened blood vessel.

if possible, and wrap your fingers in some cloth (from a shirt or handkerchief). Apply pressure to the point, but more gently than before—the tissue inside the mouth is more sensitive to pain than the outer lip. And if you're not doing it to yourself, ask first to make sure the victim is comfortable with your fingers in his mouth.

Keep up the pressure. It'll take a few minutes for the blood to clot and stop flowing, so don't remove your fingers prematurely.

Keep the nose pinched and pressured for 5 to 10 minutes. If the victim is upset or scared, use this holding time to take his mind off the situation. Speak about any simple, neutral, or pleasant topic that comes to mind: the weather, a good story you read in the newspaper, or the great sandwich place you went to for lunch.

STEP 3
Prevent nosebleeds, short-term

You can do a few things right away to help prevent the bleeding from starting again.

Leave the nose alone. As the blood dries, it may feel itchy or odd, but resist the temptation to touch this area. If you disturb the nose by picking or blowing it, you may send yourself back to Step 1.

Don't pack it in. Stuffing the bleeding nostril with cotton may keep the blood from spilling, but it's not a good solution. The cotton may be difficult to remove once the blood has dried.

Hang tight. Try to sit quietly for several minutes, even if the bleeding has stopped. Any sudden motion or exertion may reopen the clotted blood vessel. If you can avoid it, don't bend over.

STEP 4
Prevent nosebleeds, long-term

There are also a few things to keep in mind for the long term, which can help reduce the number of nosebleeds suffered.

Nosebleeds often occur when the air is very dry, so keep a humidifier in the room, especially in wintertime.

Don't dry out. Keeping the inside of your nose lubricated can also be helpful in dry climates. One of the best remedies is tea-tree oil (now available at health-food stores and even some major supermarkets). Gently rub a few drops into the nasal passages. If you don't have any tea-tree oil on hand, take a pea-sized amount of first-aid cream or white petroleum jelly on the end of your finger, and rub it inside your nose. Both remedies work well before bedtime.

Encourage kids not to pick their noses, since it can easily lead to nosebleeds. Encourage them to blow their noses instead, using a cloth handkerchief to remove dried mucus from their nose. In the interim, keeping their fingernails trimmed short will reduce the chance of nosebleed.

Learn**2** Treat a Bee Sting

Time

- Stinger removal and allergic-reaction treatment: as fast as possible
- Soothing treatments: 10 to 20 minutes

What you'll need

For allergic-reaction treatment:
- A bee-sting kit, sometimes called an anaphylaxis kit

For soothing the sting:
- Ice

Optional:
- Soap and water or alcohol wipes
- Toothpaste
- Paste made from baking soda and water
- Onion slices
- Meat tenderizer

Whether you escape to the mountains every weekend or stay tucked away in a well-manicured backyard, chances are you'll have a close encounter with a bee a few times in your life. Bee stings can be painful at best, and fatal if you're allergic to them.

BEFORE YOU BEGIN

A bee stinger is one of nature's little wonders: after a bee stings you and deposits its stinger, the stinger continues to pump venom into your bloodstream for up to 20 minutes. A self-contained unit, the stinger has a barb to pierce your skin, a venom sac to hold the stuff that stings you, and a set of muscles to push the barb and venom deeper into your skin. It even has a hormone that makes other bees in the area more aggressive and prone to sting. Current research indicates that swift removal of the stinger is preferable to a more careful removal that takes even 5 seconds longer. Unfortunately, no matter how fast you act, getting stung will always be

Key words

Anaphylaxis: A life-threatening type of allergic reaction.

Bee-sting kit (also known as an anaphylaxis kit): Contains a syringe and one or more doses of adrenaline, which is often preloaded in the syringe. While instructions are generally provided, it's best to consult a health-care professional about how to use the kit. Sold under several brand names such as Anakit and Epipen.

painful, and you'll be left with a big welt to remind you of nature's little dangers.

Of course, it's better to avoid getting stung in the first place. When they see a bee fly near them, many potential sting victims start swinging at it. Oddly enough, the bee interprets this behavior as aggressive; if it gets half a chance, it'll probably sting the aggressive person. Instead, let the bee fly around you (yes, even land on you), and you'll probably watch it fly away within seconds. Try it—you'll be amazed how well it works. It takes some self-control, but the payoff is immediate and satisfying.

STEP 1
Search for the stinger

When a bee stings, the stinger detaches from the bee's body and often remains in the wound. The bee goes off to die, since a part of its nervous system is left in the stinger.

Look for the raised, reddening area on the part of the body that has been stung. If the victim has received multiple stings, first look for areas on the head, neck, and torso. Once the sting area has been located, look carefully in the center for a small, dark object that resembles a small splinter. This is the stinger.

STEP 2
Remove the stinger

Act quickly and simply. While a stinger remains in the wound, it continues to

pump venom. It's imperative that you remove it as quickly as possible.

Maybe you've read that you should use a pair of tweezers or a flat edge (such as a credit card) to scrape the stinger out of the wound. This view encourages people to take their time and remove the stinger carefully. Instead, recent research suggests you should get the stinger out as fast as possible, any way you can.

STEP 3
Ask about allergies

Bee-sting allergy occurs in 4 percent of the human population. For these people a bee sting can be life-threatening and requires prompt medical attention. Multiple stings can cause severe reactions even in nonallergic people, especially in children and the elderly. So your first move is to find out whether the victim is allergic to bee stings.

If the answer is yes, ask the victim and any bystanders if anyone has a bee-sting kit (also known as an anaphylaxis kit). If a kit is available, follow the directions inside for treatment. If no kit is available, dial 911 from the nearest phone and request an ambulance.

If the answer is I don't know or no, continue on to Step 4 while observing the victim for the following symptoms: headache, muscle cramps, fever, drowsiness or unconsciousness, and difficulty breathing or swallowing. If any of these are observed, call 911 and request an ambulance.

STING SOOTHERS

SOAP + WATER

H2O

ALCOHOL WIPES

ALCOHOL

ICE

TOOTHPASTE

ONION SLICES

STEP 4

Soothe the sting

There's a wide variety of sting remedies, and people who get stung regularly have favorite remedies that they swear by. This one is certain to ease the pain: wash the sting area, using soap and water if available. If not, and you have a first-aid kit with alcohol wipes, use them.

Apply a cold compress. Try putting ice cubes in a plastic bag or washcloth. If there is no ice available, use a cloth that's been soaked in cold water.

In addition, apply any of the following home remedies: toothpaste; paste made from baking soda and water; raw onion slices; or meat tenderizer.

Learn2 Treat a Pulled Muscle

Time

- Mild strain: 30 minutes a day for 3 days
- Severe strain: 60 minutes a day for 7 days

What you'll need

One of the following:

- A combination ice and heat pack
- A tray of ice cubes and a towel
- A paper cup filled with water and frozen
- A bag of frozen peas
- A towel or washcloth

Optional:

- A tub of hot water
- Homeopathic remedies such as arnica ointment
- Anti-inflammatory and painkilling drugs such as ibuprofen, naproxen, aspirin, or acetaminophen

Whether you're a weekend warrior or you exercise every day, you've probably felt the effects of overly intense physical exertion. Most pulled muscles (also known as muscle strains) are the result of overexertion—by a person without the proper foundation of fitness or a more seasoned athlete who ignored some early-warning signs of potential injury.

Strained muscles are commonly recognized by restricted range of motion, stiffness, and pain, which intensifies during the first 24 hours and then declines. For most folks, they occur in the hamstrings (back of thighs) and calves (back of lower legs), abdominal muscles, lumbar region (lower back), and trapezius (neck and upper back). Fortunately, with rest and simple home remedies, you can nurse a strained muscle back to health.

BEFORE YOU BEGIN

What have I done, you ask, to develop a strained muscle? Muscles are made of long fibers of tissue. These fibers can be overstretched, with either a sudden jerky movement or through extended overuse, and you experience that overstretching as pain and reduced movement. There are three progressively severe grades of muscle strains, ranging from the common strain that heals in a week or less to a complete tearing of the muscle fiber, sometimes separating it from the tendon. This 2torial shows how to treat the first grade of strain and how to avoid muscle strains in the future.

Note: After 24 hours, if the pain and stiffness is such that you can't move easily, or if there are any bulges or asymmetries visible in the muscle, make an appointment with your health-care professional.

STEP 1
Learn the RICE guidelines

RICE is short for rest, ice, compression, elevation. These are the home remedies that are very effective for low-grade strains. If carefully followed, this simple formula will speed up and improve the healing process considerably. Note, however, that RICE isn't in chronological order. You should elevate the injured muscle as you ice it; and you shouldn't compress it until you've applied ice and elevated the injured muscle. (More details to follow.) Rest, however, is certainly the

first step on the road to complete recovery.

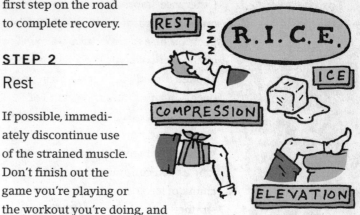

STEP 2
Rest

If possible, immediately discontinue use of the strained muscle. Don't finish out the game you're playing or the workout you're doing, and limit the area's use as much as possible for the next 24 to 48 hours. Lay off whatever activity you were doing when you strained the muscle, try to be patient, and stay active with other, less intensive forms of exercise. A forced or hastened recovery often resurfaces a month later as a more serious and debilitating injury. If you take time for the healing process to complete itself, you'll enjoy fewer injuries in the future.

STEP 3
Apply ice

Ice application is crucial to the healing process. The moist cold from the ice penetrates deep into muscle, slowing down the flow of blood to the area. This reduces the swelling, which can lead to pain and restricted movement.

Choose a pack, any pack. Here you have some options, depending on how well prepared you are. If you train regularly (say, 5 days a week), consider investing in a reusable combination cold and hot pack that you place in the freezer and then apply to the muscle.

Key words

Homeopathy: A 200-year-old school of medical theory and practice that tries to work with the symptoms of the body, rather than suppressing them.

Tips

- Accept your injury. If you continue to train by masking the pain with anti-inflammatory drugs like ibuprofen, you're probably setting yourself up for a more severe and debilitating injury. If you take some time off and do light cross-training, the injury will fully heal and you'll soon be back to 100 percent capacity.

Otherwise, improvise with whatever is on hand. Regardless of the type of cold pack, be sure to cover it with a towel or cotton cloth of some kind. Exposed ice applied directly to your skin can produce a burn—a superficial kind of frostbite. (The exception is the paper cup filled with water and frozen. That you can apply directly to the skin, as long as you continuously circulate the chunk of ice around the area of the strained muscle. Tear off horizontal strips of the paper cup as the ice melts down.)

Ice down the muscle in increments of 20 minutes: 20 minutes of ice, 20 minutes with no ice, and repeat. Continue with this schedule for up to 2 hours per session, with at least two sessions per day. Do this for the first 24 to 72 hours, depending on the severity of the strain. More severe strains will require additional days of ice treatment beyond 72 hours. If you're doing any alternative exercise, be sure to ice down the muscle very soon after finishing. For additional reduction of swelling, elevate the injured area as you ice it (see below).

How are you feeling? Here's the list of sensations you'll feel when you apply ice to an area: cold, stinging, burning, and the last stage, numbness. Remove the ice pack once the area feels numb, even if 20 minutes hasn't passed. If you're alone for the ice application and you're lying down, set a timer that will wake you up in case you fall asleep. You might think that a big lump of ice would prevent snoozing, but numbness does set in. College

athletes have fallen asleep with an ice pack on them and have woken up an hour and a half later with a frozen nerve, an injury that requires 6 months of intensive physical rehabilitation.

Some physical therapists recommend heat as well as ice after 48 hours have passed. Evening is a good time for heat application, once you've completed the ice treatments for the day. The heat must be moist: a compress purchased for this purpose (heated in a pot of boiling water) works best. Apply for a single session of 20 minutes. (Lacking a compress, soak the area in a tub of hot water for 10 minutes.) Heat will bring extra blood circulation to the area and will decrease the possibility of muscle spasm. Note: Some trainers swear by heat, others strongly recommend against it. See what effect it has on your injured muscle.

STEP 4
Compress

When possible, compressing the injured area with an Ace wrap or other reusable elastic bandage helps in two ways: it reduces swelling through the pressure of the bandage, and it supports the muscle and limits its movement somewhat, thereby reducing the possibility of additional strain. Compression is best after a session of ice application and elevation and before you do any activity, so don't strap on an Ace wrap as you go to sleep for the night.

START WRAPPING AT OUTER END OF LIMB & WORK TOWARD BODY

LEAVE WRAP ON UP TO 2 HRS.

Wrapping the bandage is an art in itself. You want a supportive compression, but you don't want to cut off too much circulation, either. To avoid turning an Ace wrap into a tourniquet, start wrapping at the edge of the injured area that's farthest from the body, and wrap toward the body. If you've strained your calf muscle, then start the wrap at the ankle and wrap toward the knee. If you've strained your thigh, then start the wrap above the knee and wrap toward the hip.

Keep the wrap on for up to 2 hours; if your schedule allows it, ice and elevate the injured area immediately after unwrapping it. Note: Keep an eye on the wrapped limb; if it turns white or blue, then unwrap it immediately, and wrap it less tightly next time.

STEP 5
Elevate

Elevation reduces pain and swelling by helping to drain fluids from the injured muscle. It is usually accompanied by an ice application.

Get comfortable. If the muscle is in your arm or leg, use some pillows to prop up that limb higher than the heart—that means you may want to lie down so that you aren't propping your leg up on 5 feet of pillows. If the muscle is in your neck or back, just lie on your stomach or in a position where you can be comfortable. Get a book or magazine, put on an ice pack, and move as little as possible.

STEP 6
Medicate

Athletes are turning more and more to homeopathic remedies to speed up and improve the healing process. While you should read up on homeopathic diagnoses or visit a homeopath (a doctor practicing homeopathy) before trying any oral remedies, topical remedies like arnica have proven to be very effective on muscle and joint strains.

Helpful Western medications include ibuprofen and naproxen, effective anti-inflammatory agents. These will reduce swelling as well as pain. Aspirin and acetaminophen also can be helpful for reducing pain and swelling. All of these drugs can upset your stomach, so give a trial to discover which drug you tolerate best.

STEP 7
Avoid strained muscles

Now that you're laid up with a strained muscle, you have a little extra time on your hands. Use it to learn to train safely and reduce injuries.

Stretch before you work out—and

not just the main muscle group you'll be working. Runners, for example, will often only stretch their hamstrings and calves, not realizing that stiff abdominal and back muscles can stress other parts of the body. Just remember to proceed gradually; overly enthusiastic stretching can result in muscle strain that reduces your flexibility and makes you more prone to injury. In general, do 10 minutes of stretching before the activity and 10 minutes afterward. The key to a good stretch is slow, deep, and regular breathing—not forcing the body into a particular position. And never bounce on a muscle as you stretch in an effort to go farther. Instead, go deep into the stretch until you can almost feel some discomfort; then slightly back off the stretch until you feel comfortable. Hold the stretch for at least 20 seconds, preferably 30, breathing deeply in and out.

Train gradually, whatever the activity. Some folks get overly enthusiastic as they experience the higher levels of energy and vitality that come with increasing levels of fitness. If you drastically increase the amount of training, you're probably on the road to emotional and physical burnout. So start slow and increase your workouts gradually; instead of focusing on the amount you train on any given day, focus on how many consecutive weeks you've been training. That's a truer indication of a commitment to physical fitness. And if you've been sick for a week or unable to train for whatever reason, consider reducing your workout for a week when you start up again.

Cross-train: Whatever your main training activity is, alternate it with other activities: swimming (or water aerobics and deep-water running in a pool), cycling, or jogging. Changing the activity works a different set of muscles, giving a rest to the ones you use regularly. If you train every day, consider taking 2 or 3 days per week to cross-train with other activities. And if you do strain a muscle, light cross-training allows you to stay active and keep the circulation moving through the injured area.

Equipment: If you run, keep track of your weekly mileage, and once you run more than 300 miles on a pair of shoes, it's time to retire them. When you buy a new pair, be certain that the width accommodates your foot—remember that your feet will swell up as you run.

Get a trainer: Consider working with a trainer for your main activity once a week for a month or two. Poor form in any activity can translate into inefficient movements that lead to injury. Trainers may seem expensive or an indulgence, but they're cheaper than doctors and surgery. You'll also get greater enjoyment from the activity, since you're doing more and spending less energy doing it.

Rest: Once every 20 to 30 days, if you feel like it, take a scheduled exercise day off; at the least, if you're feeling low in energy, reduce the length and intensity of the activity. The next day you can have a more thorough workout.

Learn**2** Blow a Gum Bubble

Blowing bubbles is that playground pleasure many of us practiced until we mastered, so we could look really cool. No matter what your age, blowing a mean bubble is still a quick and cheap way to impress your peers.

BEFORE YOU BEGIN

Chances are, blowing bubble-gum bubbles won't come immediately. Like all great body arts (whistling, snapping your fingers, belching on demand), blowing bubbles requires time to get it right.

STEP 1
Prepare the gum

Chew a fresh piece of bubble gum until it's nice and soft. Push the gum around with your tongue so that you make many different shapes with it in your mouth. Keep your mouth closed at all times, and avoid the urge to replenish the taste of the gum with a new piece. Adding to the wad will make it more difficult to blow a bubble. Use your teeth and the roof of your mouth to pull and push the gum around as well.

You're ready to advance to the first stage of the bubble. With your tongue, make a ball out of the gum, using the roof of your mouth as a rolling area. Push the ball to the front of your mouth, right behind the front teeth. Smash it against the back of your front teeth with your tongue. Your mouth should remain closed.

Bracing the edges of the ball with the back of your teeth and gums, gently push the middle of the ball with your tongue so it makes a small patty-like form as if it were dough being rolled out. If you need to, help flatten the ball into a patty against the roof of your mouth.

Time

1 to 2 hours a day to practice until you've got it; fortunately, this is something you can do while multitasking.

What you'll need

- A pack of bubble gum
- A quiet place to practice where you won't disturb anyone

Tips

- The stronger the gum, the better results you'll have. Once you're confident in your blowing abilities, any old gum will do, though the results won't be as spectacular. Be wary of gum that's also billed as a breath freshener—the minty flavors may irritate your tongue if worked too much.

ROLL GUM INTO
A BALL AGAINST
ROOF OF MOUTH

PUSH BALL AGAINST
BACK OF TEETH TO
FORM SMALL PATTY

PUSH FARTHER
INTO PATTY
TO FORM THIN
LAYER OF GUM

BRACE GUM
WITH LIPS

BLOW
FROM
LUNGS

Tips

- A fun thing to try is to see how many pieces of gum you can fit in your mouth and actually blow a bubble with. Chances are, you'll get a huge bubble, and a huge pop.
- *Please* dispose of your used gum properly! If you're old enough to read this, you're too old to think you can get away with jamming it under a chair or table somewhere. Is it so hard to return it to its wrapper and throw it away?

STEP 2

Blow the bubble

Transfer the gum back to behind the front teeth. Brace the edges of the patty against your gums and top and bottom front teeth. Now, with your tongue, push farther through the patty until a very thin layer of gum covers your tongue. Withdraw your tongue. If the layer breaks, you must reprepare the patty. Keep in mind that absolutely no hands are allowed at any time in the process. It's strictly tongue-in-cheek.

Using your lips to brace the layer, blow from your lungs, not your lips, to form a bubble. Blowing from your lips won't give the bubble the strength it needs to endure. Blow carefully and slowly so you'll get the size needed to form an actual bubble. Let it go as far as it wants until it pops.

STEP 3

Cleanup
(in case of explosions)

- Gum in carpet: To attack the pieces that projected into the carpet, try hardening them with an ice cube and then scraping them out with a dull knife. After most of it's out, try a warm, wet sponge and a very small drop of dishwashing liquid; gently rub in a circular motion.
- Gum in hair: Particularly large bubbles may explode not only out, but up and sideways as well—right into your hair. Don't reach for those scissors! Work in a little peanut butter or cooking oil, and comb it out with a fine-toothed comb. Wash and style as usual.
- Gum on furniture: Cooking oil also works for most hard surfaces and is nontoxic. Rub that gum shrapnel until it's thinned into a substance any cleaning material can take care of. WD-40 also works but causes horrible fumes and may be too harsh for your furniture. Also, very sticky tape—particularly duct tape—will pick up gum particles.
- Gum on walls: A sponge dipped in water and a little dishwashing liquid will take care of most debris splattered on walls. Don't rub too hard, or the gum may get ground in.

Learn**2** Build a Campfire

There are two kinds of campfires in this world: the campfire that you build to enjoy and the campfire that you build to survive. If you're in a situation requiring the latter, your best bet is to carry any one of a number of widely available fire "helpers." Often based on either magnesium shavings or a flammable paste, these burn at extremely high temperatures and can ignite wet material in an emergency. The techniques described below are still valid, but under really wet conditions, don't depend on natural materials.

The following is a guide to building a fire without any such helper materials. If survival isn't the issue, all you need is a source of fire, a bit of patience, and some consideration for your environment.

Time

5 minutes to clear the area, 10 minutes to gather materials, 15 minutes to build the fire

What you'll need

- A handful of any of the following: pine needles, dry grass, birch bark, dead leaves, or toilet paper
- A handful of skinny twigs or sticks about 3 to 4 inches long (8 to 10 centimeters)
- Some dry sticks or dead branches about 6 to 8 inches long (15 to 20 centimeters) and ½ inch in diameter (1 centimeter)
- Some larger dry sticks or dead branches about 12 to 18 inches long (30 to 45 centimeters) and 1 inch (3 centimeters) in diameter

- 2 chunks (about the size of your arm) of dry, split wood or dry found wood
- A matchbook or a few wooden matches in a waterproof case

Optional:
- A camping saw and/or ax
- A pocket lighter (the butane type seems to be the most reliable)

BEFORE YOU BEGIN

Most important, remember that fire is destructive if not controlled. Check that fires are permitted at your campsite, and keep water handy. Also, be aware that deforestation is a problem in many areas. Use as little gathered wood as possible, and consider bringing in your own firewood if you're not backpacking.

Choose the dryest, least green materials available; build the fire starting with small pieces and moving to large; carefully control the ventilation; and politely ignore any misguided suggestions from casual observers.

STEP 1
Prepare the site

Fire will ignite any flammable materials underneath it. Building yours on top of a metal fire pan is the surest way to control it. In any case, you'll minimize the risk by clearing an area at least 3 feet wide of debris. If no established fire pit is available, get down to bare earth, or to rock if you can, and put a ring of stones around it for aesthetics and extra protection.

Consider the wind, and attempt to find an area that's shielded from the strongest gusts. Consider also the possibility of rain, and see if there's a sheltered nook around. But be careful of flammable branches and tree trunks.

STEP 2
Gather the fuel

You need three types of materials: small stuff (tinder and kindling), medium stuff (½-inch-diameter sticks and 1-inch-diameter sticks), and large stuff (big chunks of wood).

Small stuff:

A large supply of tinder and kindling is the foundation of a good fire.

Tinder is very lightweight and dry material that will burn quickly and ignite the heavier materials. Examples of tinder are pine needles, grass, leaves, paper, and thin tree bark. Don't strip any birch bark off an upright tree, even if it looks dead. This can kill a tree by exposing it to disease, insects, and dehydration.

Kindling is small sticks; search around the base of shrubs and small trees for dead branches. Don't break any piece of wood off an upright tree, even if it looks dead. It's bad for the tree, and the wood won't burn well.

Medium stuff:

These ½-inch- and 1-inch-diameter sticks will be used to build fire-establishing structures. Search under larger shrubs and trees for the medium stuff. The same guidelines for gathering kindling apply here: leave the upright trees alone. Break longer branches into 6- or 8-inch pieces with this technique: rest one end of the stick at a 45-degree angle to the ground. Grasp the stick about 16 inches from the end on the ground, or simply rest the top end against a large tree. Stand with the ground end of the stick just outside one of your feet. Lift that foot and stomp down on the branch. It should snap with a satisfying sound. If it doesn't, try again, perhaps with your hand a little higher on the stick, or kick a little lower toward the ground.

Large stuff:

If you're in an established campsite, large chunks of wood will be available for purchase. Aside from being convenient, this option also conserves the limited and highly used resources of established campsites. If you're far away from civilization and established campsites, look around for fallen trees. If you have an ax, split the wood into chunks about the size of your arm or a little larger. Avoid any mushy wood—this has rotted and won't burn well.

TINDER

KINDLING

"TEEPEE"

STEP 3

Place the tinder and build the teepee

Put a handful of tinder in a compact pile (a little bigger than a golf ball) on the ground. This will be the heart of two simple structures: a "log cabin" built directly over a "teepee."

Using the kindling, build a small teepee around the tinder. Gaps will form naturally as you place the twigs. That's okay; you'll be dropping a match through one of those gaps.

STEP 4

Build the cabin

Now you'll take up the dry sticks and branches that are about ½ inch in diameter. Build a cabin around the teepee:

• Place two sticks on the ground parallel to each other on opposite sides of the teepee. Form a square by placing another two sticks perpendicular to the first two sticks, with the ends perched on the ends of the first two. The sticks will overlap at the corners (see picture).

"CABIN" OF STICKS

– GIVE ROOM FOR FIRE TO "BREATHE"

Tips

• Take extra care in gathering the fuel. To avoid denuding the campsite, forage some distance away. Aside from natural-beauty concerns, these materials form a part of the local ecology. The dry leaves and grass at the base of the trees decompose and enrich the soil, which makes for healthy, disease- and insect-resistant trees. Removing too much of this material has a negative impact on the forest ecosystem.

Tips

- Wet starts: Perhaps you have some good tinder and kindling and, although it's not raining, the other fuel is a little wet. The medium stuff can be prepared by carving small curls up the side of each piece with a knife. This will help it ignite from the tinder's flame. Once the fire is going, use it to dry out large chunks that you place on the perimeter of the fire. If it's pouring or all available fuel is soaking wet, consider using a chemical fire starter.

- If you're in the wilderness and you've built a ring of stones, scatter them about the area again before you leave. Remember, always practice minimal-impact camping.

- Then place four more sticks directly on top of the first four. Again, the corners should overlap, but this time make the square a little smaller.

- Repeat this a few times, until the teepee is loosely surrounded.

- Put a loose roof on top. Remember to leave several ½-inch gaps in it that match the gaps in the walls. With this design, the flame will be able to "breathe." You should still be able drop a match in between the gaps.

STEP 5
Place the larger stuff

Now you'll create a chimney effect by the careful placement of 1-inch-diameter sticks and large chunks. This will give the young fire a good flow of air, which will get it burning well.

- Put one of those good-sized chunks of wood right next to the cabin. Put another one on the other side.

- If you have one chunk of wood, lean some 1-inch-diameter sticks against the chunk and over the cabin. If you have two chunks, rest the sticks on the two chunks, suspended over the cabin.

STEP 6
Spark it up

If there is a breeze, wait for it to die down. Shield the area from the wind with your body if you have to. Assuming you've collected solid (not rotted), dry materials, you should be able to light the fire with a single match.

Kneel down and strike a match.

Shielding it from the wind, drop it through the gaps onto the tinder inside the teepee. If this is not possible, sneak the match through the bottom side of the cabin. Once the larger sticks are burning, you can let the other folks gradually and gently place larger wood on top. To encourage a struggling fire, kneel down beside it. Inhale deeply, and blow gently and steadily along the ground and into the base of the fire.

STEP 7
Extinguish the fire

When you're ready to sleep or leave the campsite, make sure that the fire is fully extinguished. Use generous amounts of water or whatever other liquid is available (hint, hint, guys). If you're in the backcountry and far from a water source, throw many shovelfuls of dirt on the fire. Avoid using moist, rich-looking dirt with decomposed leaves and wood—this material is flammable. Scrape up a bit of ground with a stick or trowel, checking for smoldering bits of material under the dead coals.

Put your hand on the surrounding ground to feel for heat. Believe it or not, half-extinguished campfires can smolder and continue burning under the surface, especially if years' worth of compressed debris is present.

Learn**2** Choose Wine

Time

At least ½ hour in
the wineshop, more
if you like to browse

What you'll need

- A local wine store
  that carries some-
  thing besides jug
  wines
- A cork pull
- A notebook in
  which to record
  your preferences
  (optional); keep it
  next to your wines

If you would like to become extremely knowledgeable on the subject, you should spend a good deal of time reading wine books and tasting a variety of wines. If, however, you would simply like to have a reasonable shot at finding a good wine, take a few minutes here to learn the basics.

BEFORE YOU BEGIN

For our purposes, wine comes in three basic forms: red, white, and sparkling. Sparkling wine when it comes from the Champagne region of France is called champagne. There are also blush or rosé wines, which are rarely taken seriously by educated wine lovers but which can be very pleasant on a summer afternoon.

STEP 1
Know your wine regions

Quite a few areas of the world are well known for producing good wine.

- The United States makes great wine. The best generally comes from California, with Napa and Sonoma counties being the best-known regions. Some very good wine is also made in Oregon.
- The French have been famous for wine for ages. Wines from the Bordeaux and Burgundy regions are probably the most widely available, along with champagne, of course.
- Italian wines can be marvelous. Chianti and other wines from Tuscany

are the best known worldwide. Spumanti is a popular Italian sparkler.

• The Spanish make very good sparkling wines, called Cavas, along with their riojas (reds) and sherries.

• Chilean wines are known as good values. The United States imports a lot of reasonably priced but very good Chilean red wine.

• Australia is an up-and-coming wine producer on the world market, and its Shiraz is generally a good bet.

STEP 2

Know your grapes

Different types of grapes make different-tasting wines. There are a few types, or "varietals," that are commonly available.

• Cabernet Sauvignon grapes make full, rich red wines that go well with hearty food. Wine made from Cabernet Sauvignon grapes ages well, although it's often blended with other grapes such as Merlot or Cabernet Franc, making it enjoyable to drink with no aging at all. Bordeaux wines are very often Cabernets.

• Pinot Noir grapes also make full, rich red wines that are usually a bit softer than Cabernets. Burgundies are most often made from Pinot Noir, and classic champagne and sparkling wine starts here.

• Merlot grapes make lighter, softer red wines. California and Chilean Merlots are among the best and can be real crowd pleasers.

• Zinfandel grapes are a California specialty. Red Zinfandel is a full, strong wine with a noticeably spicy taste. White Zinfandel is a sweeter blush wine that has become very popular.

• Syrah grapes make a very full red wine, which first gained fame in France. Lately, Australia has been making Shiraz with great success out of this varietal.

• Petite Sirah grapes make a somewhat lighter, peppery red wine and should not be confused with the similar-sounding but very different Syrahs.

• Chardonnay grapes are generally made to produce an elegant white wine that pairs well with food. White Burgundies are predominantly Chardonnay, and California is also well known for these wines.

• Sauvignon Blanc grapes make a crisp white wine (often sold as Fumé Blanc) that is a good choice for drinking on sunny days and with picnic foods. White Bordeaux wines are often made with these grapes.

• Riesling grapes make a very refreshing wine. Germany first popularized this varietal, and a German Riesling will be dryer and crisper than its California cousin.

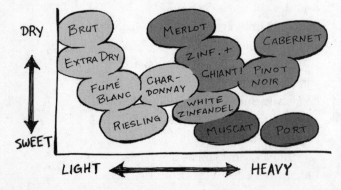

STEP 3

Understand vintages and aging

Each year another crop of wine is grown, picked, and stored in some fashion. Good wine generally has the year that it was produced (vintage) on the label somewhere, and some years are considered better than others. If you would like to know more about vintages, there are several pocket guides that will give you the lowdown.

Most red wines benefit from a little aging, and some varietals are known for improving with ten years or more in the bottle. Much of the wine produced today, though, especially from California, is distributed so that it tastes very good as soon as it appears in the store.

A winery will probably not distribute a red wine for at least two years after it is produced. An additional few years in the bottle will generally help Cabernets, Pinot Noirs, and Zinfandels to fully develop their taste, but don't worry too much about it unless you're specifically looking for a bottle to put away for a while. In that case, find a spot in your house that's always cool and dry, and get a specific wine recommendation from a reputable wine store or book.

Most white wines and sparkling wines generally do not need aging and are ready to drink at the time of purchase. The notable exceptions are sweet dessert wines and champagne, which can improve greatly with a few years in the bottle.

STEP 4

Understand pricing pressures

When you go into a wineshop, you'll find a wide range of prices. In the United States that range is from about $4 a bottle to more than $30. What makes one 1994 Cabernet Sauvignon worth twice the price of another?

• The grapes: All grapes are not created equal. Some vineyards produce better-quality grapes than others, and wineries pay premium prices for those lots. As a general rule, wine that is made of juice from an ideal vineyard is more expensive than wine that is blended from the juice of many lesser-quality vineyards.

• The method: Some methods of making wine are more costly than others. Storing wine in wooden barrels, for instance, is more expensive than storing it in stainless-steel vats. If the winegrower wants the wine to taste a certain way, certain methods must be used, and those methods often increase the cost of making the wine.

• The final product: When a wine is ready to be bottled (and often before that), the winemaker will evaluate it. Each wine is judged by its characteristics, including color, aroma, acidity, and overall complexity. A wine that has superior characteristics will cost more than a wine that does not. A wine that is set aside for additional aging before release will also command a higher price than one that has been released early.

• Availability: If a wine is made from small lots of very good grapes, there won't be a lot of it. Similarly, if a winery has an excellent reputation, a lot of wine stores will want to carry that wine. The rule of supply and demand dictates that those bottles will cost more than others.

STEP 5
Know your need

Everyone has his own opinions about a bottle of wine. That's because everyone has a different set of taste buds.

With meals:
- When eating heavier meats, such as beef and venison, choose a full red wine. Heavier Cabernets, Syrahs, and Zinfandels are likely candidates.
- For lighter meats, such as lamb and pork, a medium-bodied red is a good bet. Merlots, Pinot Noirs, and Petite Sirahs are all good choices. These wines also pair well with tomato-sauced pastas.
- Chicken and fish dishes can be overpowered by most reds. Try a Chardonnay or Sauvignon Blanc instead.
- With no-meat dishes try Chardonnays or a spicy, fruity red such as a Zinfandel. A dry white Blanc de Blanc should go very well with delicate fish and vegetarian entrées.

Wine by itself:
- Many medium-priced Pinot Noirs, Merlots, and some Cabernets are made in a softer, more accessible style and can be very nice to sip while sitting in your easy chair at night.

BEEF — Cabernet, Burgundy

PORK, VEAL — Merlot, Petite Sirah

POULTRY — Chardonnay, Sauvignon Blanc

FISH — Blancs, Fumés

PASTAS — Riesling, Chardonnay, Zinfandel

- When picnicking, try a slightly sweet blush, such as a white Zinfandel, or a lighter red, perhaps a chilled Beaujolais. If you're looking for a crisp white wine, Sauvignon Blanc is a good choice. Rieslings and Chenin Blancs are good for those who prefer sweeter whites.
- Champagne and other sparkling wines are great for celebrating, store well, and can be a nice change when served with appetizers. A brut wine is the dryest; extra dry is a little sweeter.

Learn**2** Eat Sushi

No, *wasabi* is not Japanese for "crying baby."

Sushi is one of Japan's most delightful foods. Though many people in the United States and other Western countries cringe at the thought of eating raw fish, millions across the globe salivate at the thought of sweet seaweed, fluffy rice, fresh vegetables, and tangy spices arranged in a detailed, painstaking fashion.

BEFORE YOU BEGIN

Sushi preparation is an art form, performed in public. Sushi chefs traditionally prepare the rice and raw materials before opening but actually make each piece of sushi on demand, in full view of the waiting diners. If a restaurant's offering simply emerges from the depths of the kitchen, it's possible it's not being prepared by a sushi specialist.

Establish a budget. Almost everything served at a sushi bar is à la carte. And while the price per order may not seem like much, once you've sampled from the intriguing list of fishes, fish roes, hand rolls, soup, sides, and pickles, you may go into shock when handed the bill.

STEP 1

Understand what's on the menu

Most sushi bars have diagrams or picture charts for non-Japanese-speaking customers, but it's great to be able to communicate exactly what you want to the chef instead of gesticulating wildly and mumbling "tuna . . . white . . . that, yes." Here are a few basic sushi staples. For those of you who are health-conscious, it's reassuring to know that all these items have low calorie counts. We'll give you approximations (per piece or a sixth of a roll) where possible.

Nigiri:

This slightly more expensive sushi is essentially a hand-shaped rice pad with raw fish on top. Types of fish include salmon (soft pink color), tuna (dark pink or red color), fatty tuna (looks like salmon but has large lines of white fat running through it), halibut (white with silver edges), and mackerel (white). Calorie content can vary wildly. One of the fattiest is the roasted eel (one of the few in which the fish is traditionally served hot).

California roll:

This sushi-bar basic contains vegetables including fresh avocado, cucumber, or carrot, with a little crabmeat or tuna. All this is wrapped in a thin sheet of seaweed and then packed against rice. 20 calories.

Maki:

These are all single-item rolls wrapped in thin seaweed and packed in rice. **Kappa** is cucumber, **tekka** is tuna, and **oshinko** is pickled ginger. These are small and sweet, and usually served in quantities of six or more. 15 calories.

Maguro and toro:

Tuna and fatty tuna. Mostly packed as *nigiri,* tuna sushi, like most art, can be served a number of ways. Regular tuna is a dark pink or red, but fatty tuna looks almost like salmon and has wide, white lines of fat through it. 25 calories.

STEP 2

Lay the groundwork

Wipe your hands. Once you're seated, your waitress will arrive bearing an *oshibori*—a moist, steaming, rolled white hand towel—in a basket or on a tray. Use it to wipe your hands, then place it, loosely folded, back on the tray (or, if no tray is available, to your right at the edge of the counter).

Prepare your *hashi* (chopsticks). Remove the paper wrapper, then separate the joined pair into two sticks. If your chopsticks are splintered, you may rub them together to smooth them, but please be discreet. Better sushi bars offer quality chopsticks that don't require sanding.

Rest the chopsticks. If your place setting includes a *hashi oki* (chopstick rest), position it so that your chopsticks lie about 2 inches (about 3 cen-

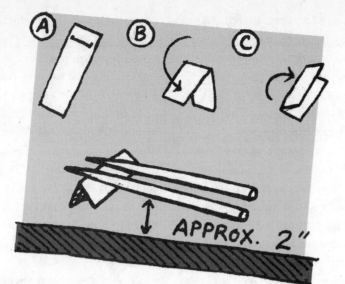

APPROX. 2"

timeters) away from and parallel to the edge of the counter. If not, make your own rest by folding the wrapper in half crosswise, then lengthwise, to make a V-shaped form. Turn it over so the rest stands stable, and position in front of you as above. Alternately, fold the wrapper into a simple knot: the triangular result lies flat on the counter, with openings to slide your chopsticks into.

Mix your wasabi. Usually, you're served a green substance that looks something like mashed avocado. Don't, repeat, *do not* eat it like it is! It's a spicy horseradish. Even if you're not fond of hot substances, mixing a little of this with your soy sauce can take some of the salt out of the soy sauce (12 calories per tablespoon) and season it besides. This is fiery stuff: some folks are almost macho about how much they can stand to apply, while others swear that the slightest amount is painful. Tread cautiously, and find your own limit. Don't look at the habits of your more experienced friends as any sort of guide.

STEP 3

Learn what you can order and from whom

As far as pronunciation goes, Japanese is basically a monotonal language, meaning that no one syllable in a word is accented more than any other. As a result, what most Americans, for example, call "sah-*shee*-mee" and "tem-*poor*-ah," the Japanese refer to as "sah-shee-mee" and "tem-poo-rah." Intimidated? Don't be! Because even if you flub, your chef or waiter will admire you for trying.

The crabmeat conundrum: There's one deception that's becoming increasingly common in even the best sushi restaurants (at least in the United States): items billed as containing crabmeat are actually made with surimi, or imitation crabmeat (usually

Tips

- Cleanliness reigns supreme, as does freshness. So while a restaurant's popularity could be merely the result of slick marketing savvy, it also suggests that the fish you see glistening in the display case were likely swimming earlier in the day. A smart sushi chef only orders what he knows he can sell quickly.

whitefish dyed and processed). Surimi is much rubberier than real crabmeat, and while some don't mind the substitution, you might resent paying for something you're not getting. Most restaurants will give you an honest answer when asked directly.

Your waiter or waitress takes care of everything else: drinks (green tea, sake, and beer are the preferred); soups (most often miso); *tsukemono* (pickled vegetables), and certain other snacks. Some sushi bars offer little nibbles with your drink: don't pass on the *edamame*—whole cooked soybeans, salted in the pod and eaten like roasted peanuts in the shell.

STEP 4
Start simply

Is there really a "right" way to season and eat sushi? There is an accepted etiquette, but as far as which dishes are the best and how they're best seasoned, it's up to you. The best bet is to start simply and work up from there as your palate becomes more educated.

Miso soup and salad greens make wonderful appetizers. Greens usually consist of cucumber strips and a wonderful, seasoned white vinegar. Miso soup is a warm soy broth with chunks of tofu, and often with strips of vegetables. Sip this with both hands on the bowl, letting yourself be wild without a spoon.

Choose a basic roll. On any sushi menu there are several standard rolls: small pieces of fish or vegetables surrounded by seasoned white rice and wrapped in thin sheets of seaweed. They are usually all small and served in quantities of six slices, though the servings may vary from place to place. They include cucumber or carrot rolls,

HOLD SOUP BOWL WITH BOTH HANDS

avocado rolls, salmon and tuna rolls, and the ubiquitous California roll. Dipping the ends of these in the soy sauce–wasabi mixture will surely delight—just make the dip quick, to prevent the roll from getting mushy.

You can eat rolls with chopsticks or simply pick them up and pop them into your mouth—there's no absolutely correct method. In fact, tradition maintains that sushi rolls were originally invented as a convenience food, to be eaten by hand much like sandwiches.

STEP 5
Step up to more elaborate dishes

After warming up your taste buds with the rolls, you may move on to the larger, more engaging fish. With *nigiri* you get larger slabs of fish, atop pads of sweet, seasoned sushi rice, sometimes accompanied by roe (fish eggs) or sesame seeds. These can be difficult to eat because of their size. If you can manage it without the whole thing falling apart, take it in two bites. If not, just don't talk with your very full mouth.

You should eat *nigiri* with chopsticks, but if you're not adept with these instruments, take consolation in the fact that not much action is necessary. Just pick up the whole, dip it quickly in the soy-wasabi mix, then pop it into your mouth. If you can't manage a whole piece of *nigiri*, there's no shame in asking for a knife, then cutting it in two.

Refresh yourself between bites with pickled ginger. With so many different treats to tantalize your taste buds with, it's nice to have a break between bites. In many cultures, water clears the palate, but in the sushi bar it's pickled ginger, or *oshinko* (only 15 calories per tablespoon). Small bites of this sweet root clear sinuses and palate alike, so eat it slowly. Wasabi does the same thing but is used as a seasoning for your soy sauce too.

Trust your tongue. Even the biggest sushi aficionados don't love all kinds of sushi—it's about variety, so don't be afraid to build your own personal list of favorites and ignore peer pressure of any sort. If you don't like clam or salmon roe or whole sweet shrimp, just smile and pass on that round. A world of flavors is always just another order away.

Key words

Nigiri: Raw fish on top of rice pads.

Miso: Japanese soup consisting of soybean broth with tofu chunks and vegetable strips.

California roll: Fish and vegetables packed in seaweed with rice.

Kappa maki: Cucumber in seaweed and rice.

Tekka maki: Tuna in seaweed and rice.

Oshinko maki: Pickled ginger in seaweed and rice.

Maguro: Tuna.

Toro: Fatty tuna.

Oshibori: A moist, steaming, rolled white hand towel.

Hashi: Chopsticks.

Hashi oki: Chopstick rest.

Wasabi: Green horseradish.

Tsukemono: Pickled vegetables.

Edamame: Whole cooked soybeans, salted in the pod.

Learn **2**   Hold a Wine Tasting

If your enjoyment of wine is
increasing, you'll begin to
develop a taste for certain styles
and form opinions about wine in
general. After speaking with
some of your friends, you'll probably discover that they've developed their own tastes and
opinions as well. What could be
better than inviting them over
and tasting a bunch of wines
together?

BEFORE YOU BEGIN

Many of us consider it sinful not to
swallow any good wine that has
passed our lips. However, a traditional
wine tasting allows the wine to be
tasted in three ways, yet leaves us
sober enough to drive home.

STEP 1
Set the scene

Ask each party to bring a bottle of
wine that they find interesting. One of
the basic differences among wines is
the level of tannins, acids that give
wine an astringent quality. They can
nicely balance a fruity taste or overwhelm the mouth with acidity. A more
tannic style is often an acquired taste
but one worth developing.

On a table set out a single glass for
each guest. Along with the crackers or
bread, have some room-temperature
water for rinsing mouths and glasses
(cold water numbs the taste buds). Put
the clean cloth where it's easily accessible.

Collect the bottles from your guests,
and open them up. Since it's difficult to
decant several bottles at once, pour off

a half glass from each bottle of red, so that there's more surface area exposed in each bottle. This will help the wine breathe a bit (see next point). White and blush wines should be chilled slightly before opening.

If you are decanting your red wines, try the wine again periodically, say, every 10 or 15 minutes. As the wine breathes, it will change a bit. If you make a note of your timing preference, you'll know how to serve that wine in the future.

When tasting many wines, it's a good idea to start with lighter, simpler wines, and move on to dryer, heavier ones. White wine's charms can be obliterated in a mouth that has been puckered by tannic reds. By the same token, swirl some water around the glass after emptying it of wine. Take the clean cloth and dry it out, so that the next wine is not diluted with water.

STEP 2

Taste with your eyes

There's a common expression we'll paraphrase here: first you taste the wine with your eyes, then with your nose, and finally with your mouth. In other words, a wine may be judged on its color, its aroma, and its taste. That's what most tasting boils down to, and those are the characteristics of a wine that you most want to understand.

Take a clean, dry glass, and pour a small amount of wine into it, perhaps a third full. Hold the wine up to the light, and note the color. Is it a deep purple or a lighter ruby color? Is it

tinged with green, or is it yellowish brown? Does it appear clear or cloudy? As you gain experience, you'll come to expect the wine to taste a certain way when it looks a certain way.

If it's a red wine, tip the glass gently back and forth, then hold it still and look at it closely. The wine will flow back down the sides of the glass, and some wine will form little rivulets, or "legs." Legs are considered desirable, as they indicate a higher glycerin presence, which means an ability to retain flavor and aroma.

STEP 3

Taste with your nose

Swirl the wine around a bit while holding the glass a little distance from your nose. This helps to increase the amount of scent that is available for smelling. Now move the glass under your nose, and inhale deeply through your nose. Then move the glass away from your face while you think about it. This will allow you to judge the "nose" of the wine, without being overwhelmed by the most dominant of the available aromas. At this point, you may be able to smell fruit or yeast, grass or earth in the wine. You may smell quite a lot or not very much at all.

SMELL . . .

Tips

- When storing wine, remember that certain wines improve with age, while others do not. The amount of tannin in the wine is one indicator of whether or not it will age well. Tannic qualities often become less apparent with age, and a bottle that you would like to keep for some years should have enough of them to start with, otherwise it won't develop much more character and will "die" rather quickly.

Tips

- There are several products on the market to preserve wine once the bottle has been opened. The two most effective seem to be the cans of inert gases that settle over the surface of the wine in the bottle, and the vacuum pumps that expel most of the air from a bottle and seal it with a rubber stop. Both of them work on the principle that wine changes character as it's exposed to air, and minimizing exposure will slow that process.

Again, experience will lead you to expect certain things from the wine by what you smell in it.

STEP 4

Taste with your mouth

Rest with the aroma of the wine for a few moments, then take a sip. Push the wine up to the front of your mouth, and inhale through your teeth. Slosh it around in your mouth, and cover your tongue. Even chew it if you like.

As the wine enters your mouth, you'll gather a first impression of it, and a predominant taste may become apparent. If it's a more complex wine, other tastes may appear, secondary notes that accompany the initial impression. Perhaps you can taste the wood from the barrels that the wine was stored in. Is that wood taste complementary or overwhelming? Different varieties of grapes are grown in various soils and in varying weather, then stored in various ways for varying periods of time. The wine in your mouth will reflect all of these factors.

Now spit the wine out into the provided container. You'll notice that you can still taste the wine, even though it's gone. Aftertaste or "finish" is an important feature of some wines, so consider: Is there much of it? Does it linger? What does it remind you of? Did you spill any on your blouse or shirt?

Take a minute or two between wines to rinse your mouth with a little water. If you like, take a bite of an unsalted cracker or bread to clear the taste of the previous wine from your mouth before you taste the next one. While you're at it, rinse your glass with water and dry it with the clean cloth.

STEP 5

Add a wine to your list of favorites

As if an evening of tasting good wine weren't rewarding enough, you have also performed valuable research into your own wine preferences. The next time you buy a bottle or order in a restaurant, you'll be prepared to make a well-informed choice.

Sometimes you'll find a wine that you like very much. Buy as much as you dare. Go so far as to try to buy bottles from the same case, or cases that arrived at the store at the same time. Wine can change from case to case, especially if it's been mishandled, and there's a good chance that a popular wine will sell out quickly.

Learn**2** Improvise a Compass (Day and Night)

Time

- Method 1:
  5 minutes
- Method 2:
  about 1 hour
- Method 3:
  5 minutes

What you'll need

For Method 1:
- Bright, direct sunlight
- A watch with rotating hands
- A straight, stiff, very thin stick, approximately ⅛ inch wide and a couple of inches long (a pencil or pen will do in a pinch)

For Method 2:
- Bright, direct sunlight
- A straight, somewhat sturdy stick, about 8 inches long

For Method 3:
- 2 sticks, straight and of uneven length, around 1 foot long

Whether climbing in the Annapurna Sanctuary or wandering in the local park, it's a good idea to know your direction. Knowing that the sun sets in the west doesn't do the trick. Celestial navigation is reliable but not much help on a day hike.

This 2torial will cover three methods, two by day and one by night. Each method will enable you to better understand your locale.

BEFORE YOU BEGIN

If you become lost, don't panic. Relax, sit down, and come up with a solution to the problem—or at least a plan. If it is daylight saving time, turn your watch back an hour before you calculate your direction.

Method 1
Use your watch (daytime)

STEP 1
Prepare your watch

Hold your watch flat, with the face toward the sky.

STEP 2
Position the stick

Place the stick upright (toward the sky) at the tip of the hour hand.

STEP 3
Adjust your watch

Turn the watch until the hour hand points to the sun. The shadow of the stick should fall exactly over the hour hand.

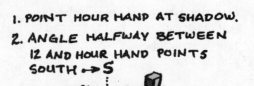

1. POINT HOUR HAND AT SHADOW.
2. ANGLE HALFWAY BETWEEN 12 AND HOUR HAND POINTS SOUTH

Method 2
Use a stick (daytime)

STEP 1
Position your stick

Find a sunny patch of level ground. Poke your stick into the ground, tilted so it points into the sun and casts no shadow.

STEP 2
Be patient

Wait at least 15 minutes until the stick casts a shadow around 6 inches long

STEP 3
Add the finishing touch

Draw a line straight across (perpendicular to) the shadow line.

STEP 4
Read the results

Voilà! You've got your compass. The stick is your west point, and the end of the shadow is the east. The cross line goes from north (on the right) to south (on the left).

Method 3
By the stars (night—
Northern Hemisphere only)

STEP 1
Find the North Star

Follow up the outside edge of the bail (scoop) of the Big Dipper. Follow that line through the sky. The North Star is the biggest, shiniest star in that direction. It is also the first star in the handle of the Little Dipper.

STEP 2
Plot the placement of the sticks

Draw an imaginary line from the North Star to the ground. Stand facing the point where that line touches the ground. Along the line between you and the point, poke holes into the ground a couple of feet apart.

STEP 3
Order the sticks

Place the sticks in the holes so you see the tip of the shorter one first, then the tip of the longer one, then the North Star.

STEP 4
Finish it off

Draw a line in the dirt between the two sticks. The stick closest to you is south; the one farthest is north.

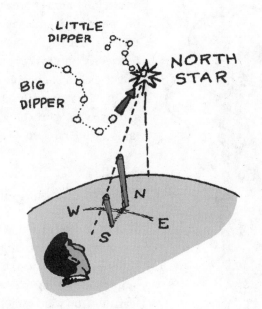

Tips

- Need quick and easy compassing? At twelve noon, place a stick straight in the ground. The shadow it throws points north in the Northern Hemisphere; south in the Southern Hemisphere.
- If you are lost on a foggy or overcast day, make safety and shelter your first concern. Fog will often clear off by late morning. But dark, thick, heavy clouds indicate precipitation, so it's more important that you remain dry and warm. Wait for the weather to break before attempting to determine the sun's position.

Learn2 Juggle (Three Balls)

Time

About three ½-hour sessions to get the hang of it, then another hour and a half of practice before you're ready to perform in public

What you'll need

- 3 beanbags, or 3 handkerchiefs or socks and a few handfuls of change
- A table (above knee height)
- A room with few breakable objects

Juggling has delighted people for centuries, and in recent years it's also served as a handy synonym for "doing more than one thing at the same time." This is a little ironic, because juggling doesn't involve multitasking skills—it's really just doing a single thing repeatedly, albeit with enough speed to create the illusion of confusing complexity.

That single thing is the simple act of throwing a ball in such a way as to leave your hand open to catch another. If you can do that, you can juggle . . . with a little patience.

BEFORE YOU BEGIN

Warning: When learning to juggle, you will look silly. Don't let this discourage you. When you get the hang of it you'll probably never forget how, but until then it's probably a good idea to practice alone, in a derision-free zone.

You can learn to juggle in any room with a minimum of breakable objects, but we recommend making use of a table as well, preferably of a height between your kneecaps and your waist; your kitchen table will probably do fine. Clear away the chairs, and stand so you're brushing against the table, facing forward.

STEP 1

Make practice juggling "balls"

When learning to juggle, the last thing you want to toss around is anything spherical and bouncy; you'll spend more time hunting for it than actually learning. You want something that'll stay in one place when it gets dropped—beanbags are ideal, but not everyone has three beanbags of equal size hanging around the house.

You can easily create a good starter set by raiding your spare-change jar. Lay out three handkerchiefs or socks on a table, then place a mound of change into each of them—about enough to fill your cupped hand. Try to get the mounds as even as possible. Then fold and knot them as shown in the illustration.

As your skill develops, you'll get a sense of how the balls fit in your hand;

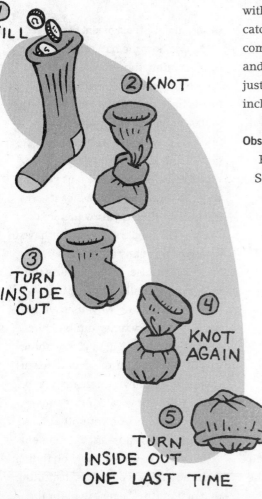

① FILL

② KNOT

③ TURN INSIDE OUT

④ KNOT AGAIN

⑤ TURN INSIDE OUT ONE LAST TIME

they should land in your palms solidly (not bouncing out) and not require a lot of effort to toss. If you find yourself throwing rather than tossing them, or if they just flop about in the air rather than tracing a neat arc, try adding coins.

STEP 2
Just toss a ball around

Now that you've made three juggling balls, the next step is to lay two of them aside and concentrate on playing with just one. Toss it up in the air, then catch it (with the same hand) as it comes down. Do it with your palm up and only lightly cupped, and toss it just hard enough to send it only a few inches higher than your head.

Observation 1. The role of rhythm:

Keep doing it for several minutes. See how there's a rhythm to it? Try standardizing the height of the toss, making each one send the ball to the same spot. With a little practice it should be easy to make the ball go up and down monotonously. But notice that monotony—see how the rhythm has become stronger?

Eventually, that rhythm will help you tell where balls are in the air, just as surely as your eyes will. That's because the rhythm corresponds to the amount of time each ball is in flight; toss a ball higher or lower, and you'll get a different rhythm.

Observation 2. Relying on peripheral vision:

Keep tossing. But now, instead of concentrating on the ball, try paying attention to your hand (the one that's doing the tossing). Eventually you'll observe something important: the fact that you can look at your hand and still keep track of the ball's progress. This might take a while, but it'll come. It's peripheral vision at work, and an ability you'll soon strengthen.

People often wonder which ball a juggler looks at when juggling. The answer? None. Jugglers usually don't track the motion of any particular ball, but just trust to peripheral vision to get a working sense of them all at once.

Observation 3. The tossing position *is* the catching position:

This is one of those Zen-like observations that can make a huge difference in understanding what juggling is all about. Look at what happens to your hand in terms of its physical position: not much, right? You cup your hand to toss, and it stays cupped for the catch. The position for both is essentially the same.

Observation 4. The abundance of free time:

Now that you're looking at your hand, notice how little time it's actually occupied with the ball. It really has lots of leisure opportunities, hasn't it, so long as it's there to catch the ball when it returns. Heck, at least half the time your hand is actually empty!

Much of juggling is simply taking advantage of that time. Here's an experiment. Keep tossing, but this time try snapping your fingers while the hand is unoccupied. Don't try to turn tossing and snapping into a single hurried motion—you'll find there's plenty of time to do both. You should be able to toss, snap, then reopen your palm and let the ball fall back in. If you can do this, congratulations. You've just mastered a skill that, in motor-coordination terms, is every bit as difficult as juggling itself.

Observation 5. The moment of apogee:

Notice how the ball reaches its highest point, then stays suspended for a fraction of a second before it heads back down? That moment—the split second before gravity takes over—is the apogee, and it's the juggler's friend. When you graduate to multiple balls, you'll use it as your timer. When one ball reaches its apogee, it's time to throw the next. Three-ball jugglers never, ever have to do anything at any other time.

Next exercise: when you toss the ball, try to visually pinpoint the moment of apogee. Now try saying the word *beep* every time your ball hits apogee (aren't you glad you're doing this in private?). After several dozen "beeps," you can graduate to the next step. Instead of vocalizing, try snapping your fingers on your other hand (the one not tossing) at that moment.

Now you've got a handle on timing. Quite soon now, you'll be substituting that action (the finger snap) for the

TRY BEEPING AT MOMENT OF APOGEE...

"BEEP!"

"SNAP!"

...THEN SNAPPING

action of tossing a second ball. Do you see why one ball's apogee is another's ideal launching moment? Because it doesn't disturb the rhythm.

Observation 6. Tossing doesn't require much movement:

To send that ball repeatedly up over your head, how much motion does it really take on your part? All you need to do is push your hand up smartly and keep your palms open. Try keeping extraneous movement to a minimum. In the beginning you'll be lunging all over catching stray tosses, but as your tossing gets consistent you'll find you need to move only the area from your elbows to your hands. Let momentum and gravity do most of the work.

STEP 3

Arc your tosses

We've got a little more single-ball work to do before the fancy stuff. This warrants a step of its own because you'll be mastering a new skill: tossing a ball back and forth from one hand to

the other. Sure, you can probably do that right now, but for juggling you'll need to streamline your technique.

Toss the ball up in the air, as in the previous step. Only this time angle your hand slightly—just enough to send it sailing, not in a straight up-and-down path, but in a gentle arc to your other hand. While practicing this, keep these thoughts in mind:

The key word is toss. You're not throwing the ball *at* your other hand, you're letting its arc spread so that its launching and landing are two different points.

Trust in the apogee. Focus your attention on the ball when it hits the point of apogee; that's how you'll know exactly where it's going to land. It's like this: the arc of a ball is a perfect curve, and the path taken to get to apogee is *always* mirrored, in exact reverse order, by the remainder of the arc. What comes down equals what goes up. That means the behavior of the ball in reaching its apogee is a preview of what's going to happen next. If a ball hits apogee at a sharp angle 2 feet away from the throwing hand, that means it'll come down at an equally sharp angle 4 feet from the point of origin. Catching it is simply a matter of positioning your hand.

Use your peripheral vision. Try this experiment: cast your eyes upward, in the general area where most of the apogees seem to occur. Pick a spot on the ceiling, and keep your eyes there. Try not to move your head, just trusting to peripheral vision and your sense of apogee.

Now toss and catch your ball, without looking at either hand. You probably won't get it at first, but with a little practice you'll find you can watch the ball sail through your field of vision and adjust your catching hand accordingly. Just fight the temptation to track the ball through its complete arc, and trust in your hand's innate sense of position.

Practice in both directions. You've probably been favoring one hand throughout your practice, and why not? You've only needed one up till now. But juggling is a bidirectional activity, and you'll be tossing and catching equally with both hands. It doesn't matter which hand you use to start your toss/catch routine, but now's the time to even out the flow. Keep the one ball shuttling back and forth as much as possible. To get comfortable with this motion (and to strengthen your peripheral vision), just look casually around the room while you're doing it.

Once you get the hang of this, it's time to move on to some actual juggling!

STEP 4

Do the jug

Ready to start juggling? You're going to master the basic mechanism in this step, even though you're still a few steps from tackling all three balls. Let's move up to two for now.

What's the basic mechanism? It's what we noted in the introduction as "the simple act of throwing a ball in such a way as to leave your hand open to catch another." We call this action "the jug."

First, warm up by doing your arc toss again of a single ball from one hand to another. By now you should have both throwing and catching down pretty well; the tosses are pretty consistent, and you don't have to move much to catch them—and when you do move, you're moving your arms, not your whole body.

Now, do the same thing—only this time, hold a ball in each hand. Hand 1 tosses a ball to hand 2—but oops, hand 2 is already occupied with a ball. What does it do? It gets rid of its current ball by throwing it in an arc that just happens to take it in the vicinity of hand 1. That's a jug.

At about this point, it's natural for panic to set in. When do I throw it? How do I keep the balls from hitting? Relax.

You throw it when the first ball is at its apogee—remember that second exercise you did with snapping fingers? Your balls won't collide, because you can judge the arc of ball 1 pre-

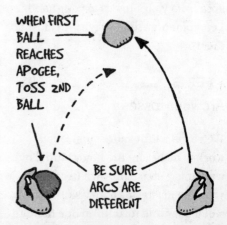

WHEN FIRST BALL REACHES APOGEE, TOSS 2ND BALL

BE SURE ARCS ARE DIFFERENT

cisely. You simply toss ball 2 in a slightly different arc, one that takes it on a path to the inside of the other. You'll find that only an incredibly slight inward tilt of the wrist is all it takes to alter the arc.

In the beginning, don't even try to catch the second ball. Just focus on how the second hand clears itself by tossing what it currently holds.

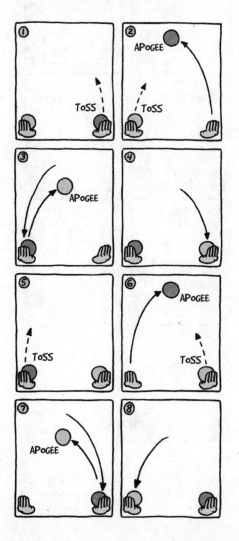

STEP 5
Do the double jug

Okay, now we're getting to the point where illustrations explain more clearly than words. The next step is to simply repeat the jug in alternate directions, as in the diagram below. With a little practice, you should be able to catch the balls every time.

Keep in mind that the hard part is past you now. Once you get the hang of throwing and clearing with the same hand, you've perfected the mechanism of juggling.

STEP 6
Start juggling!

Got the double jug down? Good. You are now on the threshold of becoming a full-fledged juggler. It's time to introduce the third and final ball.

Real juggling is no more complicated than the double jug, except that for the starting toss you've got to hold two balls in one hand. That shouldn't be too hard: try holding them side by side as in the illustration on page 72, and keep a grasp on only the one you want to stay.

Which hand should you launch from? In general, it's probably easiest to start from your dominant hand— that is, if you're right-handed, start with your right hand.

Eventually you should be able to start from any direction, but it's sort of a moot point: once the initial ball has been tossed, the pattern is exactly the same: ball gets tossed. At its apogee, next ball gets tossed. At *its* apogee, next ball, and so on.

At first it'll take some perseverance to keep the juggling going beyond a few seconds. That's usually because chaos intrudes into your carefully established order: one ball wanders a little too far, and in moving your hand to catch it you throw off the arc of the next, and so forth, until you find yourself wildly grabbing at thin air.

Relax. This is a necessary phase, not a sign that you weren't cut out for this sort of caper. Work on the regularity of your tosses and catches, and when things start going wild, don't break your rhythm and range of motion to accommodate them. Just let the ball fall short or long, pick it up, and start again. You're in charge here, and the goal isn't to keep the balls in the air at all costs but to find your own pace.

Hooray! Even if you can keep them up for only a few seconds, you're now an official juggler. What you've been working on is the primary juggling pattern, often called the "basic cascade." Once you're thoroughly comfortable with it, you might want to try these variations on the three-ball theme: try tossing all of them in big overhand loops, or reversing direction suddenly. You can also do a double jug in a single hand, sending two balls up and down in that hand while you do mischief with the other (this is how the old eating-a-juggled-apple trick is done).

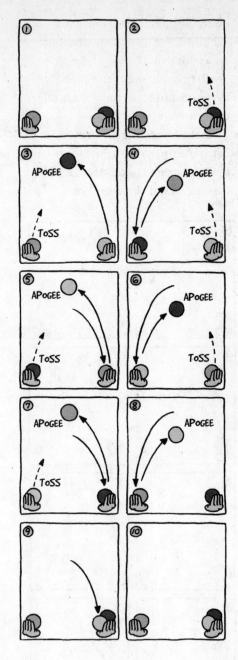

Learn2 Light a Pilot Light

Let's say you're arriving at a cabin for a weekend in the country. You're ready to enjoy a much needed getaway, but the gas furnace and water heater aren't working. They've been shut down in order to conserve fuel, and if you don't want to freeze your tail off, you'd better know how to start them up again.

BEFORE YOU BEGIN

There are many different models of gas appliances out there, so some of you may have difficulty applying these guidelines to your unit. Always get the advice of a plumber or licensed professional if you're not sure how to proceed.

Most units operate using a gas-supply valve, which is linked to a thermostat. Gas is distributed on demand to a burner, where it's ignited by a pilot light (see "Key words").

STEP 1

Find the appliance and see if it's operating

Locate the appliance you want to start up. They're generally located in a closet attached to a central hallway, in a utility room or basement, or next to the kitchen.

Listen for noise coming from the appliance. You may hear a rushing or rumbling sound. Put your hand next to the wall of the unit—carefully. It may feel warm.

Locate a removable panel on the front, usually near the bottom. Peer into the peephole, if there is one, or remove the panel and look for a blue flame. These signs—a rumbling

Time

About 15 to 20 minutes

What you'll need

- A flashlight
- Matches or a butane lighter
- A wrench

ACCESS MAY VARY...

OPEN A DOOR...

OR,

IN THE HOLE!

FROM THE BOTTOM...

REMOVE A PANEL

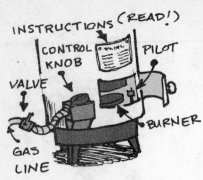

INSTRUCTIONS (READ!)

CONTROL KNOB

PILOT

VALVE

BURNER

GAS LINE

Key words

Pilot: A small flame or electric spark that ignites gas when an appliance comes on. A pilot light (flame) stays on indefinitely. An electric pilot will only spark on demand to ignite the main burner.

Burner: A flat disc, a series of discs, or a long, flat sausage shape located in the bottom half of the appliance. The burner distributes a gas-powered flame to the heating chamber of the appliance.

noise, a warm unit wall, a blue flame—all indicate that the appliance is already on. If this is the case, the pilot is already lit—you're done. Now locate the thermostat and adjust it to your desired level of comfort.

If there's no heat, no blue flame, no rumbling noise, the appliance is definitely turned off. Read the instructions printed on the unit. Most gas appliances will post printed instructions about how to turn on the gas and light the pilot. Follow these to the letter. If there are no instructions, follow the steps below carefully to turn the appliance on safely.

STEP 2
Be familiar with the parts

Connected to the unit will be a pipe with an on/off valve that looks something like a faucet. This is the main gas line. Modern gas lines have a length of flexible pipe connecting them to the appliance. The gas is turned off when the handle on the main gas line is perpendicular to the pipe. A one-quarter turn (90 degrees) of the faucet handle makes it parallel to the pipe that opens the gas line to the appliance. There's usually only one way to turn the handle.

GAS LINE

CLOSED

OPEN

Look at the control knob on the unit. Usually it's a round knob marked with three positions: off, pilot, and on. An arrow on the appliance itself indicates which setting has been selected on the knob.

Locate the pilot-light fixture, usually a small metal pipe that originates at the gas line and is located on the side of the burner unit. Sometimes it looks like metal cylinders, with a small pipe that resembles a candle wick. If you're lucky, it may even be labeled. Notice that you'll have access to the pilot-light fixture either from the wall of the appliance (through a hole or removable panel) or by reaching up from the bottom. Sometimes there'll be just enough access to put in a match held with your fingertips.

Have your equipment within easy reach. Having another person around to assist is a great idea.

STEP 3
Turn the gas on

First you want to switch on the main gas line so that gas feeds into the appliance. Sniff around for the sweetish smell of gas—none should be escaping from any valves into the air around you. If you do smell gas, turn the gas off and call a plumber or licensed professional.

Start with the off position of the control knob. Then move the gas valve one-quarter turn (90 degrees) so that it's parallel to the pipe. Use a wrench to turn the valve handle if necessary.

STEP 4
Turn the pilot on

Turn the control knob so that the word *pilot* lines up next to the marker arrow. You should hear a small hiss. That's a flow of gas going to the pilot-light fixture.

Light a match or a butane lighter on its highest setting, and hold it as close to the pilot fixture as possible for a few seconds. The flame should jump onto the fixture. If nothing happens, return the knob to off and check your pipelines to be sure they're all open.

STEP 5
Light the burner

Once you've established a flame on the pilot fixture, turn the control knob on the appliance from pilot to on.

Set the thermostat as high as possible. Check the burner unit on the appliance. A blue flame should jump across the gap from the pilot to the burner. The flame will continue to move around the burner unit until the burner is fully lit. Then you can turn down the thermostat to your desired setting. You're all set.

If you're sure all the valves in the gas line are turned on and the pilot refuses to light (sigh), professional service may be required. Turn the main valve off, and call the local gas company or a plumber. You may need to pile on some extra clothes, boil water on the electric stove, or stoke a big fire in the fireplace while you wait for the repairperson to come in the morning. But at least you'll be happy knowing you didn't blow up the house.

STEP 6
Troubleshoot

Let's say you've lit the pilot, but nothing happens to the burner when you turn up the thermostat. Check the control knob to make sure it's on the "on" setting. Knobs can become loose or wobbly and not read accurately.

If you still don't get any response, then turn the control knob to off and wait about 5 minutes. Sometimes it takes a while for natural gas to charge the line fully. After 5 minutes, turn the knob to pilot and try lighting again.

Having difficulty locating the pilot fixture? Look at where the gas line enters the appliance (usually at the control knob). Find a small pipe that leads out from the main gas line, and follow it around. You're looking for a small fitting with some kind of a nozzle, wick, or cylindrical attachment located within an inch or so of the burner.

Some units have a start button, usually red and next to the control knob. Push this after turning the control knob to pilot. Keep the start button pushed in while holding the flame to the pilot fixture. Release the button when the flame jumps to the pilot.

Does the pilot light go out frequently? Check the air vents. If they're too close to the fixture, gusts of wind can snuff out the pilot. Deflect wind with a board, or change the angle of the vent shaft.

Tips

- Natural gas is odorless; gas companies add the distinctive scent. If you smell gas, immediately extinguish any live flames. Then look for the faucet handle on the gas line and turn it off— turn it perpendicular to the pipe. Open doors or windows. Check all gas appliances if the smell persists. If the pipeline is turned off and you still smell gas, call the local gas company immediately.
- Natural gas burns cleanly; it creates heat but no carbon monoxide, soot, or other contaminants to the air. Even so, be sure that gas appliances have adequate ventilation—air vents in both the ceiling and the floor near gas appliances.

Learn **2** Open a Coconut

Time

3 to 4 minutes

What you'll need

- A clean screw-driver
- A cup or glass
- A heavy knife or cleaver
- A hammer or mallet (optional)

Coconuts are seemingly designed to be as difficult as possible to open. Many of us have given up trying to crack that tough, brown husk in an elegant manner and instead just beat the darn thing with a hammer until it shatters. When you know the secret of the coconut, however, you not only have a great party trick, but you won't get shell fragments in your coconut meat.

BEFORE YOU BEGIN

To find a good coconut, buy one that has no cracks. When you shake it, you should be able to feel liquid sloshing around inside. The liquid is coconut water, and it's often used in recipes or simply drunk by itself. You'll collect this liquid before cracking the husk.

STEP 1
Drain the liquid

Collecting the coconut water means that your kitchen will stay a lot dryer.

Find the three "eyes" of the coconut, on the smaller end of the husk. Now take that clean screwdriver, and tap the end of it about 2 inches into one of the eyes with the cleaver/knife/hammer/rock. If a knife is your tool of choice, use the back of it to tap the end of the screwdriver through. Remove the screwdriver, and pour the liquid off into the glass.

STEP 2
Crack the husk

Place the coconut firmly on a flat surface, and locate a point about a third of the way down from the smaller end. With the back of the knife blade, give that spot a light whack.

Rotate the coconut slightly, and hit it again the same distance from the end. Repeat this several times as you rotate the coconut on the flat surface. There's a natural fracture point that will become apparent as you lightly whack the nut. Once you see the fracture develop, insert the tip of the knife into it and pry upward. The coconut should separate in such a way that you can easily get at the white "meat."

Tips

• Tapping two eyes will help drain the coconut water more quickly.

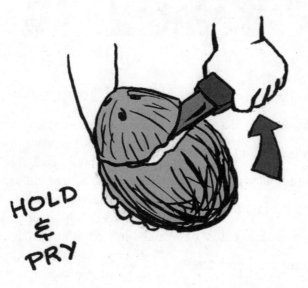

HOLD & PRY

Learn 2 Open and Serve Wine and Champagne

Time

1 to 2 minutes to open the bottle; ½ hour for red wine to "breathe"

What you'll need

- A cork pull (see Step 2)
- Wineglasses
- A decanter, for best results with red wine (optional)

Now that you've gone and spent a few bucks on a good bottle of wine, wouldn't it be nice to be able to open it with a casual flair? Apart from the rigidly enforced "dozen cardinal rules" of wine service, there are some simple guidelines that will help convince your new in-laws that you've been doing this all your life.

BEFORE YOU BEGIN

Remember that anything involving wine should be enjoyable. When you successfully pour a cork-free glass of red wine that has been allowed to breathe properly, appreciate it. On the other hand, if the cork breaks in half and won't come out, what the heck! Push it into the bottle, pick out the bits of cork, and stop worrying.

STEP 1

Think ahead

Champagne, sparkling wine, and white wine are best when served well chilled. Red wine, on the other hand, is best opened when only slightly cooler than room temperature. Put white wine in the refrigerator at least 2 hours before you plan to open it. Champagne or sparkling wine can go in even earlier than that.

Red wine (really any wine) should not be kept in sunny areas or on top of the refrigerator. Find a cool, dry place where the temperature remains fairly consistent year-round. Generally this means places like dry cellars and basements, as well as less obvious places, such as under the stairs or in ground-floor closets. It is important not to disturb wine bottles too much before opening them. Some red wines have sediment, which should be allowed to settle. Sparkling wines should not be agitated if the server wants any of it to remain in the bottle after opening.

STEP 2

Choose your weapon

There are quite a few different cork pulls on the market nowadays, and we'll cover three of them: the traditional waiter's pull, the winged pull, and the two-pronged "dishonest butler" (so named because it doesn't destroy the cork).

First, remove the foil completely from the bottle's neck. Use a sharp tool to slice the bottom edge of the foil, and peel it off by turning your hand around the bottle. Wipe off the top of the bottle with a cloth or napkin to remove any metal residue.

Using a waiter's pull:

Place the bottle upright on a flat surface or securely hold it between your knees at a slight angle, with the top easily accessible. Firmly place the point of the corkscrew into the center of the cork, and twist it straight in, until the screw part is completely in the cork. Pivot the cork pull so that the forked indentation grips the edge of the bottle's mouth and the pull's handle is pointed down. Grasp the handle firmly, and pull straight up.

Using a winged pull:

Place the bottle upright on a flat surface. Position the point of the corkscrew over the center of the cork. Firmly grasp both the bottle neck and the barrel of the pull under the wings with one hand. Twist the corkscrew by the "key" at the top until the round mouth of the pull is seated over the mouth of the bottle. Allow the wings to rise until they won't go up any farther. Put a hand on each wing, and push them all the way down. The cork should draw out of the bottle. If any part of the cork remains in the neck, grasp the entire cork pull in one hand and gently pull it straight out.

Using the "dishonest butler":

Place the bottle upright on a flat surface. Gently insert the tip of the longer prong between the edge of the

Tips

- Be careful not to allow any bits of cork to fall back into the bottle when the cork comes out. Pour a small amount of wine into the host's glass for tasting to make sure it's fit for the guests. Any bits of cork should be left in this "tasting glass."
- To quickly chill a bottle of white or sparkling wine, put the bottle into a mixture of ice cubes and a little water. Turn the bottle every few minutes, and give it as long as you can (at least 15 minutes) before popping the cork.
- Have a glass handy when opening sparkling wines. A fizzing bottle can be saved by pouring its contents off quickly into the glass.

bottle and the cork. Now bend the pull so that you can insert the other prong between the other side of the cork and the edge of the bottle. Once you've got both prongs between the cork and the bottle's edge, grasp the top of the pull and rock it back and forth. The prongs should sink further in with each movement. When the handle is right up against the top of the bottle, pull the cork out with a slow twisting motion, clockwise for righties, counterclockwise for lefties.

Opening a bottle of sparkling wine:

The first method is the one to use when you would like the wine to taste its best. Use the second method when consumption is not as important as the fun of watching the cork fly around the room.

For either method, begin by securely holding the bottle at a slight angle, with the top easily accessible. Remove the foil-and-wire cage, being careful not to aim the bottle at anyone.

• Correct method: Firmly grasp the cork with your palm over the top of it, and gently twist the bottle, not the cork. You'll be able to feel the cork sliding free by itself, and you'll need to keep it under control so that it "pops" as little as possible. Try to ensure that it only makes a little "gasp" when it comes out, and the wine shouldn't froth.

• Fun method: Grasp the bottle by the neck with both hands. Press your thumbs against the sides of the cork, and press first on one side, then the other. By rocking the cork like you mean it, it will first creep out, then pop

out of the bottle. After it flies across the room, froth will pour out and everyone will laugh. Have those glasses handy to catch the bubbly.

STEP 3
Serve

It's nice to have the proper glasses to drink from. Red-wine glasses are wider at the mouth and rounder than white-wine glasses to allow for swirling and sniffing. White-wine glasses are generally taller and have longer stems to keep the wine cold longer. Sparkling-wine glasses are typically much narrower, so that the bubbles last longer.

White wines may be served immediately after opening, whereas good red wines will benefit from being allowed to "breathe" for half an hour. The idea is to get as much surface area as possible, to allow as much wine as you can to come into contact with the air, without disturbing it too much. This process is called decanting.

Decant wine by gently pouring it into another container. Not only does this provide the necessary surface area, but it allows any sediment present (most likely in very old or unfiltered wines) to stay in the bottle. If no decanter is available, pour off a half glass 15 to 30 minutes before serving, and let both the glass and bottle sit.

When pouring sparkling wines, wrap the bottle in a cloth napkin for effect and to insulate the bottle from your warm hand. Tilt the glass, and pour down the side of it to minimize frothing.

Learn2 Shoot a Basketball Free Throw

Time

At least 1 hour of continuous practice to get the hang of it, then at least 5 minutes practicing every time you're shooting hoops

What you'll need

- A basketball, soccer ball, or similar spherical object
- A hoop, ring (approximately 18 inches or 46 centimeters in diameter), or peach basket
- For small children, a half-sized ball and basket

Like the drum solo at a rock concert, the free throw is the star turn of basketball: it's just you in the spotlight, and nothing but skill between you and success. The best shooters spend hours a week at the free-throw line, maintaining their overall rhythm while working on sneaking in those extra points come game time.

BEFORE YOU BEGIN

To find your most comfortable way of holding and shooting the ball, take it slow, and avoid the temptation to move back and fling the ball up. It's even a good idea to start halfway to the free-throw line (about 10 feet out) to get the feeling down first, then step back.

STEP 1
Position the ball

Shooting a basketball is all in the fingertips and wrist snap.

With your dominant hand, take the ball and pull your wrist to a cocked-back position until it shows wrinkles. Next, bring in your dominant elbow as far under the ball as feels comfortable, and lift the ball to a comfortable place at a height around your shoulders.

With your nondominant hand, hold the ball with your fingertips on the nondominant side like a bookmark. Bring your nondominant elbow up (around 8 inches or 20 centimeters) from your body.

STEP 2
Bend your legs

Crunch down and bend your legs, as if you are ready to jump. Your feet should be shoulder width apart—if you drew an imaginary line from your shoulder joint to the ground, your feet would be directly in that line. Then point your dominant foot at your target and set it about 4 inches (10 centimeters) in front of the other foot.

STEP 3
Extend from the legs

Just before you shoot, bend your knees a little more, then extend. Shooting involves bringing the ball up at the same time as the legs extend, then releasing the ball just before the top of the motion. To propel the ball, snap the right wrist and point your fingers (called a follow-through) where you want the ball to go. Try to get the ball to spin backward on its way.

STEP 4
Aim continuously

Keep your eyes on the target the whole time. Shoot for the back of the rim. This way, if you throw either a little too short or too long, the ball can still fall in. At the end of the shot, you should be standing just on your toes. Your dominant arm should be extended, and your wrist should be bent, with your fingers following through at the rim. Your nondominant hand should remain as it was, to the side or in front of your face.

Listen attentively for the *swish* of the ball going through the net.

EYES ON BASKET

BALL UP!

ELBOW IN

BENT

TO BASKET

Learn**2** Speak Wine

Time

10 minutes to become familiar with the terms; 20 minutes to a few hours to taste and discover what characteristics you can pick out

What you'll need

- Wine
- A corkscrew
- Wineglasses
- A fellow wine lover (or at least someone interested in sharing the wine-tasting experience)

Since the taste of a wine is a subjective experience, a wide variety of terms have developed to describe it. Some people might consider these terms an example of elitist snobbery, but actually they are a useful and enjoyable way to explain what you are tasting.

BEFORE YOU BEGIN

Wine is generally judged on its color, smell, and taste. Speaking about wine is merely an attempt to convey your opinion about these characteristics in descriptive terms. Many of those terms have become widely accepted and will pop up in most wine conversations. Some are fairly straightforward, while others are more obscure and require explanation. Interestingly, you'll find that many are applicable for more than one aspect of wine.

Key words

Tannins: Acids that give wine an astringent quality. They can nicely balance a fruity taste or overwhelm the mouth with acidity. A more tannic style is often an acquired taste but one worth developing.

STEP 1

Know your wine regions

Read Step 1 on page 51.

STEP 2

Smell it

When you smell the wine, it may remind you of certain things.

• *Aroma* is almost a synonym for *bouquet.* It is sometimes used to describe the grapelike smell of young wine, as opposed to the more complex smell of a mature wine.

• *Bouquet* describes the fragrance of a wine. Sometimes used to specifically denote a complex "winey" smell, rather than a simple grapelike smell.

• *Corky* refers to an unpleasant musty odor or taste in wine, often caused by a moldy cork.

• *Flinty* is used to describe the fragrance or taste of some white wines, especially a white Bordeaux. If you can remember what flint smells like when struck with steel, you'll have an idea of this characteristic.

• *Fruity* is used to describe a wine that has few tannins. It may smell or taste like any number of fruits, most commonly berries and citrus. A fruity wine is not always sweet.

• *Grassy* is used for a wine that has a smell or taste reminiscent of fields of grass.

• *Heady* is used to describe the smell of a wine high in alcohol.

• *Herbaceous* is almost a synonym for *grassy.* Depending on the other qualities present in the wine, it can be used to denote either an unpleasant "weedy" quality or a pleasant, flowery one.

• *Musty* is often used as a synonym for *corky* but is more pronounced and unpleasant. Mustiness can arise from a bad cork, excessive moisture, or storage in a moldy wooden cask.

• *Nose* is a synonym for smell. It's often used to describe how much of a smell the wine has, as in, "This wine has a huge nose."

• *Sour* is used for a wine that smells or tastes somewhat spoiled, often due to improper storage.

• *Spicy* is used to describe a variety of aromas or tastes, such as pepper, cloves, or nutmeg, that give the wine a distinctive character. Zinfandel, Cabernet Franc, and Gewürztraminer are considered spicy varieties.

• *Stemmy* describes a wine with an unpleasant aroma of grape stems. This will sometimes happen when too many stems are left in the fermenting wine.

• *Woody:* Discerning wood in the wine can be very desirable. Sometimes, though, a wine will have an excessive smell or taste of the wooden barrel in which it was stored, and this term will be used to describe it. Barrels made from American oak tend to give more of their flavor to wine than do barrels made from French oak.

• *Yeasty* indicates a wine that smells of the yeast used in fermentation. Most often found in younger white and sparkling wines.

STEP 3

Taste it

When the wine is in your mouth, more than one flavor may become apparent. After the wine leaves your mouth, additional tastes may surface. Here's a simple chart that gives you an idea of the directions a wine can take as it tip-toes through your taste buds.

• *Acrid* describes a wine with overly pronounced acidity. This is often apparent in cheap red wines.

• *Body* is a term that covers a lot of ground. It generally describes how "full" a wine is, or how much flavor is apparent.

• *Buttery* is associated with some white wines, notably California Chardonnays. It refers to both flavor and texture or "mouth feel."

• *Complex* is used to describe a wine that has a number of discernible characteristics (generally good ones), rather than one or two. Good wines that have aged well will be complex.

• *Dry* is used to describe a wine that is not sweet.

• *Earthy* describes a wine that tastes of the soil in which it was grown. Red wines most often have this characteristic.

• *Finish* is a synonym for aftertaste, used to describe the characteristics of a wine that remain after you have swallowed.

• *Flat* indicates a wine that does not have enough acidic qualities. A synonym for *uninteresting*.

• *Hard* is generally used to describe a young wine that has a lot of tannins (see "Key words").

• *Jammy* is used for a red wine that has the taste of dense ripe fruit. A wine can become overly jammy when not balanced by good tannin levels.

Tips

• There are, of course, many more terms that are used to describe wine. As you may have noted, most of them are descriptions of what the wine reminds a person of. As everyone sees, smells, and tastes things differently, people frequently disagree about the wines that they're tasting. While you may grow to respect one person's opinions, don't dismiss another's simply because that person doesn't find the same qualities in a wine that you do.

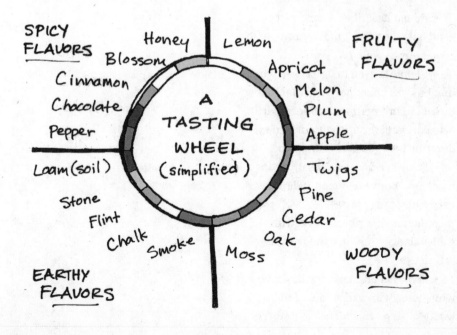

SPICY FLAVORS
Honey
Blossom
Cinnamon
Chocolate
Pepper
Loam (soil)
Stone
Flint
Chalk
Smoke
EARTHY FLAVORS

Lemon
Apricot
Melon
Plum
Apple

A TASTING WHEEL (simplified)

FRUITY FLAVORS

Twigs
Pine
Cedar
Oak
Moss

WOODY FLAVORS

Tips

- Remember, as you taste a wine, you're not looking for unpleasant characteristics at the start. There are few wines that have no redeeming qualities, and for the most part what's in your mouth can be enjoyed in one fashion or another. Try to appreciate a wine rather than knock it.

- *Neutral* is generally used to describe a wine without any outstanding characteristics but with no particular bad ones, either.

- *Nutty* refers to a wine with an oxidized character—one that has had exposure to air. This can be a good thing in smaller quantities, but too much oxidation will make a wine taste like sherry when it isn't.

- *Oaky* is used for a wine that has a noticeable taste of the oak barrel in which it was stored. This term can be used in both a positive and negative context.

- *Plummy* is used to describe wines with an overripe quality, usually resulting from the grapes having been left on the vine too long.

- *Rough* usually describes a poorly made wine, one that has a raw quality to it—although it can also refer to a quality wine that happens to be immature.

- *Round* describes a wine with a good balance of fruit and tannins, with good body as well.

- *Simple* is used to describe a wine that has few characteristics that follow the initial impression. Not necessarily a disparaging term, it's often used to describe inexpensive, young wine.

- *Strawberry* is used mostly with blush and nouveau wines. It denotes a very fruity, tangy taste.

- *Supple* describes a wine with well-balanced tannins and fruit characteristics.

- *Toasty* is often used to describe a white wine with a nice hint of the wooden barrel in which it was stored.

Sweeter wines are rarely described this way.

- *Vinegary* is used for a wine that has the excessive acidic qualities that indicate it has turned to vinegar. This generally occurs through cork failure, which exposes the wine to air; exposure to excessive heat while in storage; or excessive aging of the wine.

Learn**2** Spin a Basketball

Time

10 minutes

What you'll need

• A basketball or similar ball (kickball, soccer ball)

No matter how many 2torials you read, chances are you'll never be able to hit a home run in the World Series or slam a football through the goalposts after the winning Super Bowl touchdown. But of all the skills of athletic coordination, spinning a basketball is one of the showiest and easiest to learn.

BEFORE YOU BEGIN

Find a place where a bouncing ball will not upset anyone or anything. Stand with your weight balanced evenly on each leg. Ready to spin? Think fast. Think stable. Think *spin!*

STEP 1
Use your hands

It doesn't matter which direction you spin the ball; choose the way that feels most comfortable to you. Keep in mind it's your fingertips, not your palms, that really do the spinning.

Hold the ball about a foot and a half in front of your face, with your arms bent at a 90-degree angle and one hand on either side of the ball. For the best spinning, bring one hand closer to you and put one farther away.

Tips

- Speed and stability of the spin are your allies.
- Keep your knees bent to lean with balance.
- Don't show this trick off in the living room.

STEP 2

Start spinning

Now throw the ball up with one quick snap of the wrists, rotating your hands. Cross one arm over the other, and follow through with your fingers pointing in opposite directions.

Get used to spinning the ball (about two feet in the air) a few times and letting it drop, just to get up your speed and steadiness.

Speed is the most important factor in the spin. A spinning top is simply a top with a vigorous twist and will stay in place when rotated with force. With that in mind, spin it a few more times—still letting it drop right below—by increasing the opposing force with your hands.

STEP 3

Lift a finger

Now, when you spin the ball, don't let it drop. Instead, quickly slip your stiff index fingertip under the spinning ball. Don't worry about finding the grooves of the ball, and don't throw the ball up into the air—it will be tough to catch. Just let the momentum of the spin perpetuate itself, and place your fingertip at the ball's axis.

If you have balanced the spinning ball for just a second, you have succeeded. Practice and patience will do the rest.

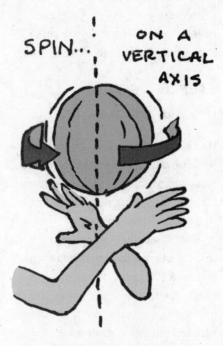

SPIN... ON A VERTICAL AXIS

Learn2 Throw a Flying Disc

Flying discs (what most of us call Frisbees) now come in various sizes, generally defined by weight. A lighter disc will travel faster and be more maneuverable than a heavier one. A heavier disc, however, will be more stable and travel farther. Heavier discs are better for windy conditions, such as the beach, and make great all-purpose discs to keep in your car's trunk.

BEFORE YOU BEGIN

There are two main factors to consider when throwing a disc: forward momentum and centrifugal force (spin). In other words, a well-thrown disc will have both sufficient wrist snap and force behind it. Wrist snap is often overlooked by novices but is essential to throwing the disc successfully.

Two additional important considerations are the angle to the ground and the point in the throw at which the disc is released. If this sounds confusing, don't worry too much. With disc in hand, your physical instincts will kick in and grasp the mechanics fairly quickly. You'll learn two throws here that will serve you well in most situations.

Method 1
The basic backhand throw

This method provides the foundation for building your throwing skills. Subtle variations in angle and release point will produce straight, right-banked, or left-banked throws. The necessary force is produced not only by arm strength but also by your body's mass moving forward with the throw.

LEVEL HEAD

WRIST SNAP

"FOLLOW THROUGH"

WEIGHT MOVES FORWARD

Time

Practice, practice, practice!

What you'll need

- A Frisbee or other flying disc that weighs at least 5 ounces (135 grams) (look at the packaging)
- Sunglasses (optional)

STEP 1

Stand corrected

Our natural tendency is to directly face the person we're throwing the disc to. Unfortunately, this often results in throws that veer wildly off target. So, position yourself accordingly.

If you're right-handed, stand with your right shoulder toward your target; left-handers should stand with their left shoulder facing the target.

Spread your feet about hip width apart, so that you have a more stable platform to throw from. Flex your knees slightly, so that your body is not rigid.

STEP 2

Get a grip!

Your grip determines the angle to the ground at which the disc is held.

Hold the edge of the disc firmly but not in a death grip. Place your thumb on top and your first two or three fingers underneath and slightly behind the thumb.

Bring your arm backward so that the disc is next to your rear leg and you feel your weight shift slightly back. Your forearm should not be parallel to the ground but dropped a bit, so that the disc is at about a 45-degree angle.

STEP 3

Gain force

Remember, the force in this throw comes not only through arm strength but from your weight and body mass shifting forward as well.

Bring your arm forward with some force. This is not a desperate heave but a smooth, disciplined action. The disc should remain at an angle to the ground, although that angle may be decreased in a natural, swinging motion. Practice a few times, back and forth, before releasing the disc.

As you bring your arm forward, shift your weight forward and take a slight step ahead with your front foot. This will add force to the throw, so that your arm doesn't have to do all the work.

STEP 4

Release

Here's where it all comes together—with the final two components, release point and wrist snap.

Be aware of where the disc is while your arm is in motion. The point in the motion at which you release the disc will determine where the disc goes: left, right, or straight ahead.

As you release the disc, snap your wrist forward, so that the disc "jumps" off the side of your first finger. This will impart spin to the disc and stabilize it in flight. The harder the wrist snaps, the more spin the disc gains and the better the throw.

Be careful to keep your wrist in line with your arm as you snap it. If you allow your thumb to lift upward, you'll lose control of the disc and it won't go anywhere near its target.

Continue your arm motion after the disc jumps off your finger. Following through directs the disc toward its target.

Method 2
The basic sidearm throw

This throw is more difficult than the basic backhand but is very useful when playing games such as Ultimate. Again, subtle variations in angle and release point will produce either straight or banked throws.

STEP 1
Stand corrected

Your stance here will be quite different from the backhanded throw.

If you're right-handed, stand with your left shoulder forward, your torso turned slightly toward your target. Left-handers stand with their right shoulder forward, torso turned slightly toward the target. Keep your feet shoulder width apart and your arm behind your rear leg. Flex your knees so that your body's not rigid.

STEP 2
Get a grip!

Your grip determines the angle to the ground at which the disc is held. Hold the edge of the disc firmly but not in a death grip. Place your thumb on top and your first two or three fingers underneath and slightly behind the thumb.

Bring your arm backward, so that the disc is next to your rear leg and you feel your weight shift slightly back. Your forearm should not be parallel to the ground but dropped a bit, so that the disc is at about a 45-degree angle.

STEP 3
Gain force

In this throw, most of your force will actually come from the wrist snap and weight transfer; your arm will move only a short distance.

Bring your arm forward with considerable force. Your elbow will be the pivot point, and your hand will actually stop with a jerk before it reaches your front leg. As you bring your arm forward, the foot facing your target should step forward a bit as your weight shifts forward. Your wrist needs all the help it can get.

STEP 4
Gain more force and release the disc

The importance of the release point and wrist snap are magnified with this throw.

Since your arm travels only a short distance, the possible release points are much closer together. Even a slight variance will greatly affect the flight direction.

A good starting point is to release the disc just after your wrist crosses your rear leg. The disc should be at a fairly steep angle when released. Snap your wrist quite firmly as you release. This throw will not succeed without good spin. After the disc leaves your hand, your first two fingers should remain firmly extended. You don't need to follow through.

Learn**2** Tune a Guitar

Time

- Beginners: 10 to 15 minutes
- Intermediate players: less than 5 minutes
- Advanced players: 1 minute or less
- Allow more time for a guitar that's completely out of tune or being strung with new strings

What you'll need

For relative tuning:
- A guitar that stays in tune (don't underestimate the importance of that; otherwise you'll perform an exercise in frustration)

For concert tuning:
- A tone source: for example, a tuning fork, another guitar already in tune, a piano, or a pitch pipe

It's true: you can play a lot of great music without knowing how to tune a guitar. But guitars naturally go out of tune as you play them for a while. And if your guitar-tuning friend isn't around when your instrument starts to go sour, you're stuck. Fortunately for beginning guitar players, tuning is a pretty easy skill to master.

And it'll improve your ear (your listening skills), which will become increasingly important as you progress in your playing.

Note: This 2torial is for acoustic and electric guitars, except those electrics with Floyd Rose–type whammy bars, in which case you're on your own.

BEFORE YOU BEGIN

With the guitar, "in tune" means that all strings have the proper tension in relation to one another. The proper tension produces the correct pitches, or sounds. These pitches sound good when the relationships are correct, and they sound dissonant (noisy and disorderly) when they're not.

STEP 1

Understand the fret board

You probably have one of three types of guitars: a standard steel-stringed folk guitar, a nylon-stringed classical guitar, or some variety of electric guitar. All of these types have six strings, arranged in size from thickest to thinnest, with the thickest on the top. Confused? If you hold the guitar on your lap horizontally (not with the guitar on its back but in the standard playing position), the thickest string should be closest to the ceiling. The strings are often numbered 1 to 6, with 6 referring to the thickest string.

Frets are the thin strips of metal that are inlaid on the wood of the *fret board,* and the number you have will vary a bit, depending on your guitar. Folk guitars have clearance (you can play notes) to fourteen frets, classical guitars to twelve, and electrics up to twenty-four frets. Frets are numbered 1 to 12 (or 24) starting from the head end of the guitar neck. The tuning pegs are the six small metal mechanisms located on the head of the guitar (at the end of the long, skinny neck). These are responsible for changing the tension of the strings.

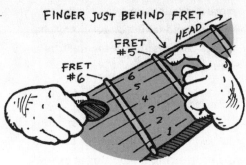

FINGER JUST BEHIND FRET
HEAD
FRET #5
FRET #6
6 5 4 3 2 1

STEP 2

Listen for the wave

The main skill for tuning a guitar is to listen and identify notes that are not in tune. By adjusting the tuning pegs, you can tune those unwanted notes out of existence.

What does "out of tune" sound like? Two strings that are similar in pitch but not in tune do something interesting. When two out-of-tune unison notes are plucked one right after the other, the resulting sound is wavering and wobbly. Think of it as a siren that's yelling, "I'm out-of-tune! I'm out-of-tune!"

STEP 3

Tune the sixth string

You start the tuning process with the sixth string (the thickest one). Here you have two options. *Relative tuning* is suitable for the beginner or the intermediate guitarist who's feeling a bit lazy. *Concert* or *absolute tuning* is for more experienced guitarists who are playing with other musicians, or for the very keen beginner guitarist. Actually, concert tuning isn't much

Optional:
• An electronic tuner (unnecessary for all but professional musicians who need to tune in a noisy environment)

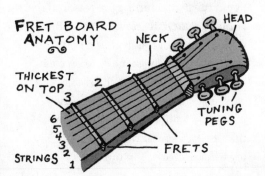

FRET BOARD ANATOMY
HEAD
NECK
THICKEST ON TOP
1
2
3
6 5 4 3 2 1
TUNING PEGS
FRETS
STRINGS

Tips

- Don't skip around. If you tune two strings well and the third one is a struggle, resist the temptation to jump ahead. You won't finish with a tuned guitar, even if you tune the rest of the strings correctly to that stubborn string.

- If you've tried and tried and still one string doesn't sound right, forget about it. Just start playing, and maybe you won't even hear the difference. The renowned bluegrass picker Doc Watson was overheard before a live gig saying this to one of his band members who was taking extra time to tune perfectly: "Oh, that's close enough for folk music!"

more difficult to do, but a beginner should avoid taking on too many challenges and possibly becoming frustrated.

Relative tuning:

This method doesn't use an external source to certify that, for example, the sixth string is vibrating at exactly the right speed. Instead, you pick a tone that sounds and feels good. It should be a nice deep tone, but listen for the signs of excessively low string tension. If a string is too low, it'll rattle on the frets or make a buzzing sound. If you hear that, tighten up the tuning peg for the sixth string until you hear the pitch rise and the buzz disappear.

If the string is difficult to press down or, heaven forbid, the tuning peg is difficult to turn, you've overtightened the string and you need to loosen the tension. Loosen slowly, or the sudden change of tension may cause the string to break.

Concert tuning:

With concert tuning you use a separate device to determine the absolutely correct tone for that string, no matter what guitar you play or where in the world you are. Examples of such devices are tuning forks, pitch pipes, a piano that is in tune, or an electronic tuner.

Let's say you're using a tuning fork. Take a look at it and see what letter is written on it—usually *A* but sometimes *E*. You'll be producing a tone with the tuning fork and matching the string to that tone. Use an A tuning

fork to tune the fifth string, an E fork for the sixth string.

Strike the fork on some firm but soft-edged surface, like your knee. (You never want to strike a tuning fork on something rigid like a bookshelf or a chair leg—that'll eventually ding up the fork and impair its tone.)

Quickly do these two actions: place the base of the tuning fork (not the forked part) gently on the guitar just by the strings. You should hear the sound of the tuning fork resonate in the guitar. Very soon after that, play the string that matches the pitch of the tuning fork. (If it's an A fork, you're tuning the fifth string with it. Afterward you'll go on to tune the sixth string by matching it with the fifth. If it's an E fork, tune the sixth string, and tune the rest of the strings as you would with relative tuning.)

STEP 4

Tune three more strings

In this step you'll learn the pattern for tuning that will work for almost all the strings. The one exception, the second string, is discussed in Step 7.

Assuming you have a good tone with the sixth string, you're ready to begin the actual tuning process. You're going to match the tone of the sixth with the tone of the fifth, and you'll do this by playing the same note on each string, one after the other. This is where you listen for the wave—the wavering, wobbling sound tells you that the two sound waves aren't together and aren't in tune.

For concert tuning:

If you have used an A tuning fork to get a true A pitch for the fifth string, you'll adjust the sixth string's tuning peg to match that string's pitch with the fifth string's. If you have used an E tuning fork to get a true E for the sixth string, you'll turn the peg for the fifth string to tune the fifth string to the sixth.

For either relative or concert tuning, proceed as follows:

Place your nondominant hand's index or middle finger on the fifth fret of the sixth string as shown in the diagram on page 93. Don't, however, put your finger exactly on the fret—it should be just behind the fret on the side closer to the head of the guitar (farther from you).

Which two notes do I compare? you may be wondering. Using your dominant hand's thumb or a guitar pick, play the sixth string while you are fretting it at the fifth fret with your other hand. Very soon after that, play the fifth string open—no fingers on any fret. Listen to the two tones. Hear the wave?

Now what? Amazingly, the slightly obscure theory in Step 2 has a very practical application to guitar tuning. Try to match the pitches of the fifth and sixth strings: you can do this by playing the notes with your dominant hand and then very quickly reaching over to adjust the appropriate string's tuning peg, depending on whether or not you've tuned one of them to concert pitch (see "concert tuning," above). If you are doing relative tun-

ing, adjust the fifth string to match the pitch of the sixth. Now listen for the speed of the wavering sounds. If the waves seem to speed up, you're putting the string even further out of tune. If you hear the waves slow down, you're getting closer to the right pitch. Once you hear the waves slow down and gradually disappear, you've got it. Well done!

Most important: Any time you try to match two tones (one that is correct and one that isn't), start the out-of-tune string lower than the string that's in tune. That is, loosen the out-of-tune string until it's lower (much lower, if you're not sure you're going in the right direction) than the correct one. You should always arrive at the right tone from below (by tightening a string that's too loose), not from above (by loosening a string that's too tight).

Repeat this process with the fourth and third strings. Once the fifth string sounds good, fret it at the fifth fret, and play the fourth string open. Again, listen for the waves and adjust the fourth string's tuning peg to match the sounds. Keep going to tune the third string: fret the fourth string on the fifth fret, play the third string open, and match the sounds.

STEP 5

Tune the second string

Now all hell breaks loose. Prepare for your world to turn upside down as you try to tune the second string. Actually, it's not bad at all.

What's the difference between this

Tips

- Find a quiet place to tune. Any other music or even loud conversation will hinder your ability to listen for the wave.
- Take a break if you feel yourself getting frustrated. You'll probably return in 5 minutes and finish tuning any remaining strings.

Key words

Flat: In the context of tuning a guitar, this describes a note that is lower than it should be.

Fret board: A thin overlay of wood that lies on top of the neck.

Frets: Thin strips of silver-colored metal that are inlaid on the fret board.

Neck: The long skinny part of the guitar that points away from you as the guitar sits on your lap.

Sharp: In the context of tuning a guitar, this describes a note that is higher than it should be.

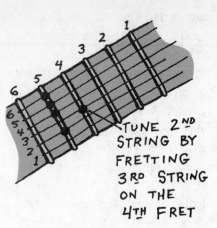

TUNE 2ND STRING BY FRETTING 3RD STRING ON THE 4TH FRET

string and the others? When you tune the second string, you have to fret the third string on the fourth fret (not the fifth, as you have been doing) and play the second string open, and adjust the second string's tuning peg. It's that easy. And remember—start the out-of-tune string lower than the string that's in tune. So, loosen the out-of-tune string until it's lower (much lower, if you're not sure you're going in the right direction) than the correct one.

Listen again for the speed of the wavering sounds. If the waves seem to speed up, you're putting the string even further out of tune. If you hear the waves slow down, you're getting closer to the right pitch. Once you hear the waves slow down and gradually disappear, you've got it.

STEP 6

Tune the first string

Tune the first string by fretting the second string on the fifth fret, and play the first string open. Match the two tones, and you're done.

STEP 7

Tune to a chord (optional)

Due to the laws of music theory and the limitations of guitar construction, a guitar cannot be tuned perfectly to every chord at the same time. To tune it perfectly to one chord will make the guitar slightly out of tune in another chord, although not offensively so. For this reason, try out your tuning skills in a chord that you might be playing in the near future, or just an open chord that you find easy to play, like the major chords of A, C, D, E, or G.

Slowly play each note of the chord successively. Hear any sour notes? If something doesn't sound right, play all the notes of the chord again, and identify the bad apples.

Fix the bum notes by playing the whole chord again and quickly reaching over with your dominant hand (which has just strummed the chord) to the tuning peg of the out-of-tune string. Give it a quick twist down to loosen the string, and turn it back up with the chord still ringing. You should hear the note match with the rest of the chord as you bring it up to the correct pitch. If it still doesn't sound right, repeat this action as necessary.

Here's an alternate posture for tuning to a chord: Push the guitar across your lap so that the head is closer to your body. It'll be easier to adjust the tuning peg right after you play the chord.

Learn**2** Use Chopsticks

Time

3 minutes a day for
3 days

What you'll need

- Some small
  pieces of food
- A set of chop-
  sticks, preferably
  tapered

Would you eat a sandwich with a spoon? Or use a fork to eat ice cream? Certain foods taste better when eaten with the appropriate utensils. Chinese and Japanese foods are no exception: they taste better eaten with chopsticks.

BEFORE YOU BEGIN

Many of us labor under a misperception about chopsticks—that both sticks are moved together in your hand as you pick up a morsel. Actually, one chopstick is held in place while you pivot the other to meet it.

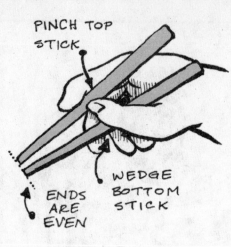

PINCH TOP STICK

ENDS ARE EVEN

WEDGE BOTTOM STICK

Tips

- Practice with a salad. Start with large pieces, and decrease the size as your skill improves. Soon you'll be plucking sesame seeds out of midair.
- As with any other motor skill, repetition is the key to success. Several short sessions over a period of time is more effective than a big chunk of time spent in one day.

STEP 1

Position the chopsticks

Place the first chopstick so that thicker part rests at the base of your thumb and the thinner part rests on the lower side of your middle fingertip. Next, bring your thumb forward so that it traps the stick firmly in place. At least 2 or 3 inches of chopstick should extend beyond your fingertip.

Relax. Now position the other chopstick so that it is held against the side of your index finger by the end of your thumb. Tap the ends of both sticks on the plate, while holding them at a slight angle to the table. Allow them to slide just a little so that the ends line up.

STEP 2

Pivot the top chopstick

Place a little pressure on the top chopstick. It will pivot on your index finger just above the second knuckle. Remember, the bottom chopstick is stationary. The tip of the top chopstick will move toward the tip of the bottom chopstick. Encourage this. Hold those tips together firmly enough to grasp a piece of food and lift it off the plate. Place delicately into your waiting mouth. You may wish to lean over your plate a bit during your first attempts. It might save you a cleanup.

That's about it. With a little practice you'll be able to fabricate stories about your life as an industrial spy in mainland China. Just remember to cook your rice so that it's sticky enough to pick up with the sides of the chopsticks. (See "Learn2 Cook Rice.")

Learn**2** Whistle

Time

Practice 5 minutes a day in the mirror, and you'll have it in a few weeks (at the most)

Whistling is a funny skill: folks who can whistle wonder how anyone could have a problem with it. Folks who can't wonder how anyone could ever produce such a sound. For those of you who can't, consider learning—a quick, loud, penetrating whistle has many useful applications and can be mastered with relative ease.

BEFORE YOU BEGIN

If you've set aside time to practice (highly recommended), then wash your hands first. It's good to be picky about what you put inside your mouth.

Method 1
The fingered whistle

STEP 1

Tuck away your lips

First, your upper and lower lips must reach over to cover your teeth and be tucked into your mouth. Only the outer edges of your lips, if anything, are visible.

STEP 2

Choose your finger combination

The role of fingers is to keep the lips in place over the teeth. Experiment with the following combinations to discover which works best for you, depending on the size of your fingers and mouth. Regardless of your choice of fingers, their placement is the same: each is placed roughly halfway between the corners and center of lips, inserted to the first knuckle. (Again, this will vary depending on the size of your fingers and mouth.)

Your options are
- A U shape created with thumb and middle finger, or thumb and index finger, of either hand
- Right and left index fingers
- Right and left middle fingers
- Right and left pinkie fingers

Now that your fingers are in place, be sure to follow these two matters of form: (1) your fingernails should be angled inward, toward the center of the tongue, not pointed straight in and toward the back of your mouth; and (2) your fingers should pull the lower lip fairly taut.

STEP 3

Form the crucial shape

Steps 3 and 4 happen very closely, if not simultaneously.

Draw the tongue back so that its front tip almost touches the bottom of the mouth a short distance behind the lower gums (about ½ inch/1 centimeter). This action also broadens and flattens the front edge of the tongue, allowing it to cover a wider portion of the lower back teeth.

The sound is produced by air flowing over a bevel, or a sharply angled edge. In this case, the upper teeth and tongue direct air onto the lower lip and teeth.

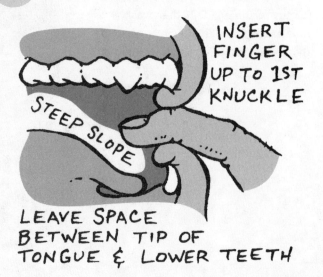

INSERT FINGER UP TO 1ST KNUCKLE

STEEP SLOPE

LEAVE SPACE BETWEEN TIP OF TONGUE & LOWER TEETH

STEP 4
Blow

Inhale deeply, and exhale over the top side of the tongue and lower lip. Some extra downward and outward pressure by the fingers onto the lips and teeth may be helpful. Experiment with the position of the fingers, the draw of the tongue, the angle of the jaw, and the strength of your exhalation. Adjust these until you succeed.

Start off with a fairly gentle blow. You'll produce a whistle of lower volume at first, but you'll also have more breath to practice with if you don't spend it all in the first three seconds. As you blow, adjust your fingers, tongue, and jaw to find the bevel's sweet spot. This is the area of maximum efficiency, where the air is blown directly over the sharpest part of the bevel. Once you locate the sweet spot, your whistle will have a strong, clear tone, as opposed to a breathy, low-volume sound.

As you practice, your mouth will learn to focus the air onto the bevel's sweet spot with increasing accuracy. You'll probably hear a breathy, low-volume tone that suddenly, as you adjust your fingers, mouth, or jaw, switches to a clear, full, high-volume tone. Success! You're on the right track—your task now is to reproduce the mouth and hand position that led to the better whistle.

Method 2
The fingerless whistle

The fingerless whistle is a natural outgrowth of the fingered whistle. In the first method, you use your fingers to keep the lip taut and in place. With the next method, instead of using your fingers, you rely on the muscles in your lips, cheeks, and jaw. Since this requires greater control of those muscles, it may be easier to master the fingered whistle first, then move on to the fingerless method.

STEP 1
Draw back the lips

Begin by extending the lower jaw slightly, and pulling the corners of your mouth back a bit, toward your ears. Your bottom teeth should not be visible, but it's fine if your upper teeth are. Your bottom lip should be quite taut against the lower teeth; if you need help with this movement, press an index and middle fingertip on either side of the mouth to draw the lip slightly out to the corners.

Note: This action is not an insertion of the fingers into the mouth, as the first method indicated. In this instance, you're simply stretching the lower lip a bit, and the fingertips aren't in the airstream.

TUCK LIPS INTO MOUTH

ONLY OUTSIDE EDGES OF LIPS SHOULD SHOW, IF ANYTHING.

STEP 2
Draw back the tongue

Now comes the crucial part. Steps 2 and 3 happen very close together, if not simultaneously.

Draw the tongue back so that it sort of floats in the mouth at the level of the lower front teeth. This action also broadens and flattens the front edge of the tongue, yet leaves a space between the tongue and the lower front teeth.

The sound of the whistle comes from air that is blown over a bevel, or a sharply angled edge. In this case, the upper teeth and tongue force air onto the lower lip and teeth.

STEP 3
Blow

Inhale deeply, and exhale—the air should flow under your tongue, up through the space between the tongue and teeth, and out of the mouth.

Experiment with the position of the fingers, the draw of the tongue, the angle of the jaw, and the strength of your exhalation.

Start off with a fairly gentle blow. You'll produce a whistle of lower volume, but you'll also have more breath to practice with if you don't spend it all in the first 3 seconds. Using your upper lip and teeth, direct the air downward and toward your lower teeth. The focus of the air is crucial for this technique—you should be able to feel the air on the underside of your tongue. And if you hold your finger below your lower lip, you should feel the downward thrust of air when you exhale.

As you blow, adjust your tongue and jaw to find the sweet spot. This is the area of maximum efficiency, where the air is blown directly over the sharpest part of the bevel. This results in a strong, clear tone that's constant, as opposed to a breathy, lower-volume sound that fades in and out. The sound you'll start with will resemble the sound of air being let out of a tire. Every now and then, the clear and full tone will come through, and you'll know that it's only a matter of time before you're hailing every pet and taxi in your community.

Learn**2** Write a Speech

Thorough preparation is a great solution to public-speaking panic. A well-written speech or presentation fills you with confidence and provides a solid base for your ideas. (You do have ideas, don't you?) What's more, there's no English teacher who'll grade down for punctuation or spelling errors. So relax. As long as you address the main points of your message (you do have a message, don't you?) with clarity and sincerity, you'll come across as a good public speaker.

BEFORE YOU BEGIN

You should know the speaking time allotted to you. If the correct speech length isn't obvious to you, ask the folks who asked you to speak. If they're too polite to give you a time limit, enforce one on yourself.

STEP 1

Consider the context

Look at a speech as a detective might, noting these factors:

• The subject: Determine your topic for this speech, for example, political action. What will you speak about? Whether it's on ancient forests or Japanese baseball history, you

Time

Spend three times the length of the speech on preparation. So if you're speaking for 20 minutes, plan on preparing for at least an hour. Technical subjects may require additional planning time.

What you'll need

• A pad of paper and a pen
• A clear mind
• Something to say (if you don't have a topic, ask the people who invited you to speak to suggest one)

Tips

• Research, then write. Spend an afternoon in the library to widen your range of knowledge on the subject. Using relevant statistics or studies strengthens the force of your argument. Avoid reciting too many numbers, though. You don't want to numb the brains of your audience.

should have a clear idea of the subject before you start writing. Speak with the organizer of the event if there are any doubts.

• The audience: This will determine your voice—your tone and the degree of formality in your word choice and sentence structures. Are you talking to fellow scientists or hyperactive nine-year-olds? Your language should change accordingly.

• The purpose: The objective that will define your subject, for example, "to argue for the possibility of a world without starvation."

• The title: Don't worry about an exact title at the outset; this will develop. Likewise, your subject may shift as you acquire more knowledge, but you must start somewhere.

STEP 2
Write anything on the topic

That's right: anything. Don't sit down to write the speech—just set down on paper some thoughts and feelings on the general subject of the speech.

Don't worry about posterity and popularity, just let it flow. This is an especially good step for those with writer's block. If you have trouble getting into the spirit, try it in the form of a letter. Write Aunt Nancy in New Iberia about the speech you're going to give, and describe what you plan to say.

During the early

stages of your writing, beware of the impulse to overedit or, rather, to edit yourself to a standstill. You don't have to forge the whole speech right now. Just sketch it out.

STEP 3
Turn it into a speech

Now that you're got a pile of verbiage, it's time to turn it into a speech. Go through it with a critical eye, picking out the gems and discarding the dross. Then arrange it in a structure that suits both the topic and your perception of the audience. An outline is one option, but you may prefer to detail a list of the things you want to say and go back later, numbering in the margin the items in order of importance. Then trim the list, maybe by half.

Repetition is essential for retention of a message. The old standard still holds true: say what you're going to say, then say it, then say what you just said.

Establish your voice by letting your personality manifest itself on paper. When you finally speak, a comfortable style will provide you with a more relaxed environment in which to express yourself.

STEP 4
Estimate the time

To best approximate how long your speech will be, simply read aloud three pages of written material at normal speed. Time it, then divide by three: you'll then know how many pages you

YOUR HEAD: SHOULD BE CLEAR!

TEXT: SIMPLE, STRAIGHT-FORWARD, POLITE

AUDIENCE→ WHO ARE YOU SPEAKING TO?

NOTES: SIMPLE REMINDERS

need to write per minute of your speech.

STEP 5
Polish the intro

The first objective is to get your audience's attention. Make your entrance fit your personal style, staying clear of a gimmick unless it really works for you. A few options to make use of are

• Anecdote: Tell a relevant story ("Upon his arrival in India, Sir Falkham searched . . .") that perks up the audience's ear to your topic. The key word here is *relevant*—an extraneous anecdote will just confuse them.

• Surprise: Propose an exciting or outrageous question ("What if the world ended tomorrow?"). That gets the audience thinking.

• Quote: Restate a well-known quote ("Ask not what you can do . . .") to introduce a point. But once again, make sure the link to your topic is clear.

• Fact: Make a factual statement that will impact your audience ("According to the *Daily Journal,* one in three of you will . . .").

• Straight: Go right to it and announce your topic ("Our management stinks!").

STEP 6
Build up the body of the speech

Be consistent and concise. If you want to present yourself as a knowledge-able source, back up your statements.

Obviously, a best man need not assure the audience of his friendship to the groom; however, your statements about the oil crisis or the burgeoning popularity of Albanian cuisine will require examples and/or statistics.

• Bad example: "Baloosa is sinking, you know!"

• Good example: "As reported by Frank Ford's senatorial task force, the city of Baloosa is sinking at a rate of three inches a year."

Don't go overboard, detailing every single item with five references, but be consistent. Cut out any redundancies.

STEP 7
Write the conclusion

Close with a statement summarizing the content of your speech. You need not write, "In closing" or "In conclusion"; a summary will be blatant enough. You may choose to thank those who invited you to speak and thank your audience for their time.

STEP 8
Edit

Expert speechwriters go through many levels of rewrites; you should do at least three. Be your own worst critic, and ask someone else to read it as well to get an outside perspective: you'll most certainly miss a few obvious mistakes.

Tips

• Know your audience. A fantastic speech written for jaded teenagers flops if delivered to the local chamber of commerce, and vice versa. Try to visualize a "typical" member of the audience as you write, but language thrown in solely to appeal (such as an adult tossing out teenage slang) tends to come across as insincere and patronizing. Knowing your audience doesn't mean pretending you're one of them.

• Use unstapled papers or cards that you can shuffle without rustling. Take care not to spill them, though, before speech time.

• Don't be afraid to write something and cut it out later.

Learn 2 Avoid Repetitive Stress

Ever wonder why you're in such a bad mood after working on your computer? Have you been experiencing wrist pain, tired eyes, or neck and back pain? Well, you're not alone: there are more people working on keyboards and in front of monitors than ever before, and many of them have been experiencing what is now termed repetitive stress injury, or RSI.

BEFORE YOU BEGIN

Let's face it: computers are not good for our physical health. Eye strain, wrist pain, back troubles, and a fat butt are what we get from working too long in front of our computers. We can,

however, minimize these complaints by setting up our work areas properly and using some common sense.

STEP 1
Consider your desk

If you or your firm has a spare desk hanging around, the temptation is almost irresistible to simply plop a computer on top and declare it a workstation. That's fine—so long as the desk offers at least a majority of these features:

- Your elbows can be bent at a 90-degree angle when you work. The best way to achieve this is by having an adjustable keyboard surface that descends to the required level.
- The desk should not shake or quiver when used. This means a heavily built, properly braced piece of furniture, with legs adjusted for full contact on the floor. Use shims if necessary.
- The desk should be deep enough to allow the monitor to be placed at least 20 inches away from your eyes. You can pull the desk back from the wall to make extra room, but don't balance the monitor precariously on the far edge.

STEP 2
Consider your chair

If you can't afford a good new chair, buy a good used one. It should be

adjustable in several different ways. It should adjust vertically to allow your forearms and thighs to be parallel with the floor when working. It should have an adjustable backrest that supports your lower back when sitting upright. It should also have armrests and wheels to roll back easily.

STEP 3

Consider your monitor

There is no substitute for a good monitor. You'll be staring at this thing for hours at a time, so insist on the following features:

- The "dot pitch" should be no greater than .28 for 17-inch or smaller monitors, .30 for monitors larger than that.
- It should not appear to flicker. If it does, then it probably doesn't have a high enough "vertical refresh rate." A vertical refresh rate of at least 68 hertz (Hz) is generally sufficient. To get a good sense of a monitor's flicker rate, try looking at it obliquely, out of the corners of your eyes.
- It should be sufficiently bright and should not distort at the edges.
- It should have an adjustable angle so that you can look directly at it without craning your neck.

STEP 4

Consider your keyboard

Your keyboard should have a springy feel when you hit the keys. You'll be amazed at the difference in typing effort from one keyboard to the next.

TOP OF MONITOR LEVEL WITH EYES .. 20 inches min.

CHAIR ADJUSTS:
HEIGHT
BACK
ARMS
SWIVEL

FEET FLAT OR TILTED UP

FOREARMS AND THIGHS EVEN WITH FLOOR

Some newer keyboards are being made in a split configuration, which allows a more natural hand position. These are highly recommended by people who use them but are not to everyone's taste.

STEP 5

Pay attention to your posture

If your equipment is adjustable, you should be able to follow these guidelines to minimize back and neck pain:

- Your keyboard should be just below elbow height, so that when your wrists are straight and your fingers are on the keys your forearms are parallel to the floor.
- Your back and neck should be straight when you look directly at the monitor. You may need to raise the monitor or lower your chair. Don't slouch!

Learn **2** Balance Your Checkbook

Time

First time: 60 minutes; subsequent balances: 30 minutes once a month

What you'll need

- A calculator
- A pencil
- One or two months' worth of your most recent bank statements
- Your checkbook (checkbook ledger included)

Tired of assessing your net worth from an ATM printout? Bouncing checks because you're "not an accountant"? Let's get those growing piles of bank statements under control. The effective handling of your finances will eliminate considerable stress and confusion from your life.

BEFORE YOU BEGIN

Calm yourself for the task at hand. Try to scrape up your ATM card, debit card, and deposit receipts, and have your checkbook ready.

STEP 1

Pick your financial type

First of all, classify yourself into one of the following categories:

- **Mostly:** This means you actually register your checks and deposits in your checkbook ledger but can never put together all the pieces.
- **Sort of:** You have a few receipts, some things written down, and can sometimes keep up with your finances.
- **Nope:** Your idea of record keeping is finding receipts in the laundry.
- **Regardless** of what type you are, the objective is the same: to understand the balancing process.

STEP 2

Assess the situation

Believe it or not, most checkbook discrepancies are easy to find and fix. The first step is to get ahold of the pieces necessary to complete the puzzle. Unbalanced accounts are usually the result of a combination of five factors:

• Uncleared checks: These are checks written but not yet cashed by the recipient. They are the archenemy of the checkbook balancer.

• Unregistered ATM- or debit-card withdrawals: Although banks are very tidy with their records, the average person is not. Money seems to slip out of ATM's unnoticed.

• Uncleared deposits: Deposits will usually clear the bank immediately, but it also takes a few days for your statement to arrive.

• Interest earned or bank fees due: These have their own line on the statement. Note: ATM- or debit-card fees will show up under "Withdrawals."

• Human error: A mistake in carrying a number can throw off your initial estimate by hundreds of dollars.

STEP 3

Keep track of debits

Sort your canceled checks (the ones returned to you) in numerical order. Then compare your canceled checks with those entered in your checkbook ledger. If you are a Nope and have trouble entering these items, write them down now—in pencil. In the future, try writing in the ledger before you write the check. Make sure the ledger entries correspond to the canceled checks. Watch for the transposing of digits, an easy error to make (like $23.21 to $21.23). As the checks in your ledger match the canceled checks, put a check mark next to them in the ledger to indicate they've cleared.

Arrange ATM-withdrawal receipts by date. Compare these with your records. Add any you've missed (the amount, date, and location) on the corresponding place in the ledger. You may have to consult the bank statement for these withdrawals if you haven't kept the receipt. As with the checks, put a check mark where the ATM withdrawals correspond in your ledger.

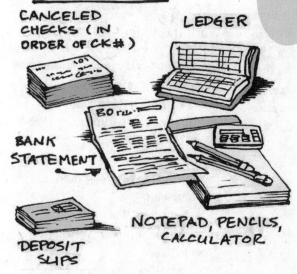

ORGANIZE:

CANCELED CHECKS (IN ORDER OF CK#)

LEDGER

BANK STATEMENT

NOTEPAD, PENCILS, CALCULATOR

DEPOSIT SLIPS

Look under the "Checks" section for any additional fees you may have accrued such as returned- (read: bounced-) check charges or monthly fees. If you were charged for anything you feel was a mistake, call your bank and inquire.

STEP 4
Note your deposits and earned interest

Compare your deposit records (ATM and bank visits) with those from the bank statement, making any amendments necessary in your ledger. Since deposits clear almost immediately (unlike that check you gave to Uncle Harvey for his eight-track player), you should contact your bank about any discrepancies.

Also check and record the interest paid to your account.

STEP 5
Work the ledger

Now calculate all of your transactions. If this is your first month of balancing, start with your bank statement's "beginning balance" and work through all the transactions to the "ending balance." By now you should have each transaction tracked down and accounted for.

So here goes. Work on the back of your statement (use the worksheet if provided):

- Write down your checkbook's current balance.

- Add any uncleared checks or earned interest to that balance. This is a discrepancy between your records and the bank's records, and the goal of balancing is to reconcile them.
- If there are any bank charges or uncleared deposits, subtract them from your balance.
- Check for any errors you may have made—that is, misplaced or miscalculated deposits or withdrawals (ATM's!). Adjust your balance accordingly.

Your final balance should match your bank statement. If it doesn't, don't worry. Step 6 will give a few ways to check your work. If it does match, you've done it! You're balanced.

STEP 6
Find the culprit(s)

If your numbers are not adding up, don't be frustrated; here are some steps to follow:

- Recheck your ledger calculations. Did you account for everything?
- Recalculate your checkbook ledger from the beginning of the month.
- Is your "beginning balance" the same as last month's "ending balance"?
- Still haven't found anything? Take a break and come back to it later. There's no reason to drive yourself into the ground.

Learn**2** Break In a Baseball Mitt

WORK IT !

Time

Anywhere from a few days to several weeks

What you'll need

- Mitt oil (or other oil designed for leather care)
- A baseball (one you don't need for play)
- A few thick, strong rubber bands
- Water and a basin

Baseball mitts are very special things. Far from being ready to use straight from the store, they demand individual effort to fully realize their enormously wonderful potential. It's the nature of leather to adapt to usage, and the only true way to optimize a mitt's condition is by using it to play.

BEFORE YOU BEGIN

What you want to do is soften the leather in the palm of the glove. At the same time you'll be training the glove to close over a baseball in such a way as to grip it firmly but provide easy access when the ball needs to be transferred to your other hand.

Method 1
The lumpy-bed approach

STEP 1
Oil it up

Rub some oil into the palm of the glove, and work it in well using your fingers. Rub some more oil into the crease in the palm that extends to the heel of the glove.

Put your hand in the glove, and flex
it back and forth. Guide it closed with
your other hand, so that it folds correctly along the crease.

STEP 2
Add the ball

Place the baseball in the webbed
"pocket" of the glove. Secure the glove
around the ball with the rubber bands.
Then put the glove under your mattress and sleep on it. Wrap it in a towel
first to keep the oil from staining the
mattress.

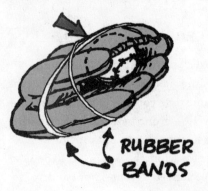

BALL HERE

RUBBER
BANDS

STEP 3
Play ball

Go out and use the glove in pickup
games and with your buddies.
    The more time you can spend oiling
and flexing the glove, the better. Sleep
on it for several more nights, and
you'll find the glove opening and closing easily.

Method 2
The big-band approach

STEP 1
Wrap the ball

Place the baseball in the webbed
"pocket" of the glove. Secure the glove
around the ball with the rubber bands.

STEP 2
Soak the glove

Soak the glove (wrapped around the
ball) in water for an hour or two. Then
set aside and let dry completely; this
could take a couple of days.

STEP 3
Oil it up

When the glove is dry, rub oil all over
the outside of it, as this method tends
to dry out the leather.

STEP 4
Play ball

Go out and use the glove in pickup
games and with your buddies.

Learn**2** Calculate Tips

The practice of tipping can be an anxiety-ridden ordeal for both parties involved, but that anxiety can easily be reduced with a little mutual understanding.

BEFORE YOU BEGIN

If the principles of tipping seem complex, remember that a tip is usually calculated in one of three ways: a percentage of the total bill for the services rendered; a flat rate for a service; or an amount per person or item (for example, luggage).

Note: The following suggestions are for situations in the United States, and all dollar amounts are in U.S. currency. Although tipping is practiced in big hotels in large cities worldwide, there are enough differences in local economies and tipping practices to preclude the formulation of any useful worldwide guidelines. Finally, this 2torial doesn't cover the practice of giving what the Chinese call *hyeung yao,* or "fragrant grease"—the reward (what some might call a bribe) for special services that won't be given without prior payment. Tipping in these situations is up to your discretion and bartering skills.

STEP 1

Identify good service

Tips shouldn't be thought of as mandatory. They are a bonus for employees who care about doing their job well. So take a minute to consider what good service is and when tips are appropriate.

Good service should be attentive without being intrusive. A good server speaks clearly and pleasantly and deals with questions in a positive and enthusiastic manner yet shouldn't be overly familiar unless the customer encourages such an interaction. A good server also acknowledges and sincerely apologizes for a mishap or a mistake in service and offers to compensate for the error.

If you're treated with superior service, then tip generously; if the service is halfhearted, terrifically inexperienced, or (heaven forbid) rude, then tip minimally or not at all. And remember, good service isn't a saccha-

Tips

• An easy way to calculate 15 percent: Let's say the bill is $44.38. First, locate the decimal point, that little dot after the second 4 of 44 (no, it's not a fly dropping). Take 10 percent of this number by moving the decimal point one place to the left, so that it's between the 4's. You now have $4.40 (skip the 38 cents) as 10 percent of the bill. Halve that number to figure out 5 percent of the bill; that will give you $2.20. Add the figures of $4.40 and $2.20 to get 15 percent: $6.60. If the service was adequate but slow or impersonal, then leave $5 or $6. If the service was decent but not fantastic, leave $7. If the service was superior, tip $8 or $9.

rine voice and smile. That's demeaning to both the customer, who's being treated like a dollar sign, and to the server.

STEP 2

Tips on land

This may seem like a long list of services and tips to keep straight, but remember that they can be divided into one of three categories: a percentage of the bill, a single charge, or a charge that increases depending on the number of people or items in your party. See "Tips" for help on calculating 15 percent of the bill.

Restaurants:

• Waiter or waitress: 15 percent of the bill.

• Headwaiter/maître d': None, but if he provides a special service for you, about $5.

COPY CLIP & SAVE

• Wine steward: 15 percent of the wine bill.

• Busboy: None.

• Server at a sit-down counter: 15 percent of the bill.

• Bartender: 10 to 15 percent of the bar bill if you're setting up a tab; if you're paying by the drink, add 50 cents to $1 per drink—don't plan on tipping at the end, especially if the bar is crowded. The waitstaff may assume you're not a tipper and won't be looking to serve you promptly.

• Coat-check attendant: $1 for one or two coats.

• Rest room attendant: 50 cents to $1.

• Car-park attendant: $1; if the attendant helps with luggage or packages, $3 to $5.

Hotels:

• Chambermaid: $1 per night; $5 to $10 per week for longer stays. For less-than-adequate service, leave a few dollars at the end of your stay, unless the service is offensively bad. (Note:

COPY CLIP & SAVE

Some folks don't leave a tip at all if they're staying only one night.)

• Room service waiter: 15 percent of the bill.

• Bellhop: $1 to $3 for opening and showing the room; $5 for bringing you to your room with luggage. (These amounts double for more expensive hotels.)

• Lobby attendant: None for opening door or calling taxi from stand; $1 or more for help with luggage or finding a taxi on the street.

• Desk clerk: None unless special service is given during long stay; in that case, $5.

Train and plane:

• Dining-car waiter: 15 percent of the bill.

• Steward/bar-car waiter: 15 percent of the bar bill.

• Redcap (luggage porter): Posted rate plus 50 cents.

• Airport skycap: $5 or more for full baggage cart.

• In-flight staff: None.

Tours and transportation:

• Tour guide (daily tour): For less-than-adequate service, don't tip. Otherwise $1 to $2 per person in your party, depending upon the quality of service.

• Tour guide (extended tour): For less-than-adequate service, $1 per day per person. Otherwise $1.50 to $2 plus per day per person, depending upon the quality of service.

• Tour-bus driver: Same as tour guide.

• Taxi driver: 15 percent of fare, no less than 25 cents.

• Car-park attendant: $1; if the attendant helps with luggage or packages, $3 to $5.

Personal services:

• Hairdresser: 15 percent of the cost, generally a minimum of $1. At a beauty shop where more than one person works on hair: 10 percent of the bill to the person who sets hair; 10 percent divided among others.

• Manicurist: $1 to $3 or more, depending on cost.

Tips

• Automatic tips: In some restaurants, a gratuity is included for large parties (in some cases, for a party of any size). It's often 15 percent, and there's always notice given when this policy exists, usually at the bottom of the menu. This relieves you of the obligation to tip—unless, of course, the service was extraordinary and you'd like to give an extra 5 percent.

RECIPIENT	AMOUNT
DINING-CAR WAITER	15% OF BILL
BAR-CAR WAITER	15% OF BAR BILL
LUGGAGE PORTER	POSTED RATE + 50¢
AIRPORT SKYCAP	$5 OR MORE
TOUR GUIDE (DAILY)	$1-$2 PER PERSON
TOUR GUIDE (EXT.)	$1.50-$2+ PER
TAXI DRIVER	15% OF FARE

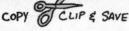

COPY CLIP & SAVE

PERSONAL SERVICES	
RECIPIENT	AMOUNT
BARBER SHOP	
HAIR CUTTER	15% OF TOTAL
BEAUTY SALON	
ONE OPERATOR	15% OF TOTAL
SEVERAL OPERATORS	10%: HAIR SETTER
	10%: ALL OTHERS
MANICURIST	$1-$3 OR MORE

COPY CLIP & SAVE

STEP 3

Tips at sea

Navigating cruise-ship tipping policies can be a bewildering experience at first glance, since there are many different kinds of staff, and the main bill (food, lodging, and travel) is usually paid in advance. Some cruise lines provide envelopes with specific suggestions and guidelines for tipping staff that have provided good service, so follow those if they're provided. A few ships, often the most expensive, have a no-tipping policy.

• Cabin steward (this person performs both housekeeping and room-service duties): $3.50 per day per person in your room.

• Dining-room waitstaff: $3.50 per night per person; half that amount to the busboy.

• Bartender and lounge waiter: on most ships, a 15 percent gratuity is automatically added to any beverage purchases. Exception: Wine stewards are usually given 15 percent of the total wine bill per night and are generally paid that night.

• Personal services: Hairdressers and beauticians are tipped 15 percent as services are rendered, just as on land.

• Don't tip: Headwaiters aren't tipped unless they've performed a special service for you. And never tip any of the ship's officers.

out to Sea

RECIPIENT	AMOUNT
CABIN STEWARD	$3.50/PERSON/DAY
WAITSTAFF	$3.50/PERSON/DAY
BUSBOY	$1.75/PERSON/DAY
BARTENDER	(TIP INCLUDED)
WINE STEWARD	15% OF WINE BILL
HEADWAITER	NONE
SHIP'S OFFICERS	NONE

COPY CLIP & SAVE

Learn2 Capture a Mouse

If you see a mouse scurrying in the corners of your home, you've probably got more than one—or will soon. Mice reproduce quickly, spread disease, and chew their way through just about anything short of concrete, leaving an entryway for their less-than-charming cousin, the rat.

BEFORE YOU BEGIN

Choose your weapon! There are a number of mousetraps available at any good-sized hardware store. The right one for you depends on the kind of fate you're comfortable imposing on mice.

• Snap traps slam a metal or plastic bar over the creature, thereby snapping its neck or spine and putting an end to its career. When they work as intended, death is instantaneous—but they don't always work as intended. Brace yourself for some unpleasant cleanups and the occasional mercy killing.

Time

15 minutes to bait traps, decide on placement, and place them; depending on the approach you take, you may not see results for 4 to 10 days

What you'll need

• At least 1 mousetrap; for best results, try about 3 per room
• Bait; peanut butter, chocolate bars, oatmeal, cooked bacon, or raw meat all work well (contrary to all those cartoons, cheese is not the best bait)

Tips

- If you don't have a humane trap, here's an alternative to killing the mouse. Keep a black umbrella on hand. If you see a mouse, open the umbrella with part of it flat toward the ground. Have someone else chase the mouse toward the umbrella. When the mouse runs into the umbrella, close it. Put the closed umbrella in a shoe box with holes (if a small umbrella), or put a rubber band around the top. Then dispose of it at least half a mile from your house.
- You might be able to prevent mice from visiting you in the first place by being a little more meticulous in your cleaning. Keep food covered, wash dishes right after you use them, wipe up crumbs and

- Humane traps are small cages with doors that shut as the mouse eats the bait. They're clean, painless, and mess-free but have a slightly less effective track record. They present the issue of disposing of the live mouse: Can you set it free without it turning into someone else's problem?
- Glue traps are not recommended in this 2torial because they're disgusting and cruel. They don't kill mice—just permanently fuse their flesh and fur to a sticky surface, making it impossible for them to do anything but quiver and starve to death.

STEP 1

Pick your trap locations

Choosing where to locate your traps is a key step. Along baseboards, in corners, and behind furniture are good locations, since mice gravitate to darkness and avoid wide-open spaces. You want places where other factors (such

FIND THE HOLES

LOOK FOR THESE

(NOT THESE)

as rattling doors or thudding feet) aren't likely to set off the traps but that aren't too hard for you to check and to retrieve the traps from.

Try finding the holes from which the mice are entering your rooms and placing the traps as close to them as possible. These holes probably won't be the archwaylike mouseholes you see in the cartoons; more likely they're the open spaces around the entry points of plumbing fixtures, or gaps between the baseboard and the floor. Remember, many mice can squeeze through an area significantly smaller than the diameter of a dime.

STEP 2

Bait and place the traps

First, bait the trap. You don't need a large amount, just a lump well under the size of a marble. You're not providing a meal, just something that smells appetizing. If you're using a snap trap, avoid getting smeary bait on the latching mechanism (the little metal ridge that keeps the trap from springing prematurely).

When placing the traps, try not to touch things in the area any more than necessary or to introduce anything that might bear your scent. You want the mice to smell the bait, not you. Orient the traps so that the bait is as close to the wall as possible: mice really don't travel any more than they have to, and placing the bait inches away may cause them to pass it up.

STEP 3
Check the traps

Every morning, check your traps—
even if you didn't hear a snap in the
night. If you don't get results after
three days, try new locations; you may
have misjudged the critter's movement
patterns. If another few days doesn't
do the trick, replace the bait and move
on to Step 4.

STEP 4
If you still haven't caught one

Move the furniture around. This
sounds wacky, but it works. Mice will
investigate the new arrangement and
will be more inclined to come across a
trap.

  If that yields no results, consider
poison or calling in an exterminator
(hey, it's war!).

STEP 5
Dispose of your mouse

Here are some suggestions:

  • If you're using the humane trap,
you'll have a live mouse wriggling
around inside. Resist the temptation to
set it loose in the vacant lot out back;
mice can very easily find their way
back to your home (and theirs).
Instead, go for a drive and find a spot
at least half a mile away from your
home (common courtesy dictates that
this spot not be someone else's resi-
dence).

  • If you've used a snap trap and the
creature is indisputedly deceased, you
can attempt to remove the body and
save the trap for further use or toss the
whole thing. In either case, wrap it in a
plastic bag and dispose of it with the
rest of your trash—unless you feel
compelled to give it a decent burial.
Whatever you do, do *not* flush it down
the toilet (yes, people have done that).

  • If the snap trap has trapped but
not dispatched the rodent, you have an
ethical choice to make. You can opt to
release it at a remote site (see "Tips"),
but if it's seriously wounded, you may
want to put it out of its misery. In that
case, one method is to place the mouse
in an airtight jar for a day or so. But
not too big a jar—mice have tiny lungs
and can survive a long time even in a
closed container.

scraps from coun-
ters and floors,
and always keep a
lid on the
garbage. If you
have a pet, pay
special attention
to the area around
its food bowl.
Check underneath
your sinks and
inside cupboards
for holes around
plumbing fixtures
or elsewhere.
Stuff some new
steel wool in the
cracks; mice
won't be able to
eat through it.

• Rats aren't just
big mice; they're
smarter, more per-
sistent, and more
serious pests. If
you suspect that
your problem isn't
mice but rats,
consider calling in
an exterminator.

Learn 2 Change a Diaper

Time

5 to 10 minutes

What you'll need

- A clean diaper (disposable or cloth)
- For babies under one month old or with diaper rash, you'll need cotton balls and warm water along with a dry washcloth; otherwise, diaper wipes

Optional:

- Ointment to help get rid of diaper rash
- Cornstarch to absorb wetness, which can lead to diaper rash

During the early months of infancy, diaper changing can take place as often as hourly during a baby's waking hours. Frequent changing and care will help prevent diaper rash.

BEFORE YOU BEGIN

Make sure you have everything you need accessible on the changing table or in the diaper bag.

STEP 1
Prepare

Wash and dry your hands thoroughly, and remove jewelry that can scratch delicate baby skin.

MOBILES ARE GREAT DISTRACTERS!

BEWARE OF "OLD FAITHFUL" - KEEP 'EM COVERED

HANG ON! HOLD BOTH LEGS WITH ONE HAND

STEP 2
Cover the changing surface

Place a towel, protective cloth diaper, or changing cloth over the table. If the baby is on a table from which he could fall, don't leave or take your attention from him, even for a second. Always keep one hand on the baby.

STEP 3
Entertain!

Your job will be much easier if you can keep the baby entertained long enough to hold still while you do the changing. Think of it as a minishow. Either you or someone else can create the diversion, or use a mobile overhead.

STEP 4
Remove the soiled diaper

As you remove the dirty diaper, pay attention to how it was secured. This will help you with putting on the new diaper. Hold the baby by the ankles, and carefully lift the hips. Remove the diaper with the soiled part folded in.

IMPORTANT!
WIPE ♂ = BOYS "UP"
♀ = GIRLS "DOWN"

STEP 5
Wipe

With a warm washcloth or diaper wipe, wipe girls from front to back and boys from back to front. Keep a fresh diaper draped over a baby boy's penis (as a defensive measure) while changing him.

STEP 6
Dry

If you used water or premoistened wipes, you'll want to pat the baby dry. Then use diaper ointment, if indicated, or dust the diaper with cornstarch to an equal height, usually from 1 to 2 inches up.

STEP 7
Put on the fresh diaper

Place the clean diaper underneath the baby. With disposable diapers, make sure that the diaper is going in the right direction. Bring the bottom half of the diaper up through the baby's legs. Aim a boy's penis downward into the diaper to prevent him wetting his shirt.

STEP 8
Seal it up

With disposables, secure the back corner over the front with the attached tape or adhesive tabs. Take care not to stick the tape to the baby's body.

If you are using cloth diapers, pin the diaper, always keeping your hand between the skin and the diaper to avoid sticking the baby. With pinned diapers, add a pair of rubber pants. The diaper should be tight enough to protect leaks but not so much that it irritates the baby's skin.

STEP 9
Get rid of the diaper

Put any formed stool into the toilet. Fold over paper diapers, and retape them before throwing them away. Cloth diapers should be rinsed and tossed into a tightly covered diaper pail until wash day. If not at home, place in a plastic bag until you get home.

STEP 10
Change wet or dirty baby clothes

Change any clothes or linens that require it.

STEP 11
Wash hands

Wash your hands (you don't need a 2torial for that, do you?).

Tips

- Change the baby often to prevent diaper rash.
- Lotions and powders are not essential to the changing process. Regular baby powder can actually cause problems (talc can be irritating) and prevent the diaper tape from sticking properly. Most baby-powder manufacturers make an all-cornstarch product as well; this can be used freely.
- If the baby has diaper rash, try to leave her undiapered for a little while to air out her bottom.

Learn 2 Convert Measurements

Time

A few minutes a day for 2 weeks will have you well on the way to metric fluency

With international trade, CNN, and of course the Internet, the global village is becoming better acquainted with itself. Unfortunately, a few key locations measure distance, weight, temperature, and liquids with the United States or Imperial system, while the rest of the world uses the metric system. Although there are small differences between U.S. and British imperial measures, all nonmetric measures are listed here as the U.S. standard.

BEFORE YOU BEGIN

Memorizing exact metric equivalents to U.S. measures is one skill, but the ability to make a quick and close estimate is a bit more useful. Estimation guidelines, while they aren't mathematically precise, are sufficiently accurate for most situations.

SKILL 1

Know your distance

These are arranged from smallest to largest.

Millimeter (mm): .039 inch. Estimate: 6 millimeters for every ¼ inch.

Centimeter (cm): .39 inch. Estimate: 2.5 centimeters to an inch. A small paper clip is 1 centimeter across.

Meter (m): 1.09 yards. Estimate: 3.3 feet in every meter.

Kilometer (km): .621 mile. A mile equals 1.6 kilometers. Estimate: 1.5 kilometers for every mile.

SKILL 2

Know your weights

These are listed from smallest to largest, so that you can see how all weight measures are based on the gram.

Gram (g): .035 ounce, or 1,000 milligrams. Estimate: 28 grams to an ounce. Multiply ounces by 28 to get grams. A small paper clip weighs 1 gram.

Kilogram (kg): 2.2 pounds. Estimate: 2 pounds in a kilogram. It's *twice* as hard to diet in a metric country.

Metric ton (t): 1,000 kilograms, or 2,240 pounds. Estimate: 2,000 pounds to a metric ton. It's *twice* as hard for your car, too.

SKILL 3

Know your volumes

These are listed largest to smallest, so that you can see how all volume measures are based on the liter.

Liter (l): 1.06 quart, or 2.1 pints, or .26 gallon. Estimate: only slightly larger than a quart.

Milliliter (ml): .03 fluid ounce, or .67 tablespoon, or .2 teaspoon. Estimate: Multiply milliliters by 30 to get ounces; 15 milliliters to each tablespoon; multiply teaspoons by 5 to get milliliters. It takes five to make a tea party.

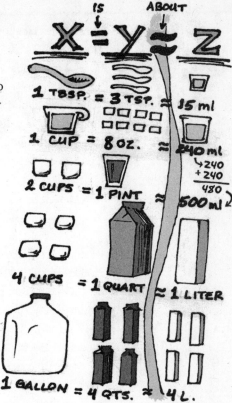

SKILL 4

Know your temperatures

Fahrenheit (F.) and Celsius (C.) are the units of temperature in U.S. and metric systems, respectively. Note that the term *Celsius* has replaced the term *centigrade*.

Estimate Celsius: Subtract 32 from the Fahrenheit degrees, then divide by 2.

Estimate Fahrenheit: Multiply Celsius degrees by 2 and then add 32.

Here are some familiar points on the scale:

- Water freezes: 0 degrees C., 32 degrees F.
- Water boils: 100 degrees C., 212 degrees F.
- Normal body temperature: 37 degrees C., 98.6 degrees F.
- Comfortable room temperature: 20 to 25 degrees C., 68 to 77 degrees F.

SKILL 5
Know your areas

Hectare: A square that's 100 meters by 100 meters (10,000 square meters), or a square 300 feet by 300 feet (90,000 square feet). In U.S. acres, a hectare is 2.47 acres. Estimate: 2.5 acres per hectare. (Heck, I can remember 2½!)

Acre: An acre equals 43,560 square feet. In metric terms, that's 4,047 square meters. Estimate: 40,000 square feet, or 4,000 square meters per acre. Or picture a square that's 200 feet by 200 feet. Get out there in your 4 by 4 to check out that land parcel.

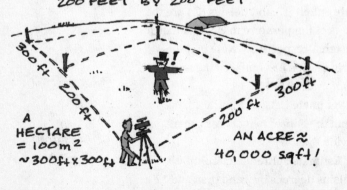

ACRE: IMAGINE A SQUARE 200 FEET BY 200 FEET

300 ft
200 ft
300 ft
200 ft

A HECTARE = 100 m² ~ 300 ft × 300 ft

AN ACRE ≈ 40,000 sqft!

SKILL 6
Know your nautical measurements

Sailors all over the world use knots to describe wind and craft speed, but they understand these measurements in terms of their respective measurement systems. To know how the other side thinks, see below.

Fathom: In U.S. measurements, 6 feet; in metric terms, 1.8 meters. Estimate: 2 meters for every fathom. U.S.: When you think of a fathom, think about being 6 feet under. Metric: The term *fathom* comes from a person's *two* arms outstretched.

Knot: A knot may also be termed a nautical mile, and it's equal to 1.151 miles, or 1.852 kilometers on land. Estimate: 1 nautical mile is equal to 1 land mile or 2 kilometers. Hey, there's knot much difference between nautical miles and miles on land.

League: 3 nautical miles; 20,000 leagues under the sea would be just over 69,000 miles on land.

SKILL 7
Know how to improvise measures with nearby objects

If you know the lengths of certain body parts or other accessible objects, you'll always have a good standard of measure on hand.

- One of the knuckles of your hand is probably close to 1 inch long. Likewise, the width of one of your fingernails is 1 centimeter.
- A U.S. standard-size piece of

paper is 8½ by 11 inches, or 215 by 275 millimeters. In other countries, A4 is the standard size, which is 210 by 297 millimeters, or roughly 8½ by 12 inches.

• Take the most common paper currency in your country, and measure its length or width. Then you'll always have a reliable standard that's equal to a certain measure.

• If you're keen on measured body parts, other good ones are your forearm, the width of your palm, the length of your foot, and how many of your strides equal 10 yards (or meters).

SKILL 8

Know your abbreviations

Note that you don't abbreviate measurements with periods.

- **m:** meter
- **cm:** centimeter
- **mm:** millimeter
- **km:** kilometer
- **g:** gram
- **kg:** kilogram
- **l:** liter
- **ml:** milliliter
- **t:** metric ton
- **ha:** hectare

SKILL 9

Know where to find exact measurements when you need them

These are very specific measurements, sometimes to the billionth of a unit. Numbers to the right of the deci-

mal point are in groups of two or three for easier reading. The characters [2] and [3] refer to square or cubic measures: 3 meters^2 is 3 square meters, 9 inches^3 is 9 cubic inches.

The basic units of the metric system are the meter, the liter, and the gram, which measure length, volume, and weight, respectively. For measuring quantities much smaller or larger than these units, simply add a prefix. These are listed below. There are many other prefixes, but they're mostly used for scientific measures.

• **Milli-** means 1/1,000. A milliliter is one thousandth of a liter.

• **Centi-** means 1/100. A centimeter is one hundredth of a meter.

• **Kilo-** means 1,000. A kilogram is 1,000 grams.

The beauty of the metric system is the ease with which you can move between units of measure. If you want to convert meters to centimeters, just move the decimal two places to the right: 2.65 meters equals 265 centimeters. For meters to millimeters, move the decimal three places to the right: .332 meters equals 332 millimeters. For meters to kilometers, move the decimal three places to the left: 4,000 meters equals 4 kilometers.

Learn **2** Drive a Stick Shift

Caution: This 2torial is intended to be supplemented by instruction from a knowledgeable driver. Do not drive unsupervised until you have been tested by a competent adult (if you can find one). Also, know that there may be some additional wear and tear on the clutch during the learning process.

Time

Allow 3 hours per day for 2 days

Driving a stick shift is sort of like riding a bicycle—only time and practice stand between confusion and second nature. Why bother? Because manual transmissions (those that require stick shifts) usually get better gas mileage than their automatic counterparts. And because you control the gears, acceleration and hill climbing will prove more effective. Also, downshifting can save wear and tear on your brakes and provides more control in icy or rainy conditions.

BEFORE YOU BEGIN

Know your way around. A manual transmission demands that the driver rather than the engine shift the gears. Most cars have four or five forward speeds, as well as reverse. In order to master the process, you need to know the following:

• The clutch pedal is located at the far left on the floor and is used when moving up or down from one gear to another. The clutch is disengaged when the pedal is pushed to the floor.

• Neutral is not a gear; actually, it is the absence of gear. When the engine is running in neutral, you can rev it up, but you won't go anywhere.

• For most cars, second gear is the workhorse. It will get you up (and down) steep hills as well as through congested downtowns.

- Reverse is somewhat different from the other gears: it's got more range than, say, first gear, but doesn't like going for too long or too fast. So, don't back up around the block to pass the time.

- Gas makes a car go. The gas pedal (at far right) works with the gears to give the engine power at different levels. As mentioned before, if you press on the gas pedal while out of gear, you will only rev the car up: this is how fifties hot-rodders showed their toughness. But if you overaccelerate with the clutch partially engaged, you'll eventually wear it out.

STEP 1
Learn the gears

Learn the location of the gears and the feel of passing through them. First learn to shift the gears without the car running, pushing the clutch in each time. Then, from the passenger seat, try it with someone else driving the car and operating the clutch. Be sure to place the stick all the way into gear—until it won't go any more—but don't force it. If you stop halfway, you will hear an incredibly unpleasant grinding sound, which means your car is not in gear.

Eventually, you will know by feel when to shift, but early on you'll have to act deliberately. Even if you've never been in a car before, you can tell when a car is in the appropriate gear: it's not coughing and chugging (gear too high), but it's not making a high-revving sound either (gear too low). If you have a tachometer, shift at around 3 (3,000 rpm) on each gear or every 15 miles per hour (first gear 1 to 15, second 15 to 30, third 30 to 45, et cetera). This is only a general rule, of course, and higher-powered autos will deviate from this. Shift before you hear that loud revving sound.

STEP 2
Start it up

Put the car in neutral before starting, or you will jump ahead. Keep in mind that most new cars will not start without the clutch pressed down. Leave the shift stick in neutral while the car warms up. Alternately, start the car in gear with the clutch pedal pushed to the floor, then shift into neutral, release the clutch, and let the car warm up.

STEP 3
Protect the clutch, yourself, and the car

The clutch is the mechanism that allows the gears to transition back and

Key words

Idling: State of the engine in which it's running in neutral or in gear with the clutch pressed in.

Revving: Increasing the power of the engine, usually by stepping on the gas pedal. The term comes from revolutions per minute (rpm), an indication of how fast the engine is turning. Low revving is idling (about 700 to 1,000 rpm), and high revving is the point where you should shift up a gear (from 2,500 to 3,000 or up).

forth smoothly. If you pull the car in or out of gear without using the clutch, or release the clutch only halfway into gear, you will hear that amazingly unpleasant sound.

It's difficult to avoid some sort of wear and tear on the clutch when learning how to drive a stick shift. If you go slowly at first and pay close attention, you can feel in your feet where the clutch engages and disengages. If you learn that well, you'll put less strain on your car. You'll also be able to drive any stick-shift car more smoothly from the get-go.

Avoid needless acceleration when the clutch is partially engaged. When at a stoplight, don't get in the habit of holding the clutch in for more than a few seconds or you will have other problems down the line. Instead, put the car in neutral while stopped for any length of time.

Popping the clutch: Invariably, you will miss your gear or release the clutch too quickly and the car will lurch ahead. Often at the outset you will pop the clutch too quickly and stall the car. Don't worry, it happens to everyone. Just get those exercises out of the way before you find yourself in bumper-to-bumper traffic.

STEP 4

Find the G spot

Here we are at the most important junction of the stick-shift experience: the door to acceleration. Driving a stick shift is all about that magical place where the clutch comes up and the gas pedal goes down: this is where the gears are shifted and the car accelerates. Let's take the shift from first to second on a flat road as an example. First gear is going steady, then you clutch in as you come off the gas quickly, then off the clutch slowly while pressing in the gas. That place in the middle where the clutch pedal is to the floor and you're off the gas is where you take the shifter from first to second. Get those feet and hands used to working together.

Here we go once more:

- You're revving high (around 3,000 rpm or at 15 mph).
- Push the clutch in and ease off the gas.
- Move the shifter smoothly from first to second gear.
- Slowly let off the clutch while pushing on the gas.
- Completely let your foot off the clutch and gas it up.
- Same time next gear!

STEP 5

Now try downshifting

Downshifting is the act of moving appropriately to lower gears while slowing down. This is the essential difference between the operation of an automatic transmission and a manual: downshifting not only helps you slow the car, but it also puts you in the right gear for the speed. Downshifting is your friend, especially in bad weather or on hills, where immediate braking can be dangerous.

Keep in mind that you may shift

down only one gear or simply apply the brakes. Again, knowing your range in each gear will help determine what's needed.

While downshifting, move from clutch to brake while in gear. This will help you slow down without revving too high between gears.

If you're driving 45 mph in fourth gear and come upon a stop sign ahead:

• Push in the clutch, and shift down to third while using the brake.

• Let the clutch out slowly to avoid high revs.

• Next, do it again into second before you stop.

• Never downshift into first.

STEP 6
Learn the subtleties of reverse

Be very careful when backing up. The reverse gear is quick and can jump out at you. To get into reverse, sometimes you need to run the shifter through the other gears first with the clutch in. The clutch is key. Let it out slowly, and push it back in while using the brake if necessary; with this simple measure you will likely be able to back out of any spot.

STEP 7
Win the hill challenge

Find a hill with little traffic. Come to a stop on an upward incline, and engage your emergency brake. When you want to go again, shift into first, start to accelerate slowly as you release the clutch pedal, then release the emer-

gency brake just as you feel the car engage the gear. This way you are using the brake to keep you from rolling back. If you stall, put on your brake and start again.

STEP 8
Remember the parking brake

It is important to note that the emergency brake is very important when parking a stick-shift car, because there is no park gear to keep the car from rolling. Some rely only on the pull-up emergency brake, usually sufficient in most situations. But for extra safety, leave the car in first gear *and* use the emergency brake.

STEP 9
Practice these scenarios

• In the neighborhood, 25 mph: Start, go to first gear, change to second gear, run either high rpm in second gear or low rpm in third. Sometimes run high to low second gear, depending on speed.

• On the highway: High rpm in third or fourth onto the highway at the appropriate speed, then fifth gear (if available).

• Going down a steep hill: Keep the car in a gear that will help you maintain the correct speed: the engine should sound like it's working but not whining. This is also helpful when you've got to come to a complete stop at the bottom of any hill.

Tips

• From the passenger seat practice helping the driver shift to get the hang of it.

• Don't downshift into first; it's too low a gear.

• Pass through the gears before you go into reverse, if necessary.

Learn **2** Gift Wrap a Present

Time

5 to 15 minutes

What you'll need

- Wrapping paper
- Transparent tape
- Scissors
- Ribbon or bow

Wrapping a gift adds a personal touch, saves money, and is really quite simple once you've mastered a few simple tricks. It's also an opportunity to express yourself creatively and to show someone that you really care.

BEFORE YOU BEGIN

Look for wrapping paper and ribbons that will look nice together. Ask a gift-wrapping attendant at a department store for ideas, or borrow an idea from a gift catalogue. If you can picture in your mind what you want the package to look like, your job will be that much simpler.

STEP 1

Set up your work space

Find a clean table or any large flat area where you can lay the above items out and where the recipient of the gift is not likely to walk in unexpectedly. Also, if your transparent tape is not in a desktop dispenser, cut yourself three 1- or 2-inch pieces. Stick them lightly to the corner of the table.

STEP 2

Measure out the wrapping paper

For wrapping purposes, let us call the four longest, thinnest sides of the box the *sides*. The two shortest sides will be called the *ends*. Be sure you have enough paper to cover all four sides of the box, plus an inch or two, and that enough paper will hang over the sides to cover the ends. Here's a quick and easy way to measure.

Lay out the paper. Set the box down 1 inch inside the side edge of the paper. Let's call the edge of the box on the paper edge A. Move the box far enough inside the end edge so that both ends would be covered if you folded the paper up over them, but don't actually fold it yet! Roll the box carefully three times so that all four sides have touched the paper. Edge A has now rolled down to the paper. This is where you cut.

Always give yourself a little extra if you aren't sure. Extra paper can be trimmed, but if there's not enough, you've wasted what you've cut.

STEP 3
Cut the paper

"Measure twice, cut once" is what the good carpenter says, and you'll be wise to follow this advice. After you have rolled out enough paper to cover the box, snip the edge of the paper to mark where you want to cut it. To make a straight cut, take the box off the paper, and fold the paper so that the edges are perfectly lined up. The fold should be exactly where you snipped the paper. Insert the bottom blade of the scissors inside the fold. Cut the paper from the inside out in one long, easy motion. If the paper snags or gets caught, stop. Use shorter, snipping cuts until the paper cuts easily again.

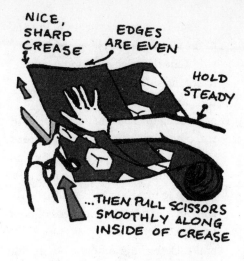

NICE, SHARP CREASE

EDGES ARE EVEN

HOLD STEADY

...THEN PULL SCISSORS SMOOTHLY ALONG INSIDE OF CREASE

Here's a second way to cut. Using a folding bone or credit card, crease the fold so that it is straight and sharp. Hold the paper down with your weaker hand so that you can run the folding bone along the inside of the crease easily and smoothly. Pull the paper so that it tears along the crease. Some papers tear more easily than others. If you need a sharper crease, fold the paper backward on exactly the same crease, then again the other way. This breaks down the threads in the paper so that it will tear more easily.

STEP 4
Wrap the sides

Place the box in the middle of the cutout section so that the "top" (the side you want up when it is opened) is on the bottom touching the paper. If you are wrapping something breakable, handle the box gently. Line up the box so that the paper you measured for the ends runs along the ends, not along the sides. That is, make sure the package is correctly oriented on the paper.

Key words

Folding bone: Any long, flat object with a straight edge you can hold easily in your hand, for example, a credit card, ruler, butter knife, or fingernail.

Swallow's tail: For the long ends of ribbon bows, an inverted V-shaped cut that leaves two skinny tails.

Take the paper that goes along one of the sides, and fold it up along that side. Line the edge up along the middle of the side that's facing you. Hold the paper in place, and run your fingers along the corner sticking up. This will crease the paper exactly where you want it, along the corners. You may need to pull up on the paper just enough to make sure the sides are smooth and tight. Take a piece of tape (remember the easy-access tape?), and stick the edge onto the box so that it will stay put.

Now take the other side of the paper and lay it to cover the unpapered portion. It should overlap the edge you just taped down. Pull it so that all four sides are smooth and tight. Use another piece of tape to hold this edge in place. Lay the tape lengthwise, centered along the edge. This second edge should lie on the face-up side of the box barely to cover the first taped edge. It should not hang over the side. If it does, trim it with your scissors, then tape it down.

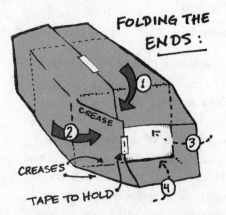

FOLDING THE ENDS:

CREASE

CREASES

TAPE TO HOLD

STEP 5

Wrap the ends

Remember, the more snug the fit, the neater the appearance.

Turn the box so that one end faces you. Remember, the box is still upside down. Fold the length of paper on the face-up side down to the end, and crease it along the edge as you did before. Tape that end down.

Now fold one side in toward the middle, and crease it. You will notice the crease creates an angle when you get to the bottom. This is good! Fold the paper into the bottom corner where the end of the box meets the paper. Crease the paper along that fold.

Carefully fold the other side in, crease it, and fit the paper into the bottom corner. One last fold for this end. You will find that the extra paper folds over onto itself, and the folded edge will run back along itself. Now you can fold up the end piece and tape it to the box. The end piece should either be a trapezoid (a rectangle with two sides caved in) or a triangle. If the end piece hangs up over the side, fold it back in on itself so that you have a trapezoid, which fits along the end, and crease it. Tape the end piece. Turn the box around, and do the same thing with the other end.

STEP 6

Add a bow

Most bows purchased today have some kind of peel-and-stick adhesive on them. Pull back the waxy paper and position the bow on top, either dead center or off to one corner.

STEP 7

Add a ribbon (nouveau style)

Again, pictures say more than words. Consult the diagrams, and go to the written directions for the specifics.

Tape one end of the ribbon about one quarter sideways in from one corner of the package. Wind the other end of the ribbon under an adjacent corner (a corner directly below or across, not diagonal). Take this end over to the corner that's diagonal from the starting corner. Finally, wrap under the remaining, unadorned corner, and tape it over the top of the end you started with. Remember to pull the ribbon as snugly as you did the wrapping paper, to make it even and taut.

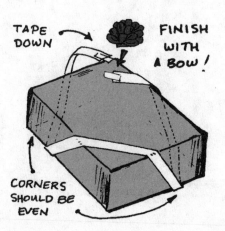

TAPE DOWN

FINISH WITH A BOW!

CORNERS SHOULD BE EVEN

STEP 8

Add a ribbon (classic style)

A classic way to add ribbon is to wrap it around the middle of the package.

Cut the ribbon so that the two ends are at least twice as long as the package. With the bottom of the package face-up, slip the ribbon underneath the top side. Cross the ribbon ends on the bottom side, and turn them sharply 90 degrees. The ribbon should fold neatly against itself and hold the package together a bit. Continue with both ribbon ends out to the two unadorned sides. Gently flip the box over, and bring the ribbon ends together at the top. Tie a bow as snug as possible. You should have enough ribbon so that there is at least as much remaining of the two ends as the length of the loops in the bow. To make it a little fancier, cut the ribbon at a diagonal or in a swallow's tail (inverted V shape that leaves two skinny tails).

If you are really good, you can fold the wrapping paper as described in Steps 4 and 5, making the creases as indicated but not using any tape. The ribbon tied in the fashion just described can hold the entire package together—with the added thrill of popping the whole thing open when the recipient pulls on one end of the bow. Neat stuff!

Tips

- In a pinch you can make your own wrapping paper with paint, markers, or stamps, or use last week's Sunday comics.
- Be sure the box is centered on the paper when you start folding. You want the end pieces to be the same length on either side.

Learn 2 Improve Your Gas Mileage

What you'll need

- A pen or pencil and paper
- A tire-pressure gauge (optional)

Tips

- Four-wheel-drive vehicles are all the rage right now, but their dirty little secret is gas mileage—it stinks. Unless you really spend a lot of time crawling along washboard roads, consider another type of vehicle instead. Front-wheel drive and snow tires will get you most places you want to go.

Let's face it: along with a thinner waist, a faster modem, and greater tranquillity, everybody wants better gas mileage. It doesn't matter if you're driving a sparkling new Dodge pickup or a barely mobile '73 Renault, that gas gauge always goes down faster than you want it to.

BEFORE YOU BEGIN

If you already own a car, there are several gas-consumption factors that you can't control: engine size and design, vehicle weight and wind resistance, gasoline quality and formulation.

There are, however, a few ways in which you are the master of your driving fate, so let's concentrate on those. All of the strategies boil down to two things: maintenance and driving habits.

STEP 1

Maintain optimum tire pressure

It sounds like a no-brainer, but when was the last time you checked your tire pressure? It takes more effort for an engine to propel an underinflated tire than a properly inflated one—the engine uses more gas to move it along.

Before you move your car in the morning, use a good-quality tire gauge to take each tire's air pressure. This is your cold measurement: write it down

TIRES SHOULD BE PROPERLY INFLATED

CHECK REGULARLY!

on a pad or slip of paper that you'll carry with you.

Look in your owner's manual (or on the edge of the driver's door), and write down what tire pressure the car maker recommends. You'll fill your tires according to these numbers rather than what's printed on the outside of the tires themselves. Compare the cold measurements with the manufacturer's pressure recommendations. If the manufacturer recommends a different pressure (higher or lower), you'll adjust the tire pressure accordingly.

Go to a gas station that has an air-pressure hose, and take your tire pressure again. This measurement will probably be a little higher, as the tire has warmed up. This is called the warm measurement.

If the cold measurement was lower than the manufacturer's recommendation, add the proper amount of air with the hose. How much? Use the warm measurement as your guide. Let's say you compare the cold measurement with the manufacturer's recommendation, and the tire needs 3 more pounds

of pressure. If the warm measurement was 34 pounds, fill up the tire until the gauge reads 37 pounds. Don't worry if the final measurement is more than the manufacturer's recommendation—tomorrow morning, when the tire is cold again, the pressure will be correct.

If the cold measurement was higher than the manufacturer's recommendation, release the excess pressure from the tire. (This is easy to do: find the valve, and press on the metal piece in the center of it with your fingernail, a key, or a small stone, until you hear a hissing sound.) Again, use the warm measurement as your guide. For example, if you knew from your cold measurement that the tire had 2 pounds of excess pressure, and the warm measurement is 38 pounds, release pressure until the gauge reads 36 pounds.

Overly inflated tires can wear unevenly or too fast and also affect the car's handling. So please don't try to improve your mileage by inflating them to a balloon shape.

STEP 2
Keep it in tune

Keep your engine tuned properly. Nowadays, most cars on the road have electronic ignitions that are simpler to maintain than they used to be, but there are still a few items that need attention.

• The air filter should be replaced when you can't easily see light through it.

Key words

Firing: The function of the spark plug—it produces a spark.

Gap: An adjustment made on a spark plug that determines the correct distance between two pieces of metal that produce a spark.

Points: Part of older ignition systems; these tend to wear out and need to be replaced when the car is tuned. They're not part of a modern car's maintenance program.

Spark plug: The mechanism that provides the spark to the compressed mixture of gas and air in the cylinder of an internal combustion engine.

Timing: A procedure that ensures the spark plugs will ignite at the proper time. In the past this was done by hand; nowadays it's generally set with a computer.

Tips

- Carpooling is one of the best ways for everybody to save gas. If there's one car on the road instead of four—well, you can do the math for yourself. Carpooling-arrangement services, both private and government-run, are cropping up in some areas; call around and find out what's available. If that doesn't work, make a sign asking other commuters to form a car pool with you, and put it up on the community board at a local food market, gym, or spiritual meeting place, or at your workplace.

UNDER THE HOOD:

CLEAN AIR FILTER

ADJUST TIMING

CLEAN SPARK PLUGS

EXHAUST IS OKAY

ON THE ROAD:

SLOW, CONSTANT SPEED

MINIMIZE AIR CONDITIONER AND HEATER USE

REDUCE BRAKING AND QUICK ACCELERATIONS

- The timing should be properly adjusted. (See "Key words.")

- The spark plugs should be clean, gapped correctly, and firing properly. (See "Key words.")

- Older cars and trucks may need the points replaced as well.

Keep your exhaust system in good shape. A hole in your muffler or along your exhaust pipe will reduce your gas mileage as well as making noise and a bad smell.

STEP 3

Change your driving habits

In general, the faster you go, the more gas you use. The defunct "Drive 55" campaign in the United States was not only about safety, it was also an energy-conservation measure: cars use less gas at 55 mph (90 kph) than at 65 mph (105 kph).

Heavy acceleration and hard braking greatly reduce gas mileage. Smooth acceleration from traffic lights and gradual braking at stop signs will help more than you might think.

Constant speeds, rather than speeding up and slowing down, help enormously. That's why highway gas-mileage estimates are always higher than the estimates for around-town driving.

In most cars, the air conditioner draws power from the engine, using a belt. Every time you turn on the air conditioner, the engine has to use more gas to keep the car moving. Although opening the windows can also reduce your gas mileage by reducing the aerodynamic efficiency, it's still better than running the air conditioner.

Overloading the car makes the engine work extra hard and consume more gas. If you can split the luggage (or building supplies) between two vehicles, then do it. This doesn't mean, however, that you ought to take two cars when one will suffice.

Learn2 Make a Fire in a Fireplace

Gathering around a cheerful blaze and staring into its fiery depths—that's something that people from all walks of life can appreciate. It calls you back to a bygone time, when early humans huddled around fires for protection from cold and animal predators. You feel some of the same satisfaction and security (even if the large predators of today are creditors and tax auditors).

WHERE'S THE FLUE?

FIREPLACE

WOOD-BURNING STOVE

BEFORE YOU BEGIN

A fire constructed with perfect form and bone-dry materials will still fizzle out if you don't understand the role of the flue. The flue is the passageway inside the chimney or stovepipe that allows air to circulate and create a draft, thus feeding the necessary oxygen to the fire. The flue has a kind of valve or doorway that opens or shuts off the flow of air through the chimney. There's a handle (or a chain or other device) that opens and closes it, usually located in the fireplace near the bottom of the chimney. For woodstoves, there's usually a handle located on the side of the stove, toward the top and at the back. Take a flashlight, and familiarize yourself with the operation

Time

- 3 to 10 minutes to gather materials
- 5 to 10 minutes to build a fire

What you'll need

- 4 to 7 sheets of newspaper
- 2 to 3 handfuls of dry kindling, about ¼ to ½ inch thick (1 to 1.5 centimeters) and 12 to 18 inches long (30 to 45 centimeters)

- 4 to 5 logs that have been split and seasoned
- A pair of fireproof or heavy leather gloves
- Long wooden matches or a butane lighter
- A fireplace screen or glass fireplace doors

Optional:

- 3 to 4 pieces of fatwood kindling—a highly resinous wood that can be used in small amounts as a fire starter
- A set of fireplace tools: a poker, a pair of tongs, a small shovel, a pail for ashes, and a broom
- A flashlight or pocket torch for rummaging around in the dark for suitable firewood (one you can easily tuck under your arm once your hands are occupied with holding the wood)

of your flue and the position of its handle or chain when it's open or closed. This will prevent the unnecessary smoke-outs and bleating smoke detectors that inevitably follow careless flue operation.

STEP 1

Gather materials

For materials, you need three categories of wood products: plain black-and-white newspaper, kindling, and logs. A few notes on these three components:

Newspaper:

As you gather newspaper, remember one word: *creosote.* Creosote is a black, dusty yet sticky by-product of wood and wood-fiber combustion. It coats the insides of chimneys and can eventually cause a chimney fire, which can be very destructive. So you're best off using a moderate amount of newspaper. It's also a good idea to avoid using newspaper with color pictures or glossy inserts. Color inks contain chemicals that at best might smell bad when burned and at worst could be slightly toxic. You don't necessarily have to cull all color from your stockpile of paper—but then again, you'll definitely want to avoid making a bonfire of your Christmas gift wrap.

Kindling:

Think of it this way: if your fire was a movie at a film festival, the kindling would get the award for best supporting actor. It has the crucial setup role

of generating flames hot enough to ignite the logs. And as they burn out into embers and slip into the background, the logs (the stars) get all of the attention.

Very soft, resinous woods like pine or Georgia fatwood can be used as kindling, a few sticks at a time. (Don't use more than that, or you're increasing the creosote levels unnecessarily.) Otherwise, use twigs and small branches that are about ¼ to ½ inch (1 to 1.5 centimeters) thick and 12 to 18 inches (30 to 45 centimeters) long. Some lumberyards sell raw scrap lumber for kindling, which is usually kiln-dried and ignites very well. Not all lumber belongs in the fireplace, however; most finished or specially treated lumber will release potentially toxic chemicals when burned, so make sure what you're getting is raw and untreated.

Logs:

Logs are the main course of this flammable feast: thick chunks of wood that will burn for up to 2 hours if they're hardwoods. Oak, hickory, ash, and cherry are examples of hardwoods, and this is the best kind of firewood available. Although all woods give off the same amount of heat when burned, hardwoods are heavier and burn more slowly and cleanly. This means fewer logs to put into the fire, fewer logs to fetch from a woodpile, and less creosote buildup inside the chimney—which means a safer fire. Softer woods like maple and elm are fine to use—just be sure you don't pay hardwood prices for them, because they won't last as long in your fireplace.

No matter what wood you choose, the key requirement with logs is seasoning—the number of seasons they've been dried. Wood consists of tiny tubes that carry water up and down the tree while it's alive. Yet when it dies, the water remains and can take years to evaporate—unless some humans come along and cut the wood into sections and then split it. If it hasn't been properly seasoned, the wood won't burn well: it'll emit a lot of smoke and require a lot of attention to stay lit. Signs of seasoned wood include darkened areas at the edges and a slightly high-pitched *clink* when struck together.

Green, unseasoned wood won't actually be green, so you can't tell by that—although the ends will bear evidence of recent sawing. Green wood will also sound a deeper, wetter *thud* when you strike two pieces together. If you buy a large volume of firewood, play it safe and buy it in the spring— it'll have six months to dry out and will be perfect for the winter season.

STEP 2
Prepare the site

A couple of inches (5 to 7 centimeters) of ash is a good base for the coals that will form from the kindling. But don't use more than that, or the fireplace area will start to get messy. Scoop out excess ash with a small metal fireplace shovel. Store the ash in metal cans or pails—embers can remain hot for a week—to be sure to avoid a fire hazard.

Open the flue. If you forget, you'll remember once the smoke starts billowing into the room and the fire alarms go crazy.

To build your fire, you'll start from the ground up, being careful to make a structure that will hold together during its early stages. A fire that collapses after the first 30 seconds may smother itself, and you'll have to start over.

STEP 3
Build the foundation

Here's where yesterday's newspaper comes in handy. The newspaper serves to ignite the kindling, which in turn will ignite the logs. Crumple up four or five full-size sheets into grapefruit-sized balls, a little smaller if you're feeling energetic. Place them on the floor of the fireplace and under the grate, if there is one. Resist the temptation to add more than seven paper balls to the fire. You'll certainly have a dramatic start to your fire, with flames blazing up the chimney, but over time excess newspaper use will create a lot of creosote.

Now distribute and place the kindling for breathing. Add two handfuls, arranging it evenly over the newspaper (or on top of the grate, if there is one) so that the logs will have a fairly uniform surface to rest on. Place the sticks of kindling at an angle to one another to allow air and flames to

Key words

Bellows: A hand-operated air pump that's used for fireplaces without doors.

Flue: The column of air inside the chimney or stovepipe that circulates and creates a draft, thus feeding the necessary oxygen to the fire.

Grate: A metal structure present in some fireplaces (not in woodstoves) that supports the weight of the logs and kindling and allows for optimum air circulation.

Tips

- Got a hot one? Here's a checklist for chimney fires. If you have a lot of smoke in the room combined with any of these signs—a load roar, shaking pipes, hot spots on the wall or chimney—you may have a chimney fire on your hands. If so, get everyone out of your home, and call 911 from a neighbor's home.

- If you regularly use your chimney even once a week, you should consider having your chimney swept once a year. If you're not inclined to stroll around on your roof, then have a professional do it. Dirty chimneys won't draw air well and, if neglected long enough, can cause a fire.

come through. Break up any kindling that extends far beyond the base of the fire or doesn't fit easily into the woodstove.

Next add two smaller logs rather than one monster log, to start with. Ideally, these logs should be split. The larger and thinner surface area of a split log allows it to ignite more easily. As with the kindling, don't lay the logs on top of each other. Place them at an angle to each other, to allow air and flames to come through.

Don't use any lighter fluid or liquid fire starters. They're unnecessary and toxic, and they increase the risk of uncontrolled fire.

STEP 4
Light and maintain

Using a long wooden match or a lighter, reach around and light the newspaper toward the back of the fire-

place. Your goal here is to set fire to the whole perimeter of newspaper, simultaneously, so have a friend help you if you like. Have your friend start on the other side, and move around to the front, finding exposed edges of newspaper to light.

Start up the draft:

Once the newspaper has caught fire, it's time to crank up the draft. This flow of air is created by the warm air that rises up the chimney and by air from the room that's drawn into the fireplace to replace the air that just went up the chimney. If you have a fireplace with glass doors (or a woodburning stove), then shut one door, and close the other partially. If the fireplace doesn't have doors, fan the flames with a bellows, your lungs, or a cowboy hat. Whatever implement you choose, you'll get the best results if you direct the air at the very base of the fire. This will increase the oxygen supply, causing it to burn more intensely. More hot air rises into the chimney, and the draft starts to flow. Now, look and listen.

Hearing is believing. You should hear the sound of air being sucked up the chimney, and you should see the effect of the draft on the fire: it'll fan the flames and spread the fire to the kindling and the logs. If you completely shut the second door at this early stage, it may have a smothering

START LIGHTING NEWSPAPER ON FAR SIDE OF FIRE

WORK AROUND PERIMETER TOWARD FRONT

effect on the fire. Let the fire burn this way until it gets established.

Feed the fire:

Watch the fire for when it really starts burning: it'll reduce the kindling to a bright pile of coals, and will burn deep into the large chunks. You can now put a screen on an open, doorless fireplace or open the doors of a wood-burning stove and put on a screen. It's also ready for another large split log or an unsplit log up to 5 inches (10 centimeters) in diameter. This should be good for 30 to 40 minutes for a smaller piece of softer wood like maple or elm, or up to 2 hours for a fat chunk of hickory, oak, or cherry.

If you have problems getting the logs to catch fire, take a careful look at what's happening. Are the logs hissing and sputtering? If they're well seasoned but damp on the outside, they won't easily ignite. You can remedy this situation by placing other damp logs just outside the fireplace or stove for them to dry out. But if you do this, *don't* leave the room unattended for a long period. They could dry out and heat up enough to catch fire. (An unlikely event, but who wants to deal with a burning home?)

If the logs are burning a little but smoking a lot, they may be green. This situation isn't so easily remedied, although it's worth trying the dry-out tactic. Whether the logs are wet or green, your best bet is to throw another big handful of kindling on the fire, under the logs if you have the

tools to manage that. Then get the draft going.

The fire may not be hot enough to set up a draft using fireplace or wood-stove doors, so you'll need to get down and blow with a bellows or your lungs. If you're making the fire purely for heating purposes, then close both doors of the fireplace or stove and leave the vents open (they're probably open already). Closing both doors produces a fire with maximum heat production.

STEP 5

Put out the fire

When it's time to leave or go to bed, put your fire to bed also. Don't close the flue, even if the flames seem mostly extinguished—you'll be inviting huge clouds of smoke into the room. For fireplaces with doors, close both doors and clear away any combustibles from the edge of the fireplace. Do the same for wood-burning stoves. For an open fireplace, wait until the fire has died down considerably, and carefully set the screen in place. Move any combustibles (matches or drying logs) away from the hearth.

That's fire starting in a nutshell—not as easy as simply lighting a match, but not exactly rocket science either. As long as you choose the materials carefully and follow common safety precautions, a roaring fire is a superlative cure for many modern ills. Now get out the marshmallows!

Tips

- Smoked out? If your flue is open but the smoke won't go up (and fills your house instead), then consider the location of your chimney. Is it on an exterior wall of your home? If so, the chimney may be too cold to draw air. To warm up your chimney, put on a fireproof glove and light a rolled-up piece of newspaper. The heat from the burning newspaper will force the cold air in the chimney outside, which will start the flow of the air through the chimney.

- Save the trees: Use fabricated firewood logs (made of compressed wood chips, sawdust, and binding materials) if you're concerned about deforestation.

Learn **2** Open a Jar

Time

Give each strategy about 5 minutes before moving on to the next one

What you'll need

Any or all of the following:
- A clean, dry kitchen towel
- Very warm tap water—heck, make it hot, as long as you don't burn anyone
- A large kitchen knife (or object of similar weight and dimension, such as a metal spatula or bottle opener); it doesn't have to be sharp, because you won't be using the blade

Things were going just great in your kitchen. Then you tried to open that innocent, perfectly functional-looking jar; now there's a thin corkscrew of metal holding fast between you and your bliss. Stuck? In a jam? Here are a few handy hints for loosening that lid.

BEFORE YOU BEGIN

Often our hands have a natural, oily residue that makes it difficult to get a good grip on slick, metallic objects. Wash your hands with a mild soap or detergent, and dry them thoroughly on a clean towel.

Jars, especially those concealed at the back of the shelf over the stove for a long time, can accumulate an oily residue from kitchen grease and smoke. Paying particular attention to the lid, rinse the jar under warm water to loosen and remove any residue. Use a drop or two of liquid detergent if the jar feels particularly greasy, and dry thoroughly with a clean towel.

STEP 1
Do the twist

Yes, we all know that you're supposed to twist it open, but not all of us know how to maximize our own body leverage. In these steps "dominant hand" refers to the hand with which you write and eat.

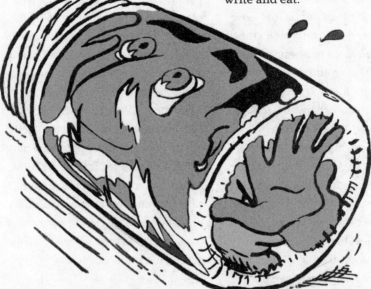

Hold the jar in your dominant hand at about chest level. The back of your hand should be facing out away from you. Hold your palm along the side of the jar (not covering the lid), and line up the thumb and index finger parallel to the lid. Wrap the thumb of your nondominant hand around the side of the lid that's facing you, and curl your fingers around to the opposite side.

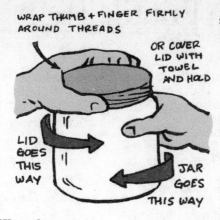

WRAP THUMB + FINGER FIRMLY AROUND THREADS

OR COVER LID WITH TOWEL AND HOLD

LID GOES THIS WAY

JAR GOES THIS WAY

Feel the lid wedged firmly in your hand. Now try to turn it by moving your hands in opposite directions at the same time. Your dominant hand (on the jar) will move clockwise, and your nondominant hand (and the lid) will move counterclockwise.

Elbows up, relax, and take a deep breath. As you exhale, grip tightly while turning your hands. Don't strain yourself, but do remember that it's just a jar, and you're certainly better than the jar!

Didn't work? Don't sweat it. Simply move on to Step 2.

STEP 2
Heat up the lid

Turn on your hot-water faucet, and let the water warm up. Being careful not to scald your hand, run very warm water over the lid of the jar for a minute or so while holding the jar itself angled away from the water stream. Metal lids absorb heat quickly, and when they do they expand. Hot water can serve a second purpose by loosening any sticky material that may have become fixed between the threads of the lid.

Turn off the tap, and dry the jar, the lid, and your hands thoroughly. Now repeat Step 1.

STEP 3
Bring out the knife

Set the jar on the counter, and hold it steady with one hand. Using the back of the knife (no slashing!), rap the rim of the lid twice, firmly, on the edge. Turn the jar one-fourth to one-third of the way around, and rap the lid twice again. This should break most stubborn seals.

Now put the knife down (you should be feeling better already), and return to Step 1. Place your hands squarely opposite each other, and do the twist.

You may repeat the rapping maneuver every inch or so around the jar as necessary, but be advised that this method often permanently dents the lid. Once open, even a battered lid should be serviceable for reclosing, but it may never again hold an airtight seal.

Learn 2 Package Fragile Items

Time

About 15 minutes

What you'll need

- An appropriate box or container
- Packing material (see Step 2)
- Post office–approved packing tape, and a way to cut it

Pack it up, I'll take it!" Fragile items need to be packed properly, or else they break. The shipper who handles your items may be doing its best but may handle too many packages to take the kind of care your package requires. In addition, many items must be packaged properly when shipped, or else the warranty becomes void. Heck, even getting Aunt Violet's best china into the car can be an adventure in itself.

BEFORE YOU BEGIN

What's on the outside of your package can be as important as what's inside. If the package is being shipped through a commercial service, find out if there are any specific requirements. For instance, many shippers will not accept a package that is wrapped in paper or has no return address. Now there are packaging stores, which sell new packing materials. They're good at providing odd-sized containers for items like bicycles and mirrors and are generally knowledgeable about shipping regulations.

The best packing material is the original packing material. Especially when you buy electronic equipment, try to save the foam pieces that hold it inside the box. Carefully break down the original box, and put it all in the attic or basement.

It's often cheaper to ship two smaller packages, rather than one large one. Find out how the shipper sets rates.

STEP 1

Select the container

The most common container used is a cardboard box. Some have thin, one-layer sides, while others are thicker, having two layers sandwiching a third, corrugated one. Use the second kind; it's much more protective. Clean, new boxes are best for shipping. They often have preprinted areas for the address and are less confusing to the shipper than a used box, with graphics and writing all over it. Use a box that will provide adequate room for the packing material around the item. Don't put a large item into a box where it can touch the sides.

Boxes can be made to fit odd-shaped items by creasing, folding, and reinforcing with tape. Don't cut the cardboard if you want it to retain any strength.

STEP 2

Choose your packing materials

There are three basic packing materials that are widely available: foam "peanuts" (choose the biodegradable kind, please), popcorn, and newspaper.

Peanuts are generally the best material: they're quite resilient and absorb shock well. They also "pour" well into odd-shaped areas. Please save any peanuts you receive for reuse.

Popcorn (air-popped) is a nice, environmentally friendly packing

material. It's cheap and absorbs shock almost as well as foam peanuts. It's not as resilient, though, and is generally best used once.

Newspaper, when crumpled into fairly tight balls, works almost as well as the other two materials. It's the cheapest of all, if you have old ones lying around, and it's interesting to unpack a box years later and read about old happenings. It is not very resilient, though, and is adversely affected by humid storage.

STEP 3

Tackle the tape issue

You're going to need more tape than you think. When you rebuild a new box, you'll reform it by taping the

PEANUTS!

POPCORN!

NEWSPAPER!

Tips

• When labeling packages for shipping, put both the destination and return address on more than one side of the box. When your package is piled with others, it will move faster if the addresses are always visible. In addition, write with a bold black permanent marker, and cover the writing with clear tape. Rainy days have a way of smearing things.

Tips

- If you put a list of contents in the box just before closing it, the person unpacking it will have an easier time.
- When packing hollow objects, such as vases, stuff them with packing material such as newspaper balls.
- When accepting packages from a commercial service, take the time to inspect any damaged or broken parcels while the delivery person is still there. If you discover damage later, save everything—from the broken shards and "peanuts" to the box soaked with somebody's morning coffee.

seams and reinforce it by taping the edges and sides. With a used box, reinforcement is even more important, so don't skimp. You'll even want to tape the corners of very heavily packed boxes.

Reinforced tape has nylon filaments running through it, making it really tough—excellent for closing and strengthening very heavy boxes. Make sure it's at least 2 inches (5 centimeters) wide.

Plastic tape is not nearly as tough as the reinforced kind but works well for all but the heaviest boxes. The clear kind is generally a bit heavier than the brown kind, which makes for easier handling. In any case, make sure it's at least 2 inches (5 centimeters) wide; 3 inches (8 centimeters) is better.

Paper tape is now less common; it needs to be wetted with a sponge for the adhesive to stick. It's good for closing boxes, less so for reinforcing edges. Again, 2 to 3 inches (5 to 8 centimeters) wide is best.

STEP 4

Put it all together

Make sure that packing materials cover the bottom of the box, before you place anything into it.

Ensure that the objects do not touch the sides of the box. If you can, keep at least an inch of packing material between the objects and the sides of the box, and you'll do just fine.

Pack things tightly, and leave as few gaps as you can. When you finally close the box, it should feel like you're compressing the materials slightly.

Pick up the box and shake it, if you can. You should not hear anything rattling around. Once satisfied, seal the box with a piece of tape that's long enough to extend several inches down either side of the box.

Reinforcing the box with tape is very important, especially when shipping commercially. Use continuous pieces for each wrapping edge.

Learn2 Parallel Park Your Car

Time

- 5 minutes

What you'll need

- A parking spot
- Clean windows (optional)

The cars are honking, Aunt Stella's whining, and the dinner reservation is slipping through your fingers. After scanning eight city blocks, the only parking spot appears way too small, but you refuse to hand your keys over to the valet guy. If you scored low on the parallel-parking part of your driving test, it's likely you're now backing up repeatedly against the curb. So pull over a moment, catch your breath, and learn these simple steps.

BEFORE YOU BEGIN

Get a sense of your car's proportions so you can better evaluate prospective spots. Next time you're out on the road, try this formula: pull your car up next to a spot you think will just fit it. Take a long look at the spot, and take into account that you'll need an additional 2 feet of space to accommodate both the bumper and your perspective. If you can't get in after several minutes of trying, you're probably better off finding another spot. It's not worth ruining your day.

STEP 1
Find a space

In the lane closest to the curb, cruise steadily, always looking a bit ahead for an opportunity—better to keep a view of the whole street and *not* have to slam on the brakes after passing a prime spot.

STEP 2
Pull up

Put on your turn signal. Pull over carefully, stopping just past the spot. That should put you 2 to 3 feet out from and parallel to the car in front of the empty space. If a car is just leaving your space, pull up behind the space to allow room for its exit. This move will both warn oncoming traffic and mark your territory.

STEP 3
Wind back

At this point, your back bumper should match up with the adjacent car's back bumper. Be certain to look back all the way over your shoulder (the one toward the curb) so you can see oncoming cars as well as your destination. Back up slowly, turning the steering wheel sharply toward the curb. Stop when you've backed up half the length of your car.

STEP 4
Turn back

Changing direction at the halfway mark is the key to success. Without moving further back, turn the steering wheel in the opposite direction (away from the curb) so the front end moves toward the curb. Move very slowly at this point, and be careful not to hit either bumper, in front or behind. Your car should slide right into the spot.

STEP 5
Adjust

Don't fool yourself: only the pros get in there by Step 4. If you back up and hit the curb too soon, reverse and move forward, adjusting the wheel all the way back and forth as needed to fit in the spot. Be sure to turn your wheels (pointed away from the curb going up and toward the curb going down) if on a hill.

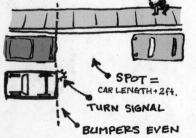

SPOT = CAR LENGTH + 2 ft.

TURN SIGNAL

BUMPERS EVEN

WATCH FOR TRAFFIC

SLOW!

Learn2 Set a Table

Time

At least ½ hour
before guests arrive

What you'll need

- Matching place
  settings (plates,
  glasses, and uten-
  sils) for every per-
  son at the table
- Placemats
- Napkins
- A clean towel
- A decorative cen-
  terpiece, such as
  flowers (optional)

You've invited the boss and his wife to dinner at your home, and TV trays just won't do. Or you want to impress that special someone with a hot, home-cooked meal but can't remember which side the fork goes on. Never fear. Here are some basic table-setting guidelines and rules of etiquette for everything from intimate tête-à-têtes to banquets for a crowd.

BEFORE YOU BEGIN

The basic place setting discussed here has developed over centuries of European and American dining. Some differences exist from country to country and even family to family, and these are often argued with remarkable passion. Still, a few basic guidelines are generally accepted and will be adhered to in most American banquet halls. This 2torial will show three types of place settings: a basic setting, a formal banquet setting, and a variation on the formal setting.

Tips

- Try not to set out any flatware that diners will not be using; this only creates confusion. The one basic exception is the spoon, which completes the basic knife-fork-spoon combo. Place a spoon whether the meal requires one or not.
- When multiple courses are served, have the plates and flatware removed from each place setting before bringing out the next dish.

STEP 1
Check what you have

Take out the flatware, dishes, glassware, and tablecloth or placemats that you intend to use. Are they dusty or soiled? Often the worst culprit will be a little dust. Use a clean dish towel to rub the dust from glasses and plates. Use a polishing cloth to shine up your flatware.

If you use a tablecloth, make sure it's clean and pressed. You don't want any stains to remind visitors of last year's Christmas dinner. Inspect your tablecloth, placemats, and napkins early to be sure they are presentable. Give yourself time for a last-minute wash if needed.

STEP 2
Understand the basics

- Rule 1. Everyone at the table gets a place setting, whether or not they intend to eat. Anyone can change his mind at the last minute, and only a careless host would be caught unprepared.
- Rule 2. Flatware is placed evenly on either side of the plate in a manner comfortable to use by a right-handed person (sorry, lefties, this one never varies). Forks go on the left, knives and spoons on the right. The cutting edge of the knife should point toward the plate. Spoons go to the outside of knives.
- Rule 3. Place the flatware in the order it will be used, with the first utensils set farthest away from the plate. The idea is to avoid rooting around for the appropriate fork or confusing your guests.

STEP 3
Master the standard place setting

It may take a bit of fussing around the first few times out, but nothing impresses a guest so easily as a perfectly set table. A place setting helps you feel important on that special occasion when you turn off the television set and eat in the dining room.

If you are using placemats, set each one square to the edge of the table where each chair will be. The bottom of the placemat (the side closest to the chair) should be about an inch (3 centimeters) from the edge of the table. Although this distance may vary from one occasion to another, every place setting at a table or banquet should be exactly consistent with every other place setting.

The dinner plate (the big one) goes dead center on the placemat; if you are using a tablecloth, put the bottom of the plate 2 inches (6 centimeters) from the edge of the table. The napkin goes lengthwise on the left of the plate. Fold square napkins once to make them rectangles, then lay them in the same direction the utensils will go. The crease goes next to the plate.

Utensils should be about ½ inch (1 centimeter) from the plate and from each other. The fork goes on the left, tines up, on top of the napkin; the knife goes on the plate's right, cutting edge toward the plate. Place the spoon to the right of the knife.

The water or drinking glass goes above the knife, about 2 inches away from the tip; the wineglass is placed to its right and down a bit, above the spoon.

STEP 4

Master the formal place setting

Generally, the more formal the occasion, the more courses are served, which of course means more flatware. There should be a different set of utensils for each course: salad fork, dinner fork; dinner knife, bread knife; and so on. Some dishes such as oysters have special utensils. These can be brought with the food but generally are placed on the table in order of course. When oysters are served as an appetizer, for example, set the oyster fork to the right of the soup spoon.

Building from the standard setting (see above), the following utensils may be added:

• On the left side of the plate put the salad fork to the left of the dinner fork.

• If soup will be served, add a soup spoon to the outside of the dinner spoon on the right of the plate. Place the soup bowl above the soup spoon and to the right.

• The bread plate goes to the left, about 2 inches above the fork. Place the butter knife across the bread plate at a diagonal, upper left to lower right.

• Small salad plates go to the left

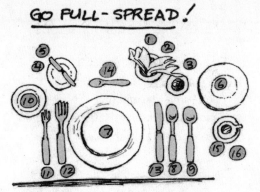

GO FULL-SPREAD!

① Napkin
② Water Glass
③ Wineglass
④ Bread Dish
⑤ Bread Knife
⑥ Soup Dish
⑦ Dinner Plate
⑧ Dinner Spoon
⑨ Soup Spoon
⑩ Salad Plate
⑪ Salad Fork
⑫ Dinner Fork
⑬ Dinner Knife
⑭ Dessert Spoon
⑮ & ⑯ Coffee Cup & Saucer

and a little lower than the bread plate.

• Dessert spoons, or in some cases knife and fork, are placed about an inch above the top of the plate with the handle(s) on the right side.

• If you have some specialized pieces of silverware that you're dying to show off, think up a dish you can use them for, and add it to the menu. Got shrimp forks? Use them for shrimp, not fondue.

The largest glass on the table is the water glass (see above for basic placement). It may be filled and iced when guests arrive or left empty to be filled at each diner's request. If wine or some other beverage is served, set the appropriate glass to the right and a little lower than the water glass.

Key words

Flatware: A set of matching knives, forks, and spoons. They are usually silver, but stainless sets and sometimes gold plate are also used.

Place setting: A space on the table for each guest. This includes flatware, water glass, wineglass, and napkin.

STEP 5
Master the formal variations

One way to vary table settings is through napkin folding—an art in itself—and placement. Here are two simple and exotic variations for when you really want to show off.

Variation 1. Do the fan:

Open each napkin completely and lay it flat on the table. Fold it back and forth like a fan, then press it down so the creases are sharp. Fold it in half lengthwise, and place the center in an empty water glass. Open the two ends of the napkin sticking out of the glass into fan shapes. Set the glass in its original placement (see above) or directly in the middle of the dinner plate.

Variation 2. Do the triangle:

An easier method is to open the napkin flat and fold one corner on top of its opposite corner. Take one of the other corners, and fold it over onto its opposite. Fold these corners on top of the other ones, and crease. Take the corner of the resulting triangle (which used to be the center of the napkin) and place into an empty water glass. Or you can open up the folded triangle a little bit and set it directly on the dinner plate.

STEP 6
Adapt to your circumstances

Left-handed diners: If you know you'll have left-handed diners, try to seat them at the left end of a long table. But please don't insist upon it. The result could mean an embarrassed guest.

Small tables: Small tables and numerous guests make crowded gatherings. If you find you are running out of room for your place settings, rearrange each setting with the utensils grouped more closely together. The most important thing is that the settings look identical.

Tablecloths versus placemats: Placemats seem to be a matter of taste and convenience rather than convention. An attractive set of placemats can add color to the table and initiate an enjoyable conversation, and you can certainly use both simultaneously. But if you are showing off with a fine linen tablecloth, topping it with placemats is probably unnecessary.

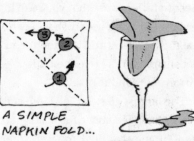

A SIMPLE NAPKIN FOLD...

THEN TUCK IN GLASS, — OR — STAND ON A PLATE

Learn2 Tie Basic Knots

Time

2 to 5 minutes to learn each knot; ½ hour or longer to practice; seconds once you are a pro

What you'll need

- A rope or piece of heavy string about 3 feet (1 meter) long that bends easily and doesn't fray—a section of laundry line works well

Gnarled knotting have you in a bind? Do you get sidetracked by a simple square knot? Want to learn the loops that'll link those lines? This 2torial untangles the basics of nine knots that make life easier.

BEFORE YOU BEGIN

Put some tape around the ends of your string, or tie figure eight knots (see below) at both ends so they won't come apart. Now you have a practice rope.

This 2torial will provide step-by-step instructions for knots with the following uses:

- Securing a line: half, double half, and clove hitches
- Tying ropes together: square or reef knots, the sheet bend
- Loops that'll hold fast: the bowline
- End knots: The figure eight

Pick the category you most want to learn, skip to that section, and follow the basic steps. Practice tying until you're comfortable, then pick another category. Oh, no, knot again!

With most knots presented here, parts of the line will be referred to as the working end and the free end. The working end is the part of the rope already tied to something—for example, a dog, a boat, or a kite. The other end, with which most of the maneuvering is done, is the free end.

Knot 1
The half hitch

This is the most basic of knots. In a slightly different form it's popularly known as an overhand knot, which is the first step to tying shoelaces. The half hitch, though insufficient for most uses by itself, is a necessary building block for most of the other knots in this 2torial.

STEP 1
Hold it

Hold one end of your practice rope in your nondominant hand. Call this the working end. Mostly you just want to keep the working end out of your way. With your dominant hand, pick up the free end, the end you want to tie.

STEP 2
Wrap it

Pass the free end under and around your leg. Pretend that your leg is an object you need to secure with the rope.

STEP 3
Cross it

Take the free end, and pull it up parallel to the working end. Cross the free end over the working end. Push the free end under the loop created by the crossover. Pull the free end to snug down the knot.

Knot 2
The double half hitch

This knot is just one of many kinds of hitches. It's great to use for securing rope to an object that you want to hold fast, such as tent stakes and laundry lines. As a bonus, it's easy to tie and untie. Start by tying a half hitch (see above).

STEP 1
Hold it

Take up the free end of your rope, which should be trailing from the loop of the half hitch. Pull the free end parallel to the working end. The working end should be straight.

STEP 2
Tie another half hitch

Cross the free end over the working end in the same direction as the first half hitch formed. Pass the free end behind the working end (notice the new loop you've just formed), and push the free end through the new loop. Snug down the two loops by pulling on both ends.

STEP 3
Tighten it

Pull the knot firmly against the object by sliding the double half hitch along the working end of the rope. This knot will also tighten naturally by pulling on the working end. Notice how the hitch puts a bend in the rope, which prevents it from slipping. This bend is called a bight.

"CLOVE HITCH":

Knot 3
The clove hitch

This knot is another quick and easy way to tie a rope to an object so that it doesn't get away. The difference is that the knot will be tied around the object rather than the working end of the rope. Clove hitches are commonly used for tying horse tethers to a hitching post. They're also good for tying up bundles of stuff like kindling or poles.

STEP 1
Drape it

Start by looping the free end over your leg (for practice) or a post. Then pass the free end under the object. Bring the free end up, and cross it over the top of the working end.

STEP 2
Loop it

Pass the free end over and under the object again in the same direction as the first loop. Leave the place where the rope crosses over the working end rather loose. Bring the free end up again. Note that the two loops don't cross or overlap but lie parallel.

STEP 3
Feed it through

Pass the free end through the place where the rope crosses over. Pull the hitch tight by tugging on both ends.

Knot 4
The square

A square knot, also called a reef knot, is used to join two lengths of rope about the same thickness. It's quick to tie and untie. Use it when you're in a hurry to tie two ends together to hold light to medium stress. Like the double half hitch, it consists of two half hitches. But it's a very different knot, and you'll see why.

"SQUARE" OR "REEF":
① OVER + UNDER
② UNDER + OVER
NOTE "SQUARE"

Key words

Bight: A bend or kink placed on a rope.

Fray: The strings and fluff that occur when a rope unravels.

Free end: The long end you use for tying knots.

Line: A length of rope that is being used for something.

Tail or tailing end: The little piece of rope that sticks out from a knot after it's tied.

Working end: The end of a rope that is already attached to something.

Knot security: No, it's not a knot having good self-esteem—it's a knot's ability to resist untying or breaking the line, despite the stress of weight, vibration, or jiggling. For example, a slip knot is more secure than a square knot.

Tips

- To pull a double half hitch tighter between two secured objects, pull it away from the object it secures to make the loop bigger. The bight or bend created by the knot should hold the rope taught.

- If you intend to untie a knot in the near future, make it easy on yourself. The final time you feed the free end though a loop, don't push the entire free end through. Instead, push only a section through, creating a new loop. Snug down the knot to secure it. This creates the "slipped" variation of whatever knot you've just tied—a slip double half hitch or a slip sheet bend. To untie, simply pull on the free end, and the last loop will slip open.

STEP 1
Loop it

Loop the rope around a stationary object (any leg, yours or a table's, will work fine). Bring the two ends up evenly on either side. You're now holding two free ends.

STEP 2
Tie it

Cross the two ends of rope you want to join. Pass the end that crosses on top (end A) over the other end (end B), and pull it back up again. This creates an overhand knot, which is actually a half hitch in a slightly different form.

STEP 3
Tie it again, but differently

Hold the two ends above and away from the overhand knot. The end that crossed on top (end A) must cross on top again. Notice that end A is now going in the opposite direction from where it went the first time. Push end A over end B, down and through the loop between the two hitches (*hitch* is another word for a simple knot).

STEP 4
Tighten it

Tighten the knot by pulling evenly on the two free ends. The center of the knot should have a diamond or square shape—hence the name. It also should look like two loops linked together.

STEP 5
Remember it

Here's an easy way to remember this: think of left and right. If, for the first hitch, the end on the left goes over and under, then for the second hitch the end on the right goes over and under. Or think about the movements of your dominant hand—over and under, then under and over.

Knot 5
The sheet bend

A sheet bend is more secure than a square knot but a little more difficult to untie. It's useful for joining together two lines of different sizes or quality. Use a sheet bend if you're going to put heavy stress on the knot, if one end is hard to bend or tie, or if you don't want the knot to come undone anytime soon.

STEP 1
Loop it

Bend one end—end A—into a J shape, where the working end is the long part of the J. Hold it in your nondominant hand.

STEP 2
Thread it

Take the other end—end B—in your dominant hand, and move it under the loop of the J. Then thread end B up through the loop of the J.

STEP 3
Wrap it

Wrap end B around the short side of the J. Pass end B all the way under the loop and up the long side of the J.

STEP 4
Thread it

Now you want to pass end B across the loop. Push end B through the section of itself where it first snakes up through the J. Then pull end B out—it should pass over the short side of the J. If you were to walk end B across the J, the pattern would be over, under, and over again.

Pull tight on end B. Then pull the two working ends to secure the knot.

STEP 5
Tie ropes of different qualities

If you are joining two ropes of different qualities, notice which end is harder to tie. Is one thicker, stiffer, or rougher? This should be end A. The thinner, more flexible, or more slippery of the two ends should be end B. Then tie the sheet bend as described above.

Knot 6
The bowline

Sometimes you need to make a loop that'll stay a loop at the end of a rope. The bowline (pronounced "bo-lin") is a critical knot used to make a loop that's secure and will stay open for as long as you need it. An old mariner's saying goes, "I could make the devil himself a good sailor if he could learn a bowline."

STEP 1
Hold it

Hold the working end (the longer end) of the rope in your nondominant hand. It should trail up and away from you.

STEP 2
Loop it

Make a loop by passing the free end over the working end. For purposes that will soon be clear, call this loop the hole. Hold the hole with your nondominant hand at the point where the two ends cross over.

Note: When you make this loop, it's critical that the free end pass on top of the working end. It's also a good idea to make it relatively small, because in the bowline there's a second, larger loop that should be easy to distinguish.

STEP 3
Thread it

Move the free end under the hole, and pass it up through the hole. (Leave enough rope hanging down on this free end. Later it will form the second, larger loop.)

STEP 4
Wrap it

Pass the free end over the working end, then around behind it, and then

Tips

- A square knot where the second hitch is tied in the same direction as the first, sometimes called a granny, doesn't hold well. It's also much more difficult to untie. Look for the little diamond shape between the two hitches. It'll remind you that you tied it right.
- The learning curve: It's easy to get confused in the early stages. To help stay focused on the knot you're tying, pull the working end out and away from you. Always assume the working end is attached to something, even if it's just coiled up on a spool. It's important to keep that working end straight, out, and away from your hands so you can concentrate on the job of tying.

Tips

- How much rope do you need? You want enough to form all the bends of the knot, plus enough trailing out afterward so that the knot won't come undone from a little slippage. How much is enough depends on how thick the rope is, how slippery it is, and how big and complex the knot is. Get in the habit of both tying and untying knots. If you realize halfway through that you don't have enough rope to finish a knot, say to yourself, "No worries!" and untie it. Start farther up the working end, and go at it again.

back down the first hole again. Be sure you pass the free end through the small loop of the knot and not through the second, larger loop you're creating.

STEP 5
Tighten it

Hold the free end and the side of the larger loop together in one hand. Hold the working end in your other hand. Pull gently on the working end until the knot is snug. Then grab the loop with one hand, the working end with the other, and pull tight.

STEP 6
Remember it

Here's a clever way to remember the bowline: imagine a woodland scene. The free end is a rabbit; the working end is a tree with a rabbit hole at the bottom of it. Say to yourself, "The rabbit comes out of the hole, goes around the tree and back down the hole again."

Knot 7
The one-handed bowline

This knot is indispensable if you have only one hand free and need a strong, stationary loop. It's exactly the same knot described above, but once mastered, it takes a fraction of the time to tie it.

STEP 1
Grab it

Pass the rope around your middle. Hold the working end out away from your body with your nondominant hand.

With your dominant hand, hold the free end about an inch or two from the end of the line with the line running up your arm.

STEP 2
Do the Macarena

Okay, so it's not the Macarena, but your hand will do some wiggling. Don't let go of the free end!

Put your hand over the working end. Wrap it under, and bring it up next to your belly (assuming you've wrapped the rope around your middle). You should have formed a loop around your wrist.

With your fingertips, wrap the free end around and up on the other side of the working end. (Which line is the working end again? It's the line that your nondominant hand is touching. Take care that you don't wrap the free end around the loop that's around your midsection.)

For the final, triumphant move, pull your hand, and the free end with it, down through the loop around your wrist. This might take some wiggling.

STEP 3
Tighten it

Keep holding on to the free end with your dominant hand. Pull the working end away from you with your nondominant hand. You should have it.

STEP 4
Practice for emergencies

Before you get stuck down a well or at the bottom of a cliff where someone must pull you up, practice doing the one-handed bowline with your rope around your middle. Once you get the hang of it, it'll be easy to wrap a loop around other obstacles, or perhaps someone unconscious, and tie the one-handed bowline in seconds.

Knot 8
The figure eight

End knots are those you tie at the end of a rope. They're good for holding the separate strands together so the rope doesn't fray. End knots also prevent rope from pulling through something it has been fed through, such as a block and tackle or an eye bolt. The figure eight, named for its final shape, is the most basic of these.

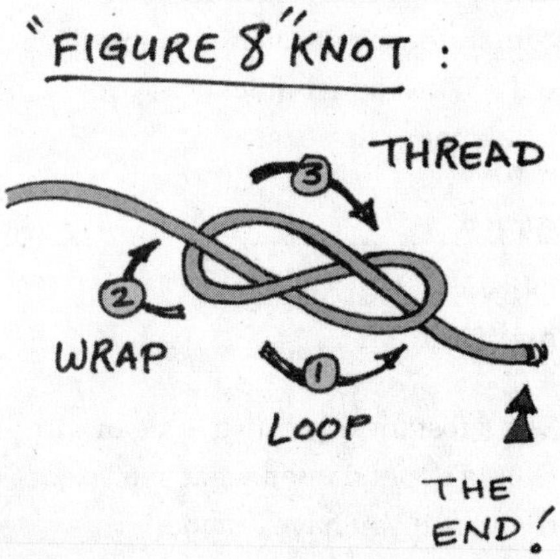

STEP 1
Bend it

Hold the rope with the long end leading away from your hands. Bend it into a U shape. The bottom of the U is where you want the knot to end up.

STEP 2
Cross it

Cross the free end over the working end. Hold the resulting loop at the point where the ends cross. Pass the free end around behind the working end. Pull it back toward you again.

STEP 3
Thread it

Push the free end down through the loop at the bottom of the U. Pull gently on both ends to snug. The finished knot will look like two interlocking loops—like a figure eight with an end trailing out of each loop.

Another way to think of this knot: make a half hitch of the first variety (not an overhand knot), and pass the free end through the loop.

"FIGURE 8" KNOT :

THREAD

WRAP

LOOP

THE END!

Learn**2** Clean a Bathroom

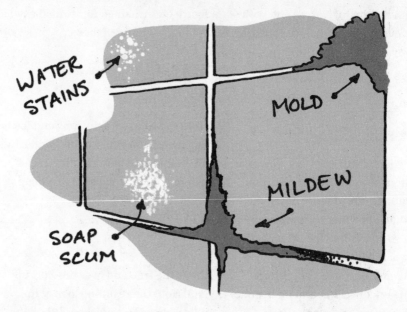

WATER STAINS

MOLD

MILDEW

SOAP SCUM

Time

If your bathroom is notably grungy, allocate about an hour for a thorough cleanup and airing out; after that, a weekly wipe-down should take about 10 minutes

Nothing else presents a cleaning challenge quite like the tiled areas of your bathroom. Add the high moisture content of a shower or tub, the limited ventilation of most bathrooms, and you've got a happy breeding ground for grossness.

BEFORE YOU BEGIN

Normally, if something gets dirty, you use plenty of soap and water to get it clean—but here soap film and water stains are components of the blight. Essentially, you've got three types of cleaning to do: removing dried-on soapy film, removing water-related stains, and removing mildew. Of course, there's dirt to be removed, too, but it'll disappear quickly as you tackle these three tasks.

STEP 1

Choose your weapons: light artillery

The substances you use to clean with should depend upon what you've got to clean: if you have a smooth-

GLASS CLEANER FOR METALS AND GLASS...

SCOURING POWDER FOR TUB AND TILE

DON'T CONFUSE !

surfaced fiberglass shower stall with no signs of mildew, a scrub-down with wetted baking soda may be all the cleanup you need. An additional rinse with diluted lemon juice can leave your bathroom sparkling, with zero caustic chemicals to trouble you or the environment. However, you may decide that stronger stuff is called for.

The next step up is diluted ammonia, the original all-purpose cleaner. A half cup (125 milliliters) of ammonia in a gallon (4 liters) of water creates a good, spongeable cleaner. You can also keep the dilution in a spray bottle for handy touch-ups; it has the added benefit of being a nifty glass cleaner as well. Be sure to rinse off well afterward, as ammonia can really irritate bare skin. This approach is recommended only if mildew is not a problem in your bathroom, because bleach is your main weapon against mildew, and it doesn't mix with ammonia (see Step 2).

Other all-purpose cleaners are stronger still, although most of them are formulated to battle household grime, not dried-on soap scum—and they tend to leave streaks on glass and mirrors. Read the labels carefully before using them: some can discolor painted or varnished surfaces.

STEP 2
Choose your weapons—heavy artillery

Next on the heavy-duty scale are the scrubbing-bubble-type bathroom cleaners, the kind you spray on and let the bubbling factor loosen up the grunge. These do require marginally less scrubbing on your part, but don't expect those dancing bubbles to whisk everything to a sparkling shine. If you don't wipe and rinse clean all the surfaces, you'll simply be left with a different kind of dried-on film. Also, it seems to leave some surfaces dangerously slippery—you'll have to experiment.

The real cleaning heavyweights are scouring powders—Ajax, Comet, and Bon Ami. These take more elbow grease, but they'll clean deep down. They can require extra effort to rinse off, though, and can scratch some surfaces (although there are scratchless equivalents). They're best used in conjunction with another cleaner, saved only for the stains and problem spots.

Effective but sometimes overwhelming are the mildew removers, most of which rely heavily on chlorine bleach in a spray-on form. These can

What you'll need

- A 2-gallon (8-liter) bucket
- A sponge (make sure it's used only in the bathroom, not in food-preparation areas)
- A flexible scrubber pad (again, keep it out of the kitchen)
- A stiff, sturdy nylon brush (the kind you can get a solid grip on)
- Rubber gloves
- Bathroom cleanser (these vary from environmentally friendly to very toxic, so be informed about your choice)

Optional:
- A used toothbrush (for scrubbing grout)
- A spray-on mildew remover
- Fabric softener (for cleaning your shower curtain)

Tips

- Don't mix bleach with ammonia! Cleansers that contain bleach can create toxic fumes when mixed with ammonia. Read and compare all labels.

- Bathtub rings? Bath oils and shaving in the tub are two big causes of these. Because they tend to be oilier than other bathroom grime, rings sometimes require separate treatment. If the overall scrubbing won't clear yours, try a bit of diluted automatic dishwashing detergent or a sponge filled with vinegar.

- Glove thyself when dealing with caustic chemicals. If you don't have rubber gloves, at least give your hands a protective coating of petroleum jelly or a nondisappearing lotion.

save you hours of scrubbing—the mildew just disappears—but you'll want plenty of ventilation and strong rubber gloves. This stuff is pretty harsh, and best only for occasional use.

Be careful when using two or more cleaners in conjunction. Remember this simple rule: *chlorine bleach and ammonia don't mix*. More accurately, they *do* mix—into a gas that's noxious and potentially poisionous. Read the labels; you may be surprised to find that most products draw their cleaning power from one or the other of these ingredients. In this case, don't mix and match!

STEP 3
Start the scrub-down

The key word here is *scrub-down*: you're going to work your way down, from top to bottom. But first, pay attention to ventilation; keep the door wide open, and any windows as well.

Scrub the bathroom in this order: sink, tub or shower, the area near the toilet, and then the floor. This way you'll be able to pick up any drips as you go along.

Fill the bucket with good clean water, and use the sponge to wet down the walls after cleaning them. It's tempting to use the showerhead to rinse the walls, but unless it's one of those detachable types, you'll probably just succeed in getting yourself wet.

Mildew (and its cousin, mold) consists of those dark spots, while water

stains and soap scum are whitish (and thereby hard to see against white tile). Make a pass at the mildew, but don't be surprised it if doesn't come right off. We'll focus on it in the next step.

Once a tiled area is cleaned and rinsed, remove one of your rubber gloves and run your fingers along the tiles: you should be able to tell if your cleaning method is working or if you missed a spot or two.

STEP 4
Battle the mildew

Now let's target the mildew itself. This isn't dirt, it's a colony of tiny organisms that flourishes in the humid conditions of your bathroom. A light scrubbing here will work for a while, but the mildew will grow back eventually. It's time for a deep cleaning and a change in the environment (see Step 6).

Bleach doesn't just clean, it kills bacteria and simple organisms (such as mildew and mold). Use a bleach-based cleaner and preferably a scouring powder for the grout between the tiles. If you really want to banish the blight, use an old toothbrush to scrub the grout.

Mildew on your shower curtain? Bleach could weaken it, so instead remove it and soak it in the tub in hot water with fabric softener added. Then rinse and dry.

If you've opted to use spray-on mildew remover, save it for last (see Step 6).

STEP 5

Clean the clear surfaces

Finish the cleanup by wiping down the mirrors, chrome, and any glass—the clear surfaces on which cleaner buildup would otherwise show.

A slightly damp rag will handle the chrome, and glass cleaner should work on all three surface types. Most glass cleaners are ammonia-based, so make sure you rinse away the residue of your bleach-based cleaners to a minimum before proceeding.

When it comes to cleaning glass, using newspaper pages is every bit as effective as paper towels. It's also a lot cheaper, and it reduces the amount of garbage in landfills.

STEP 6

Air it out

For the bathroom to be truly clean, it's got to be dry. So keep the door and any windows wide open, and pull down moisture-retaining towels from the towel racks. If possible, let it stay that way for several hours.

If you're using spray-on mildew remover, this step is especially important—you'll understand why as soon as you get a whiff of this powerful stuff. Spritz it on the mildew stains, then walk away. Unless the label says otherwise, you probably won't have to scrub the sprayed spots afterward.

STEP 7

Keep it clean!

Now that you've got it all spic-and-span, let's take a look at what you can do to keep it that way:

• If water spots are a big problem, it may be that your tap water is too hard. If this really bothers you, look into a household filtration or water-softening system. Otherwise, smile and make friends with a few water stains.

• If your basin, shower, or tub is slow to drain, it's probably retaining more grunge as a result (the stuff concentrates as it waits to be slurped away).

• If mildew keeps coming back despite your cleaning efforts, try to keep the door open as much as possible; pull the shower curtains back, too. If that doesn't do the the trick, place a moisture-capture device in the room—you can buy them at most hardware stores. These are usually plastic tubs containing silica or calcium-chloride granules; the granules draw moisture into the tub, where it condenses into water. Don't forget to check it periodically and dump out the water before it reevaporates into moisture.

Keep in mind that some cleaning chemicals can scratch or dull jewelry as well.

• If you can spend a couple of minutes each week doing a quick wipe-off with gentler cleansers, you'll save yourself a harder scrubbing later on.

• Keep a squeegee in the bathroom, and use it to wipe off the moisture on glass panels and other smooth surfaces and for clearing foggy mirrors.

• Environmentally concerned? As long as you're reading labels, look for products that are phosphate-free. These break down into simpler, less harmful compounds.

• While you're cleaning, why not chuck old medicines that have outlived their expiration dates?

Learn2 Clean Silverware

Time

Service for eight will take you about 20 minutes

What you'll need

- A soft polishing cloth
- Another soft cloth
- Silver polish or toothpaste
- Water
- Lemon juice (optional)
- Salt
- Vinegar

Tips

- If you don't have any silverware polish, try toothpaste or a paste made of water and cigarette ashes.
- When keeping flowers in a silver vase, change the water frequently to prevent discoloration.
- Polish and clean silver plate more gently than solid silver.

When the queen (or your in-laws) come for a visit, what could be nicer than brightly shining silver on the table? Well, if you're like most of us, you'll be polishing it the night before they show up.

BEFORE YOU BEGIN

Silver tarnishes when exposed to air, and there's really no way around that. But if you take proper care of your silver and silver plate, you'll have a lot less work to do after each use. Specially treated cloth bags are sold that retard or prevent tarnish from forming; these are a wise investment. They don't cost much and will save you lots of cleaning time.

STEP 1

Prevent tarnish

Wash silver by hand, never in the dishwasher, and do it before any food stuck to it becomes a permanent attachment. Some foods are particularly evil. These include fruit, salad dressing, salt, olives, and dark fruit juice and vinegar.

Rubber causes tarnish. Keep it away from your silver.

If you don't have the special cloth bags to store your silverware in, store it in plastic bags or plastic wrap after you wash and dry it. Squeeze the air out of the bag, or wrap the plastic wrap tightly around the utensils.

STEP 2

Clean up

Wash the silver by hand in mild dishwashing liquid. Dry it thoroughly.

When corrosion has been caused by salt, as happens with shaker tops, soak the silver in a mixture of salt and hot vinegar for 4 or 5 minutes. Then wash and dry as above.

STEP 3

Polish

Put a bit of silver polish on a damp cloth. You won't need more than a dab per item. Use up-and-down strokes, rather than circular, to polish the item. Polish between the tines with the edge of the cloth or a twisted bit of rag.

Finish off with a few strokes of another soft, dry cloth.

Learn**2** Clean Your Computer

Time

About 15 minutes

What you'll need

- A can of compressed air with plastic extension straw
- A few paper towels or 2 clean, lint-free cloths
- Household glass cleaner (not industrial-strength)
- A spray bottle
- A quart of water to which about a drop of dishwashing detergent has been added
- A cotton swab
- A commercial floppy-disk cleaner (optional)

Even in the most carefully kept household, dust and dirt will find their way into and onto your computer. When dust settles onto the circuit board inside your machine casing, the efficiency of the electrical pathway is compromised, and performance suffers.

BEFORE YOU BEGIN

Take a look at your monitor owner's manual. If it specifically warns not to use commercial glass cleaner, it's got a particularly delicate antiglare coating. In this case, you should follow the manufacturer's recommended cleaning procedure. This is a rare consideration.

Turn off and unplug both the computer and the monitor. If you are going to clean the inside of the computer, disconnect the monitor, keyboard, and all peripherals. Move the computer away from them, as you'll be blowing dust all over the place. Let the monitor cool down for at least 10 minutes before cleaning it, so that moisture won't come into contact with it while it's still hot.

STEP 1

Degrime the monitor

First, fill the spray bottle with the soapy water and spray some onto the clean cloth or paper towel. Wipe down the monitor's casing, being careful not to let the cloth get wet enough to drip liquid into the vents. If the casing is particularly smudged, scrub a little, but try hard not to let the cloth touch the screen. When cleaning around any control knobs or buttons, be extra sure that the cloth is not too wet.

Now spray a little glass cleaner onto your other clean rag or paper towel, not directly on the screen itself. Wipe the screen gently, making sure to get the corners. Be careful not to squeeze any liquid between the casing and the screen. If you do the screen last, any water residue from cleaning the casing will be removed.

STEP 2

Clean up the keyboard

Insert the plastic extension straw into the nozzle of the compressed-air can. Insert the end of the straw between the rows of keys, and blow out any dust that's accumulated. Be careful to use short bursts of air, as longer bursts increase the chance of condensation inside the can, which can blow into the keyboard.

Now wipe down the keys and surfaces with a clean part of the cloth sprayed with a bit of the soapy water. Again, be careful not to let the cloth get wet enough to allow any water into crevices.

Clean the keyboard cable as well, by wrapping your cloth around it and passing it through.

STEP 3

Dust the computer box, inside and out

The inside of your computer should be cleaned several times a year.

Look in your owner's manual: it will tell you how to open your computer casing. (These instructions are generally found in the section on adding expansion cards.) Check that the unit is unplugged. Before cracking the case, be careful to dissipate any static electricity by touching heavy metal objects, such as chairs and desks. Don't shuffle your feet on the carpet, and move around as little as possible while the casing is open.

Once the top of the case is off, you'll be able to see the circuit board and lots of other stuff. Using the can of air with the extension, blow out all the dust. Work in one constant direction, and reach into crevices to get it all (don't force the extension between anything, though). There's no need to touch any part of the circuit board. Finish it off by removing the extension from the can and blowing a few short blasts over the computer, to help keep any disturbed dust from settling back in. Before putting the top back on, blow out the stuff that's collected in the vents.

Once you've put the top back onto

your computer, you can clean the outside. Spray some soapy water onto a clean section of cloth, and wipe down the case. Be careful not to let water get into any openings or into the drives.

It's a good idea to clean floppy drives every once in a while. Now's a good time to do it. Just follow the instructions that come with the floppy cleaner.

STEP 4

Sponge-bathe your mouse

When your mouse starts to skip, it's time for a cleaning. You can minimize the amount of stuff that's picked up by keeping it clean and using a mouse pad. Always turn off the computer before disconnecting your mouse.

Disconnect the mouse, and turn it upside down. You'll find a little cover that either rotates counterclockwise or slides in one direction. Remove this, and take out the ball inside. Wipe the ball with the cloth that's been sprayed with cleaning water, and black gunk

will come off. Dry it off and set it aside.

Inside the mouse itself you'll find three little rollers, or rolling bars. Take a cotton swab and twirl the tip between your fingers to reduce the chance of any material coming off of it. Spritz just a little water onto it. Clean the rollers with the swab, using your fingers if necessary to pick out bits of gunk. Place the dry ball back in the mouse, and close it up.

STEP 5

Put it back together again

Make sure that everything's dry before plugging it all together again. Nothing should have gotten wet enough to be a problem. But if you're at all doubtful, wait a bit longer.

Tips

- Keyboards love feather dusters. If you have one, use it every few days to reduce the amount of grime that collects on everything.
- If the mouse still doesn't behave properly after cleaning, try using a little rubbing alcohol on the cotton swab instead of water. Using it on the ball will really clean it off but will also dry it out. Using a household spray cleaner on the casing is not recommended but can be the only way to clean off ancient grime. The danger is marring the finish, so test it on a hidden area and wait a day to see what happens.

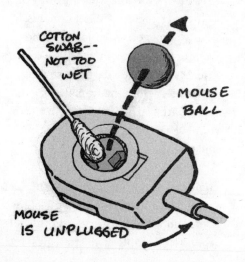

COTTON SWAB-- NOT TOO WET

MOUSE BALL

MOUSE IS UNPLUGGED

Learn**2** Darn a Sock

Time

25 minutes per sock for your first try; 10 minutes once you've done it several times

What you'll need

- A small- to medium-sized straight needle
- Sewing thread in an appropriate color and strength (see Step 1)
- A pair of scissors
- A dead lightbulb (to put inside your sock for easier darning and maneuvering)

Everyone has a favorite pair of socks. Has yours been tucked away because of a hole? Let go of your shame—just grab a needle, thread, and a favorite sock that needs darning, and in less than 30 minutes your sock will be ready to wear again.

BEFORE YOU BEGIN

A hole in your sock is made by the pressure of the foot wearing away part of the sock material. What remains, in lightly damaged socks, is the framework of the cloth, which looks like a grid. It's best if you darn the sock at this stage, before the framework gets torn apart. Darning a sock with a torn framework is a bit more difficult but still possible.

What is darning, anyway? It's a combination of sewing around the edges of the hole and thin parts of the sock, and weaving thread over the hole itself. You'll employ two strategies:

• surrounding the weakened area to limit its expansion. Use a horizontal running stitch to mark the area.

• filling in the surrounded area with a vertical, weaving-type running stitch.

STEP 1
Choose the appropriate thread

Pick a thread that's nearly the same color and weight as your sock fabric. All-purpose cotton thread works well for light- and medium-weight socks; embroidery thread works best.

For heavy wool socks, two strands of strong woolen yarn (or mending yarn or scrap yarn, as it's sometimes sold) or some embroidery floss work well.

STEP 2
Thread the needle

Don't know how to thread a needle? There's always a first time. Pull the thread from the spool, and bite or snip it off. Moisten it in your mouth or some other handy source of moisture; this will make the thread tip stiffer, straighter, and more manageable as you insert it. Now smooth the end of thread between your fingers so that no fraying occurs. This'll make the needle much easier to thread.

Hold the needle close to the eye (that's the hole at the top of the needle) with your nondominant hand. As a safety measure, keep the needle at least 6 inches away from your eye. Rest your hands slightly against each

other—try the dominant wrist resting on the base of the nondominant thumb. This will steady them while they push the thread through the needle.

Transfer the needle to your dominant hand. To keep the thread inside the eye, pull the thread through it with your nondominant thumb and forefinger. The amount of thread pulled through should be one quarter of the total length. Note: Don't knot the end of your thread when darning—you'll end up with an uncomfortable lump in your shoe.

STEP 3
Understand basic sewing

To darn a sock you only need to sew one type of stitch, the running stitch. Since you sew it two ways, however, you need to understand the difference.

The running stitch, surround-style:

Picture an earthworm (or a venomous snake, if you prefer) that wiggles through the earth, breaking through to the air and diving down into the dirt. That's what the needle will do, except it'll move through the surface of the sock fabric instead of the ground. Basically, you hold the needle above the fabric, and pierce it. Then you push the needle under the surface of the fabric but not too far. Next, you pick a spot about ⅛ inch (3 millimeters) from the first insertion point, and push the needle up through the fabric. And that's it—you've made your first stitch. To continue, pierce the

Tips

- For expensive wool socks, darning trouble spots when they're brand-new, before you ever wear them, will make them last at least four times longer.
- If you've never sewn before and need a confidence builder, practice these stitches on a clean rag before you get a sock involved.

fabric ⅛ inch further away, continuing the up-and-down motion.

The running stitch, weaving-style:

This is the actual mending structure in the darning process. It's a continuous line of thread that moves over and under, piercing the sock fabric at even intervals of ⅛ inch or so (3 millimeters) as your needle steers the thread through the sock.

STEP 4
Prepare the sock

Anchor your sock over a lightbulb—you'll have an easier time working the needle through the fabric. The needle will slide across the surface of the bulb, allowing you to weave in and out of the fabric with ease.

Trim away the ragged edges of sock (edges only). You don't want to change the shape of the hole or make it larger.

STEP 5
Surround the hole

Once your needle is threaded, work a circle (or an oval) of running stitches around the worn area or hole to mark its extent. Hold the needle above the fabric, and pierce it. Push the needle across the surface of the bulb, but don't go too far.

Pick a spot about ⅛ inch (3 millimeters) from the first insertion point. Where? Pretend your circular sock hole is a clock, and your first insertion is at the six o'clock position. Poke the needle up through the fabric at seven

o'clock. That's it—you've made your first stitch. To continue, pierce the fabric ⅛ inch further away, at eight o'clock. Continue the up-and-down motion.

After you've sewn a complete circle of stitches, sew four or five more stitches beyond. This keeps the stitches tied into the fabric without tying a knot. Once you have sewn a running stitch around the area of sock that needs darning, don't knot the ends of the thread. That would create an uncomfortable bump as you step on it or as your foot presses it against the shoe.

STEP 6
Fill the void, part 1

Locate the bottom left edge of the worn area of sock, and pick a spot just outside the marking stitches.

Beginning at the base of the hole, use the running stitch to make a series of horizontal lines of thread across the width of the hole. If the hole is simply a worn area with the cloth grid still intact, you'll weave the needle down into and back out of the sock fabric, and you'll stop at a spot just beyond the marking stitches on the opposite side.

If you have a gaping hole with no cloth grid, your horizontal lines will just be the thread, lying straight across the opening.

To make sure you aren't sewing the stitches too tightly, now and then tug the sock apart a little bit, along the line of the stitches. This pulls more thread into the stitch, which releases any tension in the thread, allowing the fabric to lie flat—not pinched or squeezed by a tight stitch.

Continue weaving, up and back across the hole, keeping the stitches parallel.

STEP 7
Fill the void, part 2

Now you want to turn your work 90 degrees; the stitching you've just done will lie vertically. You're halfway there now, well on your way to wearing your favorite socks again.

Start at a point where your needle has emerged from making horizontal stitches. Weave your needle alternately over and under each of the previously laid horizontal threads. Start and finish each row as in Step 6. Weave the thread down into and up through the grid until the worn area or hole has been completely filled up.

STEP 8
Finish it off

Once the whole area of your sock has been completely filled up with vertical and horizontal stitches, you're ready to finish your darning.

Using a running stitch, pass your needle and thread in and out of the sock fabric just outside the darned area. These four or five stitches will secure the darning stitches, that is, keep them from slipping out. You sew these extra stitches instead of tying a knot, which would not feel good to step on.

Cut off the remaining thread, and take pride in your newly mended sock: the area that was worn and torn is now much stronger than it was originally, before it ever needed mending.

Learn2 Defrost a Freezer

Time

½–2 hours, depending on the thickness of the ice

What you'll need

- Newspaper
- Cardboard boxes or milk crates
- A pot of water
- Lots of counter space
- Nontoxic cleaning supplies: white vinegar, baking soda, mild dishwashing soap
- Some old clean towels
- A vacuum, if you're really good
- A sponge mop

Tips

- Wear rubber-soled shoes. Not only will they give you traction on a wet floor, they'll prevent the transference of electric shocks.

Believe it or not, initiating freezer meltdown before the stalagmites can bar your way accomplishes a few things: it conserves energy and freezer space; it prevents confusing leftover lasagna with lentil soup; it even saves you time.

BEFORE YOU BEGIN

Empty the freezer. Wrap up the frozen food in several layers of newspaper, then pack tightly in a cardboard box or milk crate—the tighter the pack, the colder it keeps. Store the boxes in as cool a place as you can muster.

STEP 1

Shut down, then open up

With the temperature-control knob, found in the freezer or sometimes the refrigerator compartment, turn off the juice to the freezer. Or unplug the refrigerator.

Then prop open the door, and secure it so it can't whack you in the head.

STEP 2

Protect your floor

Layer some old towels on the floor in front of the freezer to catch the snow. Roll up another towel and place it at the edge of the freezer floor along the rubber door seal. This will help prevent the melting ice from pouring onto the floor.

A HOT SKILLET SPEEDS THAWING

OLD TOWELS CATCH DRIPS

STEP 3

Jump-start the process

Put a pot of water on the stove, and bring it to a brisk boil. Carefully place the steaming pot in the freezer, dribbling a bit of the hot water onto the freezer floor if it's particularly ice-bound.

Move the pot around the perimeter of the freezer so the steam can help melt wall and ceiling frost.

Boil more water as needed.

STEP 4

Dislodge the ice

After the steam has a chance to seep under the ice, try using your bare hands to pry the ice off the walls and ceiling. If it's too thick and dense, though, take one of the smaller towels, soak it in water as hot as you can

stand, and drench the icy surfaces. Repeat the soak-and-drench routine until you get down to the bare surfaces, soaking up the excess as necessary.

If your refrigerator has a drip tray (located directly under the freezer unit), empty it periodically to prevent deluges from flowing down the front of the fridge.

STEP 5

Wash up

Technically, you're done. But you may want to use this opportunity to wash your freezer's interior. Solutions of white vinegar and water or baking soda and water will remove not only residue but odors as well. For stubborn areas, use the baking soda like a scouring powder or mix with enough water to make a stiff paste. Rinse, if necessary, and dry with a clean towel.

STEP 6

Restart your engine

After you've made sure everything is dry, plug the refrigerator back in and return the thermostat to its proper position.

Remove the newspaper wrappings from the food items (they should still be frozen solid), and repack the freezer.

Tips

- Don't use an ice pick or screwdriver to gouge out the ice. At best, you'll mar the interior of your freezer; at worst, you'll chisel through a coolant line, releasing a toxic gas into the environment while rendering your freezer useless.
- Since your freezer is now fresh and gleaming, consider attacking the inside of the fridge and the exterior surfaces.
- For the overall health of your appliance, periodically remove the grate or screen that shields the compressor and fan, usually located at the very top or bottom of the unit. Remove the thick accumulated dust with a vacuum nozzle. That'll allow for free airflow, lessening the strain on the motor.

Learn 2 Fix a Leaky Faucet

Time

About 15 minutes

What you'll need

For a two-handled fixture:

- A package of assorted washers or one that matches the old one
- Both a Phillips-head and a standard screwdriver (you don't know which type of screw is inside the faucet)
- A small- to medium-sized crescent wrench

For a ball-type fixture:

- A medium-sized flat-head screwdriver
- A kit containing a special tool made specifically for disassembling ball-type fixtures, a small hex wrench, rubber O-rings, and valve seats, widely available

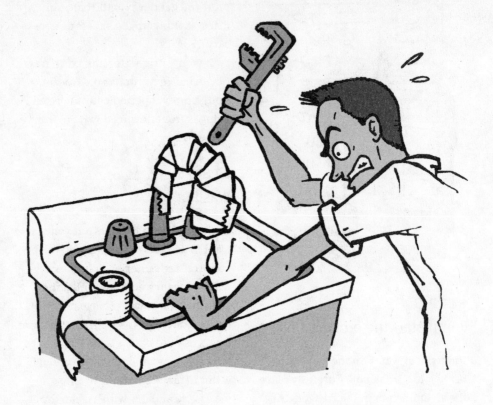

It's three in the morning, and you can't sleep anymore with that constant noise. Well, don't worry about fixing the darn thing tonight, just throw a towel under the drip for now and go back to sleep. In the morning you can fix the leak in a more permanent way.

BEFORE YOU BEGIN

There are three general styles of faucets you'll encounter. The first kind is the one that uses two different handles for hot and cold water. See the instructions below for this type of faucet. The second and third kinds both use one pivoting handle for both hot and cold water. If it's a ball-type faucet, with a rounded top, you can buy a generic kit that contains special tools, then just follow the instructions below. If it's a cartridge type, with a squared-off top, it will use one of a number of various cartridges.

Unfortunately, it's not possible to show each maker's specific unit here. The box that your cartridge comes in will contain directions for installing it; just make sure that you get the correct cartridge for your fixture. In any case, be certain to plug the drain before beginning any repairs, so parts don't fall down it!

STEP 1
Turn off the water

Ninety-nine percent of the time, you're going to find a water valve right under your sink that controls the faucet. If you don't, follow the plumbing line to the nearest one. When you find it, turn it clockwise until you can't anymore. If the valve resists being turned, put a drop or two of oil right where the stem disappears into the large nut. Then use the wrench to loosen the nut one complete turn, and tighten it back up by hand. Wait a couple of minutes and try again.

STEP 2
Remove the stem

If you have a two-handle fixture, there will be a large nut right under the faucet handle. Turn the nut counterclockwise to unscrew it completely. If you're concerned about scratches from the wrench, put some masking tape over the nut before loosening it.

Now grasp the handle, and turn it counterclockwise, as if you're turning on the water. The whole thing will lift out in your hand.

If you have a ball-type fixture, there will be a set screw on the lower surface of the handle itself. Use the hex wrench from your kit to loosen the screw and remove the handle. Then

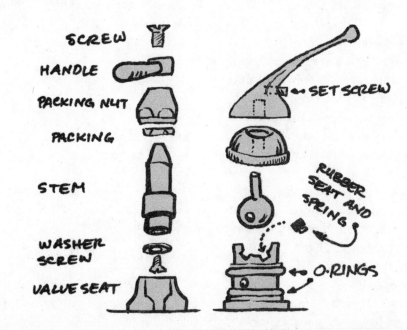

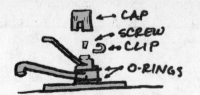

← CAP

← SCREW

← CLIP

← O-RINGS

A CARTRIDGE FIXTURE :
UNCAP, UNSCREW HANDLE
ASSEMBLY, UNCLIP AND
REMOVE , REPLACE CARTRIDGE

use the special tool to loosen the plastic adjusting ring from the knurled, rounded cap. Unscrew and remove the cap.

Pull out the ball assembly by tugging on the lever that's sticking up.

STEP 3

Replace the washer, and finish up

You're almost home now.

For a two-handled faucet:

The washer is that rubberlike thing at the bottom of the assembly in your hand. There will be a screw holding it on. Remove the screw, and replace the washer with one that's the same size. Tighten the screw firmly but without damaging the washer.

Reinsert the stem assembly, and twist it firmly clockwise, being careful not to overtighten. Replace the large nut and tighten.

Turn the water valve counterclockwise to open it.

That's it! If the darn thing still drips, call in a professional to polish

the worn valve seat or replace the fixture.

For a ball-type fixture:

Using the end of the screwdriver, lift out the rubber seats and springs. Replace them with the new ones in the kit.

Tug the spout off the base by turning it from side to side and lifting up. Then use the screwdriver to lever the old O-rings off the base. If they need to be cut off, make sure you clean off any remaining pieces. Roll the new O-rings over the base to replace them.

Reseat the faucet by turning it from side to side while pushing down. Place the ball assembly back in, and screw the rounded, knurled cap back on.

Before tightening the adjusting ring with the special tool, turn the water back on. Then tighten the ring until no water leaks, but don't overtighten. Replace the handle, and tighten the set screw.

Learn2 Fix a Toilet

Maladjusted or worn-out pieces of toilet hardware allow water to run continuously from the tank to the toilet bowl and down the pipe, eventually emptying the tank. There's also a slow-leak running toilet that's quiet and not easily detectable but will also empty the tank before long. Running toilets should be repaired for three reasons: 1) a running toilet isn't ready for use, since there's no water in the tank; 2) it's noisy; and 3) it can waste a tremendous amount of water—thousands of gallons over the course of a year.

BEFORE YOU BEGIN

Not all toilets have the design described in this 2torial, but don't let that throw you off. All toilets work on the same principles, so by taking off the lid, flushing the toilet, and watching the flush cycle a few times, you'll be able see how it works.

STEP 1

Understand toilets

There are three basic parts to toilet function: filling, stopping, and flushing. You need these three functions working together in order for the toilet to operate properly. Anytime you have a problem with the toilet running, take off the lid of the tank, flush the toilet, and watch the filling, stopping, and

Time

15 to 20 minutes, not including a possible trip to a hardware store

What you'll need

Running-toilet repair:
- A stopper replacement (possibly)
- A small pair of pliers
- A lift-arm replacement (possibly)

Slow-leak repair:
- A flush-valve seat replacement
- Food coloring
- Steel wool or fine wet/dry sandpaper
- A couple of clean rags
- A flashlight (optional)

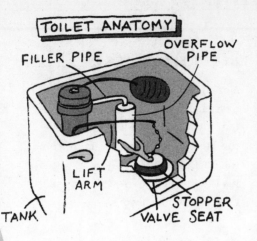

TOILET ANATOMY

FILLER PIPE

OVERFLOW PIPE

LIFT ARM

TANK

STOPPER VALVE SEAT

emptying cycle a few times. This will help you identify the source of the problem.

Filling:

The tank is the large, oblong ceramic container that's located behind the toilet bowl and at waist-to-chest level of the person sitting on it. The tank is important for two reasons: it contains the water that flushes waste down the pipes, and it contains all the hardware necessary for filling, stopping, and emptying. The overflow pipe (a.k.a. the ball cock) is a long, hollow tube fastened to the bottom of the tank. A narrow pipe usually snakes up the side of the overflow pipe and fills the tank.

Flushing:

When the tank is full and you push down the handle on the outside of it, the lift arm, which connects to the handle on the inside of the tank, pulls up either a chain or a thin, rigid, metal

rod called a lift wire. The lift wire/chain piece pulls up a rubbery black plug that's called one of many names: the stopper, flapper, disk, seal, or tank ball. As the stopper is lifted, the water in the tank rushes out the drain at the bottom of the tank, into the toilet bowl, and down the pipes to a sewer.

Stopping:

Stopping is when problems can happen. Stopping happens at the flush valve, which consists of the stopper and a flush-valve seat (a brass or plastic seal that surrounds the drain). When the tank is empty, the stopper is lowered onto the flush-valve seat (that's where the stopper "sits") and closes the drain, preventing any passage of water. A good seal at the connection between the stopper and the flush-valve seat allows the tank to be filled up.

Problem 1
Fix a running toilet

STEP 1

Adjust the stopper

Don't panic. Take off the lid of the tank and see what's happening. Chances are, the stopper isn't sitting squarely on the flush-valve seat—the chain is probably caught under the side of the stopper. You can fix the situation by pulling the chain out from the stopper; if you've ever been told to "jiggle the handle" of a running toilet, this is exactly what you're doing. A more permanent solution is to shorten the length of the chain so that there isn't excessive slack to interfere with the action of the stopper.

Use a small pair of pliers to loosen the link on top of the stopper that attaches it to the chain.

Now place the stopper squarely on the valve seat, and pull the chain taut to the stopper. Choose a link that will keep the chain fairly taut (leave a little slack, though), and attach the chain to the link on the stopper. Make sure the handle (on the outside) is up and the lift arm is down; this will put them in the correct position to pull up the chain and stopper.

No chain in your toilet? Then your toilet uses a lift wire.

Look down the length of the lift wire. If it's bent, it may be throwing the stopper off center. Remove it and try it push the bend out of it. If that's too hard or it's bent past the point of repair, you can purchase a new one at a hardware store for a few dollars.

STEP 2
Replace the stopper

Still running? Like the rest of us, stoppers get old and run-down and don't work well. If the toilet doesn't respond to the measures above, the stopper may need to be replaced. A stopper that's soft or distorted or has pockmarks or small splits near the edge is ripe for retirement.

Remove the old stopper from the chain or lift wire, and bring it down to the local hardware store. (Some brands of toilets won't accept the one-size-fits-all type of stopper, so be sure to bring the old stopper with you.) It won't cost you more than a few dollars and 5 minutes of work.

As you reattach the chain to the link on the stopper, make sure the handle (on the outside) is up and the lift arm is down. This will put them in the correct position to pull up the chain and stopper.

Problem 2
Fix a slow leak

STEP 1
Replace the flush-valve seat

If your toilet doesn't run continuously yet you can hear it refill every 15 minutes or more, the problem may be with the flush-valve seat. If you want to be sure, add several drops of dark-colored food dye to the tank. If there's a leak in the valve seat, the dyed water will seep through the seal and into the toilet bowl, right in front of your sus-

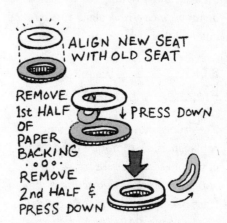

ALIGN NEW SEAT WITH OLD SEAT

REMOVE 1st HALF OF PAPER BACKING ↓ PRESS DOWN

REMOVE 2nd HALF & PRESS DOWN

Key words

Overflow pipe: A long, hollow tube, fastened to the bottom of the tank.

Tank: The large, oblong ceramic container that's located behind the toilet bowl and at waist-to-chest level of the person sitting on it.

Flush valve: The connection that consists of the stopper and the flush-valve seat.

Flush-valve seat: A brass or plastic sealant ring located at the bottom of the tank.

Lift arm: A thin metal rod inside the tank, that connects to the handle (outside) and raises the stopper.

Key words

Stopper (a.k.a., flapper, tank ball, seal, disk): The rubbery black plug attached to the wire/chain piece.

Main water valve: Located on the wall near the floor, this is a knob that you twist to turn the water supply on and off.

pecting eyes. Aha! An old valve seat won't form a good seal with the stopper or the base of the tank and will leak water until the entire tank is empty. Fortunately, it's easy to buy a replacement that can be cemented directly on top of the old one.

Most hardware stores will have a valve-seat replacement kit, which will fit most models. It won't fit all, though, and the kit's packaging will often depict what types of valve seats aren't compatible. To avoid a mistaken purchase, take a careful look at the valve seat, noting the size and any distinguishing marks, before leaving for the store. And if nothing else, note what the valve seat is made of: brass or plastic, usually.

STEP 2
Empty the tank

First, you need to clear out the tank. Turn off the water at the main water valve (located on the wall near the floor), flush the toilet to empty the tank, and remove the stopper, chain, lift arm, and anything else that might be in the way. With a clean rag, mop up any puddles of water on the tank floor.

STEP 3
Prepare the old seat

The crucial step with valve-seat replacement is thorough preparation of the old seat. If it's brass, scrub it with steel wool or wet/dry sandpaper. If it's plastic, use a nonabrasive nylon ball or sponge. After you've cleaned,

wipe down the seat again, making sure to remove any grit or moisture that remains.

STEP 4
Prepare the new seat

Most seat replacements have a self-adhesive, with a layer of peel-off paper backing. Before you peel off the backing, study the illustrations for that particular model of seat replacement, and practice aligning it over the old seat.

STEP 5
Attach the new seat

Remove *half* of the paper backing, and having aligned the new seat carefully, press it gently on the old seat. Repeat with the other side: remove the paper and press gently. Once the new seat is on and aligned correctly, press down firmly and evenly for at least a minute.

STEP 6
Place, pull, and position

Place the stopper squarely on the valve seat, and pull the chain to the stopper. Choose a link that will keep the chain fairly taut yet leave a little slack, and attach the chain to the link on the stopper. Make sure the handle (on the outside) is up and the lift arm is down; this will put them in the correct position to pull up the chain and stopper.

Turn the main water valve back on, and you're ready to flush.

Learn2 Fix a Zipper

Zippers are great until they break. There's always the chance that even the best-quality zipper could separate and develop a gap behind the slider. But before you throw away the item or rip the whole zipper out and replace it, try this simple repair method.

Time

About 20 minutes

What you'll need

- Needle-nose pliers
- A needle heavy enough to pierce the zipper's surrounding fabric
- Heavy thread
- Spray starch (optional)

BEFORE YOU BEGIN

If you have a zipper that's not separated but is merely balky or stuck, try these measures first:

- Look underneath the zipper to see if any threads are caught in it. If so, use a scissors or razor blade to cut them where they enter the slider. Pull them through to free the slider.

- Rub a bar of soap or a candle on the teeth of the zipper. Now run the slider back and forth a few times. This will smooth things out.

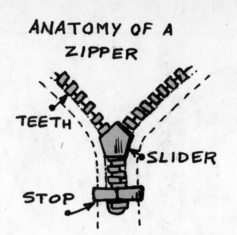

ANATOMY OF A ZIPPER

TEETH

SLIDER

STOP

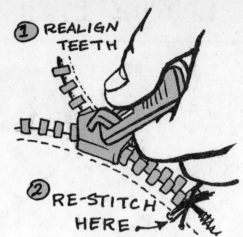

① REALIGN TEETH

② RE-STITCH HERE

STEP 1

Remove the old stop

The thick horizontal piece at the bottom of the zipper is called a stop. Take the stop in one hand and the pliers in the other. With the pliers, grasp the stop at the bottom of the teeth and work it off. Then turn the zipper over if necessary in order to access the other side of the stop.

STEP 2

Realign the slider

When the stop is removed, you'll be able to get rid of the gap.

Move the slider down the zipper, and carefully run the teeth back through the slider.

Zip the zipper completely up, so that the fabric is aligned on either side.

STEP 3

Create a new stop

Since it's just about impossible to reattach the old stop, create a new one.

Thread the needle with the heavy thread.

Starting from the back, create a new stop by placing several stitches across the bottom of the zipper. You need enough stitches to hold but not so many that it becomes bulky. On your last stitch, tie off the thread in a double knot or two under the zipper, then cut the thread.

Learn2 Groom a Cat

Is Kitty looking a little mangy? Has it shredded your couch with its long, sharp claws? Perhaps you've tried brushing it before, only to receive unsightly scratches on your arms.

What is grooming? There are three main areas: claw clipping, bathing, and brushing. If you're concerned about the relationship between your cat and your furniture, just clip its claws. (Four out of five cats strongly recommend claw-clipping over declawing.) Bathing is a good idea for outdoor cats, who may roll in pesticides, fight with other cats, or become infested with fleas and ticks. Brushing ensures a healthy coat and a strong emotional bond with the owner.

BEFORE YOU BEGIN

Cats should be brushed frequently: daily brushing is commendable but not realistic in every owner's schedule. A minimum of twice a week is sufficient for most cats, unless yours is an outdoor long-hair who likes to roll around in the dirt and collect burrs. To prevent your couch from becoming a regular scratching post, their claws can be clipped about once per month. A bath can happen every 6 to 8 weeks; in summertime, when lawn and garden pesticide use is higher, it may be wise to bathe an outdoor cat more frequently, say, once a month.

It's a good idea to do a just a little grooming at a time. Most owners have observed that cats hate water; a bath will make them very upset. If a bath is given roughly and at the wrong time, it can be a traumatic experience for everyone involved. If you're giving your cat a dry grooming (not bathing

Time

5 to 90 minutes, depending on the fur (long or short) and the amount of grooming you'll be performing

What you'll need

- A bathtub or a large plastic tub and hot water
- Nontoxic lather-and-rinse pet shampoo, available at any good pet store
- Large toenail clippers or special pet-claw cutters
- A towel you don't mind using on your cat (to dry it off)
- A pet brush
- A flea comb (optional)

- Consult a cat-care manual or your vet as to which food is best for your cat, according to your cat's weight, age, and lifestyle. The proper food can help maintain a shiny coat and healthy teeth, as well as cut down on digestive problems.

it), begin while the cat is asleep, which should not be hard considering cats sleep 16 to 18 hours a day. While your cat is groggy, it'll be more agreeable to grooming than if it's alert and playful. Have all materials ready; for example, have the clippers open—you don't want to fumble with any items. If your cat senses you're frantic or hurried, it'll get upset too.

Part 1
Clip the claws

Declawing a cat is roughly equivalent to cutting off a human's fingers; it leaves cats defenseless against anything they perceive as an enemy. Grooming habits can also fall off—cats use their claws to scratch away dead skin or old fur. Clipping is much preferable.

Back claws tend to be much thicker and harder than front claws and sometimes shatter when clipped. Since cats use their front claws to do most of their scratching damage, and since the back claws aren't sharpened regularly, you can often skip these altogether. So don't clip them unless you're convinced it's necessary and the cat is in an extraordinarily relaxed mood.

PRESS HERE

THEN HERE

STEP 1
Relax and be gentle

Help your cat to relax. Begin by petting it and speaking kind words in a low, gentle voice.

Handle your cat's paws carefully. Cats can be very sensitive about what and where their paws are touching, so gently stroke a paw before working on it.

Push a claw out of its sheath by gently pressing down on the pad of the paw with your thumb and pressing with your index finger on the top of the paw below the claw. There's sensitive skin around the claw that cats are protective of, so take care not to handle the area roughly.

STEP 2
Cut carefully

Avoid the colored part of the claw. A cat's claws are clear, so it's easy to see how far down to cut. It's very important, however, not to cut the dark- or pink-colored part of the claw, where the nerves and blood supply reside. You'll know if you've made a mistake—your cat will meow in pain, possibly bite or scratch you, and generally end the clipping session right then and there. If you do cut too far down, hold a damp paper towel to the stub to stop the bleeding. Of course, your cat will probably run away to lick its wounds in private, which is fine too. Cat saliva cleanses and disinfects.

It's best to clip in order from one end of the paw to the other. In case you're interrupted, you won't have to search for the last claw you clipped, unsettling the cat even more. Hold the claw still, and clip the tip. If you can do this without clanging the clippers around (which will draw attention to them, and cause the cat to focus on the shiny object), you and your cat will have an easier time of it, and will finish the task more quickly.

When you've clipped all the claws, clear away all clippings from its fur. This will prevent your cat from licking them up.

Part 2
Bathe

If you're doing a dry grooming (just a clip and a brush, please), skip this step and go to Step 3.

In general, watch where you stick your hands. Avoid any facial cleaning. Cats usually won't abide it. If your cat doesn't mind it, however, you can proceed with caution—just consider how you'd want your own face cleaned. If you're trying to remove fleas, you can use a flea powder, but it's safer for your cat to use a flea shampoo along with a bath. See Part 3 for an even better flea-removal technique.

STEP 1
Add water

This is going to be a messy experience, so prepare to get almost as wet as your cat. Wear old clothes or a bathing suit, and don't be afraid to climb into the tub with your cat. Avoid hovering over your cat, however, because this will make it more agitated.

Stay calm. Whether in a plastic tub, sink, or bathtub, your cat won't be delighted about a bath. Be prepared for wide eyes and loud, tortured-sounding meows. At all times, keep your movements slow and your voice soft and gentle.

Wet your cat's coat with lukewarm water. Don't pour a bucket over your cat or soak it through—that would be very unpleasant for your cat. Wet the coat gradually, using a stroking motion; you'll give the impression you're also petting it. If you're also giving your cat a flea bath, follow the directions on the shampoo bottle carefully. (Many flea shampoos require a period of waiting for the shampoo to soak in. If this is the case, it's likely your cat won't sit quietly and wait, so continue to lather and pet, thereby keeping its mind off what's happening.)

STEP 2
Lather and rinse

Pour a capful of pet shampoo on your cat's back. As you rub it in and create a lather, keep your movements linear instead of rubbing in all directions; your cat won't be familiar with that sort of petting pattern. Keep away from the face and ears at all times, but be sure to lather up its tail and legs.

After it's lathered up, you may have to wait a few minutes for the shampoo to set in, if the directions say so. Otherwise, rinse the fur in the same manner as the initial wetting. Make absolutely sure you've rinsed out all of the shampoo. Even if the shampoo is organic or nontoxic,

Tips

- For healthy claws and intact furniture, a scratching post is essential. If you've been to pet stores and balk at the cost of many synthetic posts, a great natural alternative is a chunk of cut tree trunk or any log that's taller and larger than your cat. Many cats prefer this to store-bought scratching posts: it comes from outside, it's natural, and it'll be more durable than a lot of the flimsy hollow posts you'll find in stores.

WASH USING PETTING MOTIONS

NO SCRUBBING!

Tips

- Cats can suffer tooth and gum disease if their teeth aren't cared for. You should regularly check your cat's teeth by gently lifting up a lip and noting the color of the teeth. If they are yellow or visibly built up with tartar, it's time for a cleaning. Don't attempt to clean your cat's teeth yourself. Let a veterinarian do it, since they have the proper tools and cleaning agents.

both the smell and the taste may make your cat sick.

If you're using a bathtub or sink, don't forget to clean the cat hair out from the drain, especially if your cat is long-haired. Deposit it in the trash.

STEP 3
Dry

This is the best part of the process, where you can cuddle your pet as well as dry it off. Have a huge towel waiting, and wrap it around your cat. Sit on the floor with it and gently rub its fur. If you don't spend sufficient time drying your cat, it'll have to lick itself dry; this can cause problems with hairballs. Don't be concerned when your cat licks itself for a while even after you release it; it's merely regaining its composure.

Part 3
Brush

A healthy cat is a happy cat, and brushing will contribute to the overall process of keeping your cat healthy. Brushing removes fur, which might otherwise become a hairball. It also improves blood circulation near the skin, which contributes to a healthy and shiny coat and will make your cat the envy of the neighborhood.

STEP 1
Do the brush stroke

If you have just given your cat a bath, be sure it's completely dry before

brushing it. Otherwise, the fur will be difficult to work with.

Brush your cat in the direction the fur grows. Be sure not to brush too hard, making it cringe and struggle to get away. Do as much as your cat will allow. In general, you should avoid the head. Some cats, however, are partial to cheek brushing. Some cats won't allow brushing on their underbelly. Be gentle, and discover what your cat likes best.

Brushing can be a very loving experience between owner and pet. Take the opportunity to turn it into a bonding ritual. You might want to consult some of the books available on cat massage so you can learn which techniques it likes best.

STEP 2
Remove fleas

A wonderful alternative to flea powder—and a far safer one—is to use a fine-toothed flea comb, which can be purchased at most pet stores or through your vet. By running this small comb through the fur, you can remove most of the fleas and even the flea eggs from your cat. Make sure they're dead after they're off your cat, or else they can jump on again. (If you're not sure, drop them into water with a few drops of ordinary dishwashing liquid mixed in.)

Learn**2** Make a Bed

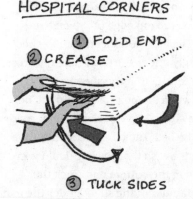

Anyone who's ever worked in a hospital, been in the armed forces, or, for that matter, gone to camp knows how to make a bed. So how come so many beds in this world are made so sloppily? Time to shape up!

BEFORE YOU BEGIN

When you've just crawled out of bed in the morning, late for work, making the bed certainly seems to be last on your list of priorities. Think how nice it would be, though, to come home to an inviting, tidy bed after a hard day's work.

STEP 1

Put on the bottom sheet

Sometimes you have a fitted sheet, and sometimes you don't. If you have one (a sheet with elastic on the ends and preformed corners), stretch it over two corners at one end of the mattress. Walk around the bed, and stretch the sheet over the other two corners of the mattress.

If you have two flat sheets, take one of them and hold the long end (the side without a hemmed edge) with both hands, and stand next to the bed. Flip the sheet out over the bed so that it billows and spreads over the mat-

tress. Position the sheet so that it hangs evenly over all sides of the mattress. Make sure the long edges are parallel to the floor and hang below the bottom of the mattress.

Take the short end of the sheet, and tuck it snugly under the end of the mattress. Make sure it lies smoothly between the box spring and the mattress. Go around to the opposite (short) end of the bed, and pull the sheet taut. Tuck the sheet under the mattress as above, maintaining the tension you've created.

HOSPITAL CORNERS

① FOLD END
② CREASE
③ TUCK SIDES

Time

About 5 to 10 minutes

What you'll need

• Clean sheets and pillowcases

Tips

- Once the bed is made completely from the bottom sheet up, only the top sheet and blanket need to be remade every morning. You can speed up the process by tucking them both under the mattress at the same time. It won't be perfect but will probably be good enough.
- If you don't like to be so confined when you sleep, just don't create as much tension when you tuck the top sheet and blanket.

Move back around to the long side of the bed. Tuck the edge of the sheet under the mattress. This should create a vertical fold, unless the short edge of the sheet is bunched under the end of the mattress.

Go to the other side of the bed and repeat the last step. Tug firmly on the sheet to create a taut surface.

STEP 2

Put on the top sheet

Now you're going to create a nice, tight, confining area to slide into at night.

If you've just used a flat sheet as your bottom sheet, you'll realize that the top sheet goes on in almost exactly the same way. Find one long end of the sheet (a side without a hemmed edge) and stand next to the bed. Generally, the sheet will have one edge with a hem of at least 2 inches; that end should go toward your head.

Flip the sheet out over the bed so that it billows and spreads over the mattress. Position the sheet so that it hangs evenly over both long sides of the mattress but has extra length at the foot end. The head end should reach the top edge of the mattress.

Tuck the bottom end of the sheet snugly under the end of the mattress. Make sure that the sheet is flat between the box spring and the bottom sheet. Move back to the long side of the bed. Tuck the sheet under the mattress, so that a vertical fold is created at the bottom end. Tuck the remainder of the sheet under the mat-

tress, but leave a foot or two of it loose at the top. This will be folded back over your blanket to form a nice, soft edge that sits next to your face.

Repeat with the other side of the mattress, creating a taut surface by tugging firmly.

STEP 3

Put on the blankets

Step to the side of the bed, and flip the blanket so that it billows over the bed. Position it so that there will be room for your head and shoulders, with the remainder hanging evenly over the other three sides.

Repeat the steps that you took with the top sheet, first tucking the bottom under the mattress, then the sides. Remember to create vertical folds by not bunching the blanket under the mattress.

Fold the portion of the top sheet that you left loose back over the blanket. Tuck the edges under the mattress to form a tidy appearance.

Place the pillowcases over the pillows, and put them aside.

If you're using a bedspread or comforter, now's the time to put it on. Flip it out so it spreads over the bed, making sure the edges at the bottom and sides are even to the floor. Fold the top edge of the spread down, and position the bottom edge of the pillow to just cover the fold (the top edge should sit about 3 inches from the head of the bed). Fold the spread over the top of the pillow, and tuck around the top and bottom edges.

Learn**2** Remove a Stain

Time

Most of these rec-
ommendations take
less than an hour,
including drying
time.

What you'll need

*Any or all of the fol-
lowing, depending
on the stain:*

- A prewash stain
  remover
- A prewash enzyme
  soak
- Laundry detergent
- Dishwashing
  detergent
- Cold water
- Ice
- White vinegar
- Salt
- Paint thinner
- Isopropyl alcohol
- Hydrogen
  peroxide
- Bleach
- Nonflammable
  stain remover (see
  "Tips")
- Shampoo

There's a whole range of products and home remedies just
waiting for you to give them a
shot and make your stains disappear.

BEFORE YOU BEGIN

On one hand, you want to treat most
stains as soon as possible. The longer
you wait before dealing with a problem, the worse it gets, right? On the
other hand, it's not a good idea to treat
a stain unless you know what it is and
how the fabric will react to treatment.
So first determine which stain is on
what kind of fabric, then act quickly.

Key words

Prewash stain remover: a liquid, gel, or solid product that is usually applied for several minutes—but sometimes up to 1 week—before laundering.

Prewash enzyme soak: A product specially formulated for protein stains like blood and egg.

Nonflammable stain remover: An evaporative liquid that is designed to be applied directly to a fabric before laundering.

Tips

• When working with nonflammable stain remover, the key is to put the fabric, stain side down, on a paper towel or clean white rag and apply the stain remover to the back of the stain. This forces the stain off, not through, the fabric.

STAIN REMOVER...
APPLY FROM BACK

PAPER TOWELS
OR RAGS

STEP 1

Read the care label attached to your garment

In some cases, the best thing for the stain is not at all right for your clothes (or upholstery). For example, normally you'd wash a white cotton blouse that's been treated for ink stains in very hot water. But you wouldn't want to do that to a purple silk. Use discretion, and err on the side of caution.

STEP 2

If in doubt, send it out

Unfamiliar, very ornate (beaded, sequined, metallic), or deeply textured fabrics may be beyond home care. Sometimes the best next step is to consult a professional.

STEP 3

Follow the stain guide

Determined that the task is within your control? Go ahead, and good luck.

Alcohol (new): Rinse with cold water. If the stain persists, soak for about 15 minutes in a mixture of tepid water, liquid detergent, and a few drops of white vinegar. Then launder in warm water.

Alcohol (old): Old alcohol stains are tough. Try rinsing with cold water, then use an enzyme presoak in warm water. Launder in warm water.

Blood: Soak the fabric in cold water (very important!). Rub some liquid detergent into the stain, then rinse in cold water. Put some hydrogen peroxide on the stain for no more than 5 minutes, then rinse clean with cold water. Now rub some more detergent into the stain. Launder in warm water.

Butter or cooking oil: First use talcum powder or cornstarch to absorb as much oil as possible. Rub shampoo on the stain, then wash in the hottest water the fabric can stand.

Chocolate: Wet the fabric with tepid water, then apply a prewash treatment and rinse. Soak in an enzyme presoak. Wash normally, but don't machine-dry until the stain is gone. If it's still there, repeat the presoak/wash cycle.

Crayons and other wax: Scrape off as much waxy substance as you can, then place the fabric between two sheets of tissue. Press gently on the area with a warm iron, to drive the wax out of the fabric. Use an enzyme presoak, or treat with a nonflammable stain remover (see illustration). Hand-wash. Repeat a few times if necessary.

Egg: Scrape off as much as you can, then soak in an enzyme presoak with cold water for a half hour. Launder in cold water.

Fruit and fruit juice: Soak immediately in cool water, then cover the stain with a paste made from colorfast bleach, a little hot water, and a few drops of ammonia. Wait for about 20 minutes, then launder as usual.

Grass: Soak the fabric in cold water, then sponge the stain with isopropyl alcohol—but first test for colorfastness on a hidden area. If the stain persists, soak in an enzyme presoak for about a half hour. Launder as usual.

Gum: Use ice cubes, or put the fabric in the freezer to harden the gum, then scrape and pull the gum off the fabric. Apply nonflammable stain remover (see illustration) and allow to air-dry. Launder as usual.

Ink: Apply isopropyl alcohol to the fabric around the stain, then to the stain itself. Place the fabric stain-side down on a paper towel. Sponge alcohol onto the stain, to drive it into the paper. Rinse well, then rub in some liquid detergent. Hand-wash in hot water.

Ketchup: Apply a prewash treatment on the stain and rinse. Then soak in an enzyme presoak for about a half hour. Wash normally.

Lipstick: First try to remove the stain with nonflammable stain remover (see illustration at left). If the stain persists, apply a prewash stain

remover, and rinse. If it still persists, rub the stain with liquid detergent, and wash in warm water.

Mud: Let the mud dry, then beat off as much as you can. If a stain remains, rub in a paste of liquid detergent and colorfast bleach. Launder as usual.

Paint, oil-based: Scrape off as much as you can, then sponge on some paint thinner, and blot the stain with a paper towel. Repeat this a few times. Once you've blotted up as much as you can, rub liquid detergent on the stain while the fabric is still wet with thinner. Hand-wash in hot water.

Paint, water-based: Get to these before they dry. Rinse the fabric well with warm water, then apply an enzyme presoak in warm water. Rinse again, then hand-wash.

Rust: Dampen the fabric with cool water, then apply a bit of lemon juice that's been mixed with salt. Boil some water in a pot, then hold the stain over the steam for a few minutes. Rinse thoroughly. Launder as usual.

Shoe polish: First scrape off as much waxy substance as you can, then clean the stain with a solution made from isopropyl alcohol and water, in equal amounts. Whites can handle straight alcohol. Launder as usual.

Soft drinks: Soak the stain in cold water. Sponge a mixture of cold water and isopropyl alcohol, in equal amounts, onto the stain. Air-dry.

Tips

- When in doubt about water temperature, use cold or warm water rather than hot. Hot water will often set the stain in the fabric. Never use hot water on blood.
- When in doubt about washing method, hand-wash rather than machine-wash. This is not only gentler on fabrics, it will keep the stain isolated to one garment.
- When in doubt about drying method, air-dry rather than machine-dry. Machine-drying, especially at high temperatures, can set the stain.
- Test for colorfastness by applying a small amount of whatever stain remover you're using on a hidden area of the fabric.

Learn2 Repair a Broken Window

Time

About 1 hour

What you'll need

- A new piece of glass, cut to size
- A chisel
- Window putty
- Some new "points" (small wedge-shaped nails)
- A hammer
- A pair of good pincers, or pliers
- Duct tape
- A putty knife
- A glass cutter
- Heavy gloves
- Linseed oil
- A rag
- 8-inch-long sections of old garden hose, slit lengthwise (optional)

Windows break all the time. If it's a newer, double-paned insulated type, it may be best to have a professional replace it. If it's an older, wooden-framed one, though, there's an excellent chance that you can replace it yourself.

BEFORE YOU BEGIN

Traditional glazier points are tough to work with. There is a newer kind available with "ears" that make for easier handling. Ask your glass supplier about them.

Remember that the new piece of glass should sit in the frame with about $1/16$ inch to spare all around (in other words, if the opening measures 6 inches by 8 inches, the glass should be $5\frac{7}{8}$ inches by $7\frac{7}{8}$ inches). This will give the frame room to expand in hot weather. If you are having the glass cut by someone else, clean out the old glass and putty first, and then take the measurements.

STEP 1

Remove the old glass

Always wear heavy gloves when handling glass. If the new piece of glass is large, use sections of slit hose to hold its edges. Keep a paper bag handy to place the old glass into.

If there are no large holes in the broken glass, use the duct tape to cover all the cracks and hold the glass together. If there are very large pieces of glass missing, don't cover them with tape. Rather, work them out as you remove each section of putty and points (working from top to bottom).

Starting from the top and working down, remove the old putty from the outside of the window with the hammer and chisel. Use the rag to brush out any putty fragments.

Seal the wood of the rabbet (see "Key words") by applying linseed oil, so that it doesn't absorb moisture from the putty.

Create two "handles" by folding a piece of duct tape and sticking it to the glass. Carefully pull out the old glass in one piece.

STEP 2

Install the new glass

Take some putty and roll it into four thin ropes (if the putty is too wet to handle well, wrap it in newspaper to absorb some moisture). Flatten the ropes of putty with your fingers all around the smaller, vertical side of the rabbet.

Lower the new glass onto the bottom section of the window frame, into the putty. Then press the remaining three edges of glass into the putty, so that the putty spreads slightly and the glass adheres. Be sure to press the edges of the glass when you're doing this. Glass has been known to crack when pressed close to the center of the pane.

Secure the new glass by tapping the new points into the rabbet with the edge of the chisel. Place the points no farther than 8 inches apart.

With the putty knife, trim any excess putty from the back of the glass.

STEP 3

Seal it up

Apply putty all around the edge of the glass, so that it fills the rabbet.

With the putty knife, smooth the putty. Ideally, the putty will form a 45-degree angle between the edge of the rabbet and the glass. If the knife sticks to the putty, wet it to reduce friction. Be tidy.

STEP 4

Finish it off

Wait at least a week, maybe two, for the putty to dry before priming and painting it. Use paint remover to get rid of any putty smears on the glass. Then paint the putty to seal it from the weather. Let the paint seep onto the glass a little to make a tight seal.

PUTTY ROPE

PRESS FROM SIDES

Key words

Rabbet: The notch in the window sash that the glass fits into.

Points: Small, wedge-shaped nails.

Learn2 Repair a Scratched CD

Time

About 10 minutes

What you'll need

- A soft, lint-free cloth or chamois; cloths made for cleaning eyeglasses are perfect
- A few smears of mild abrasive: toothpaste, metal polish, or plastic cleaner
- Water

Optional:

- A pen and paper to note the location of the CD skips
- A magnifying glass

Note: You can find special CD-repair kits, with a cloth and abrasive, at music stores, but you'll save money if you use items you already have at home, which are usually just as effective

Weren't CD's supposed to be the answer to easily damaged vinyl LP's? Alas, while they're somewhat more durable than vinyl, even a small scratch can send your CD skipping like Dorothy on the yellow brick road. But don't turn those old CD's into high-tech coasters just yet. In a few minutes, they can play like new again.

What is a skip, anyway? Vinyl LP's skip when the turntable needle hits a scratch or some dust, which makes the needle jump into another groove. Although there's no needle touching the CD surface during playback, CD's sometimes skip for a similar reason. The CD track is laid out in one continuous spiral, like an LP, although it starts at the center and winds out toward the edge (the opposite of an LP). Instead of a stylus, CD players use a laser, located below the disc inside the CD player. The laser sends a beam of light, which reflects off the shiny side and thus reads the tiny pits in the track. Since the laser follows the track, a scratch can reflect the laser in just the wrong way, and send it repeatedly to another part of the track. For this reason, scratches that run parallel to the track (or the edge of the CD) are much more likely to make a CD skip.

BEFORE YOU BEGIN

First, you should know what to expect. Most scratches deep enough to make a CD skip won't disappear completely, but that isn't your goal anyway. You want to polish the CD enough to keep the laser from misreading the pits on it. Remember to polish lightly at first, and test your work before rubbing harder—you don't want to rub the CD surface any more than necessary.

Second, it's a good idea to note where your CD skips, so it'll be easier to return to the skipping portion of the CD and test whether your efforts were successful. Play the tracks that it skips on, and write down the track time (or the part of the song) when it skips. During the postpolish test, this record will help you return directly to the repaired area of the disc.

STEP 1
Clean it

The scratches visible on the CD may not even be the source of the skipping; dust and fingerprints can cause skipping as well. It's important to keep your CD's clean: handling a CD with specks of dust on it can lead to scratches, which lead to repair jobs that might have been avoided. So before you try repairing any scratches, clean your CD thoroughly and test it for skipping.

Hold the CD by the edge, and clean it with mild soap and water (some cleaning solvents can damage the surface of the CD). Dry it with a clean,

lint-free cloth from the center straight out to the edge. Always polish in this direction; polishing in a circular motion can create the kind of scratch that can't be polished away.

STEP 2
Find the scratch(es)

First on your list is locating the scratches. Scratches on the top (label) side that are deep enough to make the CD skip are usually too deep to fix. But many scratches on the bottom (shiny) side can be repaired.

Hold the CD under a light, bottom side up at about a 60-degree angle. Scratches will appear as whitish lines that reflect off the silvery surface below.

If the CD's total track time is less than 75 minutes, some of the space toward the outside edge isn't even used. If you look closely (try a magnifying glass), you should be able to see a lighter area around the outside edge. Ignore scratches here—they won't affect playback.

A CD plays from the center to its edge, so if your CD skips mostly toward the beginning, look for scratches near the center. Scratches toward the outside edge will affect the end of the CD.

STEP 3
Smooth out the scratches

It's important to do this with a gentle touch, as you don't want to damage the

Tips

- Always hold CD's by the edges to prevent fingerprints.
- Keep CD's in the jewel boxes (clear plastic cases) they came in: don't set them down or stack them. If you must set a CD down, set it label side down.
- If your jewel boxes break, you can buy empty ones at many music and computer stores for about $1 apiece.
- Beyond repair? Don't throw the disc away; use it as a casual drink coaster, and pull out the good coasters when company comes.

Tips

- CD-ROMs can be repaired in the same way, but they're much more affected by even small scratches. As a result, CD-ROM manufacturers will often send you a new disc if you send in the old one. Contact individual companies for their policies. Here's a good reason to save your receipts!

CD further. Focus on the biggest scratches, and work gently at first, using more pressure later as needed.

Dampen a section of your cloth slightly with water, and apply to the cloth a small amount of whatever abrasive is easiest for you to get ahold of: plain white toothpaste, metal polish, or plastic cleaner. Rub the abrasive on lightly, working from the center of the disc straight out toward the edge, not in a circular motion. You may need to rub a few times, depending on the depth of the scratch. Remember, the scratches may not disappear completely. You're mainly trying to smooth out the sides of the scratch until it won't affect CD playback.

Rinse the abrasive off with water, and wipe the disc dry with a dry section of the cloth.

STEP 4

Test your work

Play the CD, listening to the tracks where you noted skipping before. If it doesn't skip anymore, congratulations! You've just saved yourself $16 on a new CD (although you've lost a perfectly good coaster). If it still skips, don't worry. Just return to Step 3, and rub a little harder this time. Most scratches can be repaired with a little effort.

NO BUFFING!

wipe gently

STRAIGHT NOT CIRCULAR

Learn2 Repair Panty Hose

Time

5 to 10 minutes

What you'll need

- A bottle of inexpensive clear nail polish
- A small pair of scissors
- A damp paper towel or cloth
- A bottle of colored nail polish (optional: only if you like a little decoration on your attire)

Whether you're dashing off to work or for a night out with your friends, all it takes is a bump against a table. Snag! Looking down at your leg, you see a hole in your new pair of panty hose; the hole becomes a run, and with every step you take the run becomes longer. Before you press the panic button, sit yourself down and fashion a patch for your hose. It's a quick and easy job, and a durable repair.

These repairs work equally well for knee-high and thigh-high stockings, as long as they're made of nylon.

BEFORE YOU BEGIN

Here's the crux of panty-hose management: be on the watch for snags and small tears. As you may be aware, these minor accidents impair the integrity of the fabric, creating long and unsightly runs that all but unravel a pair of panty hose. While a long run going down your leg is beyond repair, you can limit the damage until a replacement is available.

CLIP-OFF EXTRA THREADS

KEEP CLOTHING AWAY

PROTECT SKIN WITH PAPER TOWEL

Tips

• Use foresight when dressing. Hold off putting on your panty hose until right before you leave the house. This will prevent tears from happening while you're getting ready. Also, if you have a cat, don't put on panty hose until after you've interacted with your cat. Cats tend to find a way to snag the material.

STEP 1

Clear the area

Remove the tendrils of nylon. You may find some threads that ripped when you tore the hole, and these will become more holes and runs if left unrepaired. Carefully, so as to not cut any more of the hose, snip the thread away as close to the base as possible without getting too close to the rest of the material.

Keep your clothing away. You don't want to damage your pants, skirt, or anything else with nail polish. Protect your skin too. Keep the damp cloth handy for wiping up spills.

STEP 2

Repair holes

Dip a small amount of polish—just enough to engulf the brush, but not so much that it will drip off.

Lift away the nylon material. If your panty hose are still on your leg, hold the material away from your skin with your thumb and forefinger. If you've taken them off, hold the damaged

material away from the rest of the panty hose. Don't pull too hard on the material, or you'll cause the run to travel further. An inch (about 2 centimeters) or less is fine.

Gently dab—don't brush—around the hole. Avoid applying excess polish onto the undamaged hose, or else you'll be able to see the excess as a big, dry whitish spot. Make sure you dab all edges of the hole, because runs will take off from the hole at the first opportunity.

Clean up polish spills. If you accidentally apply polish too far beyond the hole or get it on your skin, dab it with a damp cloth immediately.

Allow for drying time. If you hurry out the door directly after applying the polish, it will get all over your skin and won't have the time to harden around the hole and make a good patch. But don't worry: nail polish takes only about 3 to 5 minutes to dry completely, and even less if it's a small dab.

STEP 3

Repair runs

Holes are easier to contain, and smaller than runs. Runs can require extra attention, as they may have lots of damaged material to be sealed off. But they can be stopped before they get larger. Be sure to seal off both ends of the run. It's also a good idea to put a little polish along the edges of the run, say, an inch or so (2 to 3 centimeters) from each end. Again, this will prevent new runs from branching off the main run.

Learn**2** Replace a Broken Tile

Ceramic tiles are used in bathrooms for good reason: they look good, and they're waterproof and easy to clean. They're not indestructible, though, and every once in a while they crack. And if the cracked tile is in a location where it's often wet, water can seep into the crack and damage the wall behind the tile. So it's something you want to take care of—and not just for aesthetic reasons.

BEFORE YOU BEGIN

Protect the tile's surrounding area with cardboard, newspaper, or an inexpensive plastic drop cloth. This will also help when it's time to clean up. If the cracked tile is around a faucet or water handle, you'll need to remove the fixture (generally by unscrewing it) before you begin.

Put on the glasses or safety goggles. Old grout and tile chips will be flying, and the last thing you want is to get some in your eye. In all phases of the project, proceed with care. Excessive force could damage surrounding tiles.

STEP 1

Remove the old grout

First you'll need to remove the old grout surrounding the cracked tile.

Using a grout saw, cut out the old

Time

Once you've collected the necessary tools and materials, about 25 minutes

What you'll need

- A grout saw (see "Key words")
- An old screwdriver
- A box of grout that matches the old grout
- A new tile that matches the old
- Masking tape
- Tile adhesive
- An old butter knife or spatula
- A hammer and chisel
- A pair of glasses or safety goggles
- A damp sponge
- A dry cloth
- A tile nipper to cut the tile to fit, if necessary (see "Key words")
- 80-grit sandpaper to smooth the cut tile, if necessary
- Rubber gloves

Key words

Grout: Grout is used to fill the gap between the new tile and the surrounding tile. It's sold as a powder, which you need to mix yourself according to the manufacturer's directions.

Grout saw: A hand tool with a thick razor on the end, used for loosening and removing old grout.

Tile nipper: A pliers-shaped hand tool with opposing, sharpened cutters on the end.

Tips

- If tiles in your exact color are no longer available, try this: tap out several surrounding tiles, and replace them with, for example, a geometric design of one or more colors. Hide any nicks and scratches with touch-up paint.

grout. Short, back-and-forth movements seem to be the most effective. Scrape out the remaining grout with the tip of the screwdriver.

STEP 2
Remove the broken tile

With the hammer and chisel, crack the tile in an X-shaped pattern. If you tap too hard, other tiles may crack. Use many soft taps rather than one thunderbolt strike. After the tile is broken into several pieces, pry them out with the screwdriver and chisel.

Chip out the old adhesive. What remains is a nice, tidy space for the new tile.

STEP 3
Shape the tile (optional)

Is the old tile next to a plumbing fixture or an outlet, or on a corner? If not, skip this step. If the answer is yes, the tile needs to be cut or shaped to fit.

Use a tile nipper, cut from the center of the tile edge. Refer frequently to the plumbing fixture or corner piece for the correct shape. If you remove too much, you'll have to start over. Don't bite off more than you can chew. Many small nips are easier on you and reduce the chance of ruining the tile.

Once you have a good fit, smooth out any

rough edges with sandpaper.

STEP 4
Spread the adhesive

With the butter knife or spatula, spread a ⅛-inch layer of tile adhesive on the back of the tile. Don't go right to the edge of the tile.

Press the tile in place, taking care that it's straight. Use several pieces of masking tape to hold it in place. If adhesive spreads into the grout space, clean it out with the screwdriver, then wipe the tile clean.

Let the adhesive cure. The package will tell you how long to wait.

STEP 5
Smooth the grout

Mix the grout according to the manufacturer's directions. Put the rubber gloves on, if you have them. Take some grout in one hand, and press it into the space around the tile with a finger of the other hand. Smooth it out to match the surrounding grout.

Use a damp sponge to wipe the excess grout off the tile. When the grout dries a bit, rub off any film that remains.

Wait for it to dry thoroughly before using the shower or tub. Check the manufacturer's directions for specific times.

PULL FINGER EVENLY ...

... TO LEAVE A SMOOTH FINISH

Learn2 Sew a Button

Beat the button-bursting blues! As we have all found, buttons generally come off at the worst possible moment. Graduations, weddings, special dinners, and big dates are all prime times to view buttons skittering down to the floor. Well, hopefully that button didn't fall out of sight or slip between the floorboards (although if you read on, you'll find out how to deal with that problem as well). Take a deep breath, try not to curse too much, and go find your needle and thread.

BEFORE YOU BEGIN

It's a good idea to keep a small sewing kit around the house and in your travel gear.

If you can't find the button that fell off, take a close look at the garment itself. There may be extra buttons sewn on at the bottom or inside it. Some clothing has a matching button that's not seen when the garment is worn, such as on the bottom of a blouse or shirt that gets tucked in. Use that button to replace the lost one, and then replace the second one from your sewing kit or from a piece of clothing that's not being worn now.

STEP 1

Prepare the site

Locate where the button should be placed by the torn threads on the garment. Clean out those threads by carefully slicing through them with a knife or cutting them with the tip of the scissors and pulling them out.

Thread your needle, trying to match

Time

About 10 minutes

What you'll need

- A small- to medium-sized straight needle
- Another needle, or a matchstick or toothpick
- Thread in an appropriate color and strength (see "Tips")
- A small knife or scissors

Key words

Shank: A short stem of thread that holds a sewn button away from the cloth.

Tips

- When forming a shank, consider the fabric thickness. Heavier fabrics need a longer shank, and you can vary how tight you pull your stitches to form the right length. Make the shank just a tad longer than the fabric thickness, and the fabric will lie flat when buttoned. Sometimes you'll have a button that's been formed with a U-shaped metal shank already. In these cases stitch the bottom of the U to the fabric, and position it so that the shank slides easily into the buttonhole without spreading it.

- For light- and medium-weight fabrics, general-purpose thread is fine. For heavy-weight fabrics, such as coats, try to use heavy-duty thread for extra strength.

the original thread color as closely as possible. If you have nothing similar, use black. Starting from the underside, take a few stitches back and forth through the fabric. Very important: Make sure that you leave enough thread handy to sew on the button (about 12 inches or 30 centimeters until you get the hang of it).

STEP 2

Attach the button

There are two basic ways to attach the button: either flat against the garment (for a decorative button) or leaving a shank, so that there's room for buttoned fabric to fasten smoothly. Shanked buttons are probably the ones you'll use most.

For a flat, decorative button:

Start off by placing the button over those first few stitches you made. Bring the needle up from the back, through one of the holes in the button.

Now bring it back down through another hole, through the fabric, and up again from the back. Pull tight after

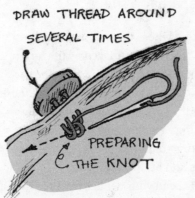

DRAW THREAD AROUND SEVERAL TIMES

PREPARING THE KNOT

each stroke. If the button has four holes, alternate holes, but cross over when the needle is behind the fabric so that the front looks neatly sewn.

After about six stitches, leave the last two slightly loose in back, then pass the needle through those stitches once or twice. Use that as the start of your finishing knot in back.

Cut off the remaining thread.

For a shanked button:

First place the button over those first few stitches you made. Place the other needle/toothpick/wooden match on top of the button, so that your stitches will pass over the top of it before going back down.

Bring the needle up from the back, through one of the holes in the button. Pass the thread over the needle/toothpick/match that's sitting on top of the button. Bring the needle back down through another hole, through the fabric, and up again from the back. If the button has four holes, alternate holes, but cross over when the needle is behind the fabric, so that the front looks neatly sewn.

After about six stitches, take away the needle/toothpick/match, and pull the button away from the fabric so that the stitches are taut. Wind the needle and thread around those stitches. This forms the shank, which creates room for fabric to be buttoned underneath. Turn the needle back into the windings, and tie a knot. Be careful not to make the shank too thick with the knot. Cut off the remaining thread.

Learn2 Wash a Car

You can prevent premature body rot if you wash your car regularly. Automated car washes may be convenient, but they strip the wax and scratch the finish. Do-it-yourself coin-operated places often use water that's too hot and brushes that are stiff and dirty. Folks who appreciate their cars always wash them by hand and take great care to avoid damaging the finish.

BEFORE YOU BEGIN

All cars have a finish, a combination of paint and clear sealant of some variety. When you wax a car, you're adding a layer that protects either kind of finish from the damaging effects of road grime, tree sap, bird droppings, dead insects, and air pollution. Whether you wax or you don't, the finish is the first line of defense against body rot, and for that reason you want to keep it intact. Once you impair the finish of the car, you invite more destructive types of corrosion to take place.

To avoid damaging the finish and wax, wash and dry your car with clean, soft all-cotton towels or car-washing

Time

1 to 3 hours

What you'll need

- A 3- to 5-gallon bucket, preferably plastic
- A handy water source with a hose and pistol-grip nozzle attached
- 2 car-washing mitts or soft all-cotton towels (for washing)
- Several all-cotton terry towels or synthetic chamois (for drying)
- A bottle of good-quality liquid car-washing detergent or "shampoo"

Optional:

- A bottle of good-quality liquid pre-wash solution
- A bottle of finish-safe wheel-cleaning solution
- A soft brush

mitts. Using the wrong cloth can create scratches and swirls, which you want to avoid at all costs. The same holds true for the cleaning solutions: dishwashing liquid will strip the car wax right off the finish, and powdered car soaps can scratch the clear coat. So use a good liquid detergent specifically designed for cars.

Park your car in the shade, and let it cool off before you start washing. If you can park on a slight incline, the water will run off more easily and the car will dry faster. Washing a car on a patch of gravel or grass is greatly preferable to washing a car on the street and sending the dirty rinse water (which contains chemicals from automobile emissions) down a storm drain. From there, the pollutants can enter a local body of water or even the water supply. Washing on gravel or grass provides a filter of stones or vegetation that will slow the spread of pollutants.

STEP 1
Clean the wheels

Wheels are a good place to start because the cleaning solution generally works best on dry surfaces. Spray on the solution as directed by the instructions, and see if it removes the dirt and dust. Use a stronger stream for stubborn areas. If all of the road grime doesn't come off, use a soft brush but don't scrub too hard. If you have alloy wheels, make sure that the cleaner is safe for the protective clear coat. Rinse the wheels if the directions call for it. Note: Keep any abrasives, like steel-wool pads, wire brushes, or even hard nylon-bristle brushes, away from the wheels.

STEP 2
Rinse

Wet the car thoroughly from top to bottom, using a hose with a pistol-grip nozzle, set for a medium-strong stream that will drive off bird droppings and other hardened deposits. Avoid those high-pressure handles that are becoming popular. They can damage a car by driving road grime into the finish rather than washing it off. Aim the hose up under the car and into the wheel wells to wash off road salt and gunk.

Prepare the car and the washing solution. If there are still some bug splats, tree sap, or other material on the surface, use a precleaning solution to remove it with a clean mitt or towel. The answer can be as simple as adding a spot of full-strength car detergent (or another product designed specifically for this purpose) to a mitt or towel. In either case, the stubborn gunk should come off with gentle wiping; don't scrub and risk scratches.

Fill the bucket with the recommended ratio of detergent to cool water (hot water will soften the car's wax). Don't use more detergent than the instructions indicate—this removes more wax. If anything, use less; many folks dilute the detergent to 75 percent of the recommended amount, and they end up with sparkly clean cars. Experiment to discover what amount works best for you.

STEP 3
Wash

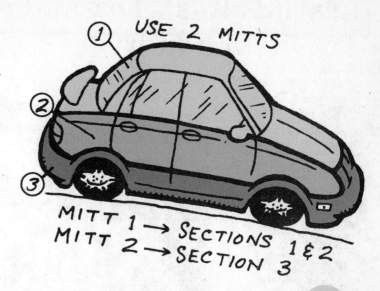

Since there's more dirt on a car's sides and panels than on the top, hood, and trunk, work from top to bottom, and switch to separate mitts and towels when you get to the dirtier areas—to keep scratches to a minimum.

Clean the horizontal surfaces (roof, trunk, and hood), then clean the sides, grille, and bumpers. Thoroughly wet down the section you'll be washing, and dunk the cleaning mitt or towel into the wash solution. Wipe gently. Dunk the mitt or towel frequently, and shake it in the solution to let the grime wash out.

Rinse each surface after it's been washed by flooding it with a low-pressure flow, not spraying with a forceful stream. Don't wash a section and then leave it to wash another before you've rinsed. The dirty wash solution can dry on the surface, and then you're back where you started.

STEP 4
Dry

Dry the surfaces of the car in the same order that you washed them. Move the towels around gently, and—you guessed it—don't scrub.

Take a clean, dry all-cotton towel or synthetic chamois (natural chamois contain acids that can strip the wax), and lay it on the surface to blot up the water. Now lay another dry towel on the surface, gently blotting up any remaining water. Continue in this fashion, wringing out the chamois and changing the towels as they're saturated, until all the surfaces are dry. Opening the doors, trunk, and hood will allow you to wipe up any water that trickled in. Finish by cleaning up the doorjambs with a damp towel—this will prevent water from dripping inside the car.

Learn2 Wash, Dry, and Fold Your Laundry

Time

When washing several loads, these tasks can be done simultaneously:

- 5 minutes to sort laundry
- 25 to 35 minutes per wash load
- 30 to 50 minutes per dry load
- 5 minutes per load to fold

What you'll need

- A box or bottle of all-purpose laundry detergent. Give it a sniff before you buy it to be certain that you like the scent.
- Laundry baskets or bags: bags work fine for carrying in dirty clothes, but baskets keep folded laundry together more neatly
- Fabric softener (optional)

For some of us it's the most difficult part of striking out from home and living on our own: battling that mysterious transformation of wardrobe into Laundry Lump. This 2torial will show you how to restore that pile of cloth to its useful state, with a minimum of hassle and time.

BEFORE YOU BEGIN

Decide when laundry time occurs, and stick to that schedule; don't wait until you're down to last year's Halloween costume and a trenchcoat. There's a wide range of views on the optimal time to do laundry. Some folks wait until two or three loads pile up. Others have a weekly date with their washer and dryer that they'd hate to miss. You'll have to decide for yourself where you fit into that range.

If going to a Laundromat, consider bringing a book or magazine, or perhaps some letter-writing materials. You'll be keeping a better watch over your clothes; theft, even of soggy clothes, is not uncommon in some parts.

STEP 1
Sort your clothes

Sort clothes by colors. Once you have one or two weeks' worth of laundry, sort them as follows: whites, light colors, dark colors, and delicates. Whites include white T-shirts with silk-screened images. Lights include striped white garments and pastels. Delicates are items that would probably best be washed by hand or dry-cleaned, such as nylons, bathing suits, sweaters, woolens, silk and rayon blouses or skirts, dress shirts, and linen.

Don't wash anything labeled "Dry clean only" in a washing machine. If you'd like to avoid dry-cleaning for financial and environmental reasons, use a gentle detergent such as Woolite, which is made for dry-clean garments.

STEP 2
Wash special clothes separately

Wash reds and any new colored garments by themselves for the first time. They can bleed and stain the other clothes in the same wash. Or you can simply dip them in almost hot water in a sink to see if they bleed. If they don't, they're probably safe to wash with other garments.

STEP 3
Pretreat stains

Rub a small amount of liquid detergent into all stains, or use one of the many sprays or liquid stain treatments. Allow it to sit before laundering.

STEP 4
Wash the remaining clothes

Most washing machines have dials that turn clockwise only. Generally, push in the dial, turn to the proper setting, and pull out to activate.

Put the soap in first, if the washer allows for it. Each detergent is different, although you should generally use no more than ½ cup of powdered detergent per full load or ⅓ cup liquid detergent. Too much detergent can cause overflow problems or clump up in the folds of your clothes and not wash out properly. Read the directions on the box to determine how much detergent to use. Most manufacturers include a scoop for powdered detergents and a measured cap for liquid.

Evenly distribute the clothes around the inside cylinder. This will prevent the cylinder from spinning off its track during the wash and ensure even washing.

Set the water temperature. Keep in mind that machines vary, and read any special notices that may be listed. There are two temperatures indicated, one for the wash cycle and one for the rinse cycle.

- Whites: hot/cold
- Lights: warm/cold
- Darks: warm/cold or cold/cold
- Delicates: cold/cold

Tips

- Bleach alternatives: If weather and real estate permit, consider doing what more traditional cultures do—hang your whites out in the midday sun. They'll usually end up sparkly clean with a wonderful, fresh-air smell.

Set the wash cycle:

- Whites: regular
- Lights: regular or permanent press
- Darks: regular or permanent press
- Delicates: delicate

Some recommend following the soap with water, some follow with laundry. May the great debate continue. Follow any instructions on the inside lid of your washing machine.

STEP 5
Dry your clothes

If you're cash-strapped, environmentally conscious, or just want to minimize your time in Laundromats, dry your clothes on a clothesline or on a folding clothes-drying rack. Both are available at hardware stores and will save you a lot of money and energy use over the long term. Otherwise, head for the dryer. Air drying is also less harsh on clothes than tumbling around in a dryer.

For some reason, most dryer dials turn both ways. Generally, push the dryer dial in to turn to the setting, and pull it out to activate. There's often an extra button that starts the process. If you open the door to check how dry the clothes are, hit the button again to start.

Important: Remove the lint from the lint trap before each load. A full lint trap sharply lowers the efficiency of your dryer and often results in very damp clothes.

Drying times depend on the effec-tiveness of the dryer. An older machine could take up to twice as long to dry the same set of clothes. Settings on the dryer are similar to the washer. There is an additional setting for timing your drying cycle. This is generally best done at 40 minutes for a full load to start. If the clothes need more time, try it 20 minutes at a time. If you dry your clothes for too long, they can shrink. It also wears and tears them a bit, too.

Jeans and towels take the longest to dry. If faced with a large load, one option is to pull out the easily dried items (like underwear) when finished early in the load to allow more heat for the others.

STEP 6
Fold

Find a flat, open space for folding. A bed or clean table or floor are all good spots. Put each folded garment out of the way in a clean space.

It's best to fold items when they are still warm. Lay the garment on a flat surface and smooth out the wrinkles. If smoothed when warm, it'll stay that way.

To fold a shirt:

Hold it by its shoulders. Flap up and down once or twice so it hangs straight. Lay it facedown and smooth out any folds. You can do an extra-neat job by pulling gently on the side seams to smooth out the back.

Now fold the shirt lengthwise along the line of the outer edge of the collar

FOLD A SHIRT :

1. SIDES IN
2. SMOOTH SLEEVES
3. FOLD IN HALF AND STACK

FOLD TROUSERS :

EVEN
ENDS

SEAMS AND A
CREASES
EVEN

SMOOTH, THEN
FOLD AT 1 TO HANG,
OR IN THIRDS TO STACK

or neck band. Smooth the sleeve out, using your fingers to pull at the seam, making it slightly taut. Fold the other side over, lengthwise, along the line of the outer edge of the collar. Repeat the sleeve-smoother technique.

Fold the shirt in half. Lift the bottom edge with both hands, and fold it up to the collar. You're done. On to the next one!

To fold pants:

The secret to flat, neatly folded pants lies is lining up the seams and hems.

Hold pants by the waist, and flap up and down several times to smooth out large folds. Lay down on the folding surface so that the seams of each pant leg are parallel. Pull gently on those seams until they're slightly taut.

Now you have two options. If you stack your pants on a shelf or in a

drawer, fold them in thirds as shown in the diagram. Hanging the pants on a hanger requires only a single fold in the middle of the pants.

Learn**2** Apply Eyeliner

Time

About 3 minutes

What you'll need

- Eyeliner: felt-tip, pencil, liquid, or cake type (the latter two require an eyeliner brush)
- Ample lighting
- A decent mirror

Tips

- Fix mistakes with a cotton swab dampened with nonoily eye-makeup remover. Remove excess before continuing.
- Instead of drawing a solid line along your lower lid, apply dots of color along the lash line. The result is less severe.
- The most common error is trying to focus on the whole eye while drawing on just one small part of it. Instead, look only at what you're lining.

All thumbs? Tired of drawing zigzags on your face when all you want is a nice neat line? Applying eyeliner is much simpler than it seems.

BEFORE YOU BEGIN

Cleanse skin and remove excess oils (for example, eye-makeup remover) from upper and lower eyelids. Apply any other eye makeup you plan to use prior to adding liner and mascara.

STEP 1
Prepare your instrument

Follow these guidelines so your liner will emit a thin, controlled line when drawn along a clean patch of skin.

If you're using a felt-tip: test liner flow by drawing very lightly on your hand. If the tip is dry, give the liner a few sharp shakes to force more fluid to the tip. If the tip is too wet, draw it against your hand (or a lint-free cloth or cosmetic paper) to remove the excess.

If you're using a pencil, sharpen the tip enough to produce a line to your liking. If it's too sharp, blunt the tip by drawing on a tissue.

If you're using a cake, moisten the eyeliner brush with clean water, then draw it across the liner cake. Paint a line to test the thickness and density. Add more water or liner as necessary.

If you're using a liquid, barely moisten the brush, then dip just its tip into the liner. Test the line; adjust fluid amount accordingly.

STEP 2
Position the lining device

Hold the lining device as you do a pen or pencil. Turn your hand so the applicator tip is parallel to your eyelid.

STEP 3
Stabilize your lining hand

This step is critical. The anatomy of your eye often determines what will work best. Feel free to modify your approach after experimentation.

Method 1:

Hold the lining device with your dominant hand. With the fingertips of your other hand, slightly stretch the eye to be lined from the outside corner. Stabilize the base of your lining hand against your other hand.

Method 2:

With your arm perpendicular to the ground, hold the lining device with your dominant hand. Stabilize your elbow with your other hand.

Method 3:

Hold the lining device with your dominant hand, and stabilize the base of your lining hand just under your cheekbone. You can hold your elbow if that seems helpful.

Key words

Cake: Solid when dry, cake eyeliner is activated with a wet liner brush (like some watercolor paint). It affords a lot of flexibility.

Liquid: Eyeliner that comes in a bottle like ink and requires a separate brush. It has a rich, lush quality but can be more difficult to control.

Felt-tip: This eyeliner looks like a felt-tip pen and has the ease of a pencil but the staying power of a liquid.

Pencil: Pencil liner is the easiest to use and ranges in texture from dry and hard to soft and pastel-like. Dry pencils can pull at delicate eye tissue; very soft pencils can bleed over time.

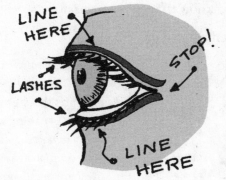

Learn **2**   Cope with Bad Breath

BEFORE YOU BEGIN

For most of us, bad breath can be traced to one or more of the following problem areas: the mouth, the stomach, and the nasal passages. If you have a problem with any of these areas, there's a good chance you have bad breath at least some of the time. Some of us, however, attend to all of these areas and still can't lose that nasty odor. Despair not!

STEP 1

Clean up your mouth

Get a dental cleaning at least twice a year. Not only will this keep the amount of plaque in your mouth down, but it'll also reduce the amount of bacteria and other nasty stuff that live at your gum line. Keeping your gums in shape will reduce mouth odors and let you keep your teeth longer.

Brush your teeth at least twice daily. This greatly reduces the amount of debris that lies rotting in your mouth. Brushing your teeth before going to bed is also very important, giving you a clean mouth for the hours of sleep ahead, not to mention preventing a night of bacteria working on your teeth.

Floss, floss, floss! Flossing regularly is the best way to remove debris from between your teeth and keep your mouth clean.

What you'll need

- Dental floss
- Mouthwash
- Toothbrush
- Toothpaste

In one old mythological tale, when a young woman pleased three spirits who lived in a pool of water, they bestowed favors upon her. One of these favors was sweet breath, so we know that bad breath has been a problem for quite some time.

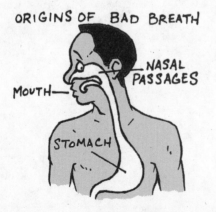

ORIGINS OF BAD BREATH

NASAL PASSAGES

MOUTH

STOMACH

Don't just brush your teeth, brush your whole mouth. Brushing your tongue may seem strange to some, but it's a good thing to do. Plaque and other bacteria grow on your tongue as well as your teeth, and bad breath results.

Use a mouthwash for short-term help, especially in the morning. Get one that "kills germs" in any flavor you want.

STEP 2
Pay attention to your upset stomach

How your stomach feels has a direct bearing on how your breath smells. An upset stomach, or even an empty one, can be a source of bad breath because of all that acid churning around in there.

Graze, don't gorge. Grazing is in nutritional vogue right now, so you'll be right in style. Have a small snack an hour before you meet that special person, and give your stomach a chance to calm down.

Chew antacid tablets, or take antacid liquid, before that big meeting. This will help neutralize stomach acids and improve your breath. These generally work pretty fast and are mint-flavored, so they're good in emergencies. Chewing parsley or mint also helps.

Don't run out of Altoids, Binacas, and Ricolas. Breath-freshening capsules are now sold at just about any large drugstore or supermarket chain.

STEP 3
Keep your nasal passages clear

Postnasal drip is a known cause of bad breath. Basically, mucus from your nose is finding its way down the back of your throat and smelling bad. If you have hay fever or other seasonal allergies, this can be a real difficulty. Use a decongestant to reduce the amount of mucus your body produces. You'll find them sold as allergy tablets in any drugstore and many supermarkets. Start with the least powerful ones available, and take them as infrequently as feasible—you may build up a tolerance before long and have to increase the dosage anyway.

Clear your passages with menthol. Mints and Vicks VapoRub are great ways to clear your passages instantly. Unfortunately, VapoRub is messy and inconvenient to use, especially before that important meeting. Luckily, mints are also breath fresheners, as well as being convenient, quick, and acceptable.

STEP 4
Make sure you're healthy

If your dentist says that your mouth is clean and healthy but your bad breath persists, there's a small chance that a medical condition is causing the problem. Respiratory-tract infections and diabetes as well as liver and kidney ailments have been known to cause bad breath and can be checked by your doctor.

Key words

Postnasal drip: The flow of mucus from your nasal passages down the back of your throat.

Learn **2** Floss Your Teeth

Flossing may not be the highlight of your day, but compared to sitting in a dentist's chair with a drill in your mouth, it's a joyful celebration. Why floss? Even the most careful brushing reaches only three-fifths of all tooth surfaces. Dental floss can go where no brush has gone before: between teeth, along the gum line.

BEFORE YOU BEGIN

It's a good idea to floss every time you brush your teeth, which for most people is twice per day. While this isn't feasible for everyone, flossing once daily should do most of the trick. Opinions differ on what time of day is the most floss-crucial, but most recommend flossing at night before bedtime.

STEP 1

Draw your weapon

The key to effective flossing is to store your ammunition carefully; this will allow you to floss each tooth with a clean section. Take out a section of floss 18 to 24 inches (45 to 60 centime-

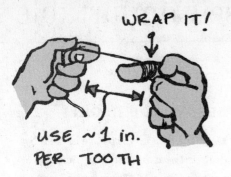

WRAP IT!

USE ~1 in. PER TOOTH

ters) long. Wrap most of the floss around the middle finger of one hand. If you like, stare in the mirror, sneer, and say, "Okay, plaque. I'm coming for you."

STEP 2
Load your weapon

You should have about 6 inches (16 centimeters) of floss dangling from one finger. Wind the dangling floss around the middle finger of the other hand. This finger will take up the floss as it becomes used.

Hold the floss tightly between your thumbs and forefingers, with about an inch (2.5 centimeters) of floss between them. There should be no slack.

"SAW" GENTLY

WORK INTO POCKETS, THEN WORK AWAY FROM GUMS

STEP 3
Fire

Using a gentle back-and-forth motion, guide the floss between your teeth. Never snap it into the gums. When the floss reaches the gum line, curve it into a C shape against one tooth. Gently slide it into the space between the gum and the tooth until you feel resistance. Victory is at hand! You have the enemy surrounded.

Hold the floss tightly against the tooth, and move it away from the gum. Slide it firmly down the tooth surface, combining this with a back-and-forth motion. Do this five or six times along the side of the tooth. Without removing the floss, curve it around the adjacent tooth and scrape that one, too. You have just eradicated the first guard in a row of hidden enemies. Victory is sweet.

STEP 4
Show no mercy

Wind the used portion of floss around your finger—the one that started with less floss. Unwind a clean segment from your storage finger, and repeat this procedure on each tooth, upper and lower. Remember to floss behind back teeth and where there is no adjacent tooth. Your mission is successfully concluded. Toss that floss—its job is done.

Don't forget to rinse your mouth vigorously with water; this will wash away any food matter that was loosened but not removed.

Key words

Dental floss: A nylon thread, also available as a tape, used to clean the crevices between individual teeth, where the toothbrush cannot reach. Dental floss comes in many different thicknesses from very fine thread to thick tape, with or without wax, and plain or flavored. Your dentist can recommend which type of floss is best for you. It became a consumer staple in 1897.

Plaque: A film of bacteria and mucus that grows on your teeth. Some of the bacteria in the plaque make acids that decay teeth enamel. Other kinds of bacteria in the plaque make toxins that cause gum disease.

Learn 2 Get a Clean, Close, Comfortable (Facial) Shave

Time

- 5 minutes prep (no kidding!)
- At least 3 minutes to shave
- 2 minutes for aftercare

What you'll need

For a wet shave:
- A manual, hand-held razor
- A shaving lubricant (cream, foam, or gel)
- Mild, nondrying soap
- A sinkful of very warm water
- A terry washcloth

Optional:
- Exfoliating lotion or scrub
- A shaving brush—natural-bristle ones are nice
- Shaving soap
- A mug with a handle (leave the coffee out!)
- A styptic pencil
- Aloe vera spray or gel (you can get it in 99 percent pure form)

Man's morning obstacle course: matching a shirt to pants, then a pair of socks to both. Running a comb through the tangled mop on your head. And then? Running a very sharp blade repeatedly across a very important part of your body. But shaving doesn't have to be scary. Follow one of the simple regimes in this 2torial, and you'll never fear the razor again.

BEFORE YOU BEGIN

Most shaving mishaps are caused by dull, dirty razors and insufficiently prepped beards. Make sure all your equipment (and your face) is clean, warm, and wet. Don't be macho, be methodical: each minute of preparation is worth ten of face scraping. Gather all of your implements before beginning, and do give your beard hairs a chance to stand to attention.

Remember to optimize your equipment: insert a new blade in your manual razor (if it needs it), or clean the heads in your electric.

If you are buying a manual razor, choose whatever you like but consider that a pivoting head can help negotiate odd angles, funny bumps, and bony places. If you find it hard to pay a lot of attention to what you're doing, this type will be a bit more forgiving than the rigid type. Also, a single-bladed razor is less irritating than a double-bladed one. Although a double-bladed razor may give a closer shave, it does so at the cost of hitting more skin. You'll need to decide if the trade-off is worthwhile.

STEP 1

Prepare your skin

Chronic razor burn? Or only at certain times of the year? Temperature, humidity, even diet and stress can alter your skin's thickness and resilience. The key to getting a clean, close, comfortable shave is prepping your beard properly. Some men feel that exfoliating their skin with a loofah once or twice a week makes their daily shave much more comfortable (see "Key words"). Find what techniques work for you and modify them to suit the seasons.

Wet your face and the washcloth with very warm water. Very hot water can dry skin and damage pores. You want the water just on the edge of hot, so that if you stuck your hand into a basin of it, you wouldn't automatically pull it out.

Soap the cloth, but not enough to make it slippery. With firm yet gentle pressure lather up the beard area, moving against the direction the whiskers grow: you want to coax the hairs up off the surface of the skin.

USE VERY WARM WATER

SOAP UP SKIN

GO AGAINST THE GRAIN

STEP 2

Soak the skin

After rinsing your face, soak the washcloth again in very warm water and place it on your beard—or over your entire face if that's comfortable. The moist heat will soften the whiskers and make your skin supple, which will reduce razor burn. Hold the washcloth there for a couple of minutes while you think about what to have for breakfast or what to wear to work.

STEP 3

Lather up

Wet shave:

A shaving brush is not obligatory but an undeniable pleasure (no, you don't need to use a straight razor with it). Regardless of the type of shaving cream you use (see Step 9), a brush is a delightful and effective way to lather up. The motion of the bristles lifts and softens the whiskers, and there's something cheering about swirling the brush around your face.

Fill the sink with very warm water. Immediately apply your shaving cream (or foam or gel) with your brush or fingertips. Work it into a lather using circular swirling motions. Spread it evenly over your face, making sure that it completely covers your whiskers—and be honest with yourself about the location of your whiskers. Don't neglect the facial areas that don't show up in a full-on mirror view, such as underneath the

For a dry shave:

- An electric razor
- A bit of cornstarch or other mild powder (such as baby powder)
- Skin toner

Tips

- Don't leave the faucet on while you shave. It wastes water and adds to your heating bill, and you never know when the water temperature will suddenly change. Fill up the sink instead. If your sink plug leaks and won't hold a sinkful of water, despair not. An inexpensive rubber sink stopper (available at hardware stores) solves that problem—take one when you travel, too.

Key words

Aloe vera: A plant whose juice or extract is known to soothe burns and irritations and aid healing.

Exfoliating lotion or scrub: A preparation that removes dead, dull, surface-layer skin cells. Exfoliation softens and smooths, keeping pores clear and ingrown hairs at bay.

Ingrown hair: Hair that changes direction, growing back under the skin instead of breaking through it. May form pimples at the surface and become infected.

WET DRY

SHAVE WITH THE GRAIN

SHAVE AGAINST IT

chin and the backward-facing part of the jaw.

Dry Shave:

After soaking your beard, dry it well, rubbing against the growth pattern. Splash on toner. Finally, dust with cornstarch or powder; the skin should be absolutely dry before using an electric shaver.

STEP 4
Get that razor swinging

Wet shave:

The direction you shave in is important. You may seem to get a closer shave going against the grain (against the direction in which your whiskers grow), but this practice damages the hair shaft and the whiskers grow back thicker and tougher. If you're in the habit of shaving this way, it'll take some time to retrain your beard. But after a few weeks of shaving with the grain, you'll get a closer shave that will also be easier on your skin.

Dunk your clean razor into the very warm water. Make a short sweep down one side of your face, with the grain. Repeat this, dunking the razor in the water, after every few swipes, until you've uncovered every centimeter of skin.

Many shaving cuts happen between sweeps of the razor, not during

the actual shaving motion. To stop the bloodshed, avoid moving the razor horizontally against your skin. Instead, lift the razor an inch or two (2.5 to 5 centimeters) off your skin and place down on the new location to be shaved.

Dry shave:

Adjust the razor—if you have the option—for your whisker type. Grasp the razor firmly, but be flexible. Turn it on.

Pick a spot, say, by the hinge of your jaw. Then move upward, going against the direction of hair growth. If your shaver has three rotating blades, circular movements are best. With a straight-bladed razor, try long, repetitive strokes. Chins can be difficult; feel free to maneuver for the best effect.

STEP 5
Master the tug

This technique plays a key role in producing a good shave. You'll need to keep the fingers of your free hand fairly dry to do it correctly.

Wet shave:

Choose an area that you're going to shave. Place the fingers of your free hand just outside the soaped-whiskers area or on a place you've just shaved. Using the fingers of your free hand, press down slightly into the skin, tugging it taut against your face. Shave this area where the whiskers are slightly lifted off. Remember to shave with the grain.

Dry shave:

The tug is easier with an electric razor because your fingers don't get wet with shaving cream and water.

Choose an area that you're going to shave. Place the fingers of your free hand on your skin, either outside of your beard or on a place you've just shaved. Using the fingers of your free hand, press down slightly into the skin, tugging it taut against your face. Shave this area where the whiskers are slightly lifted off. Remember to shave against the grain of your whiskers.

STEP 6
Rinse off

Rinse the washcloth in tepid water, wring it out, and press it to your face. Don't wipe—you don't want to irritate your face even more. The tepid water will gently close the pores that the hot water opened.

Feel around with your fingers for any missed patches, making sure to pass against the grain. Spots often missed are the rear portion of the jaw both above and below the jawbone.

Gently pat your face with a clean, dry towel. Of course, you've already thoroughly rinsed out your trusty implements, your razor, and (if you have one) your brush.

STEP 7
Cope with the bloodshed

Perhaps you were feeling a little foggy this morning and you cut yourself.

Here are some techniques to stop the flow:

• The old tried and true: Tear off a tiny piece of tissue paper, just slightly larger than the cut, and apply it directly to the cut. Leave it on for at least 5 minutes (10 for a deeper cut), then tug off. Often the wound will dry up nicely, leaving only a small red dot.

• Styptic pencils: Yow! These camphor-tipped sticks can sting a little, but they work very well and quickly for small to medium cuts. Moisten the tip, dab it onto the wound, and watch it dry up.

• If you've really slashed yourself: Swallow your pride and pull out the antiseptic and small elastic bandages. Sure, it might look a little funny, but it's not as bad as an infected cut on your face. If you're lucky, the wound will heal up enough by midday so that you'll be able to remove the bandage.

STEP 8
Moisturize your mug

Smooth on a moisturizer or aftershave balm to prevent your skin from drying. An electric razor is easy on skin; still, a moisturizing routine adds a silky finish. On the other hand, wet shaving can leave skin vulnerable to alcohol and oil: the former can burn; the latter clogs pores. Test scented lotions for mildness before slathering them on.

Some men like the invigorating feeling of splashing an alcohol-based aftershave on their faces. It has an antiseptic quality that can help heal nicks and cuts, but it also tends to dry

Key words

Loofah: A dried plant that can be used as a sponge. Loofahs are abrasive, often used to exfoliate body skin.

Razor burn: Postshave irritation. Common causes include placing too much pressure on the blade, dull blades, harsh soaps, and alcohol-containing products, to name a few.

Styptic pencil: A shaver's best friend. Stops bleeding from minor cuts like magic. Just moisten and apply.

Tips

• The best time to shave is right when you get out of the shower or while you're still in there. Your face is clean, and your skin and beard are softened by the water and steam, so you can skip Step 2. You can buy no-fog mirrors designed for the shower, or learn to shave by touch.

• As a rule, body soaps don't provide the lubrication that you need to get a close, comfortable shave. If you're stuck with soap, at least choose the kind that has moisturizing agents.

out most faces. Most men find that balms feel better. A less expensive but very effective product is aloe vera gel. It soothes razor burn and moisturizes your skin without chemicals. It's also available in a nonaerosol spray.

STEP 9

Try the ecoshave, a conservation-minded approach

If you want to create a more sustainable and less disposable lifestyle, you can start with your daily shave. You'll reduce factory pollutants and the amount of trash in the world's landfills, help shrink the hole in the ozone layer, and save money on toiletries, too.

Razors:

Try an earlier model—a double-edged (single-blade) razor that fits inside a larger metal casing. Aside from being far less expensive than disposables, you throw away only a thin sliver of metal, which will rust and biodegrade a lot faster than blades set in very durable plastic.

If you do use a disposable razor, try to use it as many times as you can.

Shaving brush:

Regardless of the type of shaving cream you use (see below), any variety can be applied, with excellent results, using a shaving brush. This accessory, too, is enjoying a resurgence in men's department stores and even large drugstores. Natural-bristle brushes are the most commonly sold; the less expensive, nylon-bristle brushes are

available in some areas and by many accounts work well enough. Some companies even sell a kit with a brush, a cake of shaving soap, and a mug in which to make the lather.

Shaving cream:

Sure, you need to lubricate your face, but that lubricant doesn't have to come in a can. Here are some options:

• Good-quality shaving cream is sold in plastic or metal tubes. Squirt a thumbnail-sized blob on a shaving brush, and massage into the skin, using a circular motion. Although the container needs to be thrown away, at least it has no gases harmful to the atmosphere. Also, it biodegrades much more quickly than a more durable metal can that's made to contain pressured gas.

• A cake of shaving soap is the option with the least amount of packaging, but it may require some experimentation to find a brand that works for you. Some men are very pleased with the lather from a good-quality facial soap, so that's another option. Carve off a chunk of the shaving soap—large enough so you can wedge it in the bottom of a coffee mug. (Wedging the cake is important—this holds it firmly in place while you're working up a lather.) Thoroughly moisten the brush with hot water, and swirl it around the mug for 30 seconds or so, until you've produced a generous amount of lather. If the lather isn't rising, drip a little more hot water into the mug. Apply the lather to your face, and replace the brush in the mug.

Learn**2** Iron a Shirt

Time

15 minutes

What you'll need

- An iron
- An ironing board (or a large, clean towel on a hard flat surface that is not sensitive to heat)
- Ironing spray or spray bottle filled with water
- Spray starch (optional)

Shirts look their best when laundered and pressed by a professional dry cleaner. But if you can't get it to the cleaners, you can do a pretty good job with an iron and a little patience.

BEFORE YOU BEGIN

If you need to wash a cotton dress shirt, use cold water on the delicate cycle in the washing machine, or wash it by hand in the sink. Hang it up to dry. The shirt should be almost completely dry before ironing.

STEP 1

Prepare the ironing board and iron

Stand the ironing board up near an electrical outlet. Be sure there is enough slack in the power cord to move the iron freely.

Fill the iron with water through the spout (if it has one). This will help steam-press your shirt.

Plug in the iron, and set the dial to the appropriate fabric setting. Be careful: the farther the dial goes to the right, the hotter the iron gets. Irons that are too hot can ruin a shirt. A tag usually found inside the back of the collar indicates the type of fabric.

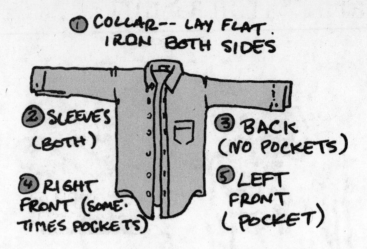

① COLLAR-- LAY FLAT. IRON BOTH SIDES

② SLEEVES (BOTH)

③ BACK (NO POCKETS)

④ RIGHT FRONT (SOME. TIMES POCKETS)

⑤ LEFT FRONT (POCKET)

Stand the iron upright so the hot area does not sit on the ironing board. Never leave the iron facedown, as it will quickly burn whatever is below it. Wait a few minutes for it to heat up.

Flick a few drops of water onto the bottom of the iron. If it sizzles, it's ready.

STEP 2

Strike when the iron is hot

If your shirt is exceptionally wrinkled, then a small spray bottle of water or ironing spray may help. Spray onto the part of the shirt you're about to iron.

If the shirt has a button-down collar, unbutton the collar. Then iron these parts of the shirt in order: collar, both sides; sleeves; back; front. For best results, iron only one part of the shirt at a time, leaving the rest of the shirt to droop off the side of the ironing board. Take extra care to iron the seams. They are the hardest to iron but can affect the appearance of the shirt the most.

STEP 3

After ironing

Hang the shirt on a hanger until you are ready to wear it.

Turn the iron off and pull the plug. Leave the iron sitting upright on the board for 15 to 20 minutes to cool down. It is then safe to put away.

Learn2 Shave Your Legs

There are people out there immune to irritating soaps, bad blades, and a brutal technique, but chances are you're not one of them. Most shaving damage results from improper products and lack of preparation. Learn what to use, how to use it, and when. After you've mastered the perfect shave, you may be able to get away with a shortcut or two.

BEFORE YOU BEGIN

Read the "Tips" and "Key words" sections for information about razors and blades, explanations, alternatives to traditional skin products, and more. Then assemble your materials at your shaving site so you can reach them easily.

Finally, optimize your equipment: insert a new blade in your manual razor, clean the heads in your electric. Regarding manual razors, choose whatever you like but consider that

• A pivoting head can help negotiate small bony places.

• A single-blade razor is less irritating than a double-blade one.

• A razor designed for women is

Time

• 10 minutes prep (no kidding!)
• At least 5 minutes to shave
• 5 to 10 minutes aftercare

What you'll need

For a wet shave:
• A safety razor
• Shaving cream, gel, or lotion
• Mild, nondrying soap
• Body lotion, oil- and alcohol-free
• A washcloth

For a dry shave:
• An electric razor, either traditional or rotating-coil system
• Cornstarch or baby powder
• Alcohol-free skin toner, body lotion
• Exfoliating lotion or scrub
• Body lotion, oil- and alcohol-free

Optional but advisable:
• A styptic pencil
• Aloe vera spray, 99 percent pure

Key words

Aloe vera: Plant known to soothe burns and irritations and aid healing.

Exfoliating lotion or scrub: A preparation that removes dead, dull, surface-layer skin cells.

Ingrown hair: Hair that grows back under the skin. May form pimples at the surface and become infected.

Razor burn: Any postshave irritation. Common causes include placing too much pressure on the blade, dull blades, harsh soaps, and alcohol-containing products.

Rotating-coil system: An electric shaver with a vibrating metal coil that circulates over the skin. It removes hairs from the root. Your legs stay smooth for weeks, and regrowth is thin and sparse. But it's too painful for some and may produce ingrown hairs.

often smaller and lighter than men's razors.

In all cases, follow the manufacturer's suggestions.

STEP 1
Prepare your skin

Chronic razor burn? Or only at certain times of the year? Temperature, humidity, even diet and stress seem to alter skin's thickness and resilience. Find what works for you, and modify to suit the seasons.

Wet shave:

Wet your legs and the washcloth with very warm water. Very hot water dries the skin and damages the pores. Soap the cloth, but not enough to make it slippery. With firm yet gentle pressure, lather up the skin, moving against the direction the hair grows: coax the hairs up off the surface. Rinse very well and leave wet. Apply the shaving potion of your choice.

Dry shave:

For a traditional electric razor, proceed as above. Then dry well, against the growth pattern. Splash on toner.

For a rotating-coil system, starting with clean skin, use an exfoliating lotion or scrub according to manufacturer's instructions. If you've used this kind of system before without pore problems, a loofah or bath brush may suffice. Dry and tone as above.

Dust with cornstarch or powder; the skin must be absolutely dry before using any electric shaver.

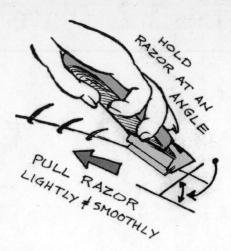

HOLD RAZOR AT AN ANGLE

PULL RAZOR LIGHTLY & SMOOTHLY

STEP 2
Bare it all

Okay. The time is now. If you've prepared your legs properly, this step should be a breeze. Good light and a place to prop your foot will make the hard-to-reach spots more accessible.

Wet shave:

Wet the razor. Good light and a sure grip help you maneuver around curves and bones. There's no need to apply pressure: just use the weight of the razor. Shaving in the direction hair grows can eliminate chronic razor burn and reduce inflammation of the pores. Rinse the razor frequently in hot water to remove hair and shaving potion.

Begin shaving around the ankle with short, delicate strokes, drawing in toward the bone. Watch what you're doing. (One technique is the "skin tug": press with your fingertips a portion of skin that's unlathered or already shaved, push it down toward your ankle, and then shave the portion above it. This helps the hair stand off the skin and also produces a flatter shaving surface.) Then, with longer strokes, draw the razor from above the ankle to just under the knees. This is the easiest part of the leg to shave, but it's vulnerable to carelessness. Easy around those shin bones!

Next come the knees. Take a good look, then bend the knee slowly and watch how it changes, for example, where curves fill in or bones recede. It only takes a few moments. Shave the flattest (easiest) sections first, then bend the knee as needed to expose other flat, easy-to-shave areas.

When you're finished, use your fingertips to feel for places you missed. Look closely at knees and ankles. Touch up if necessary. If you nicked yourself, bring out the styptic pencil. Moisten the tip, then dab on minor cuts: it works like magic. Treat deeper cuts as you would normally.

Rinse your legs well. Pat dry with a soft towel.

Dry shave:

For a traditional shaver, adjust it—if you have the option—for your hair type. Grasp the razor firmly, but be flexible. Turn it on.

Start by slowly edging around the ankle. Then move upward, going against the direction of hair growth. If your shaver has three rotating blades, circular movements are best. With a straight-bladed razor, try long, repetitive strokes. Knees can be difficult, especially if using a facial shaver; feel free to maneuver both to best effect.

For a rotating-coil system, follow the manufacturer's instructions. Note that wider movements can help prevent ingrown hairs. Also, a daily loofah or brush routine will prevent clogged hair follicles, reducing the incidence of ingrown hairs. Coarse and curly-haired legs are most at risk.

STEP 3
Aftercare: Soothe your skin

An electric razor is easy on skin; still, a moisturizing routine adds a silky finish. On the other hand, wet shaving and rotating coils leave skin vulnerable to alcohol and oil: the former can burn; the latter clogs pores. Test scented lotions for mildness.

Wet shave:

Spray your legs liberally with aloe vera. Allow to absorb a few minutes; spray again if desired. If your skin stings, wait till it feels better before slathering with lotion.

Dry shave:

Remove excess powder, then pat dry. With a traditional razor, spray an even layer of aloe vera on newly shaved skin. Wait till absorbed, then follow with body lotion. With rotating-coil systems, spray legs liberally with aloe vera. Allow to absorb completely. Follow with body lotion.

Key words

Loofah: A dried plant that can be used as an abrasive sponge.

Tips

- Ingrown hairs can sometimes be tweezed from the skin's surface. Don't dig. Infected ingrowns should be treated by a doctor.
- Persistent irritation, characterized by tender, raised red bumps, may indicate infection. If it lasts over a week, see a doctor.
- Caught without shaving potion? Rub a little oil-free hair conditioner over prepped skin, then follow with a lather made from a mild shampoo. Proceed as usual.
- Relax. Take your time. Practice. Then teach your best friend.

Learn **2** Shine Leather Shoes

Time

15 to 20 minutes

What you'll need

- A section of news-paper
- 3 clean, soft cot-ton cloths—old T-shirts and underwear work great
- Wax or cream shoe polish (can be purchased at most supermar-kets, drugstores, and shoe-repair shops)

Optional:
- Saddle soap
- A soft bristle (for example, horse-hair) brush
- A towel to kneel on

Leather dress shoes need shining. A good shine keeps them natty and preserves their longevity by moisturizing the leather. Leather, like your own skin, can dry out and crack—so shoe-care professionals use pol-ish to prevent desiccation and to restore lost moisture. You should do the same by giving your leather shoes a shine at least once a month. With a modicum of supplies, effort, and time, you can shine your shoes in almost any location.

Be advised that this 2torial teaches you how to treat leathers, such as calfskin and kidskin, that are intended to be shined. The cleaning and preservation of other leathers, such as suede and NuBuck, are not covered here. Note also that many shoes are made from a combination of leathers. For these, make sure that each type of leather can han-dle shoe polish. If you are unsure, consult the staff where you bought the shoes or a shoe-care professional.

BEFORE YOU BEGIN

Don't try to shine your shoes while they're on your feet. Leave that for the pros. It can be a messy affair, so take your shoes off your feet (we hope you're not wearing them anywhere else!), and change into some old clothes.

STEP 1

Prepare a work site

Polish is easily spilled or mishandled, so you should protect your work area. Avoid stainable surfaces—rugs, bed-spreads, couches; a tile or linoleum floor is a great location for a shine.

Clear an area of the floor. Open a section of newspaper. The funnies can provide you with some light entertain-ment while you wait for shoes to dry.

Set up your shoes and cleaning supplies on top of the paper.

STEP 2

Remove the laces

If your shoes have laces, it's best to remove them. This allows you to polish the tongue and avoid staining the laces. If you don't remove the laces, you shouldn't attempt to polish the tongue.

STEP 3

Wipe the leather

Wipe the leather with a dry, soft cotton cloth to remove any light stains and/or dust—otherwise they can become embedded or scratch the leather when you apply polish. Move from front to back—first on the left side, then on the right. Moving in a methodical way will prevent missed spots. Be sure to wipe between the heel and the sole. Use the edge of the cloth, held taut between your hands, to slip into tight areas. Repeat the process on the other shoe.

Use saddle soap on shoes with a lot of dried dirt and grime on them. This moistens the dirt and prevents the leather from being scratched. It's also effective in removing dark spots from light-colored shoes. Spots on dark-colored shoes can be cleaned and masked with polish, making saddle soap unnecessary. Shoes cleaned with saddle soap should be allowed to dry for 5 minutes before you proceed to the next step.

STEP 4

Choose the polish

Leather shoe polish comes in two forms, wax and cream. Use wax for a better shine; use cream to ensure longevity. Cream soaks into leather, moisturizing it and allowing it to breathe. Wax seals, inhibiting leather's respiration and causing it to dry out. To choose the correct color polish, fol-low these guidelines. Dark-colored shoes require a matching color polish; light-colored shoes need a neutral (colorless) polish.

Tips

- Learn fast: get a professional shoeshine. Noth-ing beats learning from a pro!
- Make sure the color of the polish matches the color of the shoe. If you're unsure, consult a profes-sional. If you're in a rush and don't have time to con-sult a shoe doctor, you can dab a small amount of polish on the heel (the closer to the sole the better) to determine if it matches.

STEP 5
Apply the polish

Wrap a small portion of the second cloth around the index finger of your dominant hand. Wrap the cloth tightly—this snug fit will give you a greater feel of the surface of the shoe and allow you to work polish into the creases, where you foot flexes.

Place your nondominant hand into one shoe. Hold the shoe on the paper.

Dip the cloth into the polish, and scoop out a thumbnail-sized glob. Note: A little dab'll do ya. The leather absorbs only what it needs. Excess polish doesn't help the shoe and takes longer to dry.

Starting from the heel, and moving forward on one side of the shoe, spread the polish on the leather evenly. There is no specific, mandatory method for putting on polish, but applying it in small circles will keep you from slopping any excess polish

inside the shoe, on the sole, or on the laces (if you haven't removed them). Cover the entire shoe, paying close attention to scratches and scuffs to ensure that they are adequately masked. As you run out of polish, apply another dab. Stop when you have covered the leather with a thin, even layer of polish.

Repeat the process on the other shoe.

STEP 6
Make them shine!

Allow the shoes to dry for 10 minutes. Now you're ready to make your shoes shine. This is the fun part, and you may want to sing a campy song while you polish.

Place your nondominant hand inside one shoe. Hold the shoe in front of you.

Take up a soft-bristle brush or your third cloth with your dominant hand, and use short, back-and-forth strokes to bring the leather to a shine. If you're using a cloth, you may want to turn it as you move from one area of the shoe to the next. This will give you a new, clean surface with which to remove the dried polish.

Repeat the process on the other shoe.

Relace the shoes, and you're ready to go!

CLEAN, SOFT DRY CLOTH OR BRUSH

USE QUICK, STRAIGHT STROKES

Learn2 Tie a Bow Tie

Sooner or later, whether it's your wedding, a gala dinner, choir concert, or the Academy Awards banquet, you will come up against the elite of contemporary neckwear: the bow tie. Most bows are pretied these days, fastened merely by clips or a hook. But tying a classic tie, known among the French as a butterfly knot, is about as easy as tying your shoelaces, once you've practiced a few times. Here are the basics of knotting this natty little fashion statement.

BEFORE YOU BEGIN

Give yourself a few extra minutes when tying a tie for the first time. Allow yourself to retie the knot higher or lower until you get it the right length. Part of good grooming means paying attention to the details.

STEP 1
Flip up the collar

Button your collar at the neck, then fold it up so that you can slip the tie easily around your neck. This helps you tie it in the right spot the first time and also helps prevent wrinkling and stretching the tie fabric.

Time

- Beginners: 15 to 30 minutes
- Intermediate and fussy: 5 to 10 minutes
- Show-offs: less than 1 minute

What you'll need

- A dress shirt that buttons at the collar
- A mirror

Tips

- Tie it in front of a mirror.
- The knot should stay snug on top of the collar button. A tie that is too tight will creep up the collar, giving you an unpleasant, strangled sensation. A loosened tie looks sloppy.
- The tabs on tuxedo shirts should remain behind the bow.

STEP 2

Adjust the length

Some bow ties have adjustable lengths. Does one end have a loop? Some ties will have neck sizes marked on the loop. If so, place the hook one number up from the number corresponding to your neck size. This will give you a somewhat larger loop but will simplify the beginner's efforts at tying the darn thing.

With other adjustable bow ties, you pull the loop through a little buckle until you have enough tie hanging down on either side of your collar to do it up. Bow ties are generally narrow in the middle and widen out to an hourglass shape on both ends. The narrow curves are where the knot will be tied. The wider places form the loops and ends of the bow.

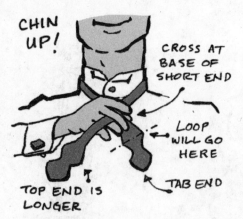

CHIN UP!

CROSS AT BASE OF SHORT END

LOOP WILL GO HERE

TOP END IS LONGER

TAB END

STEP 3

Set the stage

Put the tie around your neck, seams to the inside. Let the widening point on your nondominant side hang down from the collar button by your collarbone (so if you're left-handed, lay it on the right side). The other side should be an inch or two longer. With your nondominant hand, hold the spot just above the widening point between thumb and forefinger. This is where you'll tie the knot.

① SIMPLE KNOT

PULL SNUG

STEP 4

Form the simple knot

Cross the slightly longer end over the spot, pass it around behind and up through the top. Let it hang down. This forms a simple knot and can be pulled snug here, with the end on top still a little longer. The long end is now in your nondominant hand. Make the first loop. Fold the shorter end over on top of itself (not behind it). The wide point becomes the edge of the loop, and the narrow point should lie right on top of the actual knot. Hold this loop at its base with your nondominant hand.

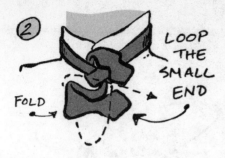

STEP 5
Wrap the second loop

Wrap the longer end carefully over and down with your dominant hand, then around behind the first loop. Do not twist the tie—wrap it around.

Now insert the longer end through the knot: push a loop with your finger through the central knot, and tug it through. This creates the second loop. Hold the first loop with your dominant hand, and carefully pull the new loop a little tighter. Be careful not to pull the ends out. When pulling the knot tight, grasp the loops and ends equally in both hands. Pull evenly. Sometimes a bow will remain unruly until you have cleaned the knot. Then you can adjust it into the final shape.

STEP 6
Primp the bow

All bow ties require some fussing to get the ends straight and the knot square. Adjust the loops and ends so that their lengths are equal on each side and both sides are even.

Some bows look great with a loop in front, end tab in back on one side, and an end tab in front, loop in back on the other side. Otherwise you may want both loops to show on the front of the tie, with the tab ends snug behind. This style may take a little more fussing around but is basically the same knot. Just give the second loop a firm twist after pulling it through. Then gently tighten and get the ends straight as before.

The last thing you should do with a bow is take a side in each hand, pull the knot firmly taut, and then pull the bow out away from the collar (which you have fastened with the collarbone buttons). A properly starched and tied bow will stand out smartly at an angle of about 30 degrees. Go get 'em, tiger!

Learn**2** Tie a Necktie

Time

- Beginners: 15 to 30 minutes
- Intermediate and fussy: 2 to 10 minutes
- Show-offs: less than 1 minute

What you'll need

- A dress shirt that buttons at the collar
- A mirror

Ascot and bertha, cravat and four-in-hand, rebato and double Windsor—there's a world of variation in fashionable neck-wear. This 2torial will walk you through the basics of tying two standard business-tie knots. Leave the clip-ons at home!

BEFORE YOU BEGIN

Which knot for your business tie? Use the double Windsor for thin materials such as silk and with wider ties. For hand-knit or woolen ties, or when you need a smaller knot, use a four-in-hand.

STEP 1
Flip the collar up

Button your collar at the neck. Then unfold it so that you can easily slip the tie around your neck. This helps you tie it in the right spot the first time and also helps prevent wrinkling and stretching the tie fabric.

STEP 2
Adjust the length

Some people prefer the ends to be exactly the same length after you've finished. Unfortunately, ties usually come in one size only, so it's hard to say where the ends will meet up. A tie that hangs only to the belly button looks cheap; one that hangs over your fly is also tacky. Even worse—when the broad end of the tie is outdistanced by the narrow end. The tip of the broad end should extend just to the top of your belt buckle. Sound tricky? Fortunately, there's a good general rule to follow.

To begin, drape the necktie around your neck so that its seam is lying along the collar. The broad end should be on the side of your dominant hand—if you're left-handed, it should be on your left side. Now for the measuring trick. Place the tip of the narrow end just above the fourth button down your shirt (the one above your navel), and eliminate the slack by pulling down on the broad end. Again, the tie seam should remain hidden in the back.

Another way to measure is to let the broad end hang down twice as long as the narrow end. To check if you've done this right, fold the broad end in half up toward your neck. The folded portion should be equal in length to the narrow end.

STEP 3
Tie the knot

The four-in-hand:

This is the basic knot fashion. Master this one, and you'll be prepared for most semiformal events.

With your nondominant hand, grasp the narrow end about 3 inches (8 centimeters) down from your neck. This is the spot where you will make the knot. With your dominant hand, take the broad end and pass it across and over the spot. Hold it there with your nondominant hand.

Bring the broad end around behind the spot, then around and over again. Then pull the broad end behind the spot and up through the V at the top. Let the broad end flop over and hang down. Now tuck it between the top wrap of the tie and the place you've been holding. Use both hands to straighten the knot and pull it tight.

Pull the knot gently but firmly. Look at the tie in the mirror. Is it straight? Does the broad end hang down too far or not far enough? Loosen the tie if necessary, and adjust the length of the narrow end as needed so that your tie will be the proper length after the knot has been tightened. The four-in-hand knot will be slightly larger on one side than the other. The knot should be smoothly wrapped, not wrinkled or folded over on itself. If you need to, take a moment to fuss with it so that it looks even and the rest of the tie hangs down straight.

Oh, and turn your collar down. Button down the collarbone buttons.

The double Windsor:

The double Windsor takes its name from the double wrap that is part of its construction. Political and business leaders seem to favor this knot, along with foreign royalty. You tie it by duplicating the wrap of the four-in-hand. It's a little more difficult to pull together in the tightening

Tips

- Tie it in front of a mirror.
- Give yourself a few extra minutes when tying a tie for the first time. Allow yourself time to retie the knot higher or lower until you get it the right length. Part of good grooming means paying attention to the details. Those who are important to you will notice and appreciate the effort.
- When slipping the broad end through the knot, push a loop through with your finger, then pull the rest through. This helps keep the knot together.

THE DOUBLE WINDSOR

BEHIND AND OUT...

OVER AND UNDER

OUT AND UP

Tips

- Look for the spot on the tie where the narrow end becomes wider. This will often be the best place to pass the broad end over the narrow end. Try tying the tie with this widening section lying on top of the narrow end's knot spot. Even if it does not make the perfect knot for you, it gives you a good way of gauging the distance the second time around. The knot should stay snug on top of the collar button. A tie that is too tight will creep up the collar, not to mention reddening your face and making it difficult to breathe. A loosened tie looks sloppy and is a sign that you are not paying attention.

stage, so go slowly and be prepared to loosen and tighten the knot as necessary. The Windsor is a bigger knot, so allow yourself a little more length on the broad end.

Grasp the narrow end about 2 inches (6 centimeters) down from your neck with your nondominant hand. This is the spot where you will make the knot. With your dominant hand, take the broad end and pass it across and over the spot. Hold it there with your nondominant hand.

Now pass the broad end around behind once, then out in front, then down through the top of the Y and back out to the same side again.

Wrap the broad end across again, behind and up through the back of the Y. Let the broad end hang down, then tuck it between the last wrap and the spot you've been holding.

Pull the knot together gently. This is a crucial step with the double Windsor. There are two actions here—tightening the funnel-shaped knot and then sliding that knot up to your collar.

While the knot is still loose, remove your nondominant hand from inside the knot and use it to grasp the bottom of the broad end. Then, while pulling on the broad end, use your dominant hand to squeeze and jostle the funnel-shaped knot into the right form. Make sure the first, smaller wrap of the knot doesn't slip down the narrow end. Instead, coax it into the larger outer wrap. Now slide the almost finished knot up toward your collar. At this point you can tighten the knot more

firmly by pulling on the narrow end. Ideally there's a dimple created just below the pointed end of the funnel-shaped knot.

Look in the mirror. Is the tie straight? Does the broad end hang down too far or not far enough? Loosen the tie if necessary, and adjust the length of the narrow end as needed so that your tie will be the proper length when the knot has been tightened. The knot should be smoothly wrapped, not wrinkled or folded over on itself. If you need to, take a moment to fuss with it so it looks even and so the rest of the tie hangs down straight.

If you followed the directions but it doesn't look right, don't despair. Many foul-looking knots have been transformed by a little knot cleaning. This involves loosening the knot slightly, removing any wrinkles in the fabric, squeezing the knot into shape, and retightening it. Try it three times, and then start again from scratch.

When untying a tie, never just pull the narrow end out. Simply follow the directions in reverse.

Learn2 Carve a Turkey

A lot of people in this world are scared to death that someday, somewhere, someone is going to ask them to carve the turkey. Less meat is wasted if the bird is cut properly, and well-cut slices can be neatly arranged on a serving platter.

BEFORE YOU BEGIN

Set up your carving board and serving platter on a solid and spacious surface. Let the bird "rest" for at least 15 minutes after being removed from the oven before starting to slice it. If you have a large serving platter handy, you can easily transfer the meat to it as you slice it. Last, but certainly not least, wash and dry your hands well.

And put on your apron. This can be a little messy.

STEP 1
Tackle the legs and wings

Place the turkey securely on the large carving board. To begin, you'll be carving only one side of the bird.

Use the large fork for balance. Depending on how steady you feel, penetrate, pierce lightly, or rest the fork on the breast. Slice down the crevice where a leg connects with the body, until you hit bone.

Pull the leg away from the body with one hand. With the other, force the edge of the knife into the joint of the leg and body. If you cut firmly, the joint will sometimes separate cleanly. If it doesn't separate, get the leg off by cutting through the joint.

Holding the leg up by the small end, rest the large end on the smaller

What you'll need

- A cooked turkey, with the stuffing removed
- A sharp carving knife for best results; in a pinch, any large, sharp knife—preferably with a narrow blade
- A large fork, at least 8 inches long
- A large carving board
- A smaller carving board or an inexpensive plate
- A large serving platter
- An apron

carving board. First carve slices off the thigh, then carve from the drumstick. Cut downward, and try to get medium-thin slices, as large as practical. Work your way around the leg.

Use the fork to pull a wing aside. Insert the point of the knife into the joint, and separate the wing from the body. Cut through the joint if necessary, and put the wing aside.

STEP 2
Carve the breast

Seat the bird firmly on the large carving board. Work from the first slice, carving down to the bone in a methodical fashion. If that serving platter is handy, you can transfer the meat with the knife blade as you slice it.

Using the large fork for balance, first cut a silver-dollar-sized slice from the most rounded area of the breast, about halfway down.

Continue to slice downward in order to get medium-thin slices, then larger ones. Picture the rib cage, and angle your slicing so that the blade of the knife is parallel to it, rather than digging in.

Work your way closer to the bone. As you expose the bones, the slices will take on some odd shapes, but keep the thickness as uniform as possible. At some point you'll start to use your fingers to get the odd bits and pieces onto the plate, but leave a little on the bone if you like turkey soup.

STEP 3
Carve the other side

The second half of the bird will be a little unbalanced, since all that weight is now on the platter. On the other hand, you've got the hang of it now, so it will probably go easier. Repeat the steps above, and you'll wind up with a turkey frame that has just enough on it for soup.

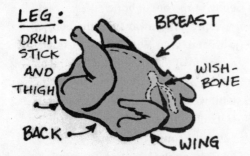

LEG: DRUMSTICK AND THIGH

BREAST

WISHBONE

BACK

WING

Learn**2** Choose a Melon

An experienced gardener knows the best way to pick a ripe melon: grasp it firmly, give a tug and a twist. If it falls easily off the vine into your hand, it's ripe. While not all varieties of melon follow the same guidelines, here are some tips that will help you choose your cantaloupes and honeydews with confidence.

STEP 1
Walk through the market stand

Just breeze through and breathe in. If you are seized by the sweet perfume of ripe melons, follow your nose to the source. If you find several varieties, sniff out the aromatic one.

STEP 2
Learn to see

A beige-skinned honeydew with distinct green veins reveals immaturity; a pale yellow version with bright, lemon-colored areas suggests time on the vine.

Cantaloupes are unripe when the skin beneath the textured "web" is green, ripe when orange or gold.

Another mark of desirability is a patch that's slightly flat and bleached

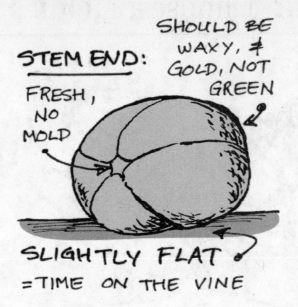

STEM END:
FRESH, NO MOLD

SHOULD BE WAXY, & GOLD, NOT GREEN

SLIGHTLY FLAT
=TIME ON THE VINE

in color. Melons that develop on the vine flatten under their own weight and lose color where they sit on hot soil. In general, stem ends should be moist, not moldy.

STEP 3
Have a feel

A good melon is firm but not rock-hard. It yields very slightly to pressure but has no soft spots. Sponginess means the fruit is too far gone.

STEP 4
Shake it up

When a honeydew is fully ripe, the fibrous net that attaches the seeds to the flesh breaks down, allowing the seeds to rattle around. Ripe cantaloupes rattle only occasionally, so it's an unreliable indicator.

STEP 5
Sound it out

Some swear by the thump test. Hold your dominant hand as if ready to knock on a door. Deliver two or three good thumps to the round side of a melon. The sound should be deep and thick, indicating a dense, full fruit. A higher, hollow sound can mean insufficient moisture, among other things.

Learn2 Clean a Fish

After the catching, or even the buying, there are a few steps between the lake and your plate. While not for the eternally queasy, cleaning a fish is not as messy as one might think. And don't worry about the guts. They're part of the full fishy experience.

BEFORE YOU BEGIN

Cover your work area with plenty of newspaper or heavy paper bags. Have a plastic bag handy for the guts and bones. Make sure to seal well before disposing.

STEP 1
Prepare the body

Wash the fish in cool running water to remove any slime.

With a sharp knife or kitchen shears, cut off the pectoral fins on both sides of the fish.

Not all fish need scaling. If you're not sure, run the blade of the blunt knife at almost a 90-degree angle to the body from tail to head. If the scales are thick and come up easily, you need to remove them. Continue until the body is smooth.

Time

5 to 15 minutes

What you'll need

- Newspaper or heavy paper bags
- A plastic bag
- Blunt knife for scaling, if necessary
- Sharp knife for cutting; if available, use kitchen shears
- A small spoon

Key words

Dorsal fin: The large, tough, spiny fin that runs along the backbone.

Pectoral fins: The small, more flexible fins attached to either side of the body.

Tips

- To prepare a fish for cooking whole, it is not necessary to remove the head, tail, or dorsal bones. It is absolutely essential, however, to completely remove the gills.

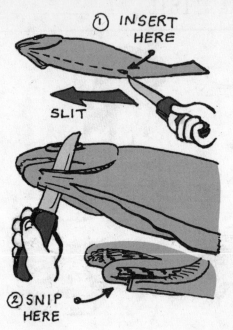

① INSERT HERE

SLIT

② SNIP HERE

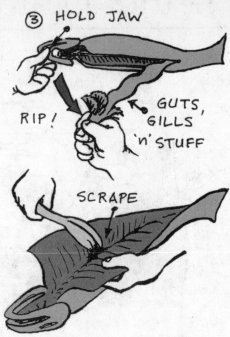

③ HOLD JAW

RIP!

GUTS, GILLS 'n' STUFF

SCRAPE

STEP 2

Gut

Now comes the fun part.

Using the sharp knife, drive the blade point into the vent (small anal opening near the tail, where the body begins to widen). Cut right through the belly all the way to the gills.

Remove the guts from the cavity.

With the spoon, scoop out the dark reddish brown kidney line that lies along the backbone.

Important: Cut out all parts of the gills.

STEP 3

Remove the head and tail

Cut the head off right below the gills. Cut the tail where it joins the body.

STEP 4

Remove the dorsal-fin bones

This step is not essential but eliminates those tiny, annoying bones that can ruin a meal.

Cut along the length of each side of the dorsal fin. Remove the fin and connected bones by giving a quick pull from tail end to head.

Learn**2** Cook Rice

Tired of burned pots and soggy, sticky concoctions that resemble tapioca pudding more than a fluffy side dish? The straightforward, no-nonsense guidelines of this 2torial will relieve these woes.

BEFORE YOU BEGIN

Many international and gourmet sections have a dozen or more types from which to choose. This 2torial will guide you through the basics of standard long-grain rice cooking. Once you have the basics down, you'll need only slight modifications to cook the more exotic varieties.

STEP 1

Measure and rinse

When making rice, expect it to roughly double in volume as it absorbs water while cooking. Generally speaking, measure ½ cup (115 milliliters) long-grain rice per person to make slightly less than 1 cup (225 milliliters) of rice per serving.

Time

20 to 50 minutes, depending on the quantity and type

What you'll need

- A 2-quart (2-liter) pot with a close-fitting lid
- 1 to 5 cups (100 milliliters) clean, fresh water—some folks say filtered spring water makes tastier and more healthful rice
- An 8-ounce (225-gram) measuring cup
- A stove with a reliable low-heat setting
- A long-handled spoon (we like wooden ones)
- ⅛ to ½ teaspoon (1 to 2 milliliters) salt (our choice: sea salt) (optional)

Tips

- Brown rice versus white: If nutrition is your first priority, the choice is easy. Brown rice has far higher amounts of vitamins E and B, minerals, fiber, and protein. These nutrients are located in the outer layer of the grain—the germ and bran. White rice is made by removing this nutritious outer layer, leaving behind mostly starch.

Measure out the rice into the saucepan. Fill the pan halfway with cold water. Stir the rice to cleanse it, and remove any floating husks or debris as the rice settles to the bottom.

Pour off the excess water. Rinse the rice lightly once or twice if you prefer sticky rice (say, for making sushi, dolmas, or other international recipes); rinse more thoroughly if you don't want it sticky. Pour off all the water carefully, or use a spoon to prevent the rice from spilling out.

STEP 2
Wet it

Measure 1 cup (250 milliliters) of water for every cup (250 grams) of dry rice in the pot. Then add 1 full cup of water "for the pot." This allows for the water lost due to steam and evaporation during cooking. If you are in the habit of burning your rice, add a little more water to the pot this time. Also, add extra water if you prefer stickier rice. Less water makes for dryer,

fluffier dishes. It all depends on how you plan to use it.

If you want to add salt, do it now.

STEP 3
Boil it

It's important that rice simmer and not simply steep in hot water. As you'll see, though, the rice needs to boil only momentarily.

Put the pan uncovered on the stove, turn the burner on high, and bring the mixture to a boil. Stir the rice occasionally, taking particular care to rub the spoon along the bottom of the pot—especially the outer edges. You want to be sure no rice grains are sticking to the bottom. They will burn even if you have plenty of water.

Bubble, bubble, toil and trouble: Boil-overs are often caused by too much liquid, pressure buildup in the pan, or heat set too high. Try reducing the heat, and watch the surface of the liquid for a very slow simmer. If boil-overs persist, try cocking up the lid at an angle to let some steam escape. This will reduce the pressure inside the pot, but be aware that too much water loss will cause rice to dry out and burn before it's fully cooked.

STEP 4
Simmer it

After the mixture is brought to a boil, keep it just barely boiling by reducing the heat to very low. You should see tiny bubbles, slightly more than in champagne or soda; the surface

① BOIL
② STIR
③ SIMMER ON LOW
✳ AND DON'T LIFT LID TOO OFTEN!

should be relatively calm, not frothing. Cover the pot with a close-fitting lid, and let simmer for 20 minutes (45 minutes for brown rice).

If after the allotted time there's still water in the pan, you probably added too much. Leave the lid off, and simmer for 5 minutes longer. If the limpid pools linger, but the rice tastes done, then simply use a slotted spoon to scoop the rice out of the pot and into a serving dish. No one will be the wiser.

Remove from the heat, and stir with your spoon around the edges and along the bottom. This will fluff it up nicely.

STEP 5
Adjust for rice varieties

• Consider organic rice: Rice grows better in good soil. Organic farmers use natural, sustainable ways of keeping minerals and nutrients in the soil; these are then passed on to the rice. Also, since the rice plants are stronger, they are more resistant to disease and pests, thus eliminating the need for pesticides and chemical fertilizers.

• Long- or short-grain rice? Long-grain rice is good with curries, pilaf, and paella, because it's dryer and less sticky than short-grain rice. Short-grain rice is fantastic with Oriental dishes and as rice pudding.

• Brown rice, available long, medium, and short grain, needs more water and more time: figure 2 cups (500 milliliters) water per 1 cup (250 grams) rice. (Note: Adding the extra cup of water "for the pot" isn't neces-

sary with this method.) Also, some experts maintain that you should heat the water first, just until it boils, then add the rice. Simmer for 45 to 50 minutes instead of 20.

• Skim that foam! Maybe you've noticed there's a foam that rises to the top of a simmering pot of rice. Some nutritional experts claim that this foam contains starches and even toxins that you're better off not ingesting. They recommend skimming it off.

• Roasty-toasty: Dry-roasting brown rice gives it a delightful, nutty quality. Heat it in a dry, hot skillet, but don't let it sit. Stir constantly until the grains are brown. Cooking instructions are the same as above, except that you reduce the simmering time by 10 minutes.

• Wild rice: Surprise! Wild rice isn't actually rice at all; it's a seed grain from an aquatic grass. Add 1 cup (250 grams) rice to 1 quart (1 liter) boiling water and simmer, covered, for 40 minutes. It's terrific as a stuffing or in a pilaf with sautéed vegetables.

Tips

• Save money: Large supermarkets, as well as traditional health-food stores, sell rice in bulk bins. Buying bulk accomplishes at least three things: you save money, you choose exactly the amount you need, and you reduce the amount of garbage in landfills.

• Make enough rice for a day or two, and reheat it as necessary. If you plan to eat it for dinner, don't bother refrigerating it—just put it in a closed container on a counter and reheat it when you're ready.

• Don't peek! Rice needs the steam that's built up in a pot with a tight-fitting lid. If you let the steam out too many times, the rice may be undercooked.

Learn **2** Make a Great Pot of Coffee

Often the simplest things are the most elusive. But the key to a great pot of coffee is no mystery; it merely depends on first-rate ingredients, good equipment, and proper technique. Buy your coffee frequently from a quality source; store it in a dark, cool, dry place for up to 2 weeks (freeze for longer storage), and follow the instructions below. You'll make a fine pot every time.

BEFORE YOU BEGIN

Make sure your coffeemaker is scrupulously clean; residual oils turn rancid over time.

If using paper filters, rinse in hot water to remove loose paper pulp and bleaching agents (if white). Also, flavor oils will thus release into the brew, not the filter.

If you must use tap water, run the faucet first to clear the water sitting in the pipes. Colder and fresher makes a tastier, livelier brew.

Warm the pot. Just a few swishes in hot water will help maintain the coffee's temperature and flavor.

Watch that water temperature! Boiling makes a bitter brew, which is why percolators are out of favor. Not heating enough produces a thin-bodied, weak decoction. In general, European-made automatics are calibrated better than their American counterparts.

Manual methods allow you to manage the amount of time the coffee grounds and water stay in contact, essential to extracting full flavor. Automatics with V-shaped filters are next best; last is the flat-bottomed drip.

Key words

French press: Also known as the plunger pot, the French press works by putting boiled water and coffee together in a carafe, steeping to extract flavor, then separating grounds from brew by pushing a flat filter through the solution.

Gold filter: A gold-plated, reusable filter, most often V-shaped. The gold filter's screen is fine enough to allow the essential oils to pass through but not the bitter grounds. And unlike paper, cloth, or other metals, gold imparts no flavor of its own.

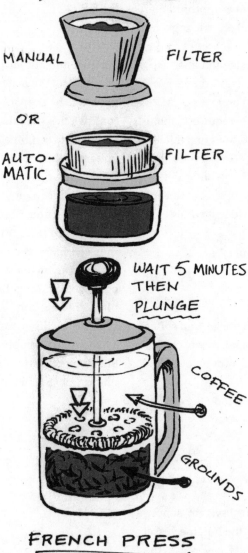

DRIP SYSTEMS

MANUAL FILTER

OR

AUTO-MATIC FILTER

WAIT 5 MINUTES THEN PLUNGE

COFFEE

GROUNDS

FRENCH PRESS
(COARSER GRIND)

Tips

- For brewing single servings, consider a mini French press or 1-cup drip system (a V-shaped cone or a straight-sided gold filter).
- Gold filters are the preferred. If you must use paper, try the unbleached variety.
- Automatic-drip machines need regular removal of mineral deposits, which can mar performance and affect flavor (tell-tale sign: when the drip process slows noticeably). Once a month, run a half pot of distilled white vinegar through the brewing cycle, then follow with two cycles of fresh water. Commercial preparations are also available.

STEP 1

Measure the coffee

This is arguably the most important step in brewing great coffee, and where most errors are made. The rule of thumb is: 1 tablespoon ground coffee for each 6 ounces of water, or 30 milliliters coffee for 180 milliliters water. This ratio (1:6) is appropriate for most manual and electric brewing systems.

A "cup" from most automatic-drip coffeemakers measures 5 ounces; adjust accordingly. For instance, a 12-cup automatic would require 10 tablespoons of ground coffee. For a milder pot of coffee, use the 1-to-6 ratio, then dilute to taste with fresh hot water. The result has more body and flavor than if you'd just used less coffee.

STEP 2

Put in the coffee

For any drip system, automatic or manual, simply add the ground coffee to the filter (be it paper, nylon, cloth, gold-plated, or some other metal). Do not pack down.

For a French press, add the coffee directly to the glass carafe.

STEP 3

Put in the water

For an automatic-drip system, simply pour the water into the holding vessel and replace the carafe, covered, to the warming unit.

For any manual method, place a pot of fresh, cold water on the stove over high heat. Watch closely until the water measures between 195 and 209 degrees F. (you'll see steam and tiny bubbles at the edge of the pot). Remove from the heat as soon as the desired temperature is reached. Do not boil.

STEP 4

Brew!

For an automatic-drip coffeemaker: If possible, set the machine for number of cups to be prepared. Then flip the "on" switch. When the brewing is complete, stir to combine (the coffee at the bottom of the pot is stronger than what's on top).

For a French press: Pour the proper amount of water directly over the grounds; stir to blend. Wait a moment, then stir again. Position the plunger mechanism on top of the carafe, wait only 3 to 5 minutes, then push the plunger to the bottom of the pot to separate the brew from the grounds. To serve, don't empty the pot completely: some bitter residue always lurks at the bottom of the pot.

Learn**2** Make a Perfect Pot of Tea

In many parts of the world, tea is an inextricable part of history and culture. In other places, serious tea drinking is just taking hold. And while the methods and serving of certain varieties differ, consider this 2torial your basic primer.

BEFORE YOU BEGIN

While we encourage you to use loose leaves in a pot, a tea ball is acceptable. Be sure it is large enough to hold the amount of tea needed for the pot. Stir before serving. Try to draw the line at prepackaged tea bags. The problem is not so much concept as execution: some large companies hide inferior ingredients in those opaque little bags; some retailers don't discard old boxes that have been sitting around for too long.

Time

10 to 20 minutes

What you'll need

- Pure, fresh water (spring or purified, if possible), 5 to 6 ounces (1¾ dL) per cup
- A nonreactive saucepan in which to boil the water (preferably glass or enamel-coated metal) (see "Tips")
- A ceramic, glass, or enameled teapot (see "Tips")
- Good-quality black, green, or oolong tea leaves, or herbal leaves and flowers; one teaspoon per cup, plus one for the pot
- A fine-meshed strainer
- A tea cozy (optional)

Key words

Tea cozy: A kind of warm hat for your teapot. Cozies are deemed essential in environments where the air temperature will chill the water in the pot to the point that it's too cool for proper steeping and enjoyable drinking.

Black tea: Tea that is dried and fermented, thus stronger than green.

Green tea: Tea that is dried immediately after harvesting.

Oolong tea: Semi-fermented tea, with an inimitable flavor.

Tips

• "Reactive" saucepans include most metals (stainless steel excepted) and can impart flavor to the water; aluminum and unlined copper are the worst offenders; glass and enamel are preferred.

If you must use tap water, run the faucet to clear the water sitting in the pipes. Colder and fresher makes a tastier, livelier infusion. Use of very hard or artificially softened water can significantly mar the flavor of tea.

Warm the teapot by letting it sit, filled with very hot water, for a few minutes. Drain, then place in the oven, at the lowest setting, till it's warm inside and out.

STEP 1
Boil the water

Pour measured fresh water into a kettle or saucepan and place over high heat. Heat the water until it just comes to a rolling boil: overboiling removes too much oxygen, imparting a flat taste to the tea.

STEP 2
Steep the tea

Add the tea leaves to the warmed teapot. Immediately pour the boiled water over the loose leaves. Cover the pot. If available, place a tea cozy over the pot. This will keep the pot warm during the steeping, which helps extract as much flavor as possible. A thick towel will do as well. To be true to the brew, steep Western teas in glass or ceramic, Asian teas in ceramic or enamel.

Steep 3 to 5 minutes for most teas, longer, to taste, for the more delicate green and herbal infusions. Stir.

STEP 3
Serve the tea

Pour the tea through the strainer into individual cups.

Specific teas traditionally use specific accompaniments:

• Serve black tea with milk or lemon and sugar, if desired. Never serve black tea with cream: it's too rich and overwhelms the flavors.

• Green tea is served without anything at all.

• Herb teas are usually served as is, with honey and/or with lemon.

Learn**2** Make Chai

What you'll need

- A saucepan, 4-quart or larger
- 1½ quarts water
- 4 bags black tea (serves 4)
- 10 cardamom seeds
- 2 cinnamon sticks, broken in half
- Pinch fresh-ground black pepper
- 3 tablespoons sugar
- Milk to taste

Tired of coffee and bored with dishwater-flavored herbal tea? Indian chai has pleased the taste buds of the subcontinent for centuries and is now making a splash in the United States.

BEFORE YOU BEGIN

Our recipe is better suited to Western taste buds than the version in which all the ingredients are boiled together for a few minutes. If you're curious, give it a try and let us know how you like it. It's quite a strong brew. Otherwise you can vary the time in Step 4 to change its intensity.

Key words

Steep: To suspend something in a hot solution to extract flavor and color, to soak.

Cardamom: Indian spice that is packaged whole (white or pale green pods) or in seed form (small, black, aromatic seeds). Now widely available.

Tips

- Take care not to burn the milk.
- Whole milk makes a richer chai.
- You may choose to reduce the amount of sugar or use honey; just know that sugar enhances the flavor of the spices.

STEP 1
Boil the water

In a saucepan, bring the water to a boil. Catch it before it has boiled too long, or the tea will have a flat taste.

STEP 2
Mix the spices

Add the tea bags, cardamom, cinnamon, and black pepper. Return to boil.

STEP 3
Add the sugar

Immediately add the sugar. Stir.

STEP 4
Steep it

Remove the pot from the heat, cover, and let stand for 5 minutes to bring out the flavor.

STEP 5
Heat the milk

Heat milk in a saucepan until warm.

STEP 6
Pour

If you want to serve your chai Indian-style, pour it into the smallest cups you can find. Add the milk until the color resembles well-creamed coffee. You may want to experiment down the line with the tea-to-milk ratio.

STEP 7
Serve to your delighted friends

For true Indian style, serve with Parve, Gluco, or Good Day Cashew biscuits. These are mind-bendingly sweet shortbread cookies palatable mostly to Indians and available only in Indian grocery stores. Any Western version will suffice.

Learn2 Make Flavored Vinegars

Vinegars flavored with spices, herbs, fruits, or flowers make a wonderful addition to salad dressings, sauces, and marinades and are an inexpensive way to liven up your dishes and give them fantastic new names. Homemade gourmet flavored vinegar also makes a great gift; it's useful, consumable, and totally unique—there's no store in the world that sells *your* vinegar.

BEFORE YOU BEGIN

In general, making flavored vinegars is a fairly carefree, foolproof process. The one exception is your choice of utensils and containers, and here's the main point: avoid metal. Vinegar is slightly corrosive and will react with the metal, adding an unpleasant taste to the mix. Stir with wooden spoons, and close the containers with corks or plastic tops. If you heat the vinegar (as you do with the infused method—see Step 3), you can use a stainless-steel pot, but after you're done heating, transfer your brew to a nonmetallic container for maturing.

If you're using a decorative bottle to hold the final product, be sure to sterilize it with boiling water first, and let it dry completely. Any foreign matter that remains in the bottle may rot and cause the vinegar to spoil.

Time

10 minutes, plus 2 to 3 weeks for maturation (depending on method)

What you'll need

- 3 cups (750 milliliters) vinegar: cider, white (distilled), or wine (red or white)

Possible additions:

- 2 to 3 sprigs of a fresh herb, such as sage, mint, rosemary, basil, parsley, marjoram, oregano, chives, savory, or dill

- 1 teaspoon (5 milliliters) black peppercorns
- 4 to 6 cloves garlic
- A 1-quart (1-liter) nonmetallic container, made of either glass or ceramic
- A funnel

Optional:

- 2 tablespoons (30 milliliters) sugar
- A decorative bottle or glass jar with at least a 24-ounce capacity (about 750 milliliters)
- Cheesecloth

STEP 1

Understand the types of vinegar

There are three main vinegars you can work with: cider, distilled (also called white), and wine. Each of these has a different source and corresponding flavor and "bite," or acidity.

Cider vinegar is made from fermented apples. Not surprisingly, it has a fruity flavor and a noticeable bite. Raw, unfiltered cider vinegar is the optimum grade.

Distilled (or white) vinegar is made from fermented grain. It's clear with a rather acid flavor and is used only with other ingredients. (You wouldn't pour it straight on a salad.)

Wine vinegars are, of course, made from fermented grapes, and their qualities vary with the type of grape used.

Tasting unadulterated vinegars will help you understand what flavorings will go well with what base. You can do this a few different ways. Add a tiny portion of vinegar to a wineglass, swirl it around, and taste it. If that's too strong, add some neutral-tasting water (perhaps filtered or bottled) before tasting. Or dip a sugar cube into a bowl with a tiny portion of vinegar, and suck the vinegar out of the sugar cube. (Take it out before it dissolves.)

For flavored vinegars, there are five main types: herb, fruit, spice, vegetable, and blends. Generally, there's a vinegar base that's best suited to a type of flavored vinegar. Here's the breakdown:

- Cider vinegars complement spices.
- Wine vinegars also complement spices, although they are more commonly paired with herbs such as sage, rosemary, marjoram, and oregano for red wine vinegar, and chives, sage, oregano, and savory for white wine vinegar.
- Distilled vinegar is a good match with fruits like cherries and raspberries and edible flowers like nasturtiums.

Note: If you're not absolutely sure something's palatable, don't add it to your concoction. Sounds like common sense, but people sometimes get carried away, perhaps adding flowers that look lovely but taste vile (or, worse yet, are toxic).

STEP 2

Know the combinations

First you need to choose your flavor scheme: the vinegar and choice of flavoring(s). Here are some examples that can serve as guidelines. If there's a combination that sounds good to you and that's different from the ones below, by all means experiment and let us at Learn2.com know about your discoveries.

In general, start off with a simple batch and gradually add more flavorings to successive batches as your experience grows. All the recipes below yield 3 cups. Go to Step 3 for the actual vinegar-flavoring process.

Fresh rosemary (or sage, marjoram, or oregano)

2 to 3 sprigs rosemary

4 to 6 cloves garlic

1 teaspoon black peppercorns

3 cups (750 milliliters) red wine vinegar

Fresh mint

1 large bunch mint

2 tablespoons (30 milligrams) sugar

3 cups distilled vinegar

Fresh tarragon-dill

2 sprigs tarragon

2 sprigs dill

3 cups (750 milliliters) white wine vinegar

Top off container with a bunch of chives, parsley, basil, or another leafy herb.

Cider thyme!

6 sprigs thyme

1 sprig rosemary

1 strip lemon peel

3 cups (750 milliliters) cider vinegar

Sour cherries

3 cups (750 milliliters) white wine vinegar

Pitted cherries

STEP 3

Make flavored vinegar

Now that you've chosen your flavor scheme, the most difficult part is behind you. Transforming ordinary vinegar into homemade gourmet flavored vinegar is simple—no magic wand necessary. Here are the two methods you can choose from.

Uninfused:

This is a really simple method that produces good but not optimal results. Simply assemble the flavorings in the correct amounts, add to the decorative bottle or glass jar, and pour the vinegar directly over the flavorings. Place the bottle in a warm, dark place (like a pantry or cabinet), or wrap it in a towel, and let it sit for 3 weeks. *Et voilà!* It's ready.

Infused:

This is a slightly more involved process, and the resulting brew matures faster and has a more potent flavor.

Measure the flavorings in the correct amounts, and combine them in a 1-quart (1-liter) nonmetallic container.

Measure 3 cups vinegar, and heat it in a stainless-steel or cast-iron pot with a baked-enamel finish. (Don't use plain cast iron.) Heat just until the vinegar boils, then remove.

Pour the heated vinegar over the flavorings, and cover the container with a double layer of cheesecloth. Let it sit for 2 weeks.

Rinse out the cheesecloth, in case any dust has settled on it. Wrap it around the mouth of the container.

Put a funnel in a decorative bottle, and pour the infused vinegar into the bottle. If you want a real hand-crafted touch, plunge the bottle's neck and cork into beeswax, and/or wrap with a bow. Another nice touch is to place a bit of the main flavoring agent in the bottle, to put it on display, so to speak. Just a twig or so, though: too much might affect the long-term flavor. Have fun!

Tips

- Don't expect to get an overwhelming punch of herb flavoring from the finished product; many herbs impart a delicate flavor. Flavored vinegars are also scented, and that is a different and subtle addition to the dish, more interesting than a powerful flavor.
- Buy some labels and labeling glue, and create your own line of flavored vinegar. Make your motto as outrageous as you like.
- If you can afford it, shop around for organic vinegar. It's better for your palate, your health, and the environment.

Learn 2 Poach an Egg

Time

About 10 minutes
from start to finish

What you'll need

- A skillet or shallow saucepan
- 1 small measuring cup, without a spout, or teacup, for each egg poached
- A perforated spatula or large slotted spoon
- A tablespoon or serving spoon
- Paper towels or an impeccably clean tea towel
- ½ teaspoon white vinegar
- ½ teaspoon salt

Poached eggs are different from fried eggs, omelettes, and scrambles in that no oil is used and no other ingredients are mixed in. Since no flavors are added during cooking, the poached egg arrives unclothed and innocent.

BEFORE YOU BEGIN

Try to find the freshest eggs possible. A fresh egg, apart from tasting superior, will be easier to handle and will hold together in the water better.

STEP 1
Boil the water

Using a relatively shallow pan makes it easier to slide the eggs in and out of the water.

Fill the pan to a depth of 2 to 3 inches (5 to 8 centimeters). Add the vinegar and salt (the vinegar makes the egg whites firm up faster), and bring to a boil.

Reduce the heat slightly to create a slow boil, rather than a rolling boil. This will keep the eggs from being damaged while cooking.

STEP 2
Add the eggs

There are two poaching methods, and the first one is nearly foolproof. After you've mastered it, you may want to try the second method, which uses one less dish.

Method 1. The teacup:

Break each egg into a small cup. Lower the cup into the water, and quickly tip the egg out. Hold the cup upside down for a moment or two to prevent the white from spreading. Don't add more than three eggs at a time, as they become difficult to handle.

Method 2. The swirl:

Create a small whirlpool in the cooking water by making tight circles with a narrow spatula or spoon. Immediately crack an egg into the center of the swirling water; the circular motion of the water will keep it together. Don't overcrowd the pan.

<u>**STEP 3**</u>

Finish the eggs

When all the eggs have been added, remove the pan from the heat and let the eggs poach for 3 or 4 minutes.

If the yolks do not appear to be cooking, spoon some water over the tops with the tablespoon or serving spoon. When the yolks are filmed over and the whites are firm and set, remove the eggs from the water with the slotted spatula or spoon.

Place the eggs on the paper or tea towels to absorb the excess water, then lift them onto warm plates, serve atop toast, or place in a cup to serve.

1. SPIN WATER

2. PUT 1 EGG HERE

WHIRLPOOL

Learn2 Prepare Garlic

Time

30 seconds to 5 minutes per clove from peeling to chopping

What you'll need

- Garlic cloves (or a head—a full knob-shaped bulb of cloves)
- A strong, sharp kitchen knife, such as a carver's or butcher knife
- A sturdy chopping board or butcher's block
- A fresh lemon (optional)

There's nothing as delicious as a home-cooked Italian meal complete with pasta, fresh tomato sauce, and garlic bread. Except maybe a pungent Thai stir-fry with snow peas, red chilis, holy basil, and garlic. Or a fiery Indian curry with cumin, coriander, cayenne, and garlic. You get the idea: garlic is good. And it's been hailed as a health tonic by traditional healers for centuries, now with the backing of modern medical research. Unfortunately, peeling garlic is the sort of culinary chore that can be tiresome for even an experienced cook. And the same is true for crushing it and mincing it.

BEFORE YOU BEGIN

You should remove all the cloves you want to use from the head before starting. Crushing garlic is recommended if you want a stronger flavor—this releases more of the natural juices. Marinades and foods such as Caesar salad and shrimp scampi demand crushed garlic. Garlic sliced or chopped coarsely will usually add a light flavor to your dish, since it's less likely to dissolve or soften. A happy medium is minced garlic, which is less pungent than crushed but still adds great flavor for recipes that require stir-frying or sautéing.

Part 1
Peel it

STEP 1
Begin at the end

Looking at the garlic clove, you'll see a tough piece at the end. This is the part that was attached to the bottom of the garlic head before the clove was removed. Place the garlic clove on the chopping block, and using the tip of your knife, slice off that end.

STEP 2
Remove the skin

Use your thumb and index finger to hold the sides of the clove as it lays on the chopping block. With your other hand, use the tip of the knife to carefully make a vertical slit from top to bottom in the skin of the garlic. Then tap the clove once or twice with the back of the knife blade. The skin should be nicely loosened at this point and can easily be pulled off in one piece.

If the skin is still not loose enough, tap the clove again.

The garlic is now ready to be crushed, chopped, minced, or used whole. Yes, you've read it correctly: whole garlic! Try it in stews or with grilled vegetables.

Part 2
Crush it

STEP 1
Have a whack at it

Place the unpeeled garlic clove on the chopping block. Grasping the butcher's knife by the handle (with the blade upside down), give the garlic a hard whack with the back of the blade. If it's not pretty well collapsed, give it another whack.

STEP 2
Start chopping

Once the garlic is well crushed, you can chop it further. Hold the knife handle with one hand and the top of the blade at the front with the fingertips of your other hand. You can then chop the garlic to your preference. Again, the more you chop the garlic, the more pungency it will add to your dish.

Tips

- In home-style Thai cooking, the garlic is often left unpeeled. Aside from saving the cook some labor, leaving the peel on the garlic in stir-fry dishes produces an especially appetizing aroma.

- Is your dinner guest less enthusiastic about garlic than you are? Don't try to convert by force with your favorite dish loaded with garlic. Using a little less garlic can grace a dish with a subtle mystery that doesn't overpower, but rather woos the garlic fearer until he is a garlic lover.

Part 3
Chop it

STEP 1
Ready, aim . . .

Place the peeled clove of garlic on the chopping block. Hold the knife with one hand and the front of the blade with the other.

STEP 2
Fire

Starting at one end of the clove, move the knife up and down until you've made pieces of the desired size. The partially chopped garlic may start to spread out away from your knife. Angle the edge of the knife toward the garlic, scoop it back into a pile, and continue chopping. Again, the thinner the piece, the more it will dissolve, and the more flavor it will impart.

Part 4
Mince it

STEP 1
Slice vertically

Place a whole, peeled garlic clove on the chopping block. Hold it steady on the sides.

Using the tip of your knife, make three or four vertical slices in the clove, being sure to cut all the way through. Try to make cuts of equal thickness.

Turn the garlic clove 90 degrees. Again, with the tip of your knife, make three or four more vertical cuts so that you have a crisscross or grid pattern.

STEP 2
Hold the clove

Two crucial points will help you at this juncture: finger position and slicing motion. With the tip of the knife, mince by cutting horizontally from the top.

Take a look at the thumb, index, middle, and ring fingers of your non-dominant hand (that's the hand you'll hold the garlic with, not the hand that holds the knife). Together these will control the thickness of the tiny garlic cubes you are about to make. The index and middle fingers are the front runners—they rest on the front edge of the garlic where you'll start slicing. Equally important is the angle of these fingers: the second knuckles are vertical, with the first knuckles (the ones nearest to the garlic) curled in slightly away from the edge of the clove. (This will prevent you from mincing your fingertips.) There should be only a small portion of the clove visible as you look down your fingers from above.

The thumb has an important function, which will be revealed to you a little later. For now let it rest on the cutting board directly behind the clove and the fingers in front.

STEP 3

Slice with rhythm

Rest the flat side of the knife against your fingers. Using this placement as a guide, make sure the knife stays on the same plane—it shouldn't move laterally, either toward your fingers or away from them.

Lift the knife off the cutting board, but keep it in contact with your fingers. Lift away from you and the garlic, toward the other side of the cutting board.

Slice downward on the crisscross, using the heel of the knife (its back edge). As you slice, also draw the knife toward you. This downward and sideways movement slices through garlic more easily, leaving you with a neat pile instead of a big sloppy mess.

Lift the knife again, up and away from you, and again slice downward and toward you. Practice this movement without even slicing any garlic. As the movement gets smoother, you'll soon realize that it's circular. Keep at it, and you'll feel the rhythm of this ancient motion.

Before you slice any further, please read on.

STEP 4

Thrust with the thumb

Now that you've got the circular motion and you're slicing with rhythm, you're ready to incorporate the thumb into this symphony of movement. The thumb is the driver of the mincing operation. As you lift the knife up and away from you, push the garlic toward it. You'll have it out just in time for the knife to descend and slice through it. Again, as the knife ascends, you push the garlic out just enough to make a small cube from your crisscross pattern. The thumb forces the garlic out into the slicing line and also prevents it from making a rear-exit escape. Its destiny is certain: it shall be minced!

Work slowly and carefully at first. Eventually you'll be able to mince with great speed using this technique, but don't rush it, or your fingers will be sorry.

As you get toward the end of the clove, you may find it necessary to angle the blade slightly in toward the fingers. But keep the flat of the blade resting on the second knuckles. Look closely where you're slicing, and you'll never get cut. As you get to the very tip of the clove, just take your fingers away and chop up the remains into small cubes. *Bon appétit!*

Tips

- To remove garlic smell from your hands when you're done cooking, cut a fresh lemon in half, squeeze the juice from one half onto your hands, and rub your hands together. Not only are your hands free from a stale garlic odor, they radiate the lovely scent of fresh lemon.

Learn 2 Season Cookware

Time

- Metal: 5 minutes to wash and dry, 30 minutes to bake
- Wood: 5 minutes to wash and dry, 5 minutes to season

What you'll need

- 1 to 5 teaspoons (5 to 25 milliliters) any vegetable oil (except safflower and corn oil, which are too sticky when dry)
- 1 teaspoon (5 milliliters) mineral oil

Did you leave half the scrambled eggs burnt on the bottom of the pan? Maybe you needed a hammer and chisel to get the cookies off the baking sheet. Perhaps it's time to season your cookware. It's got nothing to do with flavor—rather, it's the process of developing a natural nonstick finish on metal cookware and baking utensils. Also known as tempering, this simple procedure saves you some scrubbing of burned pots and pans, protects utensils against the damaging effects of moisture, and protects food from picking up any metallic flavors. You can season cast iron, stainless steel, and carbon-steel cookware.

There's also a kind of seasoning that develops with wooden utensils like spoons, spatulas, and cutting boards. Seasoning wooden items will protect the wood from drying, warping, and cracking.

BEFORE YOU BEGIN

Especially if the utensil is new, give it a thorough cleaning before you season it. For metal utensils, use hot water and a small amount of mild dishwashing soap with a stiff brush. This will remove any nasty compounds that may be hanging around from the production line.

A particularly messy cooking job will require you to scrub down the utensil with hot water and a brush. Although this is sometimes necessary, you've just removed any protective coating that was laid on the utensil. But on the bright side, you now have the perfect opportunity to reseason the utensil, having returned it to a fairly pristine state.

Utensils coated with nonstick surfaces (like Teflon or some versions of Calphalon) don't need to be seasoned. Be very careful, however, with nonstick utensils as you cook with and clean them. Any scratch in the surface can result in the absorption of toxic chemicals (from the nonstick surface) into your food. So clean these without soap or a brush: simply rinse with water and wipe the surface with a kitchen cloth or paper towel.

Part 1
Season metal cookware

Seasoning forms a protective coating by baking a few layers of vegetable oil onto the utensil. It actually works in two ways: it protects the food from the utensil and the utensil from the food.

Look at a cast-iron skillet (for example) under a microscope, and you'll see tiny peaks on the jagged surface. These peaks cause your food to stick in the pan and can also transfer a metallic flavor to the food. But they're also vulnerable—they can absorb acid and moisture from the food, which causes them to rust.

STEP 1
Oil it up

Set your oven to 300 degrees F. (about 150 degrees C.), and let the utensil warm up in the oven for about 5 minutes. If you've just washed the utensil, the oven heat performs two functions: it thoroughly dries the utensil, and it increases the absorptive ability of the metal. Don't let it become so warm, however, that you can't comfortably touch it. If it's too hot to the touch, wear a cooking glove or use a kitchen cloth to remove it from the oven.

Using either a kitchen cloth or your fingers, apply a thin, even coat of oil onto the entire surface of the utensil. Hold the utensil up to the light to look for any missed spots. For items like cast-iron skillets, grease up the handle as well—it's as prone to rust as the rest of the skillet.

Tips

- Avoid cooking large quantities of tomatoes and lemons in a cast-iron skillet. The acid in these foods reacts with the iron of the skillet, and the result is not pretty: somewhat blackened food with a metallic taste. Not a toxic combination, to be sure, but not terribly appetizing, either.

- Say no to dishwashers: None of the utensils mentioned in this 2torial should ever be run through a dishwasher. The high temperatures of water and strong detergents will shorten their life and reduce their effectiveness.

Place the utensil in the preheated oven, and let it sit for 30 minutes (20 if you need to use it right away).

Using an oven mitt or kitchen cloth, remove the utensil from the oven. The warmth of the oven may have created excess oil, which now forms a shallow pool in the skillet or pot. Go ahead and pour this off, then carefully wipe down the utensil with a kitchen cloth or paper towel. The seasoning is complete and the utensil can be stored away. Note that the surface should be slightly shiny, but the utensil should not be slippery when you pick it up.

STEP 2

Maintain

After you season a utensil and maintain its seasoning, the surface will darken in color: cast-iron items, for example, will turn black. This is the sign of a well-seasoned utensil. Sea-

soning only improves with age. After each use, don't wash metal utensils with soap. This'll strip off the seasoning, which will increase the possibility of making a big burned mess the next time you cook. Instead, soak the utensil for several minutes, and scrub off any food residue with a plastic scouring pad or a brush. Alternatively, pour vinegar or salt or both onto the utensil and scrub out the food particles with a brown paper bag—strange, yes, but many people swear by this method. In either case, dry it thoroughly by placing the utensil on the stovetop or in the oven, whichever is more convenient. This is important, as it prepares the utensil for the next step.

Now pour a teaspoon (5 milliliters) of vegetable oil—or up to 5 teaspoons for larger utensils—onto the utensil and rub well into the surface. Look at it under good light to find missed spots. Wipe down the utensil with a kitchen cloth or a paper towel to clean

SOAP ALTERNATIVE

POUR IN VINEGAR & SALT

SCRUB WITH BROWN PAPER BAG

up excess oil. Again, the surface should be slightly shiny, but the utensil should not be slippery when you pick it up.

Part 2
Season wooden utensils

As far as materials go, wood is a bit temperamental: the levels of moisture, air, and natural oil content all vary depending on how the utensil is used and cared for. For this reason, it's important to keep wood away from very hot water and frequent applications of soap or harsh scouring pads.

If you buy an unfinished wood utensil, it's especially important to season it before you use it: soaking, soaping, and drying a raw-wood implement is a sure path to warping and cracking. On the other hand, you don't want a sticky buildup of food or oil residue on wooden utensils; therefore, you may wish to scrub down and reseason a wood utensil on occasion.

STEP 1
Oil it up

The key to wood seasoning is the oil. Light, food-grade mineral oil, the kind that's made to be taken internally as an intestinal lubricant, is what you want.

Pour oil onto the utensil in increments of 1 teaspoon (5 milliliters), adding as much as you need to give the entire utensil a light coating. Rub it in with your hands—their heat will increase the absorption of oil. It's a good idea to have a few other wood utensils cleaned and ready to go; as long as your hands are oily, you can have a little seasoning party.

If you're oiling a cutting board, do both sides, even if you only cut on one side. Otherwise, moisture can penetrate the underside of the board and cause it to warp.

Let the items sit for a few minutes. You can clean up the rest of the kitchen while you wait, then wipe off excess oil with a kitchen cloth or paper towel.

STEP 2
Maintain

The best policy is to wash and immediately dry any wooden utensil—and skip the hot water and soap. If the surface starts to feel gummy with residue, then take a spatula and see what you can gently scrape off. Wash thoroughly (okay, you can use a dot of soap if the utensil has very greasy residue on it), dry it well with a kitchen cloth (not in an oven!), and season as directed above.

Season frequently. Do your spoons and boards once a month, perhaps twice if they see a lot of use. Or just reseason when they start to look dry.

Learn2 Separate Eggs

Time

1 or 2 minutes for
each egg

What you'll need

- 2 small bowls
- 1 larger bowl

One of these days, when you
least expect it, a recipe is
going to call for egg whites only,
or egg yolks only. Don't panic!
Separating eggs is easier than
you think, especially if you don't
mind getting your hands messy.

BEFORE YOU BEGIN

Wash and dry your hands well. If you
have a garbage bag or compost bucket
handy, you can toss the shells in as
soon as you've separated the eggs. If
not, just place the shells back in the
egg carton for disposal later. Method 1
is more difficult, but you may prefer it
for aesthetic reasons, or because one
of your in-laws is watching and you'd
like to show off. Method 2 is easier and
messier.

Method 1

STEP 1

Crack the egg

Place the two smaller bowls in front of
you, and crack the center of the egg on
the edge of the first bowl. Don't let the

edge of the bowl travel too far into the egg, or the yolk will break.

STEP 2
Tip the yolk

Holding the egg over the first bowl, tip it back and forth between the two halves of the shell. The idea is to let the white drop into the bowl and keep the yolk in the shell.

After all the white has been separated, put the yolk into the second bowl. Take the first bowl with the white in it, and empty it into the third, larger bowl. By doing this you make sure that a broken yolk mixes only with the egg white you're working with instead of the whole batch.

Method 2

With this method, you'll wind up with fewer broken yolks. Be careful about letting the kids watch you, though; it's been known to give them mischievous ideas.

STEP 1
Crack the egg

Place the two smaller bowls in front of you, and crack the egg on the edge of the first bowl.

STEP 2
Use your palm

Tip the whole egg into the palm of your hand. Let the white run through your fingers, into the bowl, while keeping the yolk in the palm of your hand.

STEP 3
Keep bowls separate

Put the yolk into the second bowl. Take the first bowl with the white in it, and empty it into the third, larger bowl. By doing this you make sure that a broken yolk mixes only with the egg white you're working with and not the whole batch.

Tips

- Eggshells can go in the garbage disposal and are great for keeping blades sharp.
- Think ahead: Sometimes you can slip your unused egg yolks into a recipe somewhere, such as tomorrow morning's omelette. Unused yolks will keep for a day or so in a covered bowl in the refrigerator.
- If you rub your finger along the inside of the shell, you can get an extra teaspoon of egg white out of it.

Learn**2** Shuck Oysters

Time

Set up 30 minutes before you want to eat. Open the oysters immediately before serving. Figure 1 to 2 minutes to open each oyster. Purchase the oysters no more than 2 days in advance.

What you'll need

- Fresh oysters: 3 to 4 per person for hors d'oeuvres, up to a dozen per person for a large appetizer or a full meal
- A stiff, nylon-bristle brush
- At least 1 clean, heavy-pile kitchen towel, preferably 2 or 3
- An oyster knife (see "Before you begin")
- A garbage can for shucked shells
- A platter filled with crushed ice

Not many foods embody the word *succulent* more than a bed of fresh oysters. But unless you're a professional shucker, you may not know the tricks for opening these rocky delicacies.

BEFORE YOU BEGIN

Shop for a good oyster knife at a kitchen-supply store or at your local fish market. The features to look for are a thick, solid handle made of sturdy wood or plastic, a finger guard (essential), and a short, thick blade. Strength and durability will be more important than sharpness or size.

STEP 1
Buy the oysters

Purchase fresh oysters from a reputable fish merchant. If you live near the coast, inquire whether oysters are cultivated locally. Many oyster farmers sell directly to the public, and a trip to an oyster farm makes a pleasant day outing.

Oysters are available seasonally. The old rule for shellfish generally holds: any month (in the English language) containing the letter R is a good month for shellfish. (Note: This rule works only for the Northern Hemisphere.) These are the colder months, and shellfish prefer cold water. More important, warmer waters mean an increase in bacteria levels, which can make shellfish dangerous to eat. Few experiences are harder to forget than eating a bad clam or oyster.

Pick a winner: fresh oysters should be closed tight, and kept either in fresh sea water or on a bed of ice. Never select shellfish that are open! A slack-jawed mollusk has passed its prime and very likely gone bad.

Is it still fresh? Sometimes one or two may be open slightly, especially if they are sitting in water. Test them by pressing the top of the shell near the opening. If the shell closes immediately, it's all right to purchase.

STEP 2
Put them on ice

Store oysters on ice until ready to serve. Cover them with a wet towel, or keep them in a closed container. An ice chest works well.

Feed your oysters. If they must wait for more than a few hours, try the trick that restaurants use. Put down two or three oysters between layers of crushed ice, and sprinkle cornmeal on top. As the ice melts, the cornmeal dissolves, and nutrient-rich water drips down to the oysters. This keeps them alive and fresh.

Check them periodically, and add more ice as necessary. Oysters can keep in this manner for a few days. Watch for spoilers. Remember, once they fall open, they've gone bad and must be discarded. Eating spoiled shellfish can produce severe food poisoning.

STEP 3
Set up your work space

Shucking oysters can be messy work. Set up a place of operations: in the kitchen, behind a bar, or at the end of a table if you are at a picnic. Have everything you'll need on hand.

STEP 4
Clean them off

Caution: Oyster shells have wavy ridges, which are extremely sharp. To avoid slicing up your hands, put on the shucking gloves or hold the oyster in a bar towel as you work.

Grab your first oyster. Use the stiff brush and a bucket of water to clean away any seaweed or sediment that may be on the shell. If other mollusks are attached, knock them off with the handle of the brush.

STEP 5
Unlock the hinge

Look for the hinge of the shell. It should look like an exposed seam that wraps around a smooth corner. Insert the point of the oyster knife into the seam, with the blade parallel to the seam. Gently but firmly rock the knife back and forth. Twist the blade to open the hinge a little more. Repeat this process, gradually inserting the oyster knife until you have cut the hinge completely.

Optional:

- A heavy pair of gloves—thick enough to resist sharp edges, yet not so bulky that you can't move the fingers
- 3 to 5 ounces cornmeal, if you plan to store the oysters longer than a few hours
- Condiments: fresh lemon wedges, coctktail sauce, hot pepper sauce, horseradish, or barbecue sauce

Tips

- If you've eaten a bad oyster at some point in your life, your residual distaste for shellfish doesn't have to last forever. Try one or two when they're available; soon you'll fall under their spell.

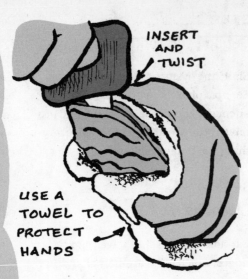

INSERT
AND
TWIST

SLIDE KNIFE
ALONG SHELL AND CUT HERE

USE A
TOWEL TO
PROTECT
HANDS

DON'T
SPILL !

STEP 6

Cut the cord

Now slide the oyster knife along the inside edge between the shell and the meat. As you work at this step, try to keep the oyster level so that the liquid inside doesn't spill out. Some oyster eaters consider this liquid, or liquor, to be the finest part of the oyster-eating experience.

Find the muscle. This looks like a thick cord, and it's what holds the shell tightly together. Use the knife to cut this cord at the point where it adheres to the shell. This can be done in a sort of scraping motion with the knife angled against the shell.

Once the cord has been cut, the two halves of the shell should fall neatly apart. Discard the empty half shell, and place the full one on the serving platter.

STEP 7

Serve with the oyster lover in mind

On behalf of true oyster connoisseurs, don't spill the juice! Set the opened oyster down gently, cradling it in the bed of ice so that the juice doesn't spill out.

Many purists enjoy their oysters neat, which is to say, unadulterated. But generally one should serve them with fresh lemon wedges and a dipping bowl of cocktail sauce. You may also offer hot chili sauce, horseradish, or barbecue sauce on the side. Do keep these condiments separate. Your guests should expect—and desire—to garnish their mouthfuls individually. It's part of the feast.

Learn2 Slice and Dice Onions

Time

3 to 5 minutes per onion

What you'll need

- A sharp kitchen knife, preferably with an 8-inch (20-centimeter) blade
- A cutting board or chopping block

Onions are one of the most versatile ingredients in cooking, appearing in everything from cocktails to appetizers to desserts. Whether you prepare them raw, steamed, sautéed, deep-fried, boiled, or caramelized, you'll have to slice or dice them. Unfortunately, onion preparation causes grief for many a budding chef, even to the point of omitting onions from their cooking.

BEFORE YOU BEGIN

Using anything less than a sharp knife and a clean, level cutting board will slow the learning process considerably. Some folks dedicate a cutting board just for onions and garlic, as their strong flavors can be absorbed into the board and transferred to other ingredients (fruit, for example).

Positioning an onion correctly makes it easier to prepare, and positioning requires that you understand the parts of the onion. The *root end* is the tough, hairy end of the onion. The other side is the *onion top,* and the line between those is called the *axis*. The axis represents the direction that the onion layers grow in; you'll need to cut lengthwise (with the axis) and widthwise (against the axis).

In order to chop or dice, you'll have to slice first, so be sure to read Step 3.

STEP 1
Cut without crying

One of the biggest complaints about onion prep is the fumes from freshly cut onions. These noxious vapors irritate the mucous membranes in your nose and eyes, and the result is discomfort and tearing. Like hiccup remedies, strategies to prevent onion tears are numerous and staunchly defended by their proponents. Here are some to try:

• Cover the onions: As soon as you slice a quantity of onion (say, half of an onion), place the sliced onion in a bowl and cover it with a plate. This prevents an accumulation of fumes and, according to Swiss culinary folklore, prevents the onions from absorbing toxins in the air.

• Wash that dirty onion: Another bit of kitchen wisdom maintains that washing an onion as soon as it's peeled will reduce fumes. As long as you're peeling and washing, peel all the onions at once. Some folks say this helps a lot.

• Chew on a piece of raw onion: If that's too much for you, chew a wooden matchstick (but not too hard).

• Experience: Probably the best remedy is to cook with onions frequently. Your eyes and nose will develop a resistance to the fumes, and they'll cease to bother you at all.

STEP 2
Clean the onion

Slice off the ends. Cut just inside the hairy root end. Keep an eye on that end—you'll need to locate it in Step 3.

Place the onion flat on an end, and slice in half, along the axis. Peel off the dry, papery layers—these can have a harsh flavor and are tough to chew.

Place the onion halves facedown on the cutting board.

STEP 3
Slice

Knowing how to hold the onion is essential to precise onion preparation. This method of holding the onion, known as the bear claw, allows you both to secure the onion so that it doesn't slide around or fall apart as you're cutting and to keep your fingertips out of the way.

For easy reference, let's call the hand that doesn't hold the knife the free hand. Place the fingertips of your free hand on the top of the facedown onion half. Your pinkie and thumb should be next to an onion end.

Push or roll those fingers forward so that the first knuckles are tucked in toward your palm. The second knuckles of your free hand will be roughly square to the cutting board and at the edge of the onion. These knuckles will act as a guide for the knife.

If you want your slices to be ¼ inch thick, pull your knuckles back ¼ inch (.5 centimeter). Try to make your slices uniform; they'll cook more evenly and

Tips

• Raw onions are too strong for some folks, so use them sparingly when cooking for someone for the first time. Cooking onions by any method softens and sweetens their taste considerably.

THE BEAR CLAW

SIDE   TOP

ROLL FINGERS FORWARD...
TUCK
1ST
KNUCKLES   2ND
KNUCKLES
SQUARE
TO BOARD

REST FLAT SIDE OF KNIFE
AGAINST KNUCKLES

SLICE 2/3

FLIP FINAL 1/3 AND
KEEP SLICING

look more appetizing. To maintain straight and even slices, rest the flat side of the knife against your knuckles. Make a slice parallel to the axis and straight down to the cutting board. Drawing the knife toward you slightly as it comes down will also help.

Lift the knife up and away from you slightly, scoot your free-hand knuckles back ¼ inch, and descend again with the knife. This motion of lifting away and drawing toward will create a circular motion that's both rhythmic and efficient.

Continue cutting until you've done two-thirds of the onion. Now flip the onion onto its other side, so that the uncut side is exposed. Using your first finger to support the remaining onion on its underside and using the outside of your thumb as a guide, start cutting.

If this seems like too much at first, here's an easier way that produces decent results. At the halfway point, turn the onion a half turn (180 degrees) so that you're working on the other end. Slice this new, uncut end until you're at the center. Use your

thumb and first two fingers to hold the final slice in place. (Hold them near the top, not at the bottom near the cutting board.)

If even that seems like too much, here's an even simpler way. Slice the onion until it's too small to hold. Then turn the remainder a quarter turn (90 degrees), and slice it. You're slicing the other way now (which some cooks forbid), but it's a good compromise if the other methods seem too precise for you.

Create crescent moons:

This is similar to slicing, but the shape is a little different—thicker at the middle and thinner at the ends. It looks lovely in stir-fry dishes and pasta sauces.

Clean the onion, and cut it in half, along the axis. Rest an onion half on its end, not facedown.

Using a modified bear claw, hold the onion and slice downward, from the center of the onion out to the edge. (Before, you were cutting across the whole length of the onion; with cres-

Tips

- How big or small? In general, the more an onion will be cooked, the larger the pieces should be. Raw onions for salad should be sliced thinly. Stir-fry dishes can handle large crescent-moon shapes. Medium onions can be quartered and added to long-cooking stews, chilis, and roasts, and small onions can be added whole to these dishes.

- That lingering scent: After working with onions, your hands can retain their odor even after scrubbing with soap. Many chefs swear by stainless steel as a scent neutralizer—just rub your hands over some quantity of the metal. You can even buy stainless-steel "bars" designed for just this purpose.

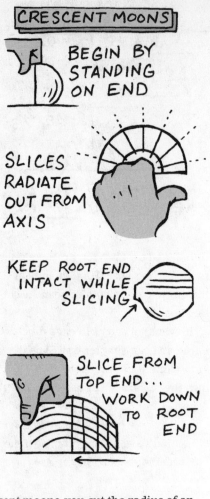

CRESCENT MOONS

BEGIN BY STANDING ON END

SLICES RADIATE OUT FROM AXIS

KEEP ROOT END INTACT WHILE SLICING

SLICE FROM TOP END... WORK DOWN TO ROOT END

cent moons, you cut the radius of an onion half.) As with regular slicing, choose a thickness and stick with it. Move the knife ¼ inch (.5 centimeter) or so with each cut, always keeping the point of the knife at the center of the onion.

STEP 4

Dice

Dicing is the cutting of any vegetable into small squares. Once those squares increase beyond a certain size (it's arbitrary), you're no longer dicing—

you're chopping. So if a recipe calls for chopped onions, just follow the directions for dicing and increase the size of your cuts (that is, make fewer cuts).

The crux of dicing lies in one detail—leaving the root end intact. If you slice through most of the onion and leave the root end intact, the root end will hold the rest of the onion together as it's sliced and diced.

After you've cleaned the onion and sliced it in half, hold it with the bear claw. The width of the slices determines the size of the dices, so some planning may be in order. If you need a large dice, starting out with thin slices won't get you there. Now slice along the axis.

If you're preparing large onions or tiny dices, you may want to make a few cuts through the center of the onion, parallel to the cutting board, after you've sliced it along the axis. Start at the onion top. Hold the knife parallel to the cutting board, and slice down the axis of the facedown onion. To prevent cutting through the root end, saw gently with the knife, rather than shoving it through. One or two of these cuts are usually all that's necessary.

To dice, hold the onion with the bear claw. Starting at the top end, cut across the axis, across the first slices you made. Continue down the onion, tucking the fingers in ¼ inch or so and slicing down.

Once you've finished half an onion, remove the diced pieces and store in a covered bowl. This makes room on the cutting board and keeps the onions fresh.

Learn2 Steam Vegetables

Time

3 to 30 minutes, depending on the vegetable and the quantity

What you'll need

- A steamer—the stainless steel, bamboo, or ceramic variety
- About 1 to 2 cups (about 125 to 250 grams) fresh vegetables suitable for steaming (see Step 1)
- A cutting board or chopping block
- A kitchen knife

Optional:

- Filtered water (see Step 2)
- Pen and paper

Steaming is perhaps the most excellent way to cook vegetables. This gentle cooking method seals in nutrients and flavor by using the steam from a pot of boiling water. The vegetables never touch the water—instead they're suspended over it by a steamer.

BEFORE YOU BEGIN

Nearly foolproof in its operation, a steamer costs a tiny fraction of what a microwave costs, cooks almost as fast with many vegetables, and, according to some nutritional experts, is much healthier to use.

Although some nutritional experts believe ceramic or bamboo steamers are more suitable for steaming, stainless-steel steamers are probably easiest to find; they're also inexpensive, and they work very dependably.

Tips

- The topping: If you'd like a little freshness added to the steamed vegetables, and extra vitamin C to boot, then garnish your plate with fresh chopped parsley or green onions. Or serve with a little lemon, olive oil, and freshly ground black pepper. If you'd like some extra protein, chopped nuts and seeds like almonds, sunflower, and sesame are superb for flavor and complete nutrition. Seeds can be lightly roasted in a frying pan for a few minutes for extra flavor. Roasting nuts takes a little longer: about 10 to 15 minutes on a baking sheet in a 350°F oven (about 165°C).

STEP 1

Select and prepare the vegetables

Virtually any vegetable can be steamed. Try spinach, summer squash such as sunburst or zucchini, broccoli, bok choy, cauliflower, cabbage, brussels sprouts, asparagus, kale, collard greens, mushrooms, onions, beets, turnips, potatoes, and sweet potatoes. Bean sprouts are not actually vegetables, but they're a great addition. Mung bean sprouts are the most common choice.

Very fresh vegetables (say, from a farmer's market) are great when steamed whole: try string beans, small summer squash, and small potatoes. And here's a great way to prepare whole spinach and bok choy leaves or even small cabbage leaves: roll them up from stem to tip, place them on their sides, and steam them in that position. Other vegetables, such as beets, yams, large potatoes, and brussels sprouts require slicing or dicing in order to have them cook in a reasonable length of time. Chop all of the vegetables beforehand, and (ideally) have different types of vegetables on separate plates or in small bowls—this makes them easier to work with.

Combinations:

Sometimes one vegetable is appropriate for a meal; other meals call out for a variety of vegetables steamed together. Try out these combinations, but be sure to add them in the order that they're presented: some vegetables require longer cooking times and hence need to be added first.

- Squash cut into rounds / shiitake mushrooms (fresh, or presoaked if dried) / whole or chopped spinach
- Carrots cut diagonally / fresh peas
- Shredded cabbage / grated carrots / mung bean sprouts
- Onions and summer squash, diced / spinach, bok choy, or chard cut into 1-inch squares
- Turnips, diced / sweet potatoes, cut into half-moons / fresh parsley, finely chopped
- Broccoli and cauliflower

STEP 2

Steam

If you can boil water, then you can steam vegetables—that's the beauty of this technique. One concern, however, may be the quality of the tap water in your home. Many municipal water supplies have been contaminated by chemical runoff from industry and conventional farming. If it's an option for you, cook it safely—steam the vegetables with filtered or spring water.

Measure the water. Put just enough water in the bottom of the pot so that it doesn't touch or boil through the base of the steamer. Cover the pot. Over high heat, bring the water to a boil. Place the vegetables in the steamer, and lower the steamer into the pot. Some folks leave the stove on high, but most prefer to turn down the heat until the water's at a low boil—there should be bubbles rising from the bot-

Is it ready yet?

	LEAFY GREENS	GREEN BEANS	ROOTS & TUBERS
TIME	3 MIN.	8-10 MIN.	30 MIN.
TEST	BRIGHT GREEN COLOR	TASTE TEST	INSERT FORK

Tips

- Don't peek! If you peek more than once or twice, you'll release all of the steam and hamper the cooking process.
- How about a quickie? A quick meal, that is. If you have leftover rice or other grains in the refrigerator, place it in the steamer with your other ingredients. Depending on the amount, the rice will be ready in 5 or 10 minutes, along with the rest of your meal.

tom of the pot, and you should hear a quiet rumbling sound. Replace the cover, and note the time that you put the vegetables in.

The general timing rule is to cook vegetables until they're crisp. Overcooking reduces their color, flavor, and nutritional value. Take them out when they're almost done. As they sit for a minute or two on the serving plate, they'll finish cooking and will arrive on your plate at the peak of perfection. Here are some timing suggestions:

- For leafy greens, wait 3 minutes or so, and watch their color. They'll change to a fresh, bright green, which indicates they're done. You might be surprised how quickly vegetables like spinach will cook.

- For green beans, try 8 or 10 minutes. Have a taste test, though—8 minutes will seem overcooked for some people; 10 will seem undercooked for

others. Here's your chance to use the pen and paper: note the vegetable and the amount of steaming time needed for vegetables prepared to your taste.

- For roots and tubers like potatoes, beets, or yams, figure on 30 minutes. You can also try the fork test: a fork inserted into the root should slide in easily. You may have to add a little boiling water if all of the original water has boiled off into steam.

When the vegetables are done, pull the steamer out of the pot or pour the contents into a colander. Trying to remove the vegetables with the steamer still in the pot often results in steamed fingers. Arrange on a warm serving plate, and garnish as desired. Enjoy!

Learn**2** Make a Kite

Time

10 minutes to an hour to assemble, depending on the kite and your skills

What you'll need

For the first kite:
- 3 plastic straws
- Transparent tape
- Tissue paper
- Crepe-paper streamers or a plastic garbage bag
- String
- Scissors
- White glue (optional)

Kite flying is a dedicated pursuit these days, an ecofriendly sport that's destined to pop up on the sports channels soon. Sponsored teams compete worldwide with dual-line, Kevlar-tethered, ripstop nylon technodreams that cost more than most people make in a week. But there's another world out there, in which kites are made from simple materials (often found) and tethered with cheap cotton string. Fortunately it's still possible to make an inexpensive kite that's fun to fly and simple to build. Get on out there and have some fun!

BEFORE YOU BEGIN

The two kites shown here each have three parts. First, there's the kite fabric, made of paper or plastic tarp, which catches the wind. The frame, made of plastic straws or wooden dowels, gives the kite its shape. And then there's the bridle, which connects the kite to the main control line (the string that you hold on to the kite with).

The first kite is quite simple, while the other requires a little more care to build. But the main difference between the two is the quality of the materials. These can be found in your local hardware store or possibly around your house. Both can be assembled inexpensively and easily.

Method 1
The paper-and-straw kite

This small, simple kite costs almost nothing to build.

STEP 1

Make the frame

You'll create an H-shaped frame, onto which you'll glue or tape some paper.

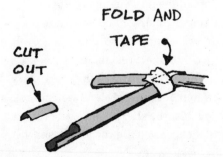

CUT OUT

FOLD AND TAPE

On each end of a straw, carefully cut 1-inch notches down the center. Now cut halfway across the straw at the bottom of each vertical cut. Half of the straw falls away, and the other half remains. The result is a straw with notched ends. This will be the center bar of the H-shaped frame.

Wrap the notched ends around the vertical midpoints of the other two straws. Secure these connections with tape.

Run the string through all four open ends of the straws. This will create a square. Tie an overhand knot and then a second one on top of the first one. Cut the string so that it's taut yet doesn't bend the straws.

STEP 2

Attach the paper and tails

Cut 1-inch squares out of the corners of a 10- by 12-inch (25- by 30-centimeter) piece of tissue paper. Place the large piece under the frame.

Fold the ends of the paper back over the straws and string. Secure the

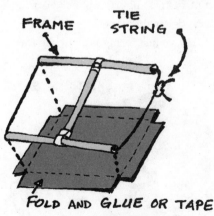

FRAME

TIE STRING

FOLD AND GLUE OR TAPE TO FRAME

For the second kite:

- A disposable plastic tarp, 2 to 4 millimeters thick, preferably in a cheerful color (available at a hardware store)
- 3 wooden dowels, ⅛ inch thick and 3 feet long
- A roll of 2-inch clear-plastic packaging tape
- Cloth tape
- A piece of 6- or 8-pound-test monofilament fishing line, 6 feet long
- A fishing swivel
- A small grommet tool and 2 grommets
- A yardstick
- A single-edged razor blade
- A permanent marker

Key words

Bridle: The loop of string that connects the frame to the main control line.

Overhand knot: You're probably familiar with this knot. It's how you tie your shoelaces up to where you make the loops. A double overhand knot is that first step repeated on top of itself. The result is a fairly secure, difficult-to-untie knot.

paper with tape or glue. The paper should be taut without bending the straws.

Cut the garbage bag or the crepe paper to make two tails, each one 3 feet long. Tie them to two corners of the kite, where the two vertical straw ends stick out.

STEP 3
Make the string bridle

Cut two small holes in the paper, just below the point where the ends of the center straw connect the two vertical straws.

Cut a piece of string about 10 inches (25 centimeters) long. Thread it through the hole closest to the tails. Loop it around the center straw and back through the same hole in the paper. Tie a double overhand knot to secure the string to the straw.

Taking the end of the main control line, feed it through the other hole and tie it to the straw on that side.

Finally, tightly tie the loose end of the first piece of string to the main control line, about 3 inches (8 centimeters) below the paper.

You've just formed the bridle for

your kite. The bridle can be adjusted by sliding the knot up and down where it's attached to the main control line. Experiment a little—by adjusting the knot in different winds.

Method 2
The classic Scott sled kite

The Scott sled is another simple kite but more durable and convenient to transport. It flies well in very light breezes, as long as the line is kept taut. Find a spacious, clean, well-lighted workplace that you can safely make cuts on (not on wood floors or rugs).

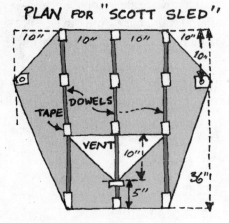

PLAN FOR "SCOTT SLED"

STEP 1
Cut the fabric to size

Spread the tarp out on the floor. Using the marker and yardstick, draw a 40-inch by 36-inch (102- by 92-centimeter) rectangle.

On the rectangle's long sides, mark off four 10-inch (25-centimeter) sections. On the short sides, make a mark 10 inches from the corners as shown in the diagram.

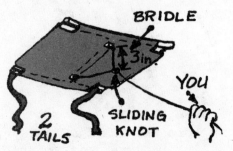

BRIDLE

3 in.

YOU

2 TAILS

SLIDING KNOT

Cut out the large rectangle with the razor blade, using the yardstick. Using the 10-inch marks as guides, cut off the corners of the rectangle. These cuts create the outline of the kite fabric. Take a look at the diagram before you start slashing away.

Use the blade and yardstick to cut out a triangular vent. Refer to the diagram for the correct location. This creates the final shape of the kite.

STEP 2

Attach the frame

This frame will make the kite fabric stiff in one direction, flexible in the other.

Lay the three wooden dowels vertically on the plastic surface 10 inches (25 centimeters) apart.

Cut small, equal-sized sections of the plastic packing tape to fix the ends of the dowels to the edges of the kite fabric. Wrapping the tape over the edge will create a strong sleeve where the end of the dowel can reside securely.

Attach the dowels to the rest of the kite fabric with more small sections of packing tape. Refer to the diagram to ensure correct placement. Don't miss the bottom of the triangular vent— that's the corner of the triangle with a 90-degree, or right, angle.

STEP 3

Attach the bridle

The bridle attaches to the outermost edges of the kite fabric (where the cor-

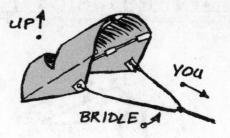

ner cuts were made). But first you need to reinforce the points where it will be attached.

Put squares of cloth tape on both of the outermost edges of the kite fabric. Consult the diagram for optimum placement. Trim the tape to match the contour of the plastic edge.

Use the small grommet tool to place a grommet ½ inch (1.3 centimeters) in from edge of the fabric, where it forms the point on both side flaps.

Fold the piece of fishing line in half to find the center. Mark the spot. At the center point tie the swivel into the line with an overhand knot.

Thread each end of the fishing line through one of the grommets. Loop this end around to the front and tie it off. Include the side of the fabric. Your bridle is now formed, and your kite is finished!

To fly the kite, attach your kite line to the swivel in the middle of the bridle, and go find some wind.

Tips

- When making cuts into the kite fabric, remember the advice of the good carpenter: measure twice, cut once.
- When making cuts, protect the work surface by placing collapsed cardboard boxes or layers of newspaper under the kite fabric.

Learn**2** Make Basic Origami

Time

Less than 10 minutes to fold a bird; less than 5 minutes to fold a cup; more complicated projects can take an hour or more.

What you'll need

- 5 to 6 squares of origami paper, each measuring between 6 and 8 inches (15 to 20 centimeters) across, or pages from magazines, or wrapping paper; if you want your cup to work more than once, aluminum foil or waxed paper
- A pencil
- A hard, smooth surface—a table, a desk, or, if you want to work on the sofa, a large, hardcover book to place on your lap.

Origami (pronounced "or-i-*ga*-me") is the Japanese art of paper folding. Learn it and you'll be able to make all kinds of paper decorations—figures of birds that you can display on a shelf, hang on a mobile, or tuck into a birthday card, for example, as a small gift. To start you off on a long and satisfying learning journey, this 2torial takes you through two relatively easy projects that will result in one decorative item and one useful item.

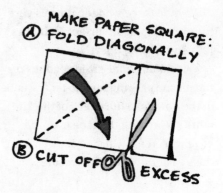

MAKE PAPER SQUARE:
Ⓐ FOLD DIAGONALLY
Ⓑ CUT OFF Ⓒ Ⓓ EXCESS

BEFORE YOU BEGIN

You may want to buy special origami paper at craft stores. It can be printed with colorful designs, or solid in color. You can also cut your own squares, if you're very careful to measure and cut precisely. If you're feeling reckless, don't measure at all. Just take a clean-edged, rectangular sheet of paper, fold one corner over to the opposite edge, and cut along the resulting square edge. See the diagram at left for more details. If you do choose to make your own, use something light, like wrapping paper or magazine pages. You'll find it easier to follow origami diagrams if your paper's front and back do not match.

Project 1
Create a bird

A crane is probably the most famous of all origami figures. In Japanese culture, the crane is a powerful symbol, and people may fold a thousand of these birds for someone they wish well. However, to fold a crane takes more than thirty steps—it's hardly the place to begin origami. The bird figure presented below takes far fewer steps but is still completely satisfying to make. When it's done, you'll have a powerfully abstracted form, distilled into a beak and a neck, wings and a tail.

STEP 1
Make the wings

Begin by clearing a place to work. If you've washed the working surface, make sure it's thoroughly dry. Starting off with soggy origami paper would be inauspicious.

Place your paper so that the prettiest side faces down. (This will give your bird a plain body but fancy head, neck, and wings.) You'll be doing mountain folds and valley folds (see "Key words").

Mountain-fold your square along a

diagonal by folding to create a peak, with the fold facing you; then unfold it, leaving it flat. The plain side should still face up. Now orient the square as a diamond, with the crease line running from top to bottom. Use a pencil to label very lightly the left corner as A. Label the right corner as B.

Fold corners A and B so they meet in the center of your diamond, bringing the bottom edges of the diamond into a flush line with the center crease. Crease these folds with a fingernail or a ruler, checking to make sure the new corner you form at the top remains neat. You can label that corner C, if you like.

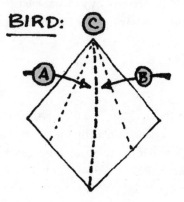

Tips

- Photocopy these instructions, including the images that accompany them. Check off each step as you complete it—this way, if you're interrupted, you'll know right where to pick up.
- A good fold is a clean fold. When you begin a fold, check to make sure that the edges or corners you're bringing together will line up exactly. You don't want them to overlap or fail to meet. Check this alignment of edges before you press down on the paper. Once you've made a good fold, crease it with your thumbnail, a finger, or a ruler, whatever you find easiest, to make it really sharp.

STEP 2
Make the bird's neck and head

At this point the paper should have a kite shape—broad at one end and narrowing toward the tail.

Locate the new top corner (C, where you'd attach the kite's tail), and fold it down to the spot where the corners A and B now meet. This fold makes the bird's neck.

Fold corner C back up a little bit, where the narrow end used to be. Don't worry about exactly how far you fold it. This fold makes the bird's head. Its beak points up, toward where the corner C used to be.

STEP 3
Help the bird sit up

Picture that you're giving the bird a base to sit on.

Mountain-fold the bird in half along the crease you made in Step 1. (Make sure all previous folds remain intact.) Turn the bird in your hand so that the neck and head are upright and face to your left-hand side. Spread the bottom edges away from each other, which will make the bird sit up.

STEP 4
Shape the neck and head

Pull the beak up, and flatten the back of the head. Squeezing the back of the head will form new angular creases. Your beak should now point up toward the sky.

Pull the neck out from the body so

the beak points forward. Pinch together the base of neck to make new creases, which will hold the neck in place.

Now sit back and admire your handiwork.

Project 2
Make a cup

A few origami figures are practical. This cup is the perfect example. Again, if you want it to work more than once, make it out of foil or waxed paper.

STEP 1
Perform the opening maneuver

If your paper has two distinct sides, place it so that the pretty side is up. Orient the square of paper as a diamond, lightly labeling the top corner A and the bottom corner B.

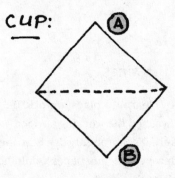

Valley-fold your paper, so that corner B comes up to meet corner A. You now have a triangle. The fold, which you can label edge C, should now be flat on the table and near you. Label the triangle's bottom left corner D. Label its bottom right corner E.

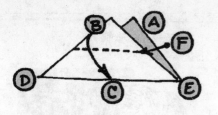

Fold down corner B, but not corner A (A lies right under B). Make corner B line up exactly with edge C. Now unfold the corner B fold (what you just did). On the right side of the triangle, mark the end of the crease you just made as point F.

STEP 2

Create the cup

This move should follow easily from the above.

Fold corner D (the bottom left corner), so that it touches point F. Mark the spot directly across from point F as point G.

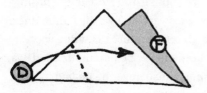

Now fold corner E (bottom right) so that it touches point G.

Fold your old friend, corner B, down in front. Fold corner A down in back.

Your cup is done. The front half of the cup should be thicker than the back.

Pour water into your cup, and observe! There's no open edge for it to leak out of.

Tips

- If you get confused while you're working, don't just throw the piece of paper away. Step away from your project for a moment, and take a few deep breaths. (Really, give this a try!) Then come back and look at the instructions again. Remember that most Japanese students learn origami by watching a master, not from printed instructions.

- When your project's complete, sit back and take a good look at it. If you made a mistake as you were going along and you find you don't like the looks of a bad fold, you might want to start all over again and produce another, perfect piece. Keep your first try for reference.

Learn**2** Make Candles

Time

For the simplest candle (one color) figure about 20 to 30 minutes, including heating the wax; the most complicated candles (such as a striped rainbow candle) can take much longer, with a day in between colors to wait for them to harden—at least 1 hour total

What you'll need

- At least 1 pound (500 grams) paraffin (available in many grocery and craft stores) or 1 pound (500 grams) of old candle stubs, or a combination
- A medium-sized cooking pot (3 to 4 quarts/liters)
- An empty coffee can or stewed-tomato can
- An old spoon or a clean, smooth stick

What a little candlelight can do! There's nothing like softly flickering candles to create a tranquil atmosphere, whether you're having a dinner party for eight, tea for two, or some quiet time by yourself. Although store-bought candles are expensive, you can make your own with minimal expense. It's an opportunity to express yourself creatively, and you get a useful and gratifying product at the end. Just imagine basking in the glow of a candle you made yourself.

BEFORE YOU BEGIN

It's a good idea to cover your work area with newspaper or waxed paper—dried wax can be difficult to remove from some surfaces. And don't plan on pouring wax over your kitchen sink—if you spill it, it'll stop up the drain.

Be aware that wax is flammable at high temperatures. Heating wax should never be left unattended. Wax should also never be heated to the point that it sputters or smokes. If it should catch fire, cover it with a lid and turn off the stove. Never pour water on a wax fire.

Method 1
Make regular or scented candles

STEP 1
Prepare a mold

Professionals use precise, expensive molds made from very durable materials, but you don't have to. You can create a mold with a variety of disposable food or beverage containers that you can reuse and give a new purpose. Here are a few guidelines:

• Make sure the mold has a mouth that's wider than the base so your candle can slide out easily.

• Oil the inside of the mold with vegetable oil. This will allow for easy removal; you don't want to have to gouge out your new creation.

• Don't use soup cans; they have ridges that will prevent the removal of the finished candle.

STEP 2
Set up your double boiler

Wax should never be heated directly in a pot; always heat it indirectly with a store-bought double boiler or a double boiler improvised in the kitchen. Since wax can be difficult to remove from pots, you'll probably want to improvise a double boiler with a coffee can in a pot of water.

Fill a medium-sized pot with a couple of inches of water, and put it on the stove over a high heat. While it is heating, place a clean coffee can in the water. There should always be some water in the pot, but not so much that it bounces the can around. Eventually the combined weight of the can and the wax will be heavy enough to keep the can from bobbing.

STEP 3
Melt the paraffin

While the water is warming up, you can start placing the wax in the coffee can. If you prefer, you may use old candles or a combination of paraffin and old candles.

To measure the wax: figure ¼ pound of wax per orange-juice container.

Cut up the paraffin into small chunks, and place it in the can. If you're using old candles, choose colors that will mix well. You'll also want to clip off any charred wick ends.

Stir with an old spoon or stick. If there are any old candles in the mix, take a fork and pull out any old wicks that have been freed from the old candles.

• Vegetable oil (1 teaspoon per mold)
• A selection of clean, sturdy containers (a milk carton, 12-ounce frozen orange-juice concentrate container, drinking glass, gelatin mold—be creative)
• Predipped wicks (available at craft stores) or thick cotton string to make your own wicks
• A pencil

Optional:
• Wax crayons in colors that you like
• Perfume or fragrant oil (such as sandalwood, patchouli, or jasmine)
• An ice pick (or a 12-inch length of thick metal wire)
• A 1½- or 2-gallon bucket or a large bowl
• Sand, enough to almost fill the bucket or bowl

Tips

- If you spill wax, the best thing to do is wait for it to harden. Then apply an ice cube to the wax, and chip it off.
- Make a base for any candle by pouring ½ inch (1 or 2 centimeters) of wax into a round or rectangular mold. When the wax has cooled but not completely hardened, remove it from the mold and place it on waxed paper. Press a completely solidified candle into the base, and leave it alone for an hour.
- If you mar the surface of the candle during the unmolding stage, you can redip the candle in melted wax. You'll have a nice smooth coat to cover up any nasty marks.

STEP 4
Color the wax (optional)

Crayons are the best way to color candles. One crayon per ¼ pound of wax provides a deep, rich color. Mix different-colored crayons, and see what you can come up with. Combining half of a white crayon with half of a colored crayon makes a softer color. Break the crayons into small pieces.

When the wax is nearly melted, drop the crayons into the coffee can. Stir to mix the color thoroughly.

STEP 5
Make your wicks (optional)

Cut thick cotton string about 3 inches longer than your mold will require.

When the wax is melted, dip the cotton string in wax. Hang your wicks from a clothesline, or place them on waxed paper, being sure to lay them out in a straight line so you'll have nice straight wicks when you need them later.

When you make your own wicks, you have the option of scenting the wicks rather than the candles. Before dipping the string in wax, soak it in a fragrance or perfume.

STEP 6
Pour the wax

Remove the can from the boiling water. You'll want to use a potholder or a kitchen cloth for this. Let the wax cool for a minute or two before pouring it into the mold. Note: If you want a scented candle, now is the time to add the scent. Mix the perfume or fragrant oils into the cooling wax, and remember to experiment with the amount of fragrance you prefer. Tilt the mold slightly, toward the can. This will improve the chances of neat, spill-free transfer.

Pour the wax slowly into the mold. Leave a little space at the top edge—it'll make candle removal easier.

STEP 7
Insert the wick

Lay your wick along the length of the mold. Add an extra ¾ inch of string for the protruding section of wick, plus an extra inch or two to wrap around the pencil.

Insert the wick into the center of the mold. Notice the amount of wick that remains outside the mold. If you have an extra 5 inches, the wick hasn't reached the base of the candle.

Wrap the end of the wick around the pencil, and lay the pencil across the top of the mold to hold the wick in place while the wax hardens.

Most candles need at least a day before you remove them from the mold. Even though your candle may look hardened, the wax inside is probably still not solid. Don't rush the cooling process, or your fine efforts will be undone.

STEP 8
Remove the candle from the mold

Be patient while removing your candle, or it might be damaged by your hastiness.

For paper molds such as a toilet-paper core or a milk carton, simply tear the paper away from the candle. For molds of other materials, try turning the mold upside down and tapping the bottom. If the candle doesn't slide out, carefully insert a knife between the candle and the mold. Jiggle the knife into that space, prying very slightly against the side of the mold. If it still won't slip out, insert the knife into the opposite side of the mold and do some more jiggling.

If your candle still won't budge, immerse the mold in very hot water for a few seconds. This will slightly melt the outside of the candle and allow it to slide out.

Method 2
Make textured candles

This technique uses sand as a mold, leaving you some freedom to create a mold of your own design. And removing a candle from this mold couldn't be easier.

STEP 1
Make the mold

Fill a bucket three-quarters full with clean sand.

Dig in the sand to create an interesting shape. You can make some very lovely rounded candles using this method.

STEP 2
Melt the wax

Melt and color the wax as described in Method 1, steps 3 and 4.

STEP 3
Pour the wax

Slowly, carefully, pour the melted wax into the hole in the sand. The sand will stick to the outside of the wax, making an interesting texture.

STEP 4
Remove the candle from the mold

Once the wax is hardened, simply lift it out of the sand. Heat an ice pick or a length of straight, thick wire—a straightened wire hanger might work well here—over an open flame from a stove or another candle. If you're using a wire, be sure to wrap the end with a cloth or hold it with a pot holder so you don't get burned.

Insert the heated pick or wire through the body of the candle. If it cools and stops melting the candle, simply reheat it and continue melting through the candle.

STEP 5
Insert the wick

Insert the wick into the hole you've just created.

Pour a small amount of melted wax on the top of the candle to secure the wick if it seems loose. Once the candle is lit, any gaps between the wick and the body of the candle will be filled in with melting wax.

Method 3
Make rainbow candles

Rainbow-striped candles take more time, but if you can make a solid-colored candle, you can make a rainbow candle. You simply pour small amounts of wax, layer upon layer, with each layer a different color of the rainbow. Rainbow candles make beautiful gifts. Plan the colors you're going to use and decide how many stripes you want to create.

STEP 1
Make the first layer

Follow Method 1 for your first, bottom color. After you have poured the colored wax into the mold of your choice, insert the wick using the technique described in Method 1.

STEP 2
Make the subsequent layers

Wait until the first layer of wax is completely hardened. Don't rush this pro-cess. You might want to make rainbow candles an ongoing process, pouring a layer every time you are making other candles.

Melt and color your next bit of wax. Let it cool down for a few minutes before pouring it into the mold. If you pour really hot wax on top of an earlier layer, it might melt the previous color, resulting in a mix of colors. This may or may not be desirable, depending on your taste. Continue adding colors until your candle is complete.

Learn**2** Make Homemade Paper

Time

About 1 hour to assemble and process the materials; an afternoon (3+ hours) to dry

What you'll need

- Scrap paper: figure 1 cup (¼ liter) of scraps, loosely packed, per sheet of paper
- A blender
- A section of window screen: slightly larger than the size of paper you'd like to make; metal-wire is best, although synthetic screens will also work
- A vat or tub large enough to accommodate the screen, three-fourths full of clean water: it should be at least 1 foot (30 centimeters) deep and the screen should fit in it horizontally, with room around the

Bring the paper chase home to roost. Making your own paper is fun, easy, and a delightful project for the weekends. Homemade paper lends a distinctive personal touch to any project, from greeting cards to a personal note or letter. And it's much easier than it sounds once you draw off a page or two.

BEFORE YOU BEGIN

The quality of paper is largely based on the fibers used. Look around your home for attractive scraps you've been saving. Many different colors can be mixed, but bear in mind what the paper will be used for. Keep the colors relatively uniform and light in hue if it'll be used for writing. A small amount of glossy, bright paper can be added to otherwise bland fibers to give a speckled effect.

Use scrap paper that contains a minimum of writing and printed ink. These could tint the paper unevenly— or worse, an unintended memo from the past could find its way back to the surface.

edges for your fingers

- 2 pieces of wool felt, slightly larger than the size of paper you'd like to make (available at fabric stores—buy the thickest you can find)
- A rolling pin
- A laundry line and clothespins (spring-loaded pins work best)

Optional:

- Small flowers, leaves, feathers, or decorative threads
- White glue
- A hand press: this uses a metal plate that is lowered by a screw mechanism to compress whatever's beneath it
- An old-fashioned laundry machine with rollers and a bucket
- Lint from a clothes-dryer lint trap

STEP 1

Find the fibers

The paper that you'll make is essentially a mesh of plant fibers pressed together to make a strong flat surface. The ingredients you choose will determine the look and quality of the paper.

Gather enough fiber to create a few sheets of paper. This need only be a cupful (¼ liter) of paper scraps, loosely packed, per standard sheet. It's good to have extra raw material on hand in order to experiment with thickness and quality. Expect to lose the equivalent of a page or two of material in the process.

Use old paper that has interesting texture. Tear a piece of it. Does it rip cleanly or leave a jagged edge? The harder to tear, the longer the fibers are in the paper. Long fibers create strong

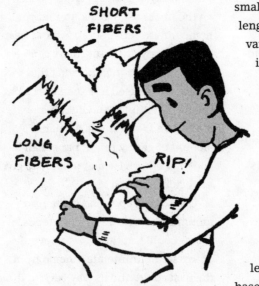

SHORT FIBERS

LONG FIBERS

RIP!

paper. Short fibers create smooth texture. Interesting yet durable paper balances these two ingredients.

Lint from a clothes-dryer lint trap is ideal paper fodder. Small flowers and leaves, bits of foil (from leftover holiday paper and champagne bottles), and colored threads also add a special touch. Grab anything you can shred and that floats. But use these specialty items sparingly; otherwise the page won't hold together.

STEP 2

Let 'er rip!

Once you've gathered enough scraps to make paper, tear them up into pieces about 1 inch (2 centimeters) square. If you're using different kinds of paper, it's a good idea to separate them into different piles.

Thread, metallic foils, and other small decorations should be cut to length using scissors. Be creative— vary the sizes from ⅛ inch to 2 inches (3 millimeters to 5 centimeters). A few long threads are interesting; too many and it looks like spaghetti. Foils and bright colors are better in small pieces less than ¼ inch (5 millimeters) across. Set any of these decorative fibers aside for now. Don't shred them in the blender.

Sort your scraps by fiber length and color, and identify the base color—the pile of scraps that most resembles the color you want the paper to be.

STEP 3

Cut the screen

Ordinary window screen works great for making paper. It should be free of dents and curves; otherwise the paper will come out in exactly the same shape. Rust-free wire screen works the best. Synthetic screen should be used with caution; it's less rigid, which can cause problems later in the process. Synthetic screen may be serviceable if used with a frame, as described below.

Cut the screen the same size as the sheets you want to make, slightly larger if you want to make a frame for the screen. If you intend to make lots of paper the same size, consider building a frame around your screen. In this case allow 2 extra inches in each direction before cutting the screen. For example, if you want to make a frame for 8- by 10-inch paper, then cut a screen 10 by 12 inches large.

Optional: Build a frame using lengths of wood ½ inch wide by 1 inch thick, or 1 inch square. You don't have to get fancy—just be sure that the inside of the frame is the same size as the paper you want to make, and that the corners are square and not too wobbly. Set your screen down on top of the frame evenly, then nail or staple it in place. You want the screen attached snugly to the frame, without any big gaps between them.

STEP 4

Blend it to bits

Now a dash of paper theory. In order to turn old paper into new paper, you've got to change it to a mushier state. Blenders accomplish this nicely, and the result is the pulp.

Fill a blender about three-fourths full with clean water. Add a handful of scraps from your base-color pile. Cover the top, and blend on medium-high for a few seconds. The water will start to look like very watery oatmeal.

Add various scraps one by one, and give a short blast with the blender each time. You want to put shorter fibers in first, then gradually add scraps of longer fibers. Otherwise all the fibers will end up about the same length—short. Add any special items (including threads) last. Don't turn the blender on at this point, as it may ruin these items or wreck the blender or both.

Key words

Fiber: Particles of variable length that hold paper together and determine texture. Long fibers make strong paper, while short fibers create smooth texture.

Sizing: Any variation of glues, bleaches, and chemical additives used to make paper. These additives help bond paper fibers and improve texture and quality.

Pulp: A solution of fibers, sizing, and decorative additions that make up a piece of paper.

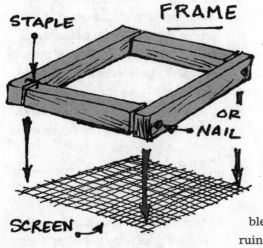

STAPLE   FRAME

OR NAIL

SCREEN

Tips

- This process works great for making paper sculpture or masks. Bend a section of metal screen into the shape you desire. Then run it through the paper tub in one direction, so that the paper pulp sticks to the outside of the form. Try to coat the form evenly with pulp. Remove the form from the water when the coating looks thick enough, hold it above the tub, and let the excess water drain off. Then set it aside in a warm dry place to dry thoroughly. A sunny windowsill is perfect. When the paper is completely dry, remove it carefully from the form by gently bending the form from behind and peeling off the paper.

Don't make a pulp more than one part scraps to four parts water—that is, don't fill the blender more than three-quarters of the way. If you're making large volumes, pour out the finished pulp mix and start again.

STEP 5
Hit the tub

In this step you'll use a tub of water to put the pulp into a liquid suspension. This will ensure even distribution of pulp onto the screen. By making one sheet at a time you can adjust the sizing or pulp-to-water ratio, as you see how each sheet comes out. You may want to test the screen with a little pulp, to check that the water can run through the screen while retaining the pulp.

Fill a large tub with clean water. Pour the pulp (the fiber and water mixture) into the tub, and swirl it around. The pulp should be distributed evenly throughout the water before you start dipping. If the mixture sits for a while before you're ready, some settling will occur. Just give it another swirl with your hands when ready.

If you're using large amounts of lint or vegetable parts (including wood-pulp paper), add a few drops of white glue to the tub, and mix it in thoroughly. Substitute a tablespoon of cornstarch if you don't have any glue. This sticky, binding substance is called sizing.

Hold the screen with the frame on top. Dip it into the tub at an angle until it's fully immersed, then move the screen back and forth until the pulp is evenly dispersed in the water and across the surface of the screen. Finish by pulling the frame straight up out of the tub.

You should have collected enough pulp on the frame to make one sheet of paper—the pulp should fill the screen to the inner edges of the frame. The water from the tub will run through the screen, depositing the pulp on top of it. Hold the frame above the tub until only a few drops of water remain on the screen. If the paper looks too thin, add more pulp to the water in the tub, swirl, and dip the screen again. Too thick? Remove some pulp from the tub, dip the screen, and collect a screenful of pulp. You can then remove the pulp from the screen by rolling it off with your fingers.

If you're not using a frame, hold the screen about 4 inches below the surface of the tub. Agitate the water by moving the screen back and forth until the pulp is evenly dispersed in the water and across the surface of the screen. Draw the screen slowly and evenly up out of the tub. Hold it above the tub, and allow the water to drain. Take care to keep the screen taut, or the pulp may "puddle" in the middle, which will produce lumpy paper.

STEP 6
Squeeze out the water

There are two actions happening here: the force applied by the roller squeezes out the water from the paper, and absorbent materials above and beneath the paper prevent the paper from reabsorbing the water.

On a flat tabletop, lay down a piece of wool felt larger than the sheet you're making. Wool felt is ideal because water runs right through it and it's strong enough to sustain the pressure of the hand press. Several felts, a stack of old newspapers, or even towels (nonterry) can be placed underneath the felt to help absorb water.

Turn the frame over on top of the felt. The freshly drawn pulp should drop out easily. If it sticks, then gently tap the frame onto the felt.

Lay another felt on top of the pulp. Cover with another sheet of felt (or newspapers or towels). With a rolling pin, press down on the pile to squeeze out the extra water. This will also bind the pulp fibers together. Start at one end, and roll firmly and evenly across the pile. Do this several times to get out as much water as possible and to press the fibers together.

The hand-press option: A small hand press is great for squeezing out the paper. Turn the paper out on a large sheet of wool felt, and cover with another sheet of felt as described above. Now squeeze the felt sandwich with the press.

The wringer-machine option: If you have an old-fashioned washing machine, assemble the felt-pulp sandwich as described for the hand press, and feed the felt sandwich through the rollers.

STEP 7

Hang it out to dry

Now carefully remove the top layer of felt and any other absorbent materials from the pulp. It should now hold together as an honest-to-goodness sheet of paper.

Carefully take up two corners of the paper by rolling them back (just a ½ inch/1 centimeter or so) with your fingers. Hold a corner with each hand, and gently peel the sheet off the bottom felt.

Clip the fresh sheet onto a laundry line with ordinary clothespins to dry. Anyplace that's warm and dry will be fine—wherever you would hang laundry. Avoid areas that are damp (mold might grow on the paper), dusty (wet paper will collect any dust in the air), or windy (your paper could be blown off the line). Drying time is about 3 hours, more if the air is humid or if there is little sun.

Tips

- Does the paper fall apart when you pick it up? Add some more sizing (glue or starch) to the tub, and mix it in thoroughly. Then proceed as before, and be sure to go firmly with the roller or press to bind the fibers together.
- Avoid placing fresh sheets of paper next to newsprint. The inks used in making newspapers will transfer to the surface of your nice clean sheet. Wool felt is ideal. If this paper-maker's dream is not available, try using a couple of hand towels. Avoid those made of terry (piled) fabric, as fresh paper will stick to them. Any pronounced pattern on the towels will be pressed onto the paper.

Learn**2** Make Paper Airplanes

Time

5 minutes to fold
the airplane, 20
minutes or more to
fly the models and
experiment with
their design

What you'll need

- A few unwrinkled
  sheets of standard
  8½- by 11-inch or
  A4 (210- by 297-
  millimeter) paper
- A hard, smooth
  surface such as a
  desktop
- A ruler (optional)

This 2torial honors and improves that time-honored tradition of basic aeronautics, the paper airplane. Here are two great methods of transforming a page of standard stationery into flight-worthy designs.

BEFORE YOU BEGIN

Paper dimensions will be more important than size. This 2torial will assume you're using 8½- by 11-inch paper, but satisfactory results can be obtained using either smaller or larger sheets. Thickness should be taken into account as well. Smaller sheets of paper can be thinner without compromising performance. Larger sheets should be thicker in order to hold a stiff-enough surface to fly. A large, very thin sheet of paper will produce a floppy model.

For the purposes of this 2torial, let's fold the paper either the long way (the fold extends to the short edges) or the short way (the fold extends to the long edges). These terms should also cover those of us with metric paper or odd-sized rejection slips. For both models described below, start with the paper lying the long way. (Hold it with the long edges vertical, then place it on the table.) It's easier to make the folds this way.

Method 1
The flying dart

The flying dart is probably the most common paper airplane. If you already know this one, skip down to the glider, or tag along to brush up on your dart finesse.

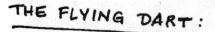

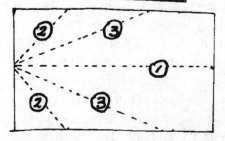

STEP 1
Make the wing folds

First, fold the sheet in half to make a center crease. Take up the diagonal edge that's lifting toward you. Fold it down to meet the center crease. (Don't fold it inward—it should meet the external edge of the center crease.) This will establish one wing. Hold it down with one hand, and crease. Take care that you don't line up the rear,

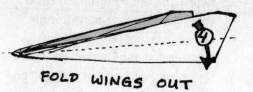

FOLD WINGS OUT

unfolded tip of the wing with the center crease. It's the diagonal edge that needs to line up with the external center crease.

Now flip the airplane over, and repeat the wing fold. Fold the diagonal edge over so it's even with the center crease. You should have the two wings.

STEP 2
Make the body folds

Fold the paper the long way, bending until the opposite corners meet. Crease the fold flat with the palm of your other hand. Run your thumbnail along the crease to make it sharp. Now open the paper again. You've just marked the two halves of the airplane and made the center crease (the bottom of the airplane). From now on, each side of the airplane should look like a mirror image of the other side.

Fold one corner into the middle. The short edge, from the corner to the center crease, will line up along the center crease. Hold the short edge down with one hand, and crease the fold with your other hand. On the other side of the crease, fold the opposite corner so that the short edges just barely meet at the center crease.

Fold the same corners again: fold one diagonal edge down to meet the center crease; hold it down and crease.

Repeat the same step on the other side. The two folds should line up along the center crease and barely touch each other. This will produce a sharp point on the front of the plane.

Fold the plane along the center crease. The two halves should line up exactly. If they don't, well, take this one as a learning experience, and pay close attention to how it flies. Skip Method 2 Steps 1–3, and go to Step 4.

Method 2
The basic glider

This airplane requires a few more folds than the dart to hold it all together, but the glider will hang in the air much longer and perform better. One distinctive feature of this airplane is its blunt nose.

STEP 1
Make the basic body folds

Fold the paper the long way, just as you did for the first two steps of the dart. If you didn't make the dart, fold the paper and line up the corners so that they're on top of each other. Hold the two long ends down with one hand, and crease the paper with the other. Use your fingernail or a ruler to get a really sharp crease. Now open the paper. You've just created the center crease of the airplane. From now on, each side should look like a mirror image of the other. This ensures that the plane will fly straight.

STEP 2
Make the tricky body folds

Fold over one of the long-edged, folded corners. Its point should touch the center crease about 1 inch (2.5 centimeters) from the point of the triangle. Look at the diagram for placement. Hold it down and crease. Fold down the other folded edge until its point just barely touches the other one. Crease this fold also. The point of the short-way fold peeks through and is a short, squat kite shape. (It shouldn't look like a square on its side or a diamond.) Turn the kite shape over the trickily folded corners and fold it down snugly. The kite shape should hold the corners in place.

Now pick up the airplane and fold it

THE GLIDER :

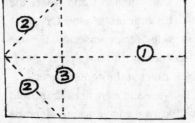

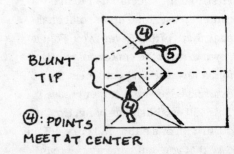

④: POINTS MEET AT CENTER

backward along the center crease so that the folded kite shape faces out. Keep the folded corners tucked in the little pockets made by the kite shape.

STEP 3
Make the wing folds

The long, folded edges are the wing edges. Lay the airplane down again. Fold the wing edge downward and outward so that it meets the center crease exactly. Hold the wing edge on top of the center crease with one hand and crease. Turn the airplane over and do the same thing on the other side. Take care that the two wings are exactly equal. You're ready to fly.

FOLD WINGS OUT

STEP 4
Prepare for takeoff

You need to unfold the wings slightly to get the best angle for flying. For both the Dart and the Glider open the wings out from the center crease, which is now the bottom of the airplane, and gently fold the two wings up. The best angle from wing to body is 60 degrees. This should make the airplane look even, like a three-pointed star, when viewed from the ends. When you release the plane the center

should open slightly, and the tops of the wings will actually float closer to parallel. You're ready to launch.

STEP 5
Fly and be free!

Most people fly paper airplanes indoors; it's a good no-wind area. If you take it outside, choose a day and a place with no wind or very light wind, unless you don't mind chasing down the airplane.

Grasp the plane almost halfway down the front end between thumb and fingers of your throwing hand. Have you ever thrown darts at a dartboard? The launching motion is similar. Hold the airplane up high, about eye level. Point it in the direction you want it to go. Bend your arm at the elbow and then extend your arm with a flick. Open your fingers and thumb and release the plane when it's pointing where you want it to go.

Learn 2   Make Potpourri

Nothing personal, but your house might be a little stinky. A little bowl of potpourri (pronounced "po-pur-*ree*") is a perfect way to give sweet breath to a stale place. What is potpourri? It's a mixture of dried flowers, spices, and aromatic essence arranged in a decorative bowl.

BEFORE YOU BEGIN

Collect all the ingredients from your local flower shop, consulting an expert while you're there. Keep an eye out for color and texture, possibly mixing some rose heads or other flower heads into the batch.

STEP 1

Choose your colors

If you're particularly sensitive to interior decorating or color coordination, you'll want to look around the prospective room and take its domi-

nant color scheme into account. Otherwise pick out colors that suit you. Try sticking to one general set of colors: red, yellow, and orange; or blue, green, and brown or purple. If you're feeling wacky, mix together whatever colors you like. Stick it in your closet if it smells good but looks a little noisy.

STEP 2

Choose your scent

As with the color scheme, most potpourris have one dominant scent with suggestions of others. Examples of dominant scents are lavender, cinnamon, and citrus. Some of these are appropriate to the season of the year: for example, cinnamon for winter, lavender or citrus for summer. Perhaps you want to coordinate with the room's decor.

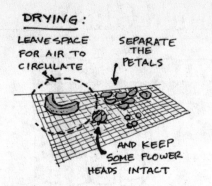

DRYING:

LEAVE SPACE FOR AIR TO CIRCULATE

SEPARATE THE PETALS

AND KEEP SOME FLOWER HEADS INTACT

STEP 3
Dry the mixture

Place the petals, leaves, and lemon peel on your screen, which will allow air to circulate. Spread the mixture out as thinly as possible for maximum circulation. Let it sit for 10 days in a light, airy room.

STEP 4
Combine

Once dry, place the petals, leaves, and lemon peel in your bowl. Save some flower heads or other particularly attractive ingredients for later. Add a bit of the essence and the orrisroot, and toss like a salad.

Once your potpourri salad is thoroughly mixed, arrange to your taste. Focus on the top layer, choosing your crowning ornaments, and placing them symmetrically. A bunch of smaller ingredients could be placed on the inner circumference or in a design around the flower heads. Here's a chance to exercise your creativity. Experiment with different designs, but handle the flower heads gently—they're delicate. If you get stuck for design ideas, ask your local florist.

STEP 5
Place in stale space

Good places for potpourri are bathrooms, hallways, foyers or entranceways, living rooms, or anywhere people congregate. Potpourri in your workplace will improve your mood and effectiveness.

STEP 6
Maintain

Every few weeks or so, remove the design on the top layer and toss the potpourri like a salad. Add two drops of essence to replenish the scent. And if you're inclined, change the top-layer design. Small details like this really can enhance your quality of life.

STEP 7
Make sachets

Sachets are basically potpourris that you can carry around with you. Dried flowers and leaves are placed in a soft cotton pouch tied with string or ribbon, depending on how fancy you like it. Fabric from a hopelessly tattered pair of jeans or khakis makes a good sachet pouch. As for the stuffing, use one dominant scent if you like—lavender, roses, or even pine needles. Keep one in your dresser drawer or purse—or near the phone at work. You'll enjoy aromatic delights while listening to the other party!

- ½ cup lavender (*Lavandula sp.*)
- ½ cup lemon-scented geranium leaves (*Pelargonium crispum*)
- ½ cup bay leaves (*Laurus nobilis*)
- ½ cup hop clover (*Trifolium agrarium*)
- ½ cup balsam needles
- Any other flower (*Flowerus randomus*) you desire for scent or color
- A medium-sized serving bowl (1½ quarts or 5 to 6 cups), as decorative as possible

Tips

- For an especially beautiful scent, seal the potpourri in a container and let it sit for 4 to 6 weeks. This allows the petals to ferment according to the original method—*potpourri* means "rancid bowl" in French! Then set it out.

Learn 2 Make Simple Stained Glass

Time

Four sessions of about 2 hours each, and a day or two to hunt down materials

What you'll need

- Pieces of colored glass, plain or textured
- A handheld glass cutter
- Thick paper, such as heavy construction paper
- All-purpose glue
- Pliers
- A soldering iron
- Copper-wire tape
- Solder rolls
- Glass cleaner
- Eye goggles
- Paper clip or piece of wire
- Work gloves

Optional:
- A glass-grinding machine

Since your local stained-glass store is charging a fortune for the sun catcher you want to buy for Aunt Ethel's birthday, you've decided you want to make a nice little piece yourself. But how do you go about this process without burying yourself in thick manuals that you know will glaze your eyes over?

BEFORE YOU BEGIN

Be sure to wear your eye goggles when handling glass. The chances that flecks of glass will fly in your eyes are slim, but it happens. Better to be safe than sorry when dealing with glass. Gloves are a good idea too, protecting your delicate paws from any scratches or slices. And if you have small children and/or pets in the house, you might want to keep them out of your work area.

STEP 1

Gather your materials

Use your Yellow Pages to find glass suppliers. Ignore the automotive and industrial-glass ads. Call a few places to ask if they have stained glass for projects. When you get there, put on your bartering boots and ask if they have any rummaging piles or broken-glass bins. Often you can find great little pieces of scrap colored glass here, which is much cheaper than buying a whole sheet of stained glass. Get pieces with different textures, color variations, and thicknesses. Avoid buying whole sheets of glass unless you plan to do a lot of projects. You can also get tools at a glass store, so you may not have to search other stores.

Search craft, sewing, and hardware stores for glass cutters, glass breakers, and a soldering iron, as well as the copper tape and solder. Ask a store clerk for referrals—they usually get a lot of people asking for obscure craft items and sometimes have a list of other resources for you.

Ask your friends and relatives. Many people, in those carefree arts-and-crafts days of the seventies and early eighties, bought stained-glass materials and have now abandoned them on a dusty attic or garage shelf. Borrow them. If you get really inspired about creating stained-glass pieces, you can always invest in your own equipment later.

STEP 2
Create a design

Stick to simple shapes. If you don't have a glass-cutting machine, you won't be able to cut rounded edges very well. For your first project, and while you're still learning the limitations of a handheld glass cutter, don't plan on creating elaborate curves and circular shapes.

When you've decided on your design, make a drawing on thick paper and separate it into numbered pieces, just like a finished piece of stained-glass has pieces. Make a few copies of

your design so you can refer to it without having it all cut up. Then carefully cut out your numbered shapes and glue them onto the glass you want for each shape. This way you can trace easily around your design with the glass cutters and cut down on skewed lines.

LAY OUT ON PAPER

GLUE EACH SECTION ONTO A PIECE OF GLASS

STEP 3
Cut the glass

With one hand holding the glass, grasp the glass cutter with the other hand as if it were a saw. Starting from the top and pressing hard onto the glass (the thicker the glass, the harder you'll need to press), slice the glass around your paper cutout shape. Keep in mind that you won't be able to make small trimming adjustments with such a bulky tool, so try to keep your slice as close to the shape as you can.

Place the mouth of the pliers onto the joint line of cut glass. Press down, and snap the glass in two. If your glass breaks or snaps apart unevenly, rendering it unusable, don't despair. This happens frequently—after all, accidents will happen. Try to trim the piece if you can.

STEP 4
Prepare to solder

Cut off enough copper tape to stretch around the perimeter of the piece of

APPLY SOLDER TO COPPER EDGE

PUSH PIECES TOGETHER

MELT SOLDER OVER TOP EDGES OF TAPE

glass. Start taping anywhere on the glass, and slowly wrap around the edges of the piece, trying to keep the tape as centered on the edge as possible. Stop every couple of inches or so, and using the length of the pen, rub the tape to make it stick, rather as if you were making gravestone rubbings. It's okay to overlap the ends of the tape. There should be a little bit of tape hanging over on the sides, depending on the width of the tape you have, but try not to make it very much. The more you have hanging over, the more you'll have to cover with solder, and a lot of thick solder on your glass isn't aesthetically pleasing. You can cut the copper-tape strip first if it's too wide, but beware of uneven cutting.

Clear your work area of any unnecessary items, then plug in your soldering iron and let it heat up for about 10 minutes. To test its heat, press it to the first tip of the solder for about a second (holding the solder over a paper towel). If the solder melts, the iron's hot enough.

STEP 5
Solder your pieces together

Unroll a piece of solder. On a paper towel, old newspaper, or cloth, melt it onto the copper edges of two glass pieces while pushing the pieces together to fuse them. Let them sit for a minute or two until you can see a slight color change in the solder, meaning it has cooled a little. Repeat the process for the other pieces until all joints are sealed.

You've fused the glass together, but you still need to cover the edges with the silver solder to create a uniform appearance. Using a wiping motion, gently melt the solder onto the outer copper tape. Give it about 20 minutes to completely dry, cool off, and harden.

STEP 6
Finish up

Use a paper towel and glass cleaner to wipe the glass free of fingerprints, sticky tape goo, or your morning-coffee stain.

To create a hanger for your piece, unfold a large paper clip and bend it so it's curved like a hook. Solder it directly onto the top of your stained glass, using thicker wires for heavier pieces.

Hang up your piece, and enjoy. Stained glass is pretty to look at, but the real beauty comes from the delicate tango of its colors with the sunlight. So put it in a window where there's direct sunlight (try to hang it out of reach of pets and children) and perhaps a bit of a breeze to make it sway. Fishing line is a good choice for tethering, as it's transparent and durable.

Learn**2** Play Checkers

Checkers is a fun, simple game that's been around for hundreds of years. Kids and adults can enjoy it together, and you can easily make your own board and pieces. The version of the game that you'll learn here is formally known as English checkers.

BEFORE YOU BEGIN

The object of the game is to advance across the board in order to capture or block your opponent's checkers until they can't make any more moves. Try

THE SETUP

REMEMBER:
"WHITE GOES RIGHT"

to make it all the way to the other side of the board—there are rewards for getting there.

STEP 1

Set up the board

A checkerboard is eight squares by eight squares. The squares alternate colors—one dark, the next light. Arrange your board so that a light corner square is to each player's right. Place twelve pieces of one color on the first three rows of alternating dark squares. Repeat with the other twelve pieces on the other side of the board, again putting all pieces on the dark squares.

Time

A few minutes to learn, a lot longer to master

What you'll need

- An opponent
- A checkerboard
- 12 white and 12 black checkers (playing pieces)

THE CAPTURE

STEP 2

Play by the rules

Black always begins play, and players take turns from there. After the game, players switch colors. Here are the essentials:

- Checkers move diagonally, one square forward, always onto a dark square. If all the dark squares diagonal to a piece already have pieces on them, that piece is blocked and another must be moved. Checkers can't move backward unless they have been "crowned" (see below).

- An opposing piece is captured by jumping (always diagonally) over it to an empty square just beyond it (the piece being captured). Take the captured piece off the board.

- Any number of checkers may be jumped over and captured in just one move, as long as each jump follows the rules. In other words, as long as you keep moving forward on the diagonal and there are available squares immediately beyond the opposing piece, you can keep jumping. Many players spend most of their time figuring out how to do this. Blocking your opponent's checkers from moving is another important consideration.

- When a single checker reaches a square on the "crown-head," or "king row" (the row closest to the player's opponent), the opponent must "crown" the piece by relinquishing a captured checker and placing it atop the piece. The stacked pieces become a "king." It's good to have a king—unlike the uncrowned pieces, a king can move forward or backward diagonally along the board.

- Officially, if an opposing piece is available to be captured, the player whose turn it is must capture that piece. If the player fails to do this, the opposing player may (a) insist that the moved piece be returned to its original position and the capture made; (b) accept the move (but the capture must be made on the next move, if still possible); or (c) remove the piece that should have made the capture from the board. In practice, many people do not require pieces to be captured because they are available. An agreement should be reached beforehand on which method to play by (especially if you're outside of your neighborhood).

STEP 3

Emerge victorious

The game is won by the first player to capture, or block, the twelve opposing pieces. Let the games begin!

Learn2 Play Chess

Time

- An hour to learn the rules
- 15 minutes to 2 hours to play a game

What you'll need

- An opponent
- A chessboard (64 alternating black and white squares, the same as a checkerboard)
- A set of black pieces and white pieces; each side includes 1 king, 1 queen, 2 bishops, 2 rooks (or castles), 2 knights, and 8 pawns

The ancient game of chess, known as the game of kings, has captivated players for hundreds of years. It's one of the best-known games of the world, spread throughout the Middle East, Asia, Europe, and North America. If you have always wanted to learn the game but felt daunted by the rules, relax. Many people think chess is complicated, but it's no more difficult to learn than many card games.

BEFORE YOU BEGIN

One player takes white and the other takes black, although chess pieces are occasionally colored differently. A traditional way of determining sides is for one player to hold a black pawn concealed in one fist and a white pawn in the other. The other player then selects a hand, and the pawn inside is the color he will play. The advantage of selecting white is that white moves first.

WHITE ON RIGHT

STEP 1

Set up the board

Most beginners quickly remember the setup of the pieces. It's easy if you think of the pieces getting shorter as they move away from the king and queen. The bishop is the tallest, then the knight, then the rook. But sometimes players have trouble remembering what order the king and queen go in. Just remember, the opposing kings are always facing each other along the same vertical line (see illustration), the queen always goes on her own color, and the board is set up with a white square on each player's right side.

STEP 2

Know the basics

Now that the board is set up, you need to learn the fundamentals.

- The object of the game is to capture the opponent's king.
- Turns alternate between the white and black sides.
- On each turn, a player may move one piece appropriately from one square to another that is either open or occupied by an opponent.
- Each space on the board may be occupied by only one piece. When an opposing piece moves onto a space

held by an opponent, it "captures" the piece and removes it from the board.

- Unlike checkers, with the exception of the knight pieces may not jump over their own or their opponent's pieces.

STEP 3

Study the pieces and their movements

There are six different pieces in the game.

- King: This piece is the object of both you and your opponent. While you are trying to capture your opponent's king, your opponent will be trying to do the same to yours. The king moves in any direction, even diagonally, one space per turn.
- Queen: The queen can move in all directions, like the king, but with one

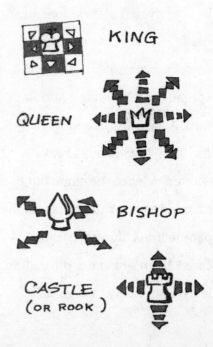

KING

QUEEN

BISHOP

CASTLE (OR ROOK)

key advantage: she can move as many spaces as desired in any one direction, as long as her path is unobstructed. She is the most powerful piece on the board. Losing your queen can put you at a serious disadvantage, but so can being overprotective.

- Bishop: This piece can move diagonally along its own color any number of spaces. Each side has one bishop that moves along the black squares and one that moves along the white squares.
- Rook: Rooks may move either horizontally or vertically any number of spaces.
- Knight: This piece has a unique moving pattern. It moves two spaces forward, then one space sideways; it can also move two spaces sideways, then one space forward or backward. This is also the only piece that may jump over other pieces. Pieces jumped over are not captured: only the piece occupying the destination square is.
- Pawn: The pawn moves one space forward, and only forward. The pawn captures, however, by moving forward diagonally. The first time each pawn is moved, it has the option of moving two spaces forward instead of the usual one space. After a pawn moves (either one or two spaces), it no longer has this option.

STEP 4
Consider your first moves

The white player moves first. Options include moving a pawn forward either one or two spaces or moving a knight

out. Black then moves; play alternates between the two. It's often helpful to move pawns out of the way as soon as possible to allow the more powerful pieces to be utilized.

STEP 5
Learn about "castling" with the king

Castling is a special move that employs both the king and the rook. This is the only time that two pieces may be moved in a single turn. To castle, a king is moved two spaces to the left or right of its original square, while the rook that the king moves toward is moved from its original space to a space adjacent to the king but on the opposite side. Castling is not allowed under the following conditions:

- If either the king or the selected rook has been moved in the game. Both pieces must be in their original places on the board.
- If there are pieces between the king and the rook. The space must be entirely open without any intervening pieces.
- If the king is in check, or if castling would move the king through any spaces that would put it in check.

STEP 6
Memorize the special moves of the pawn

You may play quite a few games before you need or care to use the following. But it's nice to have them in your arsenal.

CAPTURE "EN PASSANT"

GONE!

Pawns capture only by moving diagonally. This is the only way they can capture and the only time they can move diagonally.

When a pawn has advanced to the fifth row on the board and an opposing pawn moves out two spaces in an adjacent column, the first pawn can then declare an "en passant" capture and move diagonally behind the opposing pawn. The captured pawn is then removed as if captured normally.

If a pawn is moved all the way across to the far side of the board, it must be replaced by another piece of that player's choice. This is called "promotion." Pawns may be promoted to either a knight, rook, bishop, or queen, regardless of what has been previously captured. Promotion can also be used to exceed the normal roster of pieces (that is, several queens are possible).

STEP 7

Know the difference between check and checkmate

This is the difference between threatening to win and actually winning the game. When a king is threatened with capture, the player who threatens the king makes this known by saying, "Check."

To avoid capture, the king may be moved out of check, the threatening piece may be captured, or a piece may be moved between the king and the checking piece to effectively block check.

If there is no way out of check, "checkmate" is called and the game is over.

STEP 8

Learn how to end the game

The king may never move into check. Chess etiquette requires that the king is not removed from the board; rather, he is laid down sideways on the board.

The game is won when one king is in checkmate. A draw results when a king is not in check but cannot move without putting himself into check. This is called a stalemate and results in a tie game.

You may also offer a draw to your opponent and mutually agree to end the game at a tie.

Learn**2** Play Poker

Poker is not so much a card game as it is a psychology class. It's said that good poker players can win more consistently by making accurate assessments of their fellow players' characters than by paying attention to the cards, and that's not too far off the mark. Knowledge, patience, and luck are all important factors in any poker game, but the truth is, not much can save an amateur's money from an experienced poker professional who's determined to get it.

BEFORE YOU BEGIN

Here's the general idea. Most poker sessions are made up of many individual games, or "hands." Every player will "ante up" a token amount for the privilege of receiving his or her first cards. The ante goes into the "pot," and winning the pot is the object of the game. Based on those cards, the player will make an estimate of the chances of success—"success" hinging on who holds the best hand. Every time an additional card is added to the hand, another bet is required to continue

and another estimate is made. The difficulties lie in knowing at what point to cut your losses and fold, when to bluff, when to play a mediocre hand, and how to increase the chance of acquiring a good hand.

Each player's rhythm will gradually emerge as the session progresses, and the good player will understand those rhythms well enough to make an educated guess as to the quality of his opponents' hands. Luck, of course, plays a large role, but a crafty player can still win on a night when the cards are running against him or her.

STEP 1

Learn the common goals and the card values

The goal of most games of poker (except for oddball ones like high-low) is to either gain the best selection of five cards (as defined below) or to convince the other players that you have

Time

A few minutes to learn, much longer to become proficient. A game of poker can last as long as the players' endurance (in casual play, it's a good idea to set a cut-off time before starting, since the losing parties are always motivated to keep playing).

What you'll need

- A standard, 52-card deck of playing cards
- A table and chairs
- Ideally, 5 to 7 players (poker is a bit strange with fewer than 4 players and cumbersome with more than 8) but any number is okay
- Chips of various colors, each with an established value (you can use genuine poker chips or anything that's in abundant supply so long as everyone agrees on the value of each item)

gained the best selection of five cards (bluffing), so that they drop out of the game (fold).

Cards are ranked, or valued, in the following order, from lowest to highest: 2 through 10, jack, queen, king, ace. Suits are also valued, from lowest to highest, as follows: diamonds, clubs, hearts, and spades. House rules often allow aces to double as low cards, so make sure that the house rules are understood before beginning.

The value of poker hands, from lowest to highest, are as follows:

- High card: In a poker hand with no winning combinations of cards, the high card wins. That card is determined by the ranking above.
- One pair: Two cards of the same value, with three extra cards that do not combine in any desirable way.
- Two pair: Two pairs of cards with the same value, each pair having a different value, and one extra card.
- Three of a kind: Three cards of the same value, with the remaining two cards not combining in any desirable way.
- Straight: Five cards of sequential value and differing suits.
- Flush: Five cards of the same suit that are not all sequential.
- Full house: Three cards of one value and two cards of another value. Sometimes called a "full boat."
- Four of a kind: Four cards of the same value, with one extra card.
- Straight flush: Five sequential cards of the same suit.
- Royal flush: A straight flush that consists of the five highest-value

cards, 10, jack, queen, king, and ace.

Each level of value beats all levels below it. For instance, even the lowest three of a kind (2's) will beat the highest two pair (aces and kings). If two players have the same type of hand, the player with the higher-value cards wins the hand. For instance, the player with three jacks beats the player with three 8's. Extra cards only matter if two players have otherwise identical hands. For instance, if two players each have two pair consisting of 10's and 4's, the player with the higher-value extra card wins the hand.

STEP 2
Learn five-card draw

Five-card draw is the basic game from which all other poker games are derived. To begin, shuffle the deck of cards thoroughly, as each player antes an identical, agreed-upon amount.

The dealer gives each player five cards, one at a time, in a clockwise order starting with the person on the dealer's left.

After looking at her cards, the person on the dealer's left has several options:

- Fold: Placing her cards facedown toward the middle of the table and sitting out the rest of the hand. The cards remain on the table until the hand is finished, and her ante remains in the pot.
- Bet: Placing a wager in the pot. Often the house rules determine minimum and maximum bets.
- Pass: Choosing not to make a

wager and allowing the person to her left the same three choices.

Once a player has made a wager, the choices for the remaining players are slightly different:

- Fold: As above, the players turn their cards facedown toward the middle of the table and sit out the rest of the hand. Sorry, all the money stays in.
- Call: Matching the other player's bet by placing an equal wager into the pot.
- Raise: Placing a higher wager into the pot. All other players must call that bet—or raise it—in order to remain in the game.

After a round of betting, any remaining players are allowed to exchange up to three of their cards for an equal number from the top of the deck. After all players have done this, a second round of betting occurs. When that round is finished, the player whose bet has been called by other players must show her cards first. A winner is determined, and that person collects all bets in the pot. If all other players are unwilling to call the bet and fold, the winner is not required (but certainly is allowed) to show her cards to the other players.

STEP 3
Learn five-card stud

The most common variation on the classic draw game, stud differs in the presentation of cards and the addition of betting rounds.

Rather than receiving five cards facedown, players receive one card

down and one card face up to begin the game. All of the cards are left on the table.

Players then glance at their facedown cards, and a round of betting ensues. Betting starts with the player having the highest card face up, or showing.

After the first round of betting, each player receives another card face up. Another round of betting occurs, beginning with the player showing the highest hand. The betting continues until each player who hasn't folded has five cards total (four showing and one down). The player with the highest hand wins and takes the pot.

STEP 4
Learn seven-card stud

Another common variation, this game differs from five-card stud in the presentation of cards, and the ability to choose the best five of seven total cards to form your hand. This is often a higher-stakes game than most, and higher-value hands, such as flushes, are common.

Each player initially receives two cards facedown and one face up. A betting round ensues, and each player who does not fold is given another card face up. This continues until all remaining players have seven cards total, with the final card being dealt facedown.

Players then choose their best five cards, and the winner is determined. As before, each betting round starts with the player showing the best hand.

Tips

- There are many other poker games being played today, some of the most common being baseball, Texas hold 'em, and high-low variations. Many books on the market can tell you all about them, as well as provide strategies to maximize your winnings. If you are serious about playing poker, pick up a few, and gain some experience playing in friendly games.
- Be careful: card playing for money is one of the top ways to mess up finances and ruin relationships.

Learn 2 Childproof Your Home

The presence of a tiny tyrant, whether it's your own or another's, can disrupt any household's flow. But some simple preparations can ease the tension and increase safety, so you can really enjoy your new guest or family member.

BEFORE YOU BEGIN

"All the world passes through Gordon's mouth" goes a famous Greek saying, and it paints a good picture of an infant's curiosity. Now let's wander through a few rooms in your home, making adjustments on the way.

STEP 1

Childproof the living room

Look for any items within a toddler's reach or on top of a table platform that could be shaken or knocked over. Relocate these to higher ground or to a locked room or closet. Here are some particulars to watch out for:

• Cord yanking: If something can be pulled, you can bet toddlers will pull on it. Children can choke on miniblind cords, so keep these out of reach. For electronics and appliances, tie the various wires together or keep them together inside an old telephone cord. Another alternative is to use cord shorteners, available at most hardware stores.

• Outlet testing: A child's explorations can include knee-high electrical outlets. Place safety guards over unoccupied outlets.

• Lid closing: To avoid squishing little fingers in chests or pianos, glue a few pieces of a resilient material (for example, cork or thick felt) on the lid to keep it from slamming shut.

• Plant pulling: Keep all floor and hanging plants out of reach. Even if the child isn't hurt by knocking one over, you'll have a big mess on your hands.

• Bookcase tumbling: If you have a slightly wobbly or top-heavy bookcase, consider securing it to the wall. Use shelf brackets screwed to the side or top of the bookcase and then to the wall.

STEP 2

Childproof the kitchen

Since there are stoves, knives, and strong chemical cleaners in a kitchen,

DANGER ZONES:

COVER WALL OUTLETS

LOCK OR BLOCK OFF DOORS AND STAIRWAYS

SECURE BOOKCASES

FRAGILE! – STORE IT OR WATCH CLOSELY

one should never leave a toddler unattended in your kitchen. Here are some important items to remember:

• Secure household cleaners in a locked box.

• On the stove, keep the handles of pots and pans turned toward the wall—away from a child's reach.

• Plastic bags cause many suffocation accidents: keep these tucked away and out of reach.

• Install childproof latches (see illustration) on any cabinets and appliances within reach. For a quicker, improvised measure, tightly tie any cabinet handles together with wire, twine, or nylon line.

• Be extra careful with kitchen drips and spills: a slippery patch can send a toddler sprawling to the floor.

PULL, THEN PRESS TO OPEN

"CHILDPROOF" LATCHES

Tips

- When making preparations, pay attention to the child's changing age and size. A safety barrier that's sufficient for a young toddler may fail to constrain a two-year-old.
- Put up screen doors to keep pets out of rooms where the child may sleep.
- Keep pillows out of an infant's crib.
- Tots love the way videotapes disappear into the VCR. Keep an eye out to make sure nothing else disappears into it.

STEP 3

Childproof the stairs

A safety gate is highly recommended at one or both ends of the staircase, depending on where the child will be. They attach to the banister or rail post and often can swing open on hinges for adult access. If you don't have a safety gate, improvise one with a firmly stationed mattress or a table pushed over onto its side.

For an inexpensive and portable method of securing the staircase, purchase some 3-foot plastic mesh, available at most hardware stores, and attach it to the stair banister with plastic ties, metal wire, or twine.

If you have a deck or balcony, check that the railing slats are close enough together to prevent a small child from slipping through. If they aren't, childproof the railings with 3-foot-high plastic mesh. You can tie it to the inside of the railings with strong twine or staple in place with heavy staples and a staple gun.

TIE HANDLES TO PREVENT EASY ACCESS

STEP 4

Childproof the windows and doors

Many accidents can happen in these areas of entry and exit. But they're easily avoided with a little planning.

Window guards are a necessity; a screen is not enough to protect a child from danger. In fact, some local governments require guards on windows in their housing safety codes. Otherwise, children can fall out of windows the moment your back is turned.

An excited child running from a playmate can mistake a sliding glass door for an open doorway. To prevent a serious accident, mark the window with decorative tape or stickers to distinguish it from a doorway.

For doors, you can make a reusable doorstop with 4-inch sections of 1-inch quarter molding and coat hangers. To start, cut the molding into 4-inch sections, one for each door you'd like to stop. Then unwind a coat hanger, and using your hands (bend the wire back and forth at the same point) or a strong clipper, break off a 6-inch piece of wire for each door. Make a 90-degree bend about an inch from the end, and make another bend an 1¼ inch from the first bend. This forms a hook that will hang on the hinge. Take a moment to file the ends down so there aren't any rough edges. Hammer along this bend to drive the wire about an inch into the molding. It's ready! Just slip it over the hinge, and the door can't slam shut. Make sure that the molding rests in between the flaps of the hinge.

STEP 5

Childproof the bathroom

Like the kitchen, the bathroom has many slippery surfaces and dangerous materials requiring attention:

Be sure to lock or tightly tie off any cabinets, and move to higher ground any colorful and sweet-smelling soaps or shampoos.

Even adults can fall in the tub. For the whole household's safety, lay down a rubber no-slip mat or no-slip stickers on the floor of the tub. For optimum sticking strength, clean the tub surface thoroughly beforehand.

Lock all medicine cabinets, even if they seem out of reach. Children can improve their climbing skills on a day-to-day basis. Locks for sliding cabinets are available at hardware stores.

Pad the bathtub water spout with a store-bought cover. Or create your own with a piece of flexible rubber hosing: slit it partway down the middle to get it on, and secure it with ring clamps or nylon line.

Install an antiscald valve. This attaches to most faucets and shower-heads and prevents water from reaching a dangerously high temperature. Hot water that feels fine to adults can burn an infant.

STEP 6

Childproof the garage

Heavy tools, electric devices, and flammable materials add up to one thing: danger. Keep children out of the garage. Still, to be safe, keep any dangerous items stashed inside a wire-mesh pen. Depending on the amount of stuff you have, you can make this pen with a 10- to 15-foot section of mesh. Take the sharp edges and pull them into a cylinder shape to help you assess how large an area you need. Then staple (use a staple gun) those sharp edges to two 3-foot sections of 1- by 2-inch wood. Staple each edge onto its own piece. Make sure to bend back any sharp edges that are exposed. To lock up the pen, screw two screw eyes on the side edge of each wood piece—one toward the top, one toward the bottom. Place the screws close enough to the edge so that a padlock can be passed through the two screw eyes. Lock it up, and the tots are safe.

Store garage-door openers and buttons out of reach. Locking the doors of cars that are inside the garage is a good idea too. Parking brakes, light and windshield-wiper switches are problems waiting to happen.

Test your automated garage door. Most recent models reverse direction when they come in contact with another object. Check that yours does this. Place a cardboard box in the way of the door as it closes. If it crushes that, it can do the same to a child.

A storage freezer or a cabinet can look like a playpen to a child. Be certain to lock these doors and hide the keys.

Tips

- If you need ventilation but you want the child in the room with you, try this little trick. Install a screw-eye and hook into the door and door-jamb. Make sure you put the screw-eye on the other side of the door, so that the door can open a couple of inches. The air gets in, but the kids can't get out.

Learn2 Hang a Picture

Hanging a framed work requires the proper materials for support and stability. It takes a little planning, but the results will be evident: a carefully hung picture shows off its merits and enhances the rest of the room.

BEFORE YOU BEGIN

Before you determine the right spot to hang your picture, you need to make some decisions about the decor of the room. Look at the artwork already hanging; is there room for one more picture? Or does something need to come down and get swapped out? Perhaps the other pictures are worth being rehung in order to make way for the new beauty. While you think about these things, collect all necessary materials.

STEP 1
Survey the layout

Look at the other objects in the room. Everything there, the lamp, the couch, the ficus plant in the corner, has its own space, its breathing room, that needs to be respected. Hold your picture up, or have a friend hold it for you, and experiment with moving it closer to, and then farther away from, the other furnishings. Notice when things start to feel crowded: that means you need more space.

STEP 2

Install the right wire

Even if you've had your picture framed professionally, take a look at the back. Picture-hanging wire comes in different gauges according to weight. Is the wire strong enough to support the weight of the frame? Make sure the wire is securely anchored to the frame. Screw eyes driven into a wooden frame or sliders made for metal frames should be

located at least two-thirds up from the bottom of the frame. The wire should curve up halfway from the screw eyes to the top of the frame. It should not be visible above the top of the frame.

If you're wiring it yourself, cut wire 1½ times the width of the frame. (If you are uncertain of the wire's strength, use twice as much and double it through.)

Fold the wire in half to find its center. Feed it through both screw eyes.

Adjust the wire so the center of it remains at the center of the picture, and pull the remainder through the screw eyes evenly on both sides.

Wrap the wire around the screw eye twice, then pull the remaining wire back along itself and twist it around. This helps secure the wire to the screw eye as well as to get the remainder out of the way. Do the same on the other side.

Stick a small felt pad on each bottom corner of the picture. This protects your wall and the frame and also stabilizes the picture.

STEP 3

Find the spot

Hold the picture up by the sides of the frame in the area where you want it to hang. A friend could be especially useful now, to hold the picture while you stand back and see exactly where you want it to go. Place it so that the geometric center of the image is 5 feet 2 inches high. This allows for most people to look directly into the picture. Tall folks will be looking down, but

Key words

Anchor bolt: The behind-the-wall component of a hanging mechanism for heavy pictures.

Drywall: an internal building material with a thin cardboard exterior and compressed gypsum (looks like chalk) interior.

Screw eye: A screw with a normal body and with a circular loop of metal instead of a regular or Phillips head.

Wall stud: vertical wood beam used for anchoring drywall or plasterboard.

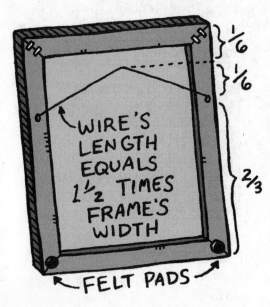

WIRE'S LENGTH EQUALS 1½ TIMES FRAME'S WIDTH

FELT PADS

Tips

- Don't use a pencil to mark picture placement unless you can be absolutely sure that the pencil marks will be covered by the frame. If you must, first hold the picture up to the proper height, then mark lightly along the top edge of each frame. Then center the picture side to side, and lightly mark the top corner of each side. The picture may then be set aside without the need to remeasure.

- When centering a picture, be aware of the effect the entire wall has on your eye. When a picture is centered and balanced, your eye will relax. This may feel like sudden clarity, and the entire wall may seem to hum and get fuzzy.

this is easier than having short people look up. Life is full of compromises.

Measure the distance on either side of the frame toward the edge of the adjoining artwork or piece of furniture. The spaces should be even on each side. Use a measuring tape if desired; a hammer's handle or the span of your hand works well too.

Start with the picture in the center of the available space. Slowly move it away from the object. Your eye will feel the moment when the room starts to balance and will relax. When you feel your eye relax, stop. That's the spot to hang your picture.

STEP 4
Mark the spot

Tuck a pencil behind your ear (this will become useful in a minute).

Now hold the picture with one hand on the wire and the other on the bottom of the frame. For the hand holding the wire, hook your middle finger on the center of the wire so that the picture hangs straight. This is where the nail or hook will hold the picture. Hold the picture up to the wall again, and make sure it is both centered and straight. The weight of the picture will leave a mark or small indentation on your finger where the wire was. Keep your hand firmly on that point, and remove the picture. Take the pencil and draw a small mark on the wall exactly where your finger held the wire. Good! Now you are ready to approach the wall.

STEP 5
Install hooks, nails, or screws

Light- to medium-weight pictures:

Place a picture hook to the wall so that the bottom of the hook is at the mark you made for the wire. Above the hook is a slot for the nail that should be directly above the mark. Hold the hook and nail steady with one hand, and use a hammer to get the nail started. Be careful not to let the nail slip down at first. This may hang the picture lower than you want it. Once you have the nail established, drive it in.

If you don't have any picture hooks, then medium-gauge nails will work fine. For lightweight pictures such as framed documents use a 1-inch finishing nail. Put a small piece of tape over the spot where the nail will go. This helps protect the wall plaster from cracking. Drive the nail downward at a

FOR HEAVIER PICTURES

45° ANGLE

DRIVE NAIL INTO STUD

IF STUD WON'T WORK, USE A WALL ANCHOR

45-degree angle. The angle is critical to ensure the picture will stay on the wall.

Heavy pictures:

For pictures weighing 10 pounds or more, use nails instead of hooks. If the room is constructed with framed drywall, center your picture along a wall stud. Unsupported nails can be ripped out of drywall by the weight of the picture alone. To support the picture's weight evenly, use two or more nails evenly spaced from the center and level with each other.

Very heavy pictures:

Where placing at wall studs is inconvenient, use wall screws with anchor bolts. These hold the wall together while supporting the weight of your picture. They can be found at most hardware stores and have instructions printed on the package. Most require you to drill a hole in the drywall just large enough to allow the anchor bolt to slip through (usually ¼ inch). Once the anchor bolt is in place, tighten the screw clockwise to secure it snugly against the back of the wall.

STEP 6

Hang the picture

Your picture should now be ready for hanging.

Pick it up carefully by the sides, and check to see that the wire hangs outward, looped toward the wall. Put the picture up higher than it will go, and

then let it down gently until the hook or nail catches the loop of wire. Adjust the picture slightly until it comes to rest evenly on the hook. The wire should be centered as much as possible, and the picture should hang straight down.

You may want to use a level on the top of the frame as a guide, or look at where the wall meets the ceiling and bring the top frame parallel to it. Be sure the sides hang straight up and down, too. Some ceilings may be crooked.

Pictures can be adjusted up and down by tightening or loosening the wire (now aren't you glad you left extra wire?). Slides at the back of metal frames make this easy. Adjusting pictures side to side is more difficult. Use a second nail level with the first, driven into the wall at twice the distance you want to move the picture. The middle of the picture hanging on both nails will be dead center between the two.

Tips

- After inserting an anchor bolt, you may want to patch over the hole. Allow the patch to dry thoroughly before hanging the picture.

- In cases where the placement is way off, you may have to renail the hook. If you're lucky, the old hole will be hidden by the picture, but you should always keep a jar of Spackle (finishing plaster) and matching wall paint handy in order to cover your tracks. Spackling should only take an hour or so, just long enough for the paint to dry.

Learn 2 Make a Compost Pile

And if you've ever thought of having a small garden (or even a houseplant), you'll end up with a fantastic supplement for the soil.

So what is compost, anyway? It's the loamy mixture produced by the decomposition of garden wastes, kitchen wastes, or other materials. Although compost contains only about $\frac{1}{10}$ to 1 percent nitrogen (the rest is carbon and trace minerals), it'll dramatically improve soil by boosting its water-retention capabilities and by providing nutrients for the vegetation. By adding compost, you allow your soil to retain water without becoming soggy. If your soil has a lot of clay, you're preventing root rot; if you have sandy soil, the moisture will be available more evenly to thirsty plants.

What you'll need

- Composting thermometer (available at garden centers)
- Dried blood, fish emulsion, or fish meal (available at farm-supply or garden centers)
- Grass clippings
- Pitchfork, shovel, or other turning implement
- Shredded newspaper
- Compost bin (optional)

Composting is the opposite of growing—nothing more than the breakdown of organic, once living materials into simpler organic materials that are easier for plants to use. It's a kind of rotting, but speedier and not as stinky (if you do it right).

Making a compost pile is a smart move for many, not just hard-core organic farmers. By recycling kitchen and yard wastes you'll keep this "garbage" out of the world's overflowing landfills.

BEFORE YOU BEGIN

You can produce compost with a minimum of effort, but first ask yourself a few questions to decide how to proceed.

- How much time do you have to devote to this activity?
- What sort of space is available for the compost pile or bin?
- How much material is available for the compost pile? How much compost would you like to have?

STEP 1

Pick your method

Composting uses naturally occurring microorganisms to transform organic materials into composted materials, and the microorganisms require oxygen, water, warmth, and materials that aren't overly acidic. Once you've constructed the pile, you have options that affect how much time you'll spend on it:

On the effort-intensive side of the continuum, you turn the pile frequently, one to three times a day. This aerates the pile—it mixes oxygen into the decaying material. When there is plenty of oxygen, aerobic decomposition takes place and the materials decompose quickly—in as little as 3 weeks. If you need immediate results and you can find the time, this way is for you.

On the other end of the continuum is the long-term method for easygoing, patient people, those who aren't in a hurry and don't want to work too hard.

Most of the work is in the construction of the pile; aside from turning the pile once every week or two, you just let it sit. The compost will be ready in about a year. If you live in a cold climate, figure about two years. But if you're continuously adding new material to the top, understand that the whole pile won't be ready at once—and this makes harvesting the compost a little trickier.

STEP 2

Find a good spot

If you live in a cold climate, you may want to locate your pile in a sunny place. Any heat the pile can get during a cold winter is a help, even though the pile may dry out a little. The opposite is true with a hot climate: the pile will require shade to keep it moist longer. If you're in a middling sort of climate, sun exposure isn't much of a factor— but monitor the location with an eye toward any unplanned moisture retention. Sometimes that great spot turns out to be underneath the rain-gutter outflow, or right under the watershed of a roof. You may need to move the site a few times before you get it right.

How large a space do you need to stake out? For estimating compost production, here's a rule of thumb: If you want to produce at least 1 cubic yard of compost, you will need 10 cubic yards of raw material. If you only want to compost a few kitchen scraps, talk to your neighbors; you may be able to donate your scraps to another compost pile that needs more materials.

Neighbors should also be taken into consideration when locating your pile: for some reason, not everyone thinks that heaps of rotting waste are a noble addition to the neighborhood. A well-planned and -maintained compost setup need not be odiferous, but you should be sensitive to prevalent breezes and obvious insect-congregation patterns. You may find it prudent to let your neighbors know what you're up to, before they draw the wrong conclusions. Heck, why not invite them to join in?

STEP 3

Collect compostable materials

If you, like many gardeners, enjoy the thrift that gardening allows, then this is the method for you. It requires that you collect your compostable materials and throw them in a pile. To make this method work, it's important to know the difference between nitrogenous and carbonaceous ingredients. This is not as imposing as it sounds: nitrogenous ingredients are high in nitrogen, and carbonaceous ingredients contain a lot of carbon. The formula is about one-third nitrogenous ingredients and two-thirds carbonaceous materials in the pile.

Carbon sources:

Carbonaceous ingredients include any plant material: tree by-products, autumn leaves, sawdust, shredded newspapers, cardboard egg cartons,

CARBONACEOUS INGREDIENTS

chopped dead cornstalks, fireplace ashes. And, if you live in or near an agricultural area, you might want to add some straw (look around for a farmer giving it away).

Go easy on the fireplace ashes. Although they're high in potash, ashes tend to raise the soil's pH balance; also, you may find they're too messy to work with. If you do include them, only add about 3 pounds (1.5 kilograms) per 1,000 square feet. And, of course, make sure they're thoroughly cold—smoldering ashes could find many flammable components in your compost.

Nitrogen sources:

Horse or cow manure is fine, especially if it's already decomposing and crumbly. If you go to a stable, look for the old stuff in the back of the pile; it's already breaking down and will speed the process in your pile (it also tends not to smell as bad as the, er, younger stuff).

The following contain nitrogen:
- grass clippings
- soft green prunings from shrubbery
- kitchen wastes, including coffee grounds, used tea bags, and vegetable, fruit, and other food scraps
- green vegetation and manure

But they may not contain enough nitrogen to get the pile cooking. Grass clippings, for instance, may have only 1 percent nitrogen.

NITROGENOUS INGREDIENTS

A compost heap cooks best at about 160 degrees F. (64 degrees C.). If you find that your pile is not heating up enough, try forking in materials that are higher in nitrogen, such as kitchen wastes. If that doesn't do the trick, try dried blood (13 percent nitrogen), fish emulsion (5 percent nitrogen), or fish meal (10 percent nitrogen), all available at your local nursery.

Crushed shells from crabs, lobsters, shrimp, or clams will give your pile calcium, a mineral that plants need in trace amounts. If you live near the seashore, add some seaweed, which contains trace minerals such as potassium. If you include soft tree or shrub prunings, fibrous kitchen wastes, or seafood shells in the pile, use a brick, shovel, or another blunt-ended garden tool to break open the stems and roots or crush the shells. The smaller the materials are, the easier they decompose. As an added benefit, the seafood shells contain a compound called chitin ("kie-tin"), which helps control pesky nematodes, a sort of midget worm that lives in the soil and damages the roots of garden plants.

STEP 4

Avoid problem materials

Not all organic substances will yield nicely to the composting process. Here are a few you should keep out of your pile:

- Weeds, especially if they have gone to seed. Seeds don't break down readily in compost piles, and you may end up spreading weeds in your garden by including them.
- Rosebush refuse. Roses get diseases, such as rusts, that affect its leaves. Some folks don't even include the petals.
- Any manure from carnivores (meat-eaters). This includes dogs, cats, and other pets—and especially human waste. This kind of manure can harbor diseases and bacterial infections to which humans are susceptible. Horse and cow manure are fine, as is the manure of any animal that has a vegetarian diet (zoos are an excellent source of exotic dung, by the way).

• Meats or meat products, even though they are high in nitrogen. Meats, raw or cooked, attract critters that could tear up your compost and leave behind unhealthy droppings to boot. Fish products, on the other hand, seem to do just fine. Dried blood (found in farm-supply stores or large garden centers) is another exception: it's a source of nitrogen, which you may opt to add to your pile.

STEP 5
Pile it on

Many gardeners have materials or space that's sufficient for only one pile at a time. But if you're starting out with a lot of materials, space, and time, consider building up to three piles: one for storing new raw materials; a second pile for actually making compost you're actively turning (at least once a day, for this method); and a third pile that contains finished compost that's ready to be added to the garden or to houseplants. As the second, active pile is completed, you move its contents over to the third pile for storage with the other finished compost, and move the new raw materials from the first pile into the newly emptied second pile.

If this seems like too much, forget about it. Just build a single pile, and harvest the finished compost from the bottom.

Start with a layer of grass clippings about 4 to 6 inches (10 to 15 centimeters) thick. Then add a shovelful of dirt. The dirt contains the microorganisms to get the pile going. Then add about 2 to 4 inches (5 to 10 centimeters) of shredded newspapers, leaves, or other carbonaceous materials. Add another shovelful of dirt. Add some high-nitrogen ingredient, such as dried blood. You may have to experiment to see how many scoops of blood to add to your pile, depending upon the type and quantity of materials you've included. (When adding manure, skip the dirt for that layer. Manure has plenty of microorganisms in it, not to mention worms to help with the decomposing process.) Continue alternating nitrogenous and carbonaceous ingredients with shovelfuls of dirt included, and boosts of fish emulsion, fish meal, or dried blood to speed up the cooking process.

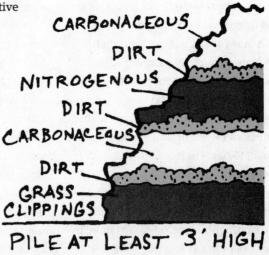

CARBONACEOUS
DIRT
NITROGENOUS
DIRT
CARBONACEOUS
DIRT
GRASS
CLIPPINGS

PILE AT LEAST 3' HIGH

STEP 6

Maintain the pile

There's one last vital ingredient in compost: elbow grease. For it to turn from a pile of rot into a potent soil enricher, you'll need to aerate it with a pitchfork, shovel, or other implement. This process is called turning. Turning sounds tedious, but it's good exercise and it goes quickly if you approach it methodically. Note: In the absence of oxygen (that is, if you don't turn the pile), anaerobic decomposition takes place; this will produce a pile of slime, which is pretty unpleasant to work with.

You should not have to turn the pile more than once per week. But if it starts to smell, it needs oxygen and may also be too wet. (If the material is any wetter than a damp sponge, it's probably too wet.) Although an overly wet pile will eventually smell, your first clue will be the temperature of the pile: it will have dropped below 140 degrees F. (54 degrees C.). To dry the pile out quickly, turn it with a garden fork, and stop watering it (or cover if the weather is rainy). Add more nitrogenous materials. Keep in mind that compost piles need moisture but shouldn't be soggy.

There are several alternatives to turning, although none are so easy and efficient as to put the manual method out of business. Some people place a couple of PVC pipes with holes bored into them into the pile. Air travels down the pipes and helps oxygen get to the center of the pile. Another method is to insert boards into the pile at intervals. This method requires a bin: the boards rest on the slats and go straight through the pile to the other side, creating small pockets of air.

After a couple of weeks, put your hand on top of the pile, or buy a composting thermometer (they're available in most garden centers or larger hardware stores). The temperature should be up to 140 to 160 degrees F. (60 to 70 degrees C.), preferably 160. If not, thoroughly mix in more dried blood or fish products.

STEP 7

Spread it around

The final step in composting is, of course, putting the end product to use. When is it ready? That depends: if you're on the relaxed plan and are turning the pile four times per month or less, you'll wait 6 months to a year—that is, if you live in a dry, hot climate. If you live in a cold climate, figure about 1 to 2 years.

If you haven't been adding new materials to your pile, you'll be able to harvest the whole pile at one time. Otherwise, scoop out the compost from the bottom.

Compost can be either dug into the garden or spread on top of an already planted garden and then lightly scratched into the top 2 inches of the soil's surface—not too deeply, or you'll disturb the roots of existing plants.

Learn2 Paint a Room

What you'll need

- Enough paint for the entire job (see Step 1)
- Quick-drying primer or under-coat, enough to cover the room once (see Step 1)
- A few 2-inch foam brushes or a 2-inch bristle brush
- A ribbed paint tray or a 5-gallon bucket with paint screen
- A 4-foot-long roller-handle extension
- Several drop cloths, cloth or plastic, enough to cover the floor and any immovable furniture
- A paint stir or small piece of scrap lumber
- A big roll of 3-inch-wide masking tape

Make no mistake about it, painting a room is messy, time-consuming work. On the other hand, it's kind of fun, not very difficult, and you can save a lot of money by doing it yourself.

First, make sure that you've got good lighting in the room, and open the windows and doors for ventilation. Toddlers and pets shouldn't have access to the area, and keep things off windowsills so they don't fall ten stories down. If you're repainting a room, you'll need to do some prep work if you want the paint to stick to the wall.

On Friday evening do the prep work. Spend the next morning covering surfaces with drop cloths, taping, and painting your first coat. When that coat is dry (about 2 to 4 hours), you'll spend the afternoon putting on the second (and possibly the third) coats and painting the trim. The following day can be spent touching up, cleaning up, moving the furniture back in, and getting some rest.

BEFORE YOU BEGIN

When it comes to buying paint and brushes, don't skimp on the expense. That cheapo paint could end up costing you more than a costly, high-quality one: the "bargain" paints rarely cover or wear as well as better paint, which means you'll either need to add multiple coats this time around or repaint sooner. And cheap brushes shed bristles, which end up stuck to your wall, looking like the proverbial fly in the ointment. You don't need to buy top-of-the-line materials, just don't cut too many corners.

Keep in mind that paint splatters—there's no way around it, no matter how fastidious your painting style. Wear old clothes and shoes. Buy a couple of those cheap paper hats that your local paint store carries. Wearing some kind of glasses (if only to keep paint from splattering into your eyes) is also a good move.

STEP 1
Prepaint planning

As with many home-improvement projects, the first tools you should use are a pencil and a piece of paper. Take 10 minutes to plan the job.

Calculate how much paint you'll need. Measuring each wall tells you how many square feet you need to cover. If a wall is 12 feet long and 8 feet high, that's 96 square feet. The approximate square-foot coverage per can is listed on the paint label.

Decide if you need a primer.

Primers help paint adhere and cover uniformly. If you're painting over a white surface in good condition with a darker color, you might be able to skip this step. Otherwise, plan on laying at least one layer of primer before painting with your final color. When tinted to match your final coat, excellent results are the norm. It might seem like extra work, but it's actually less work than laying on two additional paint coats to insure opacity.

Choose the type of paint. Generally, flat latex is used for walls and ceilings, with semigloss latex or oil used on trim for contrast. Latex paint does not adhere well when used over old oil-based paint, so be careful with your choices.

Choose your brush. Use either a 2-inch foam or bristle brush. Foam brushes leave fewer brush marks, but they fall apart quickly. A good bristle brush that is cleaned well after each use can last many years.

STEP 2
Prepare the wall

The night before you paint, or several hours before you start, you need to prepare the surface. A clean, dry, and flat surface produces optimum coverage and adhesion.

Wash the walls. Using household cleaner and a sponge, thoroughly clean any surface to be painted. A capful or two of cleaner in a bucket of hot water will do the trick. Make sure that you clean oily or greasy surfaces very carefully.

- 3 to 5 thin strips of cardboard, if you have wall-to-wall carpeting
- 1 or 2 quarts paint thinner, if you're using oil-based paints
- A household cleaner and a sponge

Optional:
- A 6-foot step-ladder. This will reduce strain on your arms, especially if you're less than 8 feet tall.
- A plastic paint shield, with handle, for quickly masking areas around trim or carpeting (see Step 7)
- A small amount of primer tint to match your final paint color (see Step 1)

Tips

- How much is enough? A gallon of good-quality latex paint will cover about 350 to 400 square feet (110 to 120 square meters). A gallon of primer will cover about 500 to 600 square feet (155 to 185 square meters). Buy a little more paint than you need, just in case of spills or a miscalculation. Raw, untreated surfaces absorb a lot of paint, so these will require more. For best results, prime these surfaces at least once, maybe twice. On the other hand, the more previous coats that have been applied, the better the coverage.

If a stain looks dark enough to show through the imminent coat of paint, an application of sealer will cover it up. This is a liquid compound similar to paint that has better masking qualities than primer. You can find it at most hardware or paint-supply stores. If the stain doesn't look too bad, ordinary primer will suffice.

Remove any picture hooks or adhesive tape on the wall. These can snag and tear a roller cover and will interrupt your painting rhythm. Any holes left by nails and hooks should be filled with putty and a putty knife.

Remove wallpaper. If you want to paint on a surface that is currently wallpapered, you'll need an extra day to remove it. See "Learn2 Remove Wallpaper" for details.

STEP 3

Protect the room

Professionals use cloth drop cloths because they're reusable and they absorb paint spills—there's no slipping and sliding on wet, unabsorbed paint. Many self-painters buy those thin plastic drop cloths, which will be with us for the next several centuries. Save money and the planet—use old bedsheets instead, if you don't want to buy new drop cloths. If you must buy the plastic kind, get the thicker variety (3 to 4 millimeters) for the floors, and the thinner ones (.5 to 2 millimeters) for draping over furniture.

Remove all of the furniture and rugs that you can. After laying a drop cloth on the floor, move the remaining

PREPARE THE ROOM

COVER ALL FURNITURE

REMOVE FACEPLATES

USE OLD SHEETS AS DROPCLOTHS

items into the center of the room. Drape them with other drop cloths, and tape down any loose flaps where paint mist might enter.

Cover the floor completely. A fine mist of paint will adhere to any exposed surfaces. Protect the edges of the floor by using strips of wide masking tape. These will cover the remaining gap between the wall and the drop cloth. If you have wall-to-wall carpeting, slide a thin piece of cardboard between the baseboard and the carpet to protect it when painting the baseboards. For better handling, use a plastic paint shield instead of the cardboard.

Remove the faceplates of electrical outlets and light switches before beginning. If you have an overhead fixture, remove its cover to avoid getting paint on it. Use masking tape to protect doorknobs and locks.

For the best results, protect the trim. These are the wooden pieces that surround the doors and windows and, in some homes, outline the walls and ceilings. Tape it where it meets the wall, pressing tape in place with a putty knife for a good seal. After the final coat of wall paint dries, you'll remove the tape and paint the trim. If the trim is being painted for the first time (raw lumber), don't protect it. Instead, cover it with the primer when painting the first coat.

STEP 4

Paint the first coat: corners

Whether you use a primer as your first coat or not, the mechanics are the same. When painting, you want to work from the ceiling down to the floor, so splattering doesn't mar your finish. This means painting the ceiling first, then the walls, and finally the trim.

There's no need to carry around a heavy gallon-can of paint. Instead, fill up a plastic quart-size container, and dip your brush into that.

Rather than soaking the brush up to your knuckles in paint and wiping it on the side of the can, try this alternative. Dip about a third of the brush into the paint. Then, with a snap of the wrist, tap the side of the brush on the side of the can, two times. This removes just enough paint so that the brush won't drip.

Paint the corners in three locations: where the ceiling meets the wall, where the walls meet each other, and where any trim meets the wall. You're doing this so that the roller doesn't have to make it all the way to the edges. When applying the paint, put the wet brush down just ahead of a freshly painted area, and brush back into it to blend nicely. Avoid leaving globs of paint. For both the ceiling and the wall surfaces, paint out from the corner about 2 inches. Use the width of your brush as a guide.

To reach corners, it's best to use a stepladder. If none is available, tape the small brush tightly to the 4-foot roller extension. You may need to retape the brush a few times to make it around the room.

STEP 5

Paint the first coat: ceiling and walls

Rollers are fun to work with, because they cover so much area in a short time. Two important points with roller technique: keep the roller fully in contact with the wall, and use zigzag strokes. Zigzag strokes prevent the visibility of clear paint lines where each roller stroke begins and ends. We'll explain how.

ZIGZAG STROKES
KEEP CONTACT W/ WALL
PAINT "M"S ON WALLS & "W"S ON CEILINGS

Tips

- Use heavily napped roller sleeves for textured surfaces and shorter-napped sleeves for smooth walls. A sleeve with a fiberglass core will last for many jobs. Cardboard-core sleeves fall apart after a wall or two.

- Is it ready? A coat of latex or quick-dry primer will generally be repaintable in about 4 hours. Ask your salesperson about the particular product that you buy.

- Flat-finish paint hides imperfections better than semigloss or high-gloss paint, which is why it's generally used for walls.

Tips

- If you want to take a 20-minute break but don't want your brush or roller to dry out, put it into a sturdy plastic bag, and tie it tightly or fasten it with rubber bands. Squeeze the air out of the bag before you close it up. This will keep the air out and your brush soft.
- If you're cleaning up oil-based paints, you need to use strong, petroleum-based solvents. *Don't pour these down the drain.* Call your local recycling center for information

Put the appropriate sleeve (see "Tips") on the roller, and screw the roller onto the extension. Pour enough paint into the tray so that the pan is full but the slanted, ribbed area is clean. Dip the roller lightly into the paint tray (or 5-gallon bucket with wire screen). Coat the roller evenly by rolling it over the ribbed area or the screen.

Now do the zigzag. With your well-loaded roller, make a narrow W shape on the ceiling. Start painting the ceiling from a corner, and work out from there. Place the paint-loaded roller against a dry area, and work back into the wet paint. Follow the angles of the W—avoid making vertical lines. Work small areas at once, perhaps 8 or 9 square feet, and try to coat the surface evenly. Don't overwork an area.

Roll the walls one at a time, starting from the top. Complete each wall before starting the next or taking a break, using those same zigzag strokes. An M shape works better on walls.

STEP 6

Paint the second coat

The first coat should be left alone for a few hours, until it is dry to the touch. Then, using your final color, repeat the steps above for the corners, walls, and ceiling.

If you used a primer on your unmasked trim during the first coat, now's the time to protect it with tape, as outlined in Step 3. Be careful not to paint the trim again with anything but your chosen trim paint.

Beware of shortcuts. If you're painting white paint onto a white wall and want a quickie job, you might leave out the corner painting when doing the second coat. Just be aware that it won't look as good (especially in the daylight) as a properly done second coat.

A third coat, anyone? Wait until the second coat is dry to the touch. Take a good look at the job so far, assessing the coverage and the blending. Is the primer showing through anywhere? Are there areas of lighter and heavier coverage? If you used good-quality paint, everything's probably fine and you can go on to the trim. If you used cheaper paint, another coat might be necessary. Curse as little as possible, and get to it.

STEP 7

Paint the trim and doors

After the final wall coat is dry to the touch, take the protective masking tape off the trim. Avoid smearing any wet globs while doing this, and have a garbage bag handy. Immediately put the messy tape into it.

Using the small-bristle brush, carefully paint the trim, including the baseboards. Use small amounts of paint for a thin coat, and brush back into the wet paint to blend it well. Brush lightly on the last strokes to minimize brush marks.

Protect the walls, windows, and ceiling surrounding the trim. Plastic shields with handles are handy to quickly protect windows and walls from the trim paint. While it's not a big deal to get wall paint on the trim, you definitely want to avoid getting glossy trim paint on the walls. Glossy paint will stand out on a flat, latex base. Wipe the shields clean after every few strokes, and you can move pretty quickly. If you prefer, use wide masking tape to protect the walls, windows, and ceiling. The tape method takes a little more time but is great for people with shaky hands.

Doors can be rolled or brushed, depending on their contours. When a door connects two different-color rooms, paint the latch edge the same color as the room that the door opens into. Paint the hinged edge the opposite color.

STEP 8

Clean up your room!

After you've been playing with brushes for all these hours, it's only right to put your tools away when you're done. Leaving brushes and rollers loaded with paint is a good way to ruin them. Clean them up and they'll serve you again.

Cleaning latex paint from brushes and rollers is easy. Just hold the brush or roller under warm to hot water and massage the paint out. Rinse thoroughly with a little soap, and you'll have a happy brush.

Cleaning oil-based paint is a little tougher. You're going to need a half-gallon bucket, a quart of paint thinner or mineral spirits, a pair of rubber gloves, and a well-ventilated work space. Paint thinner easily enters your bloodstream through your skin or your lungs, and the stuff is not exactly a health tonic. So put on some gloves, pour some thinner into a bucket, and use as little as possible. Massage the paint out of the brush, and press it gently and rhythmically against the bottom of the bucket. Don't pour any thinner down the drain. It can go right to the water table, and you might drink it someday. Contact your local recycling center for information on safe disposal.

Get it while it's wet—before it dries solid. Scrub any excess paint off of wood floors before it dries overnight. Don't let toddlers or pets in the room before cleanup, or you'll have fresh paint all over your home.

Hooray! You're done. You've acquired a valuable skill and saved yourself a bundle. Next stop—the Sistine Chapel.

Learn **2** Prepare for an Earthquake

Time

- A few hours to shop for emergency supplies and assemble them into a kit
- A few evenings to learn CPR or basic first-aid skills
- ½ hour to form an emergency plan for the family

What you'll need

- Emergency supplies (see Step 2)
- An emergency plan
- A clear head

If a serious earthquake occurs near your home or where you're visiting, there's a good chance that you're not going to be able to shop, communicate, or move about normally. If you and your family want to be as safe as possible, here's what you'll need to do before anything happens, during the earthquake and in the aftermath.

BEFORE THE EARTHQUAKE

This 2torial will present some general strategies for preparing for earthquakes. Keep in mind that not all earthquakes are serious: in many regions a little ground shaking is a part of life and nothing to worry about. A more serious earthquake, however, can be frightening and disorienting. For that reason it's important to be very familiar with safety procedures. Some planning and practice will help you stay calm: this factor more than any other will likely improve your situation.

STEP 1

Make your home or office earthquake-ready

During an earthquake, certain objects in your home seem to have minds of their own. Your water heater, for instance, wants to topple over and sever its gas and water connections. To prevent this, secure your unit to the wall. Use galvanized steel straps, with holes punched through the length of them, and screw them to the wall.

Any object on shelves will try to jump off, and the cabinetry itself may collapse. Keep the shelves against the wall with screws or brackets near the top of the unit. Don't put flammable materials anywhere but on the bottom shelf.

Learn how to shut off your own gas, water, and electricity. If any connections break inside the house or even where they enter the house, you have a problem. Your local utilities office will help you find the valves for gas and water, and they'll also warn you not to try to turn them off unless you're certain that a break has occurred. Circuit breakers are generally in the basement or under the stairs. Find yours before an emergency arises.

STEP 2

Collect emergency supplies

Emergency kits are one of those items that nobody pays much attention to until there's an emergency. Make sure that everyone in your household knows where the kit is located. Also, consider preparing a smaller version to store in your car trunk. Your kit should contain as many of the following as possible:

• A battery-operated radio and flashlight, with spare batteries.

• Candles and matches.

• A fire extinguisher.

• 1 gallon of bottled water, per person per day, for 5 days. Store in airtight containers, away from gasoline or other petroleum products. Change every 6 months (when you change the clocks for daylight savings). Keep some disinfectant with it (for example, iodine tablets—read manufacturer's instructions) in case the water becomes unsanitary.

• Nonperishable food that does not need cooking or additional water.

• A multiple tool knife with can opener.

• Extra blankets and heavy clothing, including rubber-soled shoes and work gloves.

• A first-aid kit, with essential pre-scription medications and sunscreen added to it.

• Pipe and crescent wrenches to turn off gas and water mains.

• A shovel and toilet paper; sewer lines may be disrupted during an earthquake. Avoid flushing the toilet and risking further contamination of the groundwater.

• Money: $30 to $100 in cash, depending on the size of your household.

STEP 3

Learn emergency procedures

If an earthquake happened tonight, would your family know what to do? Perhaps one person is out of the house; how would she let the rest of you know that she's all right? Where would all of you meet to count heads? Emergency plans don't have to scare anyone, and they're pretty simple to write down and put on the refrigerator. Some important points:

• Select an out-of-town relative or friend to be your contact person. When separated, family members can call this person to report their safety or to leave messages.

• Conduct practice drills with all family members, and make sure everyone knows which areas of your house and property are safer than others (see Step 4).

• Choose a place to meet following the earthquake.

• Could there be a worse feeling than seeing someone you know injured and not knowing what to do?

Tips

• Look into earthquake insurance if you are in a particularly precarious zone; understand, however, that recent legislation slashed the benefits in many states.

Consider learning CPR and basic first aid.

STEP 4

During the earthquake: find a safe place

If you're indoors, take as few steps as possible to a safer area. These include inside corners of rooms (with walls that don't face outside), under doorframes, and under sturdy furniture. Stay away from windows, bookcases, and shelving that could fall on you. And use stairs, not elevators!

If you're outdoors, get into an open area away from trees, buildings, and power lines.

If you're driving, pull over, and stay inside your car until the shaking stops. Don't trust overpasses and bridges to be safe after a major shock.

STEP 5

After the earthquake: cover the necessities

Be prepared for aftershocks. They'll happen, and they'll scare someone near you. Calming others will help keep you calm.

First check yourself for injuries, then check others. Give first aid if you know it, but don't move seriously injured people unless they're in immediate danger.

Do you smell natural gas—not gasoline—at any gas appliance, including your water heater? If so, your gas line may have ruptured. This situation requires immediate and calm action. Open all windows and doors, turn off the valve, and notify the utility company. Do not shut off the gas line unnecessarily (that is, if there's no gas smell)—it may take weeks to restore service.

Check for water leaks and electrical-systems damage. For the electrical, check for frayed wires, sparks, or the smell of hot insulation. If a utility line breaks, turn off the circuit breaker or water valve.

Check your house for structural damage: cracks on the roof, chimney, or foundation are signs of possible serious damage. Your house may not be safe during an aftershock. If so, seek out alternative temporary shelter.

Turn on your battery-powered radio for instructions and news.

If running water is available (and your gas line is okay), boil it at least 10 minutes until your local water supply is declared safe. Emergency water can be found inside a toilet tank (not the bowl), or reclaimed from melted ice cubes. Canned vegetables are often packed in water.

Keep the streets clear for emergency vehicles; avoid driving just to have a look around. This is not the time to go sight-seeing.

Keep the phone line clear as well, except to report emergencies.

QUAKE DO'S:
- STAND IN A DOORWAY
- OR UNDER HEAVY FURNITURE

DON'T:
- RUN AROUND
- STAND NEXT TO WINDOWS

Learn**2** Remove Wallpaper

Time

After you've cleared the walls and prepared your materials, 1 to 2 hours to strip the average-sized room

What you'll need

- A bucket
- Drop cloths or old bedsheets
- A garden sprayer or a scrub brush and bucket
- A squeegee

Optional:

- A 3-inch scraper (available at hardware stores)
- A scoring tool
- A few sheets of sandpaper: coarse and medium grades
- Chemical wallpaper remover or wetting agent, or white vinegar
- Goggles
- A sponge
- A stepladder
- A paintbrush

There are a few different methods of removing old wallpaper. The easiest is to strip it off the walls dry. This is possible with newer papers, which are made so that you can pull them off without assistance from water or chemicals. Using steam is another method but may not be worth the blisters on the wallboard that can result. Note: You must steam and scrape at the same time, which requires effort and time. You're also obliged to clean up the equipment and fork over extra cash to rent a steamer. The third way is the traditional wet-and-scrape method, which is the approach discussed in this 2torial.

BEFORE YOU BEGIN

Removing wallpaper takes some effort, which is well worth it—if it's necessary. But is it? Naturally, if you want to paint the walls, you'll need to remove old wallpaper. If you're planning to hang new wallpaper, it may not be necessary—as long as the old paper is a single, smooth layer that's well attached to the wall.

Tips

- Make your own wallpaper remover: it's inexpensive, effective, and friendly to the environment. Combine equal parts of white vinegar and hot water. Apply with a sponge to wet the wallpaper thoroughly. Apply a second time, and check if the paper will come off.
- To remove leftover adhesive from the wall, use a squeegee dipped in very hot water. Work in 2-foot sections, and wipe the tool frequently.

30° ANGLE

RAZOR SCRAPER

STEP 1

Determine if removal is necessary

Pass your hand over the surface of the wall. If you hear any crinkling sounds, it means the old wallpaper has buckled up and has to go. Also check the corners with a butter or putty knife: if paper peels up in large sections, it needs to come off.

If the wallpaper is vinyl or has foil or plastic films, it should be removed—even if it's the first layer and in good condition. Wallpaper adhesive will not stick well on these surfaces.

Otherwise, you can paper over a single layer of smooth, well-adhered wallpaper. Some preparation is necessary, however. Check edges and corners for any loose areas: these should be glued down with white glue or wallpaper paste. It's also a good idea to give the surface a good cleaning, too. Mix a solution of detergent and water, and scrub away. Follow this with an application of primer that's made specifically for wallpaper. It's a little extra work, but your repapering efforts will hold up much longer if you do these preparations.

STEP 2

Check the old paper

In an unseen corner, try lifting the wallpaper off the wall with a scraper or putty knife. If the wall beneath the paper has been sealed or painted, you might be able to peel it right off. However, if the paper was applied directly to the bare wallboard by some careless hurrybug, this will be a bit more challenging.

If the old wallpaper won't budge, it must be moistened thoroughly. Don't remove any electrical switches or plates. To be even safer, turn off the circuit breaker for the room you're working in.

STEP 3

Moisten the paper

Do you have an old garden sprayer used to spread chemicals all over your garden in the seventies? Well, bring it out and clean it up. Otherwise a bucket and a broad brush will do fine.

If desired, you can mix a chemical wallpaper remover or wetting agent into the water. Beware: if you use any chemical remover, always wear goggles for protection.

You may be faced with old paper that chooses not to absorb water. In this case you'll have to scratch up the surface with coarse sandpaper or a scoring tool. This will allow the water to soak into the paper.

Apply the wetting agent twice; ideally, the water will do most of the work. Then let it soak for 30 minutes. It's ready when you can scrape off pieces of paper with your fingernail.

Learn2 Repot a Houseplant

You wouldn't enjoy sleeping in a crib, but you expect your plants to grow big and beautiful while squatting in a pot from their childhood. The restrictions of cramped pot life can dry a plant's roots, sending them down through the bottom of the pot or up to the topsoil, which makes for stunted or choked greenery. There are two solutions to this travesty: repotting, which involves removing the plant and replacing the potting soil; and potting on, or moving the plant to a larger pot.

BEFORE YOU BEGIN

Pick a good time of year to do this. The beginning of the growing season is best, since the growing roots will tap the new potting soil.

If possible, work with several plants at a time to consolidate your efforts. Make sure the pots are all clean, and water the plant an hour before to soften the soil. This will prevent spillage and help the plant to slide out easily. Finally, lay down the newspapers.

STEP 1
Remove the original pot

For smaller pots, lightly tap the sides of the pot. Then place the palm of your hand on the root ball (the root system and soil), holding the main stems between your fingers. Now stand, sit, or kneel over the newspaper. Holding the root ball so that nothing slips through, turn the plant upside down and tap on the sides and bottom of the pot. The plant should slip smoothly into your cupped hand.

For larger pots, insert a flat stick or blunt knife between the pot and the soil, and work it around the circumference of the pot. While holding the plant with one hand, lay it on its side and tap a bit more firmly as you rotate the pot. If it's sticky, use a wooden block to tap the exterior of the pot and dislodge the root ball. When you're sure the plant is loose, slide it out

Time

15 minutes

What you'll need

- Potting soil (equivalent to half the pot's volume)
- Drainage materials (gravel or sand)
- Fertilizer
- A good-sized serrated knife
- Newspapers to cover the floor
- Gardening gloves (optional)

Key words

Pot-bound: This describes a plant in need of potting on: the roots have poked past the potting mixture, have collected, or have begun to spiral.

Root ball: The root system and the soil it lives in.

Topdressing: The removal of a few inches of old topsoil and its replacement with fresh potting material.

Tips

- If removing (ouch) a cactus, cover with a piece of paper to protect your hand.
- For brand-new pots: ceramic pots are porous—meaning they will need to be water-logged before they'll hold water. Submerge the pot, and watch for tiny air bubbles to rise to the surface. When the bubbles stop rising, your pot is ready.

slowly from the pot onto the newspaper you've laid out.

STEP 2
Choose your method of transfer

To evaluate whether you need to repot or pot on, you need to examine the plant's root system. If the roots have poked past the potting mixture, or if they've collected or begun to spiral, the plant has become pot-bound. You need a larger pot. If none of these symptoms are present, take the repotting option.

Caution: Don't repot or pot on just after the growing season, because the roots won't tap the new soil and old roots may rot. Also, if the plant is unhealthy, don't replant—that may be too great a shock for it.

STEP 3
Prepare the new home

Pick any moss or greenery from the top of the root ball. Discard.

For repotting, you may need to make space for the new potting mixture. Prune the roots by trimming thin slices off the root ball. Use a serrated knife, sawing gently on each side or around the circumference. Take at least a half inch off smaller plants.

STEP 4
Place in the new home

Repotting:

Line your cleaned, original pot with drainage material. Use ½ inch to 3 or 4

inches of gravel or sand, depending on the size of the plant and pot.

Place your newly trimmed root ball in the pot. Scoop on some fresh potting soil, and gently push it down the sides of the pot with your fingers. Pack the soil, and water the plant lightly.

Don't feed a plant with new soil for about a month; allow the roots to get their goodies from the new surroundings.

Potting on:

Line the pot with drainage materials. Cover the bottom with additional potting soil to bring the plant to its original level. If you're using a brand-new pot, see "Tips."

Create a mold for your plant by placing the original pot inside the new one. Using your fingers, slide in potting soil to fill the gap between the inner and outer pots.

Remove the original pot from the soil, and replace it with your plant. Fill in any gaps, and lightly water the plant.

STEP 5
Learn the art of topdressing

Topdressing is for well-established plants that have outgrown previous homes yet have no larger pots available. The plants benefit from the refreshed nutrient base that topdressing provides. Do it for your plants about once a year.

Carefully remove the top few inches of soil, and replace with new potting soil.

Learn2 Varnish a Wood Surface

For protecting wood furniture from the elements, synthetic varnish can be a strong ally. Just wander down to any yacht harbor and examine boats with shiny wooden rails and trim: nobody knows better than a boat owner how to avoid the trials of sun, storm, and salt. But a sailor also knows patience. Applying the thick, slow-drying varnish will help hone those skills as well.

BEFORE YOU BEGIN

Bring your furniture item into a temperate, dust-free room if possible; varnish is very sticky, and you'll want to avoid creating a bug-and-leaf collage. If working outside, choose a moderate, windless day.

Get your surfaces ready for varnish. Remove any excess paint, sand the surface to the desired smoothness, and dust out any residue from the corners.

STEP 1

Select the proper varnish

Most varnishes are alkyd, and those containing tung oil are more water-retardant than those with linseed oil. Alkyd is more yielding than polyurethane and often more attractive. It is the best choice for fine wood pieces.

Polyurethane is best used on everyday pieces that take a real beating. Drying time is fast (four hours instead of the usual twenty-four), and you don't need to go back and level your brush strokes. But by providing such a truly solid layer, polyurethane more resembles plastic than wood. Avoid using it on fine wood. Polyurethane varnish is so tough it often requires an electric sander to remove.

Time

2 to 4 hours, depending on the size of the furniture

What you'll need

- 1 quart of polyurethane, alkyd, or spar varnish
- A new, soft paintbrush, 2 to 3 inches wide
- A few sheets of 7/0 sandpaper
- Tack cloth
- Plenty of newspaper
- Good ventilation

Tips

- Be soft and some-what brisk with your brush strokes.
- Check the instruc-tions on the can to determine drying time.
- Keep the dog out of the room.

Use phenolic resin or spar varnish for outside work or for boats. These varnishes are too thick and will yellow too much over time for fine wood or interior work.

STEP 2
Prepare your area

Lay down enough newspaper to exceed your project's width by 2 feet in each direction. This will help protect your floor from drips. Use a tack cloth to wipe up any trace of dust or sanded paint on the surface of your furniture.

STEP 3
Learn the stroke

BRUSH ACROSS THE GRAIN

Chart out your areas of attack so you don't have to stop in the middle of a panel. Shake any dust off your brush, and dip the brush into the varnish. Brush across—not with—the grain, using long strokes. Repeat the process, making a 1-inch overlap from where your last stroke ended in order to avoid patches.

STEP 4
Even out and level the varnish surface

Once you've covered the panel, go back over and work with the grain. Use the rim of the can to remove any excess varnish from your brush, then brush lightly over the wood surface. Brush over the surface only once, making the coat as smooth and even as possible.

STEP 5
Perform the art of tipping off

Now for the last, smoothing step. Tip-ping off is a dry-brush method of using just the tip of your brush to do away with the last brush-stroke (or finger) marks. Moving in rows with the grain, hold the brush perpendicular to the wood and barely stroke the sur-face.

Repeat Steps 3 through 5 for each segment of your project.

STEP 6
Prepare properly for the second coat

It is a good idea to wait one full day before embarking on your second coat. First you must use the sandpaper to softly "take back" (usually in one pass) the first coat. Do this by sanding gently with the grain into the first layer of varnish. You want to rough up the surface enough so the second layer can set without going through to the bare wood. Clean the surfaces with the tack cloth. Now you can repeat the varnishing steps.